365 days **of Encouragement**

A Collection
of Daily Readings
given in 2020-2021
during the Covid-19 Pandemic by
John G Roberts

DayOne

© Day One Publications 2021

ISBN 978-1-84625-700-1

All Scripture quotations, unless stated otherwise, are from The Holy Bible, New King James Version Copyright © 1982 by Thomas Nelson, Inc. Used by Permission. All rights reserved.

British Library Cataloguing in Publication Data available

Published by Day One Publications
Ryelands Road, Leominster, HR6 8NZ
Telephone 01568 613 740
Toll Free 888 329 6630 (North America)
email—sales@dayone.co.uk
web site—www.dayone.co.uk

All rights reserved

No part of this publication may be reproduced, or stored in a retrieval system, or transmitted, in any form or by any means, mechanical, electronic, photocopying, recording or otherwise, without the prior permission of Day One Publications.

Printed by 4edge Limited

*This book is dedicated to my wife, Kathryn,
who has supported, encouraged and prayed for me
throughout my ministry.*

COMMENDATIONS

Thought for the Day has been a spiritual oasis for our fellowship during the pandemic. The daily devotionals are full of theological insight and practical application. You will be challenged and encouraged by the warmth of this Christ-centred, God-glorifying, Spirit-led devotional.

Pastor Kristian Dimond
Wellington Chapel, Hereford

Clear, concise and encouraging. These daily meditations were prepared during a national pandemic when sickness, bereavement and isolation had become part of daily life. But they are not tied to a national crisis. Covering 366 daily readings they are meditations from the mind of a preacher with a heart of a pastor and rooted in the depth and breadth of the Bible. For all who want to begin or close the day with a vision of their God and the challenge and encouragement of His Word, these will prove a meaningful pause for thought and I warmly recommend them.

Brian H Edwards
July 2021

INTRODUCTION

I remember, in my younger days, listening to Alastair Cook's *Letter from America* on BBC Radio. He began on 24 March 1946 and his final recorded message was on 24 March 2004. There were 2869 instalments during those 58 years of broadcasting. To rest your minds, I will not be seeking to emulate his great achievement.

Thought for the Day began in March 2020. I had just commenced a tour in the south of England and, following my first meeting in Horsham, I heard on the news that the coronavirus was on the move in several areas throughout the United Kingdom.

I decided, for the safety of all, that I should return home. It wasn't long afterwards that churches had to close their doors as the country was put into lockdown.

As I sat at home, my thoughts went out to Christians who would be deprived of vital ministry. I contacted my pastor suggesting that, as a fellowship, we should prepare and send out a daily message for any who would wish to receive it. His reply was, 'You thought of it; so go for it!'

So, on the 16 March 2020 lockdown began and so did these daily messages. I expected it to be only for our own congregation at Wellington Chapel, and for it to last for just a couple of months at the most. I was wrong on both counts. People began to receive them in other parts of the country and were grateful for the link with us.

During the autumn of 2020, a number of people began to ask if they could be published for a wider readership. When Day One agreed to publish them, the work began to put them into print. During the process, I have endeavoured to give recognition for any quotes I included, where it is due. If I have omitted anyone, I sincerely apologise and it will be rectified in any future edition.

I am so grateful to those who encouraged me to continue with these messages, but I would especially thank Keith Weber who designed the format and sent them out each morning.

I would also thank Mark, the Managing Director at Day One and the publishing committee for their willingness to publish the material and see it through to completion.

My gratitude also goes to Helen Clark for patiently going through each daily thought and correcting grammatical errors which inevitably come from a Yorkshireman who is still learning the English language.

I am grateful to those who have emailed, telephoned and sent messages of encouragement to continue when I was about to come to a conclusion.

There are many people to whom I am indebted, none more than my wife Kathryn, who has encouraged and supported me all the way. She has constantly driven me to my computer and supplied me with pots of tea whenever I began to flag.

Most importantly, I am grateful to Almighty God for guiding and enabling us to continue this project through these difficult and challenging days.

John Roberts
August 2021

1 JANUARY

Looking ahead with courage and hope

'Have I not commanded you? Be strong and of good courage; do not be afraid, nor be dismayed, for the Lord your God is with you wherever you go.'
Joshua 1:9

RECOMMENDED READING: Joshua 1

When I took my family from our home in South Yorkshire 48 years ago, it was to begin a work with what is now known as Day One Christian Ministries. Although it was a new adventure for us as a family, we soon realised we were out of our comfort zone. Everything was new: our home; the church fellowship; living in a big city. We had to adapt to a new environment and strange accents; it was like being in a foreign land. However, despite all this, one thing hadn't changed: God's presence with us. As He was with us in Yorkshire, so He was with us in Sussex.

Moses had died and God had buried him on Mount Nebo. Joshua now received instructions from God to lead the Children of Israel across the Jordan to occupy the Promised Land that God was about to give to His people (v.2).

Joshua, facing this daunting task, would naturally be filled with trepidation and apprehension, but God assured him in v.5, 'As I was with Moses, so I will be with you. I will not leave you nor forsake you.'

He then gave him clear instructions in v.9: 'Be strong and of good courage; do not be afraid nor dismayed.'

When you face a new challenge, whether it be a new school; a new job; or a new location, there is excitement, but also nervousness at what the future will hold for you. It will certainly not be a picnic in the park.

As God instructed Joshua to be strong and not to be afraid, so He says the same to us. Whatever hurdles are before us we will have the strength to jump them. Whatever battles will have to be fought, we will have the ability to fight them. Whatever difficulties we have to face, we will have the help to confront them.

Why can we be so sure? Just read the remainder of v.9: 'for the LORD your God is with you wherever you go'. God will help you over the hurdles; He will help you fight the battles; He will face the difficulties with you. You are never alone!

So, as we embark upon a new year with all its challenges ahead, remember there is One who is constantly by our side to strengthen, protect and encourage us all throughout the year.

2 JANUARY

United with the heroes of scripture

'I do not pray for these alone, but also for those who will believe in Me through their word; that they all may be one, as You Father are in Me, and I in You.' John 17:20–21a

RECOMMENDED READING: Ephesians 4:4–16

One of the most encouraging aspects of church life is the unity and support we can give to each other. This morning I want to consider our unity in Christ, and tomorrow our unity with each other.

If we are to look out for the unity in Christ's church, we are to seek lost souls; to seek out those who are to believe in Him. We cannot bring the increase, but we must sow the seed by using the gifts God has given to each one of us. We will never see the church complete as long as one soul is left unsaved for whom Jesus poured out His precious blood. Until these people are saved, the church will not be perfect and unified.

I love to read the last verses in Hebrews 11. The writer of this letter lists some of the great giants of the faith. Some names in this chapter may surprise you, but all were commended for their faith, yet none received the fulfilment of what had been promised at that time. God had planned and provided something better for all believers so that only together with us would they be made perfect.

That is truly astounding!

We are included in that great company of believers and we are in it together with Moses, Abraham, David, Samuel and a host more. We will inherit the heavenly kingdom with them. I feel so unworthy of such an honour, but the inspired writer assures us that this is so.

What this verse is saying is that saints in heaven cannot be perfect until we get there! Yes, they are part of the body, but not the whole body. They cannot be perfect as a flock until the rest of the sheep join them.

Christian unity is like conversion in that it is not of blood, nor of the will of the flesh, nor of the will of man, but of God.

> 'How vast the benefits divine
> which we in Christ possess!
> We are redeemed form sin and shame
> and called to holiness.
> Not for the works that we have done—
> all these to Him we owed;
> But He of His electing love
> salvation has bestowed.'
>
> Augustus Toplady (1740–78)

3 JANUARY

United in Christ

'... endeavouring to keep the unity of the Spirit in the bond of peace.'
Ephesians 4:3

RECOMMENDED READING: Romans 15:1–13

Yesterday we considered our unity in our Lord Jesus Christ. Today we turn our thoughts to our unity with each other.

Unity of the Spirit doesn't come naturally for any of us. We are all so different—in personality, in temperament, and in our likes and dislikes. We have our preferences and tend to think that our ways and ideas are always the best. We can feel hurt if someone disagrees with us. That is human nature.

This is why we are to work hard at maintaining unity among God's people. We must never take it for granted but be eager to maintain that which is so precious. Let us cultivate everything that would encourage unity.

If any of our brothers or sisters are sick, let us care for them; if any are discouraged, let us build them up; if any are troubled, sympathise with them; if we are aware of faults in another believer, admonish them with love and affection.

Be patient with others, as we would wish them to be patient with us. Treat one another as you would like to be treated. Above all we must, if at all possible, be peacemakers and not troublemakers.

We need to remember to walk in our brother's or sister's shoes before we knock them over.

We cannot keep the unity of the Spirit unless we follow the Bible's teaching. We want unity in the truth of God. Let us live near to Christ, for that is the best way of promoting true Christian unity.

One final, but important, thought is to remember that we all have an adversary, the devil, who will do anything to undermine our unity in the gospel.

Therefore, let us resist him at all times and strive with all our energy to keep the unity of the Spirit in the bond of peace.

As members of God's orchestra, let us ensure we are constantly in tune with each other with our eyes always focused on the conductor.

> 'Blest be the tie that binds
> our hearts in Christian love;
> The fellowship of kindred minds
> foreshadows that above.'
>
> John Fawcett (1782–1817)

4 JANUARY

Chosen to be His bride

'Just as He chose us in Him before the foundation of the world, that we should be holy and without blame before Him in love.' Ephesians 1:4

RECOMMENDED READING: Ephesians 1:1–14

The early verses of Ephesians 1 present to us five wonders of our faith that the writer Ruth Paxson (1889–1949) commented on.[1] Even in these challenging days in which we live, they should cause us to turn to God in ceaseless praise—which is exactly what Paul did from v.14.

1. The first wonder is that we are chosen. We must begin with a very simple, yet important fact; we did not choose Him! We were unable to do anything. The Bible tells us that we were blind so that we could not see spiritual truths. We were deaf so that we could not hear His voice. Above all we were spiritually dead; we were lifeless with no power to do anything. We were lost in a spiritual wilderness with no oasis in sight. We didn't even have faith, which is a gift from God.

Let us thank Him that He makes the blind to see; the deaf to hear; the dumb to sing and the dead to live. No, we didn't choose Him, but let us thank God that He chose us.

When were we chosen? Verse 4 tells us: 'before the foundation of the world'. That makes my little grey cells go into overdrive. God knew us before He said, 'Let there be light' (Genesis 1:3). Take hold of that and ponder upon it throughout the day. You will be exhausted by tonight!

Why were we chosen? Verse 4 tells us: 'to be holy and without blame before Him'. 'No chance!' you say. Let me tell you that He would not ask us to do that which is impossible.

It is possible because of Jesus. At Calvary the Son of God took our sin upon Himself and in return gave us His spotless robe of righteousness, so that when God looks down upon us, He doesn't see the real you and me but He sees His Son. Because of Jesus we are perfect in God's sight. The Christian is faultless to stand before Him. Hallelujah. What a Saviour!

> 'Pause, my soul, adore and wonder!
> Ask, O why such love to me?
> Grace hath put me in the number
> Of the Saviour's family;
> Hallelujah!
> Thanks, eternal thanks, to Thee!'

Anonymous

5 JANUARY

God's grace flows as fresh as ever

'In Him we have redemption through His blood, the forgiveness of sins, according to the riches of His grace.' Ephesians 1:7

RECOMMENDED READING: Psalm 32

Yesterday we began by considering the first wonder which is the fact that we are chosen.

2. The second wonder is that we are forgiven. If you examine v.7 carefully, there are three wonders packed together in one.

- 'In Him we have redemption through His blood.' God not only chose us but bought us at a great cost to Himself. To 'redeem' is to buy back—to release for a ransom. We are redeemed from the curse of the law (Galatians 3:13). We are rescued from the death penalty due to our guilt. The law says, 'we are condemned'. God says, 'we are His children' but at a price (1 Corinthians 6:20). The price is the blood of His Son.

- '… the forgiveness of our sins'. Psalm 32 begins with these words: 'Blessed is he whose transgression is forgiven.' These words are like a millstone removed from around our necks; like a heavy burden lifted from our backs. This morning our sins are buried at the bottom of the deepest ocean; they have been carried as far as the east is from the west, and there is no end to either. Our sins will never be remembered again. That includes all our past sins, our present sins, and the sins we commit until the day we leave this earthly scene. The blood of Jesus covers them all.

- '… according to the riches of His grace'. Notice that there is no mention of love in this verse. Neither is there any mention of mercy. It is all of grace. Love travels in three directions. God first demonstrated His love to us; then we show our love to Him; finally, we express it to others. Mercy goes in two directions. God has shown mercy to us and we can show mercy to others. We cannot show mercy to God. As for grace, it flows in only one direction and that is downwards to unworthy sinners like us. God's grace is unearned, unmerited and undeserved. Who is worthy of such a gift as grace? Yet God gives it unconditionally to all who repent and turn to Him.

'Who is a pardoning God like Thee?
Or who has grace so rich and free?'

Samuel Davies (1723–61)

6 JANUARY

God's mystery revealed

'Having made known to us the mystery of His will, according to His good pleasure, which He purposed in Himself.' Ephesians 1:9

RECOMMENDED READING: Ephesians 3

These wonders of the faith that Paul is sharing with the Ephesian church must have been a great encouragement to them, as I trust they are to us.

We have already been reminded that we are chosen and forgiven. Is there more? Indeed, there is!

3. The third wonder is that we have God's revelation. In Ephesians 3:3 we are told that this mystery was revealed to Paul by revelation. So, what is the mystery? Or should we ask, who is the mystery? Verse 4 gives us the answer: Christ is the mystery.

Paul confirms this in Colossians 2:2b–3, when he says, '… the knowledge of the mystery of God, both of the Father and of Christ, in whom are hidden all the treasures of wisdom and knowledge'.

God has revealed His will and purpose to us, and He has done this through His word which is totally reliable and trustworthy.

In Colossians 1:25–26 Paul says, '… to fulfil the word of God, the mystery which has been hidden from ages and from generations but now has been revealed to His saints'. A mystery signifies something hidden, but it is no longer a mystery once it is revealed.

In 2018 Kathryn and I celebrated our golden wedding anniversary. Our daughter Helen came over from South Africa and took us to Stratford-upon-Avon for a couple of days—my wife loves the Cotswolds. Unbeknown to us, while we were there, our son Mark and his wife Sharon, with the help of our three grandchildren, were preparing a very special event at Wellington Chapel with our spiritual family. We knew nothing about this; it was a complete mystery. When we arrived at the Chapel, I was speechless. (I can hear the comments coming!) Before we arrived, it was a mystery that would soon be revealed.

God's mystery was revealed at Bethlehem and He used shepherds to make the mystery known.

When by grace we become believers, Jesus is no longer a mystery, for He has been made known to us. What a glorious revelation!

'Rest your hope fully upon the grace that is to be brought to you at the revelation of Jesus Christ' (1 Peter 1:13b).

7 JANUARY

God's mystery revealed—part two

'... in whom also we have obtained an inheritance, ...' Ephesians 1:11a

RECOMMENDED READING: Ephesians 3

4. The fourth wonder is the assurance of our inheritance. Never has there been such an endowment heard of before. The words 'In Christ ...' give it limitless meaning. 'Giving thanks to the Father who has qualified us to be partakers of the inheritance of the saints in the light' (Colossians 1:12).

As you read this first chapter in Ephesians, you can feel Paul's excitement building. By the time he reaches the end of chapter 3, he is uncontainable. There are times when we lose the excitement, thrill and wonder of our faith. We depend on our 'yo-yo' feelings and not on the facts that are contained in God's Word. Christians should be the happiest people on earth, despite the trials that sometimes we have to face. Remember that we have bread to eat of that the world knows nothing about.

We have a glorious inheritance awaiting us that will never, ever, fade away, reserved in heaven for every child of God. Our inheritance is not down here where everything is insecure and will not last. Our treasure is in heaven and the stock market will not affect it. For the Christian the best is yet to come.

Just spend a moment reading Ephesians 3:17–21, then read again v.20.

'Now to him who is able to do ... ALL that we ask or think.' Read it again!

'... exceedingly ABUNDANTLY above all that we ask or think'. Having trouble with your eyes? Read it again!

'... EXCEEDINGLY abundantly above all that we ask or think'. You may need your eyes testing! Read it once more carefully.

It says, 'Now to him who is able to do EXCEEDINGLY ABUNDANTLY above ALL that we ask or think.'

Wow! It is in Him, the heir of the whole universe that we have our inheritance. Not even all the powers of darkness can rob you and me of our inheritance. All the blessings we have now are minuscule compared with what we have to come. Heaven and all it contains is our inheritance.

Colossians 3:24 says, '... knowing that from the Lord you will receive the reward of the inheritance, for you serve the Lord Christ.'

> 'How vast the treasure we possess!
> How rich Thy bounty, King of grace!
> This world is ours, and worlds to come;
> Earth is our lodge, and heaven our home.'

Isaac Watts (1674–1748)

8 JANUARY

The rich are not always godly, but the godly are always rich

'In Him you also trusted, after you heard the word of truth, the gospel of your salvation; in whom also, having believed, you were sealed with the Holy Spirit of promise.' Ephesians 1:13

RECOMMENDED READING: 2 Corinthians 1 (note vv.21,22)

Today we come to the fifth wonder of our faith, concluding our brief glimpse into the first chapter of Ephesians.

5. The fifth wonder is that we are sealed with the Holy Spirit. There are two prominent aspects in sealing, namely ownership and security.

In my early days as director of Day One Ministries, our council held meetings on a monthly basis at our headquarters in London. There were occasions when important documents were presented to our council to be sealed. Our chairman would insert these documents into the seal and, after applying pressure, the papers would have the Society's imprint upon them. He would then sign his name over the imprint. The documents would then be both sealed and signed. This meant they, and all they pertained to, were ours and secure in our care.

The message today is twofold.

Firstly, we are His. John 17:9,10 says, 'I pray for … those whom You have given Me, for they are Yours. And all Mine are Yours, and Yours are Mine, and I am glorified in them.'

The old hymn says, 'Now I belong to Jesus, and Jesus belongs to me. Not for the years of time alone, but for eternity' (Norman Clayton, 1903–1992).

God wants those who are His to know they are His. 'Loved with everlasting love … I am His and He is mine' (George Wade Robinson, 1838–77). That thought should lift our spirits whenever we feel low.

Secondly, we are secure. Nothing, and no one, can snatch us from His hand. He holds us securely and will not let us go. Many seals have been broken, but no one shall break this one.

You may not have seen any of the wonders of the world but, if you are in Christ, you have experienced these wonders of the faith. You may not be wealthy, as some in this world count wealth, but you have treasures laid up in heaven that should make unbelievers envious.

> 'Heirs of God, joint heirs with Jesus,
> Called and chosen in the Son!
> To his name eternal praises,
> For the wonders he has done!'
>
> John Kent (1766–1843)

9 JANUARY

Our eternal calling

'... that you may know what is the hope of His calling ...' Ephesians 1:18

RECOMMENDED READING: Ephesians 1:15-23

When we move to the second half of Ephesians 1, the apostle, Paul, turns from praise to prayer. He longs that the Ephesians may know three vital things and today we look at the first.

1. **The hope of His calling.** The word 'CALLING' in this context refers to the work of God's grace within our hearts. In other words, it refers to our conversion. 'Moreover whom He predestined, these He also called; whom He called, these He also justified; ...' (Romans 8:30).

Now let us look at the word 'HOPE'. This word takes our minds away from this earthly scene into the future. It is the fulfilment of our heavenly calling. Four experiences are prepared for us:

(a) We will be raised from the dead. 'If in this life only we have hope in Christ, we are of all men the most pitiable. But now, Christ is risen from the dead' (1 Corinthians 15:19, 20). We are living in a world that has no hope. Misery and fear are so clearly evident and the Christian feels for such people. The Christian has hope and joy, and fear is removed. Because He lives, we shall live also.

(b) We will reign with Christ in His Kingdom. 'To him who overcomes, I will grant to sit with Me on My throne, as I also overcame and sat down with my Father on his throne' (Revelation 3:21). My mind nearly explodes when I think that one day, I will reign with him. Who deserves such a privilege?

(c) We will receive an eternal inheritance in heaven. '... to an inheritance incorruptible and undefiled and that does not fade away, reserved in heaven for you'(1 Peter 1:4). It is personal, prepared and permanent.

(d) We will be transformed into the image of Christ. 'We know that when He is revealed, we shall be like him, for we shall see Him as He is' (1 John 3:2). It baffles the imagination and sends our mind into top gear. It should excite us, humble us, and cause us to fall before our Creator in continuous appreciation—just as it did Paul.

> 'Safe in the arms of sovereign love we ever shall remain;
> Nor shall the rage of earth or hell make Thy sure counsel vain.
> Not one of all the chosen race but shall to heaven attain;
> Here they will share abounding grace, and there with Jesus reign.'
>
> Augustus Montague Toplady (1740–78)

10 JANUARY

It is certainly going to get better!

'… the riches of the glory of His inheritance in the saints.' Ephesians 1:18

RECOMMENDED READING: 2 Corinthians 4

In concluding our thoughts on this first chapter of Paul's letter to the Ephesians, we note in Paul's prayer that he desires we know three vital things. Yesterday we considered, 'the hope of his calling.'

Today I want us to think about:

2. God's glorious inheritance in the saints.

We touched upon our inheritance a few days ago, but we need to revisit it again as it is such an important aspect of our faith.

Verse 18 of Ephesians 1 begins, 'the eyes of your understanding being enlightened; …'. Christians should not just be satisfied with warm feelings towards God—though important—but we must persevere in obtaining a clear understanding of who He is and those things that He has revealed to us.

When we become members of His true church, we receive an inheritance in God because of the atoning work of our Lord Jesus Christ. Is there anything in this great, vast universe that can mean more to God than those whom He has redeemed by the precious blood of His dear Son?

For Almighty God to give his only Son, whom he loved so much, and see Him suffer in such pain and agony for those who were His enemies, was a sacrifice that words cannot express.

It is therefore beyond our human understanding that the Almighty One should find an inheritance in us who are such rebellious, sinful creatures. But let us never forget that there is an inheritance in the saints which is experienced NOW. Isaac Watts (1674–1748), the great hymn writer, wrote these words: 'Grace is glory begun below.'

If we are in Christ then eternity begins immediately we become a Christian. Our future is safe and secure through the sacrifice of our Lord Jesus.

Let us by reading and studying His Word, by regular communion with Him in prayer, and by worshipping regularly with the Lord's people, know as much of heaven as we can, so that we may desire and long to be there.

> 'My Father's house on high, home of my soul, how near
> At times to faith's foreseeing eye those golden gates appear!
> Oh how my spirit faints to reach the land I love,
> The bright inheritance of saints, Jerusalem above.'
>
> James Montgomery (1771–1854)

11 JANUARY

A power far greater than our own

'But you shall receive power when the Holy Spirit has come upon you, and you shall be witnesses to Me in Jerusalem, and in all Judea and Samaria, and to the end of the earth.' Acts 1:8

RECOMMENDED READING: Acts 1:1–11

We have been considering Paul's prayer from Ephesians 1:15–23. He desires that we may know the hope of his calling and God's glorious inheritance in the saints. This morning we look at his final desire.

3. God's divine power in us (v.19).

It is humanly impossible for us to bring someone to faith in Christ. We have spent many hours talking with enthusiasm to someone about the Lord Jesus, but they remain unmoved. They seem to be deaf to our words; we just can't get through no matter how hard we try to explain the wonders of our faith. We need to realise that it takes Almighty power to do this. Notice that this power is '… according to the working of His mighty power which He worked in Christ …' (vv.19b–20a). We see the demonstration of that power throughout the life of our Lord, culminating in His dead body being brought to life again and made fit for heaven. God then lifted that body away from this earth to what our Lord calls, 'My Father's House' (John 14:2). It is a place where God dwells, and His presence experienced in a way that cannot be compared with anything else in the whole universe. And God brought this about despite the opposition from Satan's army.

Do you realise that you will experience that power when you are raised from death?

Could I conclude with a message to pastors, elders, deacons, youth workers, missionaries and in fact all members of Christ's church? Would you ask yourself this question: How much do I know of this Almighty power within my life today? Do I know it in my ministry? Do I know it in my preaching? Do I know it in my daily witness for the Lord? The church is looking for better methods; God is looking for better men and women.

Paul prays 'that you may know …' (Ephesians 1:18). May we truly know that Almighty power in our lives, so that people may recognise and acknowledge that we have been with Jesus.

> 'Spirit divine, attend our prayers,
> And make our hearts Thy home;
> Descend with all Thy gracious powers,
> O come, great Spirit, come!'

Andrew Reed (1787–1862)

12 JANUARY

God's providential care

'I was the king's cupbearer.' Nehemiah 1:11

RECOMMENDED READING: Esther 4

During the next three days I want to consider the life of a man who has inspired, challenged and encouraged me. His name was Nehemiah.

Nehemiah lived around 450 years before our Lord Jesus Christ. It was a time when the Persian monarchy was flourishing with great pomp and power. It was also a time when Greece and Rome were beginning to figure in the history books.

The account begins in Persia, whose empire was vast, extending eastward to India and westward to Greece. We are told in chapter 1:1 that Nehemiah resided in Susa, which was the capital, and v.11 informs us that he was the cupbearer to the king.

This was a very responsible position, as kings had been poisoned by their enemies, so Nehemiah's task was to protect the life of the king.

The responsibility was not given to a Persian, which may have been understandable, but to a Hebrew who was in captivity along with his fellow Israelites. This shows how much Nehemiah was trusted.

God had placed him in the right place, at the right time, to do the right job.

What about you and me? Our life is all planned out in the courts of eternity. The place of our birth, the time of our birth and even the place where we worship is arranged by God. There is nothing left to chance for the Christian; God has it all in hand.

The hymn writer, Charles Wesley, wrote, 'To serve the present age my calling to fulfil; O may it all my powers engage to do my Master's will' (1762). We were chosen and called to serve Him in this present age.

Nehemiah did not serve in the Persian court by accident, but by God's providential design. We see the extent of God's providential care as the book of Nehemiah unfolds. He could be sure that his God would care for him and meet his needs.

God always has His people in the right place at the right time and will keep His eye constantly upon them. So always be assured you are exactly where God wants you to be, and never forget that He orders our stops as well as our steps.

> 'My times are in your hand;
> my God, I wish them there!
> My life, my friends, my soul,
> I leave entirely to your care.'
>
> William F. Lloyd (1791–1853)

13 JANUARY

Always take it to God in prayer

'So I prayed to the God of heaven.' Nehemiah 2:4b

RECOMMENDED READING: Matthew 6:5–13

Today we consider Nehemiah's prayer life.

There is no doubt that Nehemiah was a man of prayer. He was in constant communion with His God. In Nehemiah 1:2 we are told that Hanani, and other men from Judah, came to Susa and Nehemiah enquired about the situation in Jerusalem. The news was disturbing (v.3). We find Nehemiah's response in v.4. What is our response to the distressing news we hear daily in the media?

Nehemiah's response was to pray. He loved the city of Jerusalem; it was the joy of the whole earth. Yet, 140 years earlier, the Babylonians had destroyed the city and it lay in ruins. He desperately wanted to return, but two major obstacles stood in his way.

Firstly, he was 1,400 miles from the city. It would take four months to complete the journey and it would be dangerous. Secondly, he couldn't just quit his employment. It was difficult getting into the Persian palace, but even more challenging getting out.

So, does he despair? Does he panic? Does he give up as many would do today? No, he prays! Notice his prayer which starts in 1:5. It begins with worship, then confession, then thanks and finally, in the last verse, he makes his appeal to God for an opportunity to speak to the king. In our prayers we tend to rush to our requests. Have we forgotten how to worship God in our prayers? Nehemiah sets a pattern we would do well to follow.

We are told in chapter 1:1 that he prays in the month of Chislev (October/November). His answer is in chapter 2:1 and came in the month of Nisan (March/April). God didn't answer his prayer for four months. He had to learn patience.

Today we live in an instant society; everything has to be done immediately. God doesn't work like that! It has to be done in His way and in His time. You cannot rush God, neither can you delay Him. Lay your requests before Him—He hears our prayers. Then let Him answer in His good time; it is always worth the wait.

> 'Have we trials and temptations, is there trouble anywhere?
> We should never be discouraged, take it to the Lord in prayer.
> Can we find a friend so faithful who will all our sorrows share?
> Jesus knows our every weakness—take it to the Lord in prayer.'
>
> Joseph M. Scriven (1819–86)

14 JANUARY

A prayer from the heart

'Then the king said to me, "What do you request?" So I prayed to the God of heaven.' Nehemiah 2:4

RECOMMENDED READING: Nehemiah 2:1–8

As we began to look into the life of Nehemiah one thing became very clear and that was God's providential care over his servant. But we also saw Nehemiah's commitment to prayer. Communion with God was an important aspect of his life, for he would not have accomplished his great task without God's help.

Today we consider His concern for Jerusalem. Most people I have met enjoy a hobby or pastime and they are often passionate about it. For some it is sport; others love reading; many enjoy walking in the beautiful countryside; others spend hours in their garden or vegetable patch. This can consume much of their time and, in some cases, their energy. Here we have a man who had a spiritual passion that was strong and God-centred.

When we turn to chapter 2, it is now four months after the events of the opening chapter. Nehemiah is once again in the king's presence, but on this occasion his countenance is downcast. This had never happened on any previous occasion, and the king notices (v.2). This is a very serious offence in the court, so we are not surprised Nehemiah became afraid.

He begins to explain to the king the reason for his sadness, hoping he would understand and accept it. It is all because of the news he had received about the state of Jerusalem.

The king then asks, 'What do you request?' (v.4). In the following verse Nehemiah sends an urgent prayer to the God of heaven.

In chapter 1 we have the main prayer of Nehemiah. In chapter 2:4 we have what I would call an arrow prayer. Sometimes arrow prayers are necessary in a time of emergency, such as a sudden, serious illness, but you cannot live your Christian life on arrow prayers alone. They are sure to make you immature and spiritually lazy. Your faith will not grow as it should.

His prayer is answered and, with the king's blessing in v.6, Nehemiah returns to Jerusalem to commence the rebuilding of the city's walls.

Tomorrow we shall see the many challenges he faced once he arrived.

'Your promise is my only plea;
to you alone I cry,
For burdened souls in you are free
and such, O Lord, am I.'

John Newton (1725–1807)

15 JANUARY

Spiritual passion

'Come and let us build the wall of Jerusalem.' Nehemiah 2:17

RECOMMENDED READING: 1 Corinthians 3:9–17

During the past four days as we have looked into the life of Nehemiah, we have seen God's providential care over His servant, his prayer life and his concern for Jerusalem. Today we consider his spiritual passion.

The king gave Nehemiah permission to return to Jerusalem to commence the rebuilding of the city's walls. This would not be a straightforward project.

There are five things to note: (a) This would be a major task. (b) There would be much opposition. Sanballat and Tobiah would make it as difficult as possible by hindering the work and discouraging the people. (c) There would be much rubble to remove before the building work itself could commence. (d) The threat of death would be hanging over Nehemiah. He, as leader, was the enemy's main target and he would need to be alert at all times. (e) He would need to find time to encourage the people in the task they had undertaken because discouragement would never be far away.

Yes, this would be a monumental effort. Yet it is amazing what you can achieve when people are united and have a passion for the work. Nehemiah 2:18b says, 'Then they set their hands to this good work.' St Augustine of Hippo (AD 354–430) put it this way: 'Pray as though everything depended on God. Work as though everything depended on you.'[2] The Christian says, 'Let us arise and build.' The enemy says, 'Let us arise and oppose.' There is no triumph without trouble. There is no crown without a cross.

The task of rebuilding the walls was completed within six months of receiving the King's commission. The circumference of Jerusalem equalled 4.5 miles (answers.com) and the city walls were completed in the amazing time of 52 days. We couldn't contemplate such a task today, even with all our technology and modern building equipment. The workforce would go on strike! But with God's guidance and Nehemiah's leadership and encouragement, the task was accomplished. Nehemiah stayed in Jerusalem for twelve years before returning to Susa.

Whatever fellowship we belong to, there is a monumental task before us. But we have a monumental God supporting us. The moral and spiritual walls of our land have crumbled before us. Therefore, let us arise and build. With God nothing is impossible. Times of revival are testimony to that fact.

> 'Give me the faith which can remove and sink the mountain to a plain;
> Give me the child-like, praying love which longs to build your house again.'
> Charles Wesley (1707–88)

h's example of prayer

'Now Hannah spoke in her heart; only her lips moved, but her voice was not heard.' 1 Samuel 1:13

RECOMMENDED READING: Luke 1:5–16

Consider the importance of prayer through Samuel's mother Hannah and relate these thoughts to the situation we find ourselves facing today:

(a) It was sincere. In v.10 we read, 'She was in bitterness of soul and prayed to the Lord and wept in anguish.' Hannah was afflicted and she prayed. In her sad condition she poured out her heart to the Lord. As the prayer came from her heart, the tears came from her eyes. May our heart and our words be united as we seek God's face in prayer during these very challenging times.

(b) It was specific (v.11). Hannah, unlike Rachel (Genesis 30:1) only asked for one child. Her desire was that he should serve the Lord. He was not to be kept but given for the Lord to use. It is important that our prayers are clear and specific, both for people who are known to us, and also for the situation in which we find ourselves.

(c) It was quietly spoken (vv.12–13). There is no need to lift the roof unless we are praying in public. Though her voice never penetrated the ears of the old priest Eli, the Lord could and did hear her prayer. It is what is in the heart, not what is on our lips that is really important (Isaiah 29:13). We are not to try and impress others around us. We are pleading with the only One who can answer us.

(d) She was falsely accused (v.14). Eli thought that she was drunk. The same accusation was made with regard to the apostles (Acts 2:13). We should not judge another's prayers. God knows the heart of all who pray to Him. Eli should have been more understanding. Let us be thankful that we have One in heaven who is (Hebrews 4:15).

(e) She was satisfied (vv.17–18). When Eli's doubts had been answered, Hannah received his blessing and the assurance that God had heard.

Let us be thankful that we have a great High Priest who hears every word we utter (Hebrews 4:14). But remember, He sees the beginning and the end and will only respond in a way that is good for us. With these thoughts in mind, 'Let us therefore come boldly to the throne of grace, that we may obtain mercy and find grace to help in time of need' (Hebrews 4:16).

'Before the throne of God above, I have a strong and perfect plea.
A great High Priest, whose name is Love, Who ever lives and pleads for me.'

Charitie L. Bancroft (1841–1923)

17 JANUARY

Persecuted but never destroyed

'As the mountains surround Jerusalem, so the Lord surrounds His people from this time forth and forever.' Psalm 125:2

RECOMMENDED READING: Jude 17–25

From the Church's conception on the day of Pentecost, two characteristics have been evident during the 2,000 years of its existence:

1. Persecution. History shows us how nations and their rulers have brought much suffering to God's people. From the time of the Roman Empire, under evil emperors such as Nero, Christians have endured severe persecution, often leading to death. Our own history in the United Kingdom covers periods of intense suffering which the Lord's people have had to endure. Many Covenanters in Scotland, and Reformers throughout England, were burned at the stake or faced other severe forms of martyrdom. Today in many parts of the world such as North Korea, China, and the Middle East, Christians are very much aware of the challenges they face because of their love and commitment to the Lord Jesus Christ. Throughout the United Kingdom there are those who are challenging the Church in more subtle and devious ways, but all with the same intent: to destroy the Church of Jesus Christ. Therefore, we must not be surprised that, as they hated our Lord, they will also hate us.

2. Preservation. Despite all the word has thrown at the Lord's people, the Church has always been preserved. No ruler, nation or empire can, or will, overthrow the Church. Individual churches may at times be in danger, but God's Church is not! She shall stand secure, even to the end. Today liberal theologians and ungodly scientists constantly seek to undermine the authority of Scripture, but they will fail. 'Heaven and earth will pass away, but My Words will by no means pass away' (Matthew 24:35). Those who would batter her walls to pieces will discover that she is impregnable. The Church is built upon a firm foundation, 'Jesus Christ' (1 Corinthians 3:11), and 'she shall not be moved' (Psalm 46:5). Throughout this day, and every day, remember that the Christian Church is the only organisation on earth that never loses a member through death. No other sect or organisation can make such a boast.

So, believer, be encouraged. We are on the victory side.

> 'Crowns and thorns may perish, kingdoms rise and wane,
> But the church of Jesus constant will remain.
> Gates of hell can never 'gainst that church prevail;
> We have Christ's own promise and that cannot fail.'
> Sabine Baring-Gould (1834–1924)

18 JANUARY

Compassion for the anxious

'Therefore, I say to you, do not be worry about your life.' Matthew 6:25

RECOMMENDED READING: 1 Peter 5:6–11

'Don't worry about it!' Has someone ever said that to you, or have you said it to someone else? Anxiety or worry is a problem we all encounter to some degree or another. In our modern culture, stress is one of the fastest growing diseases affecting all classes of society. The NHS spends vast amounts of money on prescriptions, supplying many forms of medications, to try and counteract this growing problem. Countless days are lost with people absent from their employment through stress-related illnesses.

We have before us a major problem that seems to be uncontrollable, and which affects the very young as well as those who are older in years.

Over the past year it has mushroomed due to the spreading of the coronavirus. People are worried about their older and sick relatives; their financial uncertainties; the closed shops and restaurants; and over family members who are on the front line of the NHS and other supporting agencies. I could go on! So, what is the remedy now we have identified just some of the problems?

- A good cup of strong Yorkshire tea? (I had to get it in somewhere!) Despite it being a good idea, it doesn't solve all problems.
- Meditation? After all, this is one of the fastest growing religions in the world.
- More possessions and wealth? These seem to further the problem rather than solving it.
- A chat with a counsellor? Today we have them for almost every situation we have to face.

In Matthew 6:25–34, Jesus used the word 'worry' or 'anxious' six times. He clearly understood people's concerns and took them seriously.

If you are someone who just doesn't seem to worry about anything, and speaks glibly about this disease, be careful, for it is a daily battle for many people. They are not looking for your sympathy, but for your consideration and understanding. We need to show compassion to those who suffer with anxiety as Jesus did—who knows, you could be the next to face it.

Tomorrow we will see what our Lord says about it.

'Leave God to order all thy ways, And hope in Him whate'er betide.
Thou'lt find Him in the evil days Thy all-sufficient strength and guide.'

Georg C. Neumark (1621–1681)

19 JANUARY

Do not be anxious; God is in control

'Therefore, do not worry about tomorrow, for tomorrow will worry about its own things. Sufficient for the day is its own trouble.' Matthew 6:34

RECOMMENDED READING: Matthew 6:25–34

Yesterday we began to look at the problem of anxiety or worry, which affects so many in this age of constant pressure. What is the message for us today as we face this worrying epidemic?

- Try not to be anxious and focus upon what is most important (Matthew 6:25). On the whole we tend to be anxious about things and issues that will not last. Remember that the cares of this world are only a means to an end, not an end in themselves. There are some things more important than the things of this life. We must get our priorities in their right perspective.
- Try not to be anxious and remember that God is good (Matthew 6:26). Look around you. The birds of the air … God provides for them. This doesn't mean it is handed to them on a plate. Birds, animals and insects have to work for their food, but God cares for them. God will meet our needs because He cares for us also. He will not hold back His goodness from His own children. He knows best what we need. If God meets the needs of the birds of the air and the animals of the field, He will meet ours.
- Try not to be anxious, because it's an exercise in futility (Matthew 6:27). We can all waste valuable time and energy when we become anxious. Most times the things we are anxious about never happen. Who has the power to add one inch to their height? Who has the power to add one hour to their lifespan? When God says it is over, it is over. So, try not to be anxious about what you cannot change.

As we draw to a conclusion, just spend a few moments reflecting upon God's wonderful creation. Jesus uses the example of lilies and how they grow. They don't want to be roses; they are content to be what God made them to be. Even Solomon in all his glory could not be compared with them.

So be content with who you are. Be content with all you have. God loves you. He will care for you and bring you through this world of sin and suffering. Try not to be anxious. He is in control and watching over you every moment of every day and every step of your way.

> 'The soul that in Jesus has found its repose,
> He will not, he cannot desert to its foes;
> That soul, though all hell should endeavour to shake,
> He'll never, no never, no never forsake.'
>
> John Rippon (1751–1836)

20 JANUARY

Show unity in a world of disunity

'Joseph ... said to them, "Do not quarrel on the way."' Genesis 45:24, ESV

RECOMMENDED READING: Acts 15:36–41

One of the saddest aspects of my ministry is when I meet, or hear of, believers in the Lord Jesus who have fallen out with one another.

Joseph, who was the governor of Egypt, had just revealed himself to his brothers. As he sent them home to collect their father and bring him to Egypt, he told them not to fall out or argue with each other on the journey. A very appropriate warning to them after all that had recently taken place.

Leaders of other nations may bicker and disagree, but you are members of one family, tribe and nation, so do not let our name be brought into disrepute. The way home may be difficult, with enemies to encounter on the journey, but don't fall out among yourselves.

I believe this is a timely message to all believers. Whatever our personal feelings, we must demonstrate unity at all times. Jealousy, anger, bitterness or personal disagreements must never bring division among God's people.

We must support one another always, and never demean another person's character if they are unfairly attacked. Christian love should be evident as we support each other.

One thing that is often lacking is encouragement when we are under pressure. That is why Barnabas is a great example to us all.

There may be occasions when we disagree, but we must never let it fester, even if we have to eat humble pie in the end. A day will come when we all must sit at the same table in heaven, so don't fall out on the way while we journey together here on earth.

If ever you are tempted to do so, just remember the many blessings that we share. We have all been forgiven, accepted, justified and adopted into God's great family. We must not fall out when God has blessed us so much.

Don't quarrel that 'Benjamin's sack' has extra things in it than yours; just be grateful that your sack is never empty. We all have enough; we are all safe and secure; we have all been blessed far more than we could ever deserve.

'The God of love and peace' will be with His people when His people are at peace with one another (2 Corinthians 13:11).

> 'Let us for each other care,
> Each the other's burden bear,
> To Thy church the pattern give,
> Show how true believers live.'

Charles Wesley (1708–88)

21 JANUARY

Betrayed and denied

'Now it came to pass, when the time had come for Him to be received up, that He steadfastly set His face to go to Jerusalem.' Luke 9:51

RECOMMENDED READING: Luke 19:28–40

During the next couple of days, I want to direct our thoughts towards Jerusalem and consider some important events that made an impact upon so many lives, including our own. As the Lord Jesus set His eyes towards Jerusalem, what did He see before Him? After all, nothing is going to take Him by surprise (John 18:4).

1. He saw one who would betray Him. A disciple would soon become a traitor (John 18:1–3). Judas, who had been with Jesus, seen the miracles He had done and heard the messages He had proclaimed, would soon turn his back upon Him and stand alongside His enemies. What a stark warning that is to us all! It is so distressing to hear of those who once stood with us, but now no longer do so—some even becoming enemies towards those who were once their friends.

2. He saw one who would later deny Him. On more than one occasion, when Jesus had spoken to the disciples about His suffering and cruel death, Peter defended Jesus (John 18:10) and assured Him that he would even die with Him. How easy it can be to make boastful predictions but fail to carry them out when put to the test. After Jesus' arrest in Gethsemane, it wasn't long before He was on trial facing trumped-up charges against Him. Regrettably, Peter, by this time, had found himself to be in the wrong company and the furnace was proving to be too hot to handle. That eventful night, he had been given three great opportunities to fulfil his promise to stand by Jesus. Instead, on each occasion, he denied his Master (John 18:27).

There is a clear lesson for all who profess the name of Jesus. We need to be very careful of the company we keep. Yes, we are to be a witness to unbelievers, but if we ever find it becoming too hot, that may be the time to remove ourselves from the flames before we deny Him and get burnt.

It wasn't long afterwards that Peter deeply regretted his actions, but forgiveness was not far away. Peter atoned for his sins and he became a giant in the early church. May that be encouragement for us all.

> 'For me it was in the garden
> He prayed—"Not My will, but Thine";
> He had no tears for His own griefs,
> But sweat drops of blood for mine.'   Charles H. Gabriel (1856–1932)

22 JANUARY

From rejection to resurrection

'And He went through the cities and villages, teaching and journeying towards Jerusalem.' Luke 13:22

RECOMMENDED READING: Luke 13:20–35

Yesterday we saw how Jesus set His face towards Jerusalem and saw one who would betray Him and one who would later deny Him. There are four other sights that we will consider today.

3. He saw His own people rejecting him. John 1:11 says, 'He came to his own, and his own did not receive him.' On Palm Sunday they would lay their clothes on the road, cut down branches from the trees and cry, 'Hosanna! Blessed is he who comes in the name of the Lord' (John 12:13b). But five days later, the same people would cry, 'Crucify him!' (Matthew 27:22b). Now His own people turn their backs upon Him.

4. He saw a cross that would hold Him but not keep him there. A cross that came from a tree that He had created and planted. The nails came from ore that He had placed in the ground. I hear some say that His enemies took His life. 'No!' A thousand times, 'No!' No one took His life; He freely gave it up for us all. He had the power to call ten thousand angels, but it was love for His people, such as you and me, that held Him there to the bitter end. He knew the plan, which was formed before the world began, and He followed it in obedience to His Father's will.

5. He saw a tomb that could not keep Him. Wrapped in grave clothes, with a large stone to keep Him in and guards to ensure that no one stole His body, Jesus was securely encased within the cold, dark sepulchre. However, nothing or no one could prevent His bodily resurrection. Almighty God had been watching over His Son for the past three days, and the time was coming when He would release Him from captivity.

6. He saw an enemy that couldn't conquer Him. Since His birth in Bethlehem, the devil had done all within his power to defeat God's plan. Yet, on that first Lord's Day, God overturned the devil's plans and the One the devil planned to conquer became the conqueror.

Let every Christian rejoice this day that there is no body on a cross because Jesus is alive. Hallelujah!

'Thine be the glory, risen conquering Son,
Endless is the victory Thou o'er death hast won!'

Edmond Louis Budry (1854–1932)

23 JANUARY

He supports those in the furnace

'For in that he himself has suffered, being tempted, He is able to aid those who are tempted.' Hebrews 2:18

RECOMMENDED READING: Matthew 4:1–11

When we read the Gospels, it soon becomes clear that our Lord Jesus Christ was not immune from the devil's attacks.

As He was about to begin His earthly ministry, He was exposed to temptation. Following His baptism (Matthew 3:13–17), we read that He was led of the Spirit into the wilderness to be tempted by the devil (Matthew 4:1). Despite the severity of these three temptations, we read that He came through victoriously (Matthew 4:11).

As we fast forward towards the closing days of His ministry, He again faced temptation in the Garden of Gethsemane. As well as being the Son of God, He was also the Son of Man, and here, in the garden, the anguish of the cross was clear to see. 'Take this cup away from me' (Mark 14:36). He was asking His Father that, if there was any other way to redeem mankind, then show it to Him and He would take it. It became immediately clear that there was no other way, for without the shedding of blood there is no forgiveness of sin. Finally, He said, 'Nevertheless, not what I will, but what you will' (Mark 14:36).

From that moment His eyes turned towards Calvary, although He had never lost sight of the true purpose of why He came to earth.

When we pass through deep waters or journey through the furnace of affliction, don't look at the waters or the flames, but keep your eyes upon Jesus, for he will carry us through. Because He has suffered, He is able to comfort and support us through the dark and lonesome valley of temptation.

When you are tempted, sometimes to despair, then tell Him. He knows how you feel; He knows what you are experiencing. There is nothing that you are going through, or will ever go through, that He hasn't faced already. So be honest with Him and tell Him everything. He will hear for He understands how you feel and will be there to bring you through.

We may be battered and bruised, but never defeated. As He went on to victory, so do we. Hallelujah!

Dead, dry bones live again

'Surely I will cause breath to enter into you, and you shall live.' Ezekiel 37:5

RECOMMENDED READING: Ezekiel 37:1–14

As we begin this chapter, Ezekiel is preparing to preach to God's people. But what a strange congregation he had before him! We are told in vv.1 and 2 that they were dead, dry bones lying in an open valley; and there were many of them. It is also clear that they had been there a very long time.

The people of Israel were so far from God that they were compared to a valley of dry bones. What is the purpose, then, in preaching to them? If Ezekiel were to answer that question, he would probably reply by saying, 'I have been told by God to preach to them (v.4). What God does after that is none of my business.'

Our task as Christians is to be obedient to what God has told us to do, but at the same time be always submissive to His sovereign will. We share the gospel with others, not because we know they will respond, as on most occasions, sadly, they will not. Yes, we love them, and long to see them saved, but another reason we do it is so that we can be clear of their blood. We tell them because God requires us to do so (Ezekiel 33:1–6).

In our country there are millions of people of all ages who are spiritually dead, and some have been in that condition for many years. They have become hardened to the gospel with hearts like stone. Most would not enter a place of worship, but those who do can become more hardened as the years go by. The preacher can preach his heart out, but there is no reaction to the message—that is if they are awake to hear it.

The same applies to members of our family, friends or colleagues at work. You spend years trying to witness to them, but they remain spiritually dry, cold and dead. So why bother? There's no hope for such people. That is exactly what Ezekiel may have thought when he saw the vision before him.

But once Ezekiel followed God's instructions in v.7, '... the bones came together'. Then in v.8, '... sinews and flesh came upon them'. Finally, in v.10, '... breath came into them and they lived'.

Never, ever give up in your ministry. Dead, dry bones can live! Yours did! Mine did! But never forget; only God can give life. So, keep pressing on.

> 'Lord, you have made the blind to see,
> the deaf to hear, the dumb to speak,
> The dead to live—and now I break
> the chains of my captivity!'
>
> William T. Matson (1833–99)

25 JANUARY

Keep watering and you will be watered

'And he who waters will also be watered himself.' Proverbs 11:25

RECOMMENDED READING: Proverbs 11:24–31

As I was reading this verse, it both challenged and encouraged me. I hope it will do the same for you.

1. Through teaching others, we receive instruction. How often when we minister to others, are we also ministered to in some special way. We go to teach the Bible to others and then return utterly ashamed that we knew so little about it ourselves. We share the truth that we thought we were familiar with and then realise, despite our many years as a Christian, that we were only up to our ankles in the knowledge and depth of God's love, whereas some mature believers were up to their necks. Charles Haddon Spurgeon said, 'We learn by teaching, and our pupils often teach us.'[3]

2. By bringing comfort, we receive comfort. 2 Corinthians 1:4 says, '[The God and Father of our Lord Jesus Christ] who comforts us in all our tribulation that we may be able to comfort those who are in any trouble, with the comfort with which we ourselves are comforted by God.' We seek to bring comfort to another believer who is in need of our support, yet that person brings comfort to us and meets our need. I cannot count the number of times that I have visited some elderly or sick believer to try and bring some word of comfort to them, and it is I who have received the greater comfort and blessing. Pastoral work can be demanding at times, but it can also bring unexpected blessings to us.

3. Helping others should make us humble. If we have a high opinion of ourselves, we are quickly brought down to reality when we discover there are many people in the world far better than we are. Never ask the Lord to keep us humble, because so often we are not. Instead ask Him to make us humble, because so often that is what is needed. James 4:6 tells us that, 'God resists the proud, but gives grace to the humble.' That is a lesson we all need to learn. After all, we have nothing to be proud of, as we are what we are only because of God's amazing grace.

4. By ministering to others, you receive many prayers. Spurgeon also said, 'Let me have your prayers, and I can do anything! Without your prayers I can do nothing.'[4] We all need the prayers of others. Pastors, youth workers, missionaries, and all who serve the Lord in any capacity need the prayers of others. With them do not be surprised by what can be achieved. So, keep watering and you too will be watered.

26 JANUARY

Lest we forget

'I thank my God upon every remembrance of you.' Philippians 1:3

RECOMMENDED READING: Romans 16:1–16

As my thoughts turned to Philippians 1:3, I began to thank God for every remembrance of you all. I think of my own fellowship at Wellington Chapel. During this time of lockdown, you are all greatly missed. I long for the time when we can see each other again. You may ask, 'What is happening? Is John Roberts getting sentimental and soppy?' No, I'm still a Yorkshireman, but it is in difficult times such as these that we perhaps appreciate each other much more.

When the apostle Paul was in prison, in far more difficult circumstances than we face today, he wrote, 'For God is my witness, how greatly I long for you all with the affection of Jesus Christ' (Philippians 1:8). But turning my attention more widespread, I thank God when I remember Christian friends throughout the United Kingdom that Kathryn and I have enjoyed fellowship with over many years. You are very much in our thoughts as well. I also thank God for those in our fellowships who are serving others so faithfully. For pastors, who in these days are preparing spiritual food to satisfy many hungry souls. Your labours are much appreciated and your work is not in vain.

I thank God for those who give their time and vehicles to collect groceries and medication for those who are isolated; they are always available when there is a need. Almighty God sees the kind acts you perform. Then there are those who ring around the fellowships checking that other believers are well and coping. Your concern is greatly appreciated by all.

I thank God for Christian friends in the NHS who are working long hours, caring for those who, in some instances, are fighting for their lives. For those known personally to us, we remember you and thank God for you.

For those at home who are isolated and often feel lonely, we think and pray for you. You served the Lord when you were young and strong. Now is the time to let those who care, serve you.

My sentimental mood may pass by tomorrow and I know this 'thought for the day' has been very different. However, let us thank God for each other and remember, wherever in the country or the world we live, we are members of the same family, and what a wonderful Father we have who cares so much for us all.

> 'He bids us build each other up; And, gathered into one,
> To our high calling's glorious hope We hand in hand go on.'
>
> Charles Wesley (1707–88)

27 JANUARY

We have an appointment to keep

'Thomas, because you have seen Me, you have believed. Blessed are those who have not seen and yet have believed.' John 20:29

RECOMMENDED READING: John 20:19–31

It was the day of the resurrection of our Lord. Jesus appeared to His disciples but Thomas was not with them when He came (John 20:24). It is so important that we meet together at the appointed time, in the appointed place. Some may ask, 'Must I go to church? Surely once is enough?'

If we stay away as Thomas did, we may miss something important. It is vital to be there, unless we have a genuine reason to be absent, because God may well have something to say to us which He may choose not to repeat.

Thomas was missing! When the other disciples told him they had met Jesus he was sceptical. He wanted proof and yet, if he had been present on that day, he would have had proof. How gracious and patient Jesus was with Thomas a week later! 'After eight days ...' (John 20:26). A week had gone by and this time Thomas was with them. That is exactly how it should always be. The preacher has an appointment to fulfil, after many hours of preparation. So has each member of the congregation.

Notice how the second visit was a replica of the first. It was the same day—the first day of the week; the same message—'Peace be with you'; the same position—'in the midst.'

The only difference was, this time, Thomas was there. How tenderly Jesus dealt with the sceptic! No harsh condemning words were spoken. How embarrassed Thomas must have been!

In v.25, he had made a clear declaration: 'Unless I see in His hands the print of the nails and put my finger into the print of the nails, and put my hand into His side, I will not believe.' In v.27 he had to keep his word. Thomas had not only to see, but also to touch his Master.

What a profound truth came from his lips! In v.28 he declared, 'My Lord and my God!'

May we, believers and doubters, be given assurance to make the same affirmation with total confidence. Thomas now understood the true character of Jesus.

May Almighty God open wide our spiritual eyes so that we too may say, 'My Lord and my God!'

> 'No one can truly say that Jesus is the Lord
> Unless you take the veil away and breathe the living word.'
>
> Charles Wesley (1707–88)

28 JANUARY

God is in control

'O Lord my God, in You I put my trust.' Psalm 7:1

RECOMMENDED READING: Psalm 2

During the past few years, we have seen the growth of fake news. We need to take great care in distinguishing between the fake and the facts. However, there is something even more serious and that is the need to be aware of spiritual myths which many are accepting as facts. What is especially dangerous are fictitious beliefs which contain some elements of truth. During the next few days, I want to consider some of these fictitious beliefs.

1. **The world is out of control.** I hear this quite frequently in my travels. People refer to the devastation caused over recent years by ISIS throughout parts of the Middle East and even further afield. We also hear of the growing threat of rogue nations obtaining nuclear weapons. Then we read of famines, floods and droughts in many parts of the world. We cannot forget the battle with COVID-19 which affected every continent of the world, including the UK.

Yes, to the unbeliever, it does look as though situations are out of control with governments powerless to prevent them.

For the Christian believes that all events are under God's control, and are working out perfectly, although they sometimes seem very strange to us. They not only are, but always have been, and always will be under sovereign control. God looks from heaven upon a world He created and derides man's puny efforts to control the world by himself. What an utter mess we make of it when we leave God out of our plans.

If only leaders and governments would seek God's help and direction, this world would be so different. But man thinks he has all the answers and can deal with every situation as it arises without looking to his Creator. What stupidity!

However, the Christian doesn't need to get worked up and in some frenzy. God knows what He is doing—He is the only One who does—and we can depend on Him. Nothing can happen by chance or without His knowledge. What comfort that brings to the believer.

Some situations are hard to understand and Christians don't have all the answers. But we know that God is love. He suffered as He saw His Son die in agony upon a cross at a place called Calvary. Jesus died to bring us forgiveness for our sins and peace with God.

Ignore the fake news. Stick to the facts!

29 JANUARY

In the beginning was God

'He has made everything beautiful.' Ecclesiastes 3:11

RECOMMENDED READING: Genesis 1:1 – 2:3

Yesterday we began to consider some spiritual myths that are being accepted as facts. Today we turn to the second myth.

2. Everything just evolved. Over recent decades the theory of evolution has gained increasing popularity, partly aided by a godless media. But let us never forget, it is only a theory. The Christian stands by facts. The Bible, which is God's authority, begins, 'In the beginning God created' (Genesis 1:1). I find it amazing that intelligent people can believe that life, as we know it, began with a big bang, and that over billions of years things have evolved to this present time.

Just consider the human body. We have been given all that is needed to maintain life. We have a heart, liver, kidneys, lungs and a brain, to name but a few organs. Did all these come through chance? The brain itself is more intricate than any computer system. It stores vast amounts of information. It remembers past events and plans future projects. Most of us are blessed with sight which can observe objects at a great distance and can detect amazing colours. We have hearing to enjoy the many different sounds of nature. We have speech which enables us to communicate both in conversation and in song. We can enjoy the variety of food which God has graciously given to us. He has also given taste buds which we so easily take for granted. We have a skeleton structure that enables us to walk, run and work. This is one small aspect of God's vast creation. We are fearfully and wonderfully made.

Try and imagine a major explosion in a clock factory. All the workings have been widely scattered throughout the building in minute pieces. Yet without any help or interference the pieces come together in a most remarkable way. According to many people, following the big bang, the many particles just happened to come together and brought life. It's ludicrous to even consider it. An explosion brings chaos and disaster, not orderliness. God brought the latter out of the former. It makes sense to believe that there is a great designer behind the orderliness and beauty of Creation. This designer is Almighty God, the Creator of all things seen and unseen. After all, He was there when it all happened. Were you? We need to be aware of who this God is, for one day we all, including our scientists, will bow before Him and acknowledge that He is Lord. It's better to do that now, than when we die. Charles Spurgeon regarded evolution as the abyss of absurdity.[5] John Calvin said, 'Creation is the theatre of God's glory' (Taylor 2017).[6] I agree with both.

30 JANUARY

God is not to blame

'In all this, Job did not sin with his lips.' Job 2:10

RECOMMENDED READING: Job 2:1-10

We continue to consider items of fake news that are circulating, particularly throughout the western world today, which Christians must strongly refute.

3. All tragedies are God's fault. If you don't believe in a creator who is God, how can you blame Him when tragedies occur? You cannot blame someone in whom you do not believe. Surely that is hypocrisy!

If you accept the creation account of Genesis 1, you will then begin to understand the implications of Genesis 3. Here we have an account of the fall of man into sin and all the horrific consequences that followed.

No, the fault doesn't lie with God. Instead, we have to turn the accusations upon ourselves. Tragedies in whatever guise they come are a result of the fall, and we must be honest with ourselves and with God.

Human nature loves to always pass the buck for our own sin and failures onto someone else. We never like to ask, 'Could it be my fault?'

Adam and Eve did exactly this in the Garden of Eden. You could sum up Adam's reply to God in Genesis 3:12 simply as, 'It wasn't me; it was Eve.' Eve's reply in the following verse can in turn be summed up as, 'It wasn't me; it was the serpent.' We cannot pass the buck and put the blame for our own failures upon someone else, especially God.

We are all responsible for our own sin and should have the courage and honesty to admit it.

When I look at this beautiful planet; it is us who are ruining it. When I consider the millions of hungry people around the world, it is us who throw tons of good food away each day, even in our own nation. When I think of the wars that take place throughout the world, it is our greed and thirst for power which often leads to conflict. We could go on.

No, tragedies are not God's fault; they are the result of man's rejection of God and therefore the consequences rest heavily with us.

For those who acknowledge their sin, God provided a rescuer in His Son, the Lord Jesus Christ. Although we deserve God's punishment for our failure and rejection of Him, God instead demonstrated His love by sending His Son to die on Calvary's cross so that we might be forgiven from all our sin. Our iniquity was laid upon Him instead of ourselves. What a wonderful Saviour is Jesus my Lord.

31 JANUARY

We all need God

'The fool has said in his heart, "There is no God."' Psalm 14:1

RECOMMENDED READING: Luke 12:16–21

We continue to consider another item of fake news which Christians must denounce.

4. I don't need God. How often do we hear that statement from the lips of unbelievers? It cannot be further from the truth for we all need Him.

You hear people say that they are in control of their own destiny. But what is that destiny, or where is that destiny to which they are heading?

In Luke 12:16, Jesus tells a parable of the rich farmer who had far more than he needed. Here is a man who thought he was in control of his own life and destiny:

'What shall I do since I have no room to store my crops?' (v.17).

'I will do this: I will pull down my barns and build greater, and there I will store all my crops and my goods' (v.18).

'I will say to my soul, "Soul, you have many goods laid up for many years; take your ease; eat, drink and be merry"' (v.19). His entire future is all centred around himself. It is all 'I' throughout the story.

What does God call him? 'You fool!' (v.20). That is applicable to all who put 'I' before God.

Psalm 14:1 says, 'The fool has said in his heart, "There is no God."'

It is wise to recognise that the Creator controls all that He has created. Our destiny is not in our hands, but in the hands of Almighty God.

That fact is a great comfort to the Christian but holds great terror to the unbeliever.

My friend, you need God desperately! You need Him now! You need Him always!

Do not deceive yourself and cling to fake news. Honesty is where you begin. Stick to the facts; they are there for you in the Bible. There you will read that God sent his Son, the Lord Jesus, to rescue you from sin. He gave His life and poured out his blood upon a cross to give all who believe eternal life.

> 'I need Thee, O I need Thee! Every hour I need Thee;
> O bless me now, my Saviour! I come to Thee.'
>
> Annie S. Hawks (1835–1918)

1 FEBRUARY

Not so innocent

'Blessed is he whose transgression is forgiven, whose sin is covered.' Psalm 32:1

RECOMMENDED READING: Psalm 1

We continue our series looking at fake statements that are spoken by many people today.

5. I've done nothing wrong. Who are you kidding? This statement is often said by children when they have been caught doing something that is disapproved of by their parents.

However, it is not just spoken by children. You hear it from the lips of the most prominent and powerful people in society when their misdemeanour has been discovered.

In Romans 3:23 we read, 'For all have sinned and fall short of the glory of God.'

We also read the following words in Romans 5:12: 'As through one man sin entered the world, and death through sin, and thus death spread to all men, because all sinned.'

I heard of a young minister who could not accept the doctrine of original sin. He could not acknowledge that a baby was born with a sinful nature. He never changed his view, until he had his first child. If you are a parent, have you ever had to bring up your children and teach them to be naughty? If so, I would be pleased to meet you, for you are unique.

The most difficult task of any parent is to bring up their children to be decent, good living citizens.

How often you hear people say, 'I lead a good life. I'm as good as anyone who go to church. I give regularly to charity.'

No matter how good and commendable a life may be, it does not hide our sinful condition before God. That is why Jesus came to die for sinners such as you and me.

He did not come to call the righteous, but sinners to repentance. To acknowledge that you are a sinner is the first step in finding forgiveness and peace with God.

It was for us that Jesus took that lonely journey through the streets of Jerusalem. He was then nailed to a cross of wood bearing our sin in His own body on the tree. Three days later He rose victorious from the grave and now lives forever more.

The Christian message is a message of love, forgiveness and hope of eternal life.

2 FEBRUARY

God cares for his people

'*... casting all your care upon Him, for He cares for you.*' 1 Peter 5:7

RECOMMENDED READING: 1 Corinthians 1:3–7

We continue our consideration of fake news which so many regretfully accept as fact.

6. God doesn't care about me. So, you think you are insignificant to Him? You truly believe He doesn't care about you? Let me ask you to reconsider by ignoring the fake news and turning to the facts.

When Jesus lived on this earth, He preached to vast multitudes of people throughout the land of Israel. On one particular occasion He fed over 5,000 men, besides women and children.

We are told that the common people heard Him gladly, for His message was both relevant and understandable. It was not beyond their comprehension.

Although crowds flocked to hear His message, He always found time to speak to individuals. He not only preached to them, but He gave sight to the blind, restored hearing to the deaf, brought healing to the crippled and infirm, and comforted those who mourned. Why? Because He cared for people and showed compassion to them.

He spoke to a Samaritan woman at a well. He brought comfort to a widow outside the village of Nain. He gave time to speak to a rich, young ruler about eternal life.

Although His life was full of activity, He always found time for the individual who was in great need.

Jesus has time for you if you are willing to give it to Him. He is interested in you. You are important to Him. He cares for you. He died a cruel death to save you. The big question is, 'Have you time for Him?'

Can I today encourage you to seek Him; read about Him; talk to Him; listen to Him; trust and believe in Him. You will find the time well spent.

John 3:16 says, 'Whoever believes in Him should not perish, but have everlasting life.'

An encounter with Jesus could radically change your life and your future. He does care about you and wants to be involved in your life.

Don't believe in myths and fake news; just look at the facts. Peace with God is of more value than anything the world can offer.

3 FEBRUARY

Not all roads lead to Heaven

'If I go and prepare a place for you, I will come again and receive you to Myself; that where I am, there you may be also.' John 14:3

RECOMMENDED READING: 2 Timothy 3:14–17

We continue our brief series warning people of fake news that is commonly uttered today. I leave you with another statement.

7. All people go to heaven. This has become widely accepted over recent decades. How many are sadly misled by this myth. It is always interesting to hear people's comments when well-known celebrities have died:
- 'They will be looking down on us!'
- 'They will be having a party up there!'
- 'They lived a good life and deserve to be there!'

The big question is, 'Will they be there?'

When you read the Bible, it is interesting to note that Jesus spoke more about hell than He did about heaven.

People are very comfortable joking about hell when they are alive and in good health. However, when serious illness or death strikes, people's minds automatically go to a place called heaven. Let me conclude with three very important questions. Please take each one seriously.

1. Who will not be there? Revelation 22:15 gives us a comprehensive list. If our name is not written in the Lamb's Book of Life, we will not be there. If we have not sought forgiveness for our sins, then the cross upon which Jesus died is meaningless to us; we will not be there.

2. So, who will be there? Revelation 21: 27 make it very clear: '… only those who are written in the Lamb's Book of Life.' Only those whose sins have been forgiven through the pouring out of the blood of Jesus upon the cross will be there.

3. How can I get there? Now you are asking the right question! So, let us now ignore the fake and look at the facts:

First of all, by acknowledging before Almighty God your sins, whatever they may be.

Secondly, by trusting in Jesus Christ alone for forgiveness of your sin.

Thirdly, by thanking Jesus for pouring out His precious blood upon the cross at Calvary to save you from God's anger and your condemnation.

Finally, by living a life that glorifies His Name.

You can then be assured of a place with Him in heaven for ever.

4 FEBRUARY

The Bible still speaks today

'Your word is a lamp to my feet and a light to my path.' Psalm 119:105

RECOMMENDED READING: 2 Timothy 3:14–17

During the past few days, we have been considering fake news which is being propounded throughout our nation and discredits the Christian faith. We have looked briefly at seven myths which need to be challenged because they are contrary to the Bible's teaching. Today we look at the final piece of fake news, which is the most serious of all, because our faith hangs upon the reliability of the Bible, which is God's Holy Word.

8. The Bible cannot be relied upon. We not only hear this and similar statements out in the world at large, but even more serious is that there are leaders within our churches who do not accept the Bible as their complete authority.

There was a time when the United Kingdom showed great respect for the Bible and its message. Our laws were built upon Exodus 20—'The Ten Commandments'. Many of our great national leaders in the past held this book in high esteem. Today the Bible is regretfully disregarded by many, but the truth contained within its pages remains reliable, dependable and completely trustworthy.

Predictions made in the Old Testament came to pass hundreds of years later in the New Testament, and every detail was precise and authentic. Today, throughout the land of Israel, records are being discovered and artefacts unearthed which verify the truths of the Bible.

Predictions in the New Testament have already been and will continue to be proved true and accurate. For over 2,000 years, men and women have given their lives to preserve the truths contained in this precious book.

Some say its contents and message are outdated; this book is far more reliable than tomorrow's newspaper. Others say it is old fashioned; so is breathing but hold your nose and close your mouth for two minutes and discover the result.

Men who have denied its historical truth have had to eventually acknowledge their own failings and the Bible's accuracy. God cannot lie! His Word can be relied upon!

Don't believe the fake news with promises that are lies. Read and trust the Bible because God's Word is truth.

> 'How precious is the Book divine, By inspiration given!
> Bright as a lamp its doctrines shine, To guide our souls to heaven.'
>
> John Fawcett (1739–1817)

5 FEBRUARY

Be careful how you walk

'Walk worthy of the calling with which you were called.' Ephesians 4:1b

RECOMMENDED READING: Ephesians 2:1–10

Paul's letter to the Ephesians has brought special blessing and encouragement to me over the years. We have covered chapter 1 earlier, but now, over the next few days, I want to consider chapter 4 where the apostle writes about our Christian walk.

Have you ever witnessed someone trying to walk in a straight line after they have had too much alcohol? Apart from having difficulty standing, they are literally all over the place. Their legs are completely out of control and not co-ordinating with their brain, hence their inability to walk properly.

Throughout the Bible we are instructed how to walk properly and in a manner that brings glory to God.

A young convert to Christ had, years later, become a backslider. He told a friend that, although he had drifted from the faith, he still believed everything in the Bible. The only apt reply his friend gave was, 'If you believe it, then why don't you live it?'

The more we know the truth and believe it, the greater is our responsibility to live it. Our walk should be consistent with our profession of faith.

The American evangelist, D.L. Moody, said, 'Some Christians talk like cream and live like skimmed milk.'[7]

Ephesians chapters 1–3 tell us how God sees us in Christ. Chapters 4–6 tell us how people should see Christ in us.

The word 'walk' indicates motion and movement. There are other words that do the same, such as leap, crawl, float, and drift.

The word 'walk' is different in that it indicates motion with a purpose. We see progress and perseverance; keeping on until the goal is reached.

- It involves the mind—a desire to start.
- It involves the heart—a determination to continue.
- It involves the will—a determination to arrive.

May our heart, mind and will determine how we walk, and choose carefully your companions on the journey.

During the next few days, I want us to look at the occasions when Paul uses the word 'walk' and consider what message he is seeking to convey to us.

May God help us to keep in step with him.

6 FEBRUARY

United in Christ

'Endeavouring to keep the unity of the Spirit in the bond of peace.'
Ephesians 4:3

RECOMMENDED READING: Ephesians 4:1–13

In this chapter Paul is instructing us to walk properly and in a manner that brings glory to God.

1. Walk in unity. If we were asked what the first characteristic of a Christian's walk should be, most of us would probably say, 'holiness'. After all, Ephesians 4:1 states clearly that God chose us to be holy. However, from vv.2–16, Paul shows that the first characteristic of a worthy walk is 'unity'.

In the human body, good health depends on the harmonious working of all the various organs. Just one small part that does not operate correctly can lead to disability and disease.

When we lived near London, friends took us to the Barbican to hear an orchestra playing popular classics. At the end of one particular piece, a few members of the orchestra left the stage while a larger contingent took their seats next to their instruments for the main concerto. One young lady made her way to the back of the orchestra and for the next twenty minutes just stared at the conductor. I thought she had the wrong seat and should have been in the audience. Then she picked up her triangle, struck it three times, and then put it down. She really earned her money that night. Although she only played a very small part, her eyes were on the conductor the whole time, and her part contributed to the harmony and unity of the music.

When we look at the Christian church, her spiritual health is dependent on three things: harmony; perfect co-ordination of each part; keeping our eyes upon Jesus at all times. Unfortunately, that doesn't always happen. We often lack harmony by taking our eyes off Jesus. The result is divisions that dishonour the Lord and cause the world to ridicule the church.

We are desperately in need of returning to the unity Paul desired for the Ephesians, and to seek God's forgiveness for our failure and disharmony. The unity to which God is calling His church is very clearly defined. It is laid down from v.3: '...endeavouring to keep.'

God is not asking us to create unity but preserve a unity that should already exist. The unity we are to keep is 'the unity of the Spirit' (Ephesians 4:3). The body of Christ should have unity in heart, mind, and purpose. This we should hold on to at all costs. Our unity is grounded in the truth of God's Word and operates through his love. It should be an inward unity showing itself in outward affection.

7 FEBRUARY

Pride often leads to a fall

'Walk worthy of the calling with which you were called, with all lowliness.'
Ephesians 4:1,2

RECOMMENDED READING: Philippians 2:5–13

As we continue to consider our Christian walk, in unity with each other, Paul in v.2 shows us how this unity can be achieved.

(a) In humility. The apostle Paul always had a low estimation of himself. He described himself as, 'the least of all the saints' (Ephesians 3:8).

As you read through the Bible many men and women, particularly some of the kings of Judah, began well, but sadly pride brought about their downfall. They were blessed by God with wealth, position, and power, but it went to their heads and pride consumed them. In the end God intervened and brought them down from their high position.

Pride can be destructive and this can be seen today in the lives of many who rule and govern us. There is no fear of God before their eyes. As with Judah's kings, when those who have been elevated to positions of responsibility, and then demonstrated pride, God has brought down to their knees. Power has been stripped from them.

This also applies to religious leaders who have been removed from their elevated positions because they thought too highly of themselves. So, what does the Bible say about pride?

The prophet Micah is very clear in his message to the people. In 6:8 he says, 'What does the Lord require of you but ... to walk humbly with your God?'

John the Baptist said regarding Jesus, in John 3:30, 'He must increase, but I must decrease.' That is a true sign of humility, spoken by the one who was called the greatest prophet born of woman (Luke 7:28).

It is therefore no wonder that Paul, when he writes to the Ephesians in 4:1,2 says, 'walk ... with all humility'(ESV).

John Charles Ryle, the first Bishop of Liverpool, once said, 'The best of men are only men at their very best.'[8] We constantly need to be reminded of who we are and where we came from.

I would like to close this point with one warning: 'Never be proud of your humility.'

> 'The Lord who left the heavens
> Our life and peace to bring,
> To dwell in lowliness with us,
> Our pattern and our king.'

John Keble (1792–1866)

8 FEBRUARY

Attributes to be desired

'Take my yoke upon you and learn from Me, for I am gentle and lowly in heart, and you will find rest for your souls.' Matthew 11:29

RECOMMENDED READING: 1 Timothy 6:11–16

Yesterday we saw how we needed humility in order to walk in unity with each other in the Lord. We conclude with desiring two further characteristics.

(b) **In gentleness.** This is a fruit of the Spirit that is often lacking in our Christian walk, so we need to immediately turn to our perfect example.

In our Lord Jesus Christ we have one who, when He suffered, did not threaten. He was called some humiliating names, yet He endured all the accusations that were directed to Him. He never once looked for revenge or retaliation. He never took offence even when He was provoked to do so. He was strong in His conviction, but always gentle in nature.

Are you feeling guilty and uncomfortable? So am I.

We need to cultivate a gentle spirit in every circumstance that we face in life. It is the humble heart that is gentle.

(c) **In patience.** I am sure most of us will plead guilty here!

How quickly we get annoyed when things don't happen immediately, or as we think they should. We want everything to suit our personal situation. We must not possess an irritable nature that gets easily angered at the first sign of provocation.

God, however, wants us to meet every trial with a calm and serene disposition with each thought and each temper beneath His control. Let God's purpose unfold as He chooses. God will not be rushed under any circumstances.

We need to be patient with God. Remember, He was patient with us and still is. We also need to be patient with people as we would wish people to be patient with us.

Patience is one of God's many attributes; let patience be one of ours also.

When we consider humility, gentleness and patience, we realise how unity does not come on a plate but is something to work at. We should be determined to preserve the unity of the Spirit, for in doing so we glorify our God and bring pleasure and delight to our Lord and Saviour.

Let us walk and work together in unity.

9 FEBRUARY

Truth is the best policy

'You shall know the truth, and the truth shall make you free.' John 8:32

RECOMMENDED READING: John 8:30–47

We are considering the Christian's walk, and how we should conduct ourselves so that we bring glory to God. We have seen how the apostle Paul emphasised the need for Christians to walk in unity, with humility, gentleness and patience. Today we turn to another aspect of our Christian walk.

2. **Walk in truth.** Christians should love the truth. In the prayer of our Lord Jesus in John 17:17b, it says, 'Your word is truth.' That is why the Bible is so important to Christians. It is the only book that is reliable, dependable and trustworthy. In the Bible it is God who is speaking from beginning to end, and His words are truth. If the Bible is true, then we must walk in the truth.

In Isaiah 38, King Hezekiah is sick and near to death. He prays to the Lord and says in v.3, 'I have walked before You in truth.' What a wonderful testimony from this great king of Judah.

Many godly men and women throughout Scripture testified to the fact that they 'walked in truth'. How important it is for us, not only to live by the truth, but also to speak the truth at all times.

In writing to the church at Ephesus, Paul had many practical instructions to give the church. In Ephesians 4:25 he says, 'Putting away lying, let each one of you speak truth with his neighbour.' We must never be guilty of telling lies.

We may say, 'It was only a white lie', but it was still a lie. 'It was only a slight exaggeration', but it was still a lie. 'It was only to save me from embarrassment', but it was still a lie. 'It was only to get me out of a deep hole', but it was still a lie.

Truth is important and precious whether it is read or spoken. As Jesus lived by the truth, and died by it, so we as Christians should be truthful in everything we say.

God can always be relied upon because He always spoke that which was true, and His Son is the exact image of the Father. Therefore, people should be able to rely upon us because we walk in truth.

10 FEBRUARY

Don't stumble in the dark

'This is the message which we have heard from Him and declare to you, that God is light and in Him is no darkness at all.' 1 John 1:5

RECOMMENDED READING: 1 John 2:6–11

We continue our thoughts on our Christian walk. Our conduct should walk in step with our profession of faith. We have considered our walk in unity and in truth. Today we consider a third walk.

3. Walk in light. When we read the biblical account of creation, we are told in Genesis 1:2 that, '… darkness was on the face of the deep'. The first thing God created was light (v.3). 'And God saw the light, that it was good' (v.4). When you have been in darkness, you appreciate the light.

Many years ago, Kathryn and I visited the caverns in Derbyshire. One cavern was called High Peak and our guide directed us to the heart of this enormous structure and warned us that we would experience total darkness. He turned off the lights and his words proved true. We could see nothing; it was a strange sensation. Then, to our relief, we were back in the light.

In the darkness we can stumble and injure ourselves; in the light we see clearly where to place our feet.

If it is wiser to physically walk in the light, how much more important it is for us to do so spiritually. Yet many still walk in darkness. Why? The Bible tells us, '… because their deeds were evil' (John 3:19).

In Isaiah 2:5, the prophet encourages the house of Jacob to '… walk in the light of the Lord'. The apostle John, in his first letter, encourages believers to '… walk in the light as He is in the light' (1 John 1:7).

Now Paul in his letter to the Ephesians 5:8, reminds the church that they were once in darkness, but through God's grace they now walk in the light.

There was a time when we walked in darkness, but a day came when a beam of light began to shine through the darkness. We came into contact with the light of the world—Jesus Himself.

Now you are in the light, I encourage you to continue in the light. That is the only way we can avoid the devil's obstacles and continue our spiritual journey in safety.

> 'Walk in the light, and thou shalt own
> Thy darkness passed away,
> Because that light hath on thee shone
> in which is perfect day.'
>
> Bernard Barton (1784–1849)

We love Him because He first loved us

'Walk in love, as Christ also has loved us and given Himself for us.' Ephesians 5:2

RECOMMENDED READING: 1 Corinthians 13

During the past few days, Paul has given to us many examples of how we should walk as Christians. We continue with one example that both our Lord and the apostles spoke much about.

4. Walk in love. In chapter 5:2 of his letter to the Ephesians, Paul again uses the word 'walk.' This time we are encouraged to walk in love.

The apostle John tells the believers that we 'ought ... to walk just as He walked (1 John 2:6). Then in chapters 3 and 4 he emphasises the importance of showing love to one another. This letter should be read regularly and then demonstrated in every area of our lives. In 1 Corinthians 16:14 Paul says, 'Let all that you do be done with love.' The key word in this sentence is the word 'all'. This is a challenge if ever there was one.

The Bible instructs us to fulfil every responsibility, whether spiritual or practical, in love. The implications of this command are quite staggering. If we followed this principle and obeyed it implicitly, all our earthly relationships would be totally transformed.

- The traditional family unit, now under vicious attack from some quarters in society, would be immediately strengthened. Divorce and youth crime would significantly decline.
- The frustration of job pressure would suddenly decrease because Christians would carry out their duties in love for Christ and not out of compulsion.
- Even our times of worship would become far more meaningful.

Paul instructs us in Ephesians 5:2 to 'walk in love', but we need an example to follow. In the same verse he goes on to say, '... as Christ also has loved us and given Himself for us'. Christ is our example. He is the standard before us that we should emulate. He demonstrated the depth of His love, '... in that while we were still sinners, Christ died for us' (Romans 5:8). In Ephesians 4:32 we have before us the perfect picture: 'Be kind to one another, tender-hearted, forgiving one another.' Then follows the example: '... even as God in Christ forgave you'. When Paul uses the word 'as' he tells us how do it.

You very rarely come across the word 'love' in many of the other religions, but it is at the heart of Christianity. Christ loved us. We ought to love one another. Therefore, I say to you, 'Walk in love'.

12 FEBRUARY

Walking with the Lord

'Wisdom is the principal thing; therefore get wisdom.' Proverbs 4:7

RECOMMENDED READING: Proverbs 3:13–24

The apostle Paul has been instructing us how we should walk in our Christian life. We conclude with two more.

5. Walk in wisdom. Some time ago I referred to the occasion when Tony Blair came into power as Prime Minister; it was on 2 May 1997. In his first Labour Party Conference address he said that, 'Education, education, education is my priority.'

Today more young people go to university than in any previous generation. People of all ages are seeking degrees, many through correspondence courses. Our people have heads crammed full of all kinds of knowledge. When I watch University Challenge, I am amazed at the amount of knowledge our young people possess.

But where is wisdom? Unfortunately, many seem wise in their own eyes only.

Our Parliament and judiciary comprise of many learned men and women who have attained high levels of education. But wisdom? In Job 12:17 we read that God '… makes fools of the judges'. When I read of some of the decisions made in our law courts, God's Word is pretty accurate.

Are we not seeing that is so, both by the conduct of those in authorities, and also by the godless laws which are being enacted in the corridors of power? Job 28 closes with these words: 'Behold, the fear of the Lord, that is wisdom.'

I would encourage young people to search for knowledge and educate yourselves in as many areas of life as you can. But never forget that wisdom is an attribute far more valuable to possess, and this can only be obtained from God alone.

We provide in our educational establishments ample education for the body. We saturate our minds with general knowledge. But where is the education for the soul that at one time we counted so important for our young people's future.

Today many have much knowledge, but lack wisdom, whilst some may have little knowledge but abound in wisdom.

Walk in wisdom!

Keeping in step with God

'Enoch walked with God.' Genesis 5:22

RECOMMENDED READING: Genesis 6:1–9

We have been considering the apostle Paul's instructions on how to walk the Christian life in a manner that is pleasing to God. Our final walk is the most important walk of all.

6. Walk with God. There are only two men in the Bible who are described as having walked with God. In Genesis 5:22 we read, 'Enoch walked with God.' Then in Genesis 6:9 we read that 'Noah walked with God.' What a great testimony to leave for all those who followed!

Although not directly mentioned, there are others who walked with God, such as Abraham, Moses, Ruth, John, Paul and so many more. But as we conclude our thoughts over the past few days, we must ask the big question: What about us? Do we walk with God?

When I was much younger, I developed a very bad habit that took me a while to conquer. When Kathryn and I went for a walk with friends, my mind would often be on the next sermon I was planning to preach or a project I wanted to get clear in my mind. I found it difficult to switch off and unintentionally I found myself walking well ahead of the others. Kathryn would then gently correct me by saying that it was not only bad manners, but how could she converse with me when I was so far in front. You can only have fellowship when you walk with people. I soon began to rectify it.

When it comes to our relationship with God, the danger is that we either run ahead or lag behind Him. God wants us to have communion with Him, so let us learn to walk with God. When we walk 'with' Him, He will ensure that we walk in unity, in truth, in light, in wisdom, in humility and in love. Our relationship with Him will be much more pleasant.

Therefore, as we journey on the path of life, let us ensure that we too walk with the Lord in the light of His Word. By doing this we will not go astray by deviating to the right or the left but remain on the narrow path which will take us safely to our final destination, heaven.

> 'When we walk with the Lord,
> In the light of His Word,
> What a glory He sheds on our way!'
>
> 'Then in fellowship sweet
> We will sit at His feet,
> Or we'll walk by His side in the way.'   John Henry Sammis (1846–1919)

14 FEBRUARY

Let contentment be our goal

'Be content with such things as you have.' Hebrews 13:5

RECOMMENDED READING: 1 Timothy 6:1–11

As I look into the life of the apostle Paul, I realise what an amazing man he was. From the moment of his conversion to his final days spent in a prison in Rome, the man was confronted with trials of every kind.

Just read 2 Corinthians 11:23–28, and then ponder upon the words from 2 Corinthians 7:4: 'I am exceedingly joyful in all our tribulation.' You can see that in all circumstances he knew what it was to be content. How could he be like that? Because God had promised that He would never leave Paul, the apostle believed what God had said.

Even during the final days of his life, having spent two years in prison and now awaiting execution, there was a calmness that only God could have given to him. Read those final words which he spoke to Timothy in his second letter. In chapter 4:6–8, his thoughts were on the future.

It reminds me of my brothers and sisters in many parts of the world where they can truly empathise with Paul. Many are cold and hungry and have no shelter with little clothing. For some their home is a labour camp, or a dark infested prison cell. Yet, they too are content because they know God will never leave them, and their future home is not far away. They can say with Paul in Philippians 4:11, 'I have learned in whatever state I am, to be content.'

When I compare their lifestyle with ours, it could not be more opposite. We have beautiful homes that are warm and dry in winter. Even in the midst of the coronavirus pandemic, we have ample food on our tables and clothing on our backs. Instead of looking at the walls of a cell, even though we may be confined to our homes, we have so much to be thank God for and enjoy.

Oh, may God forgive us when we grumble and complain! Can I remind you that in our free society, our lifestyles are considerably easier than those of our many persecuted families in restricted countries. There are more Christians being persecuted today than those who are free to worship in peace in this world.

I am always challenged by the words of Paul in 1 Timothy 6:6–8: 'Now godliness with contentment is great gain. For we brought nothing into this world, and it is certain we can carry nothing out. And having food and clothing, with these we shall be content.'

May we all grow old gracefully and not grumpily. Contentment—what a wonderful state to be in!

15 FEBRUARY

Preparing for the future

'For the trumpet will sound, and the dead will be raised incorruptible, and we shall be changed.' 1 Corinthians 15:52

RECOMMENDED READING: 1 Thessalonians 4:13–18

For the next few days, I want to turn our thoughts to a subject that should be important to every Christian. We are going to be considering our final destination, which is heaven.

After thinking about this subject, I want to acknowledge at the very beginning that it is far greater than any Christian can fully understand. Therefore, it is not surprising that we hear few sermons on heaven. But this subject should be in our thoughts constantly because we never know when God will call us to be with Him.

Just before I retired from Day One Christian Ministries, we were publishing a series of Travel Guides based upon the lives of well-known and greatly respected Christians from past centuries, such as Bunyan, Spurgeon, Carey and Wilberforce.

As we began the series, I had the opportunity of visiting the places of interest associated with these godly men. In other words, I had been there.

We are now about to consider a place I have never been to. Neither have I met anyone who has. All I have is a record of One who came from there, spoke about it, and has now returned. I also have an account of a vision that the apostle John had of this remarkable place in Revelation.

When we relocate to another part of the country, we investigate all about it: the shops; the transport links; the schools, if you have children; and, most importantly, a good, biblically based evangelical church.

But do we investigate our eternal destiny? Do we prepare for our forever home and ensure our hearts are ready for what will be our final move? Heaven is a place where every Christian will go and they will reside there for evermore. This is our final destiny so make sure you are well prepared for when God calls you.

So, during the coming days, we will be turning our thoughts to the Bible and see what our Lord has to teach us about our future home. At the end I pray that we will be ready to meet our Saviour.

16 FEBRUARY

'I' is always at the heart of sin

'Christ died for our sins according to the Scriptures.' 1 Corinthians 15:3

RECOMMENDED READING: Romans 5:12-19

During the next few days, we are considering the subject of heaven which should be so important to all who are the Lord's people. I will try to describe the indescribable and fathom the unfathomable.

So where do we commence our journey?

Reading the Bible helps us to understand what heaven is like, not just by telling us what is there, but also emphasising what is not there. So, let us consider certain experiences we face now in this life, but will not be experienced in heaven.

1. The first experience we face now is sin—common to the entire human race. In Psalm 51:3, David said, 'For I acknowledge my transgressions, and my sin is always before me.' Although King David lived in close communion with his God, he was very conscious of falling into sinful ways, and some very serious ones. He is not alone.

The biggest battle we face is one that is fought daily and with the same enemy. It is the battle with sin. It haunts us constantly. But we must keep fighting this battle. The enemy of our soul will not give up, so we must not give up. We must be thankful that God has given to us the equipment to fight this battle (Ephesians 6). We must wear it and use it.

What a burden sin is to us all! It follows us continually. There are times when it even brings sorrow and shame. Oh, the mind. How it plays tricks with us at the most unexpected times! Thoughts come into our head, even during times of worship, and we ask, 'who put that thought there?' The evil one is deceitful and tries many avenues to distract us from having fellowship with God.

A request for mercy is a confession of guilt. David pleaded with God to blot out his sin (Psalm 51:9). In this life, the battle with sin, whether it is in thought, in word or in action will always be evident. It is an experience we face now.

BUT THEN: Revelation 7:14 assures us there will be no more sin. The battle will be over. We will wear robes that have been washed in the blood of the Lamb. We will be, and will remain, spotlessly clean. No unclean thing will enter this place. We will enter heaven and revel in its blessings, not because of our merits, but because of His grace. Sin shall then have no more dominion over us. The battle will be finally over.

Hallelujah! What a Saviour!

17 FEBRUARY

Weeping tonight: joy in the morning

'Jesus wept.' John 11:35

RECOMMENDED READING: Luke 19:37–48

We continue to consider a number of experiences that we face in this life but will not be experienced in heaven.

2. The second experience we face now is weeping. In John 20:11, we read that on the morning of the resurrection, 'Mary stood outside by the tomb weeping.' She remained in the garden weeping, even after the disciples had gone home.

The 'staying' and the 'weeping' demonstrated the deep affection Mary had for her Master. To lose Him to the cross was one great tragedy, but now to lose Him from the tomb was more than Mary could bear. To hear Jesus speak her name, and then finally recognise Him, brought great delight to her stricken soul. She just didn't want to let Him go. Those who find Christ just long to cling to Him (John 20:17).

Most people cry from time to time. Could I remind you, especially men who want to present a tough image, that there is nothing shameful in crying. Even our Lord wept at the tomb of His close friend Lazarus. Earlier when He made His final journey into Jerusalem, He wept over the city that had rejected His life-changing message, and would, in a few days, demand His crucifixion.

During our lifetime there are occasions when we also break down and weep. We shed tears of regret, tears of unhappiness, tears of bereavement and loss, tears of despair and tears of sorrow. Expressing emotion through weeping is an experience we will all face from time to time.

BUT THEN:

In Revelation 21:4 we are told that, 'God will wipe away every tear from their eyes ... there shall be no more ... crying.' All the tears I have mentioned, and many more, will be gone forever. However, I have deep down within me a gut feeling. I wonder if there could be one form of tears in heaven—tears of joy. I love good music. When I hear the trumpets of heaven playing, and the choirs of heaven singing, I wonder if my eyes will be wet with tears. I wouldn't be surprised.

I just feel that, when I see my Saviour for the first time face to face, my eyes will be wet with tears. When I realise the suffering He went through to save my soul, I am sure there will be tears of joy and gratitude for all that He did on the cross for me. I can tell you that I will be happy to shed them. What I do know is that there will not be any tears of unhappiness, for heaven is a place of unending joy, and Jesus is already there preparing a place for us.

18 FEBRUARY

Suffering will be no more

'I know that my Redeemer lives… and after my skin is destroyed, this I know, that in my flesh I shall see God.' Job 19:25–26

RECOMMENDED READING: Psalm 66:8–12, 16–20

We continue to look at experiences we face now in this life, that will not be experienced in heaven.

3. The third experience we face now is the challenge of pain. If there was one hero of the faith who knew what it was to endure constant pain, it was God's servant Job. He suffered the loss of his many possessions, including his sheep, cattle and camels. He also lost his seven sons and three daughters. This alone would be painful enough for any person to bear.

But on top of all this, he had to endure personal, physical pain with severe boils from the crown of his head to the soles of his feet (Job 2:7). These boils were so painful and uncomfortable that he took a piece of broken pottery to scrape himself so he could get some relief. His wife even told him to curse God and die (Job 2:9).

The beggar Lazarus, who sat at the rich man's gate, had some relief when the tongues of the dogs licked his sores (Luke 16:19–21), but Job had no help at all. Instead of resting in a soft warm bed, he sat among the ashes (2:8). In the life of Job, we see the devil was not only a tempter, but a tormentor.

Yet, despite all this, we are left with a remarkable testimony. In Job 2:10 we read, 'In all this, Job did not sin with his lips.'

During our travels throughout the United Kingdom, Kathryn and I have met a number of people who have, and still are, experiencing constant pain. They hardly ever find relief, day or night. Our hearts go out to such people.

Pain is an experience that most of us will have to face some time or another during our lifetime.

BUT THEN:

Revelation 21:4 says, 'There shall be no more pain, for the former things have passed away.'

Can you believe it? No more aches or discomfort; migraines gone for ever; rheumatism and arthritis no longer an issue; your health service totally redundant. The blind will see, the deaf will hear, the lame will run and the dumb will speak.

In this life our bodies bear the marks of our sinful nature, and pain is one of its characteristics. Let me conclude with really good news. A day is coming when the Christian will receive a brand-new body, in perfect condition, and it will remain that way forever.

19 FEBRUARY

Death will die

'For as in Adam all die, even so in Christ all shall be made alive.'
1 Corinthians 15:22

RECOMMENDED READING: John 11:1–45

During the past few days, we have been considering a number of experiences we face now but will not be faced in heaven. I want to share with you one more.

4. The fourth experience we face now is death. I want to take a short journey from Jerusalem, along the Mount of Olives, to a small village called Bethany. It is the home of sisters Mary and Martha and their brother Lazarus. We find the account in John 11. Lazarus was sick. His sisters, being concerned about his health, sent a message to Jesus asking Him to come. When Jesus received the news, v.6 tells us that He remained where He was for two more days. Eventually He made His way into Judea. On the way He told His disciples in v.11 that Lazarus was sleeping and that He was going to wake him up. This seemed to confuse them and they told Jesus in v.12, 'If he sleeps, he will get well.' They just didn't understand, so in v.14 Jesus told them plainly that, 'Lazarus is dead.'

'Lazarus is dead.' These words sound so cold. The finality of losing a loved one on this earth can be heart-breaking. A loved one deceased. To be seen no more; to talk with no more; to share things no more.

Death is an experience we all will face at some time. We cannot escape it. 1 Corinthians 15:26 calls it an 'enemy', and so it is; but it is the last enemy.
BUT THEN:
Revelation 21:4 says, 'There shall be no more death.' The Greek says, 'Death shall be no more.' 1 Corinthians 15:22 says, 'As in Adam all die; even so in Christ all shall be made alive.' Note, only those 'in Christ'; only those whose sins have been forgiven. 1 Corinthians 15:54,55 says, 'Death is swallowed up in victory. O death where is your sting?'

Even Job, who is believed by many to have lived during the time of the Patriarchs, had this assurance. In Job 19:25–26 he said, 'I know that my Redeemer lives ... After my skin is destroyed, this I know, that in my flesh I shall see God.' Death is not the end for the believer.

When we die, it will be the beginning of the greatest adventure we have ever undertaken. Heaven will be beyond our wildest dreams. But the most important aspect is that Jesus will be there, and we will have eternity to express our gratitude for all that He has done for us.

20 FEBRUARY

The best is yet to come

'I saw a new heaven and a new earth, for the first heaven and the first earth had passed away.' Revelation 21:1

RECOMMENDED READING: Revelation 21

Before we conclude this short glimpse into the future, I want to share some wonders of our new home.

1. Heaven is eternal. When we were young in years, the future seemed such a long way ahead. However, when we are older the past seems such a long way behind. On earth everything is ordered by time. Here we grow old, waste away, and deteriorate, which eventually results in our death. Life will pass away. Death will come to us all. That's the bad news.

Now for the good news. Heaven will never end. We will not grow old or deteriorate. In time we cannot fully grasp eternity; in eternity we will never consider time.

2. Heaven will reveal the full character of God. In heaven, all God's attributes will be displayed. We will experience perfect holiness. No evil thing or thought will be able to enter. God's purity will shine in words, thoughts and actions. We will behold His glory. It will dazzle us. We will be lost in wonder love and praise.

3. Heaven will have all our questions answered. During my earthly journey, many questions have come to my mind. They usually start with 'How?', 'Why?', or 'When?'. At the door of heaven, we will be able to enquire within. All questions, dilemmas and doubts will be answered. We will fully understand those things that have been a puzzle to us throughout our lifetime.

4. Heaven will give full forgiveness. Stephen, the first Christian martyr, will forgive Saul of Tarsus for consenting to his death. John Newton will be forgiven by the Christian slaves he captured and ill-treated. We will receive forgiveness from those we have wronged. Those who have wronged us, we will forgive. But most of all, we will know full pardon for all our sin.

5. Heaven will bring a change in us. We will be transformed into His likeness. What we lost in the Garden of Eden will be restored in heaven. Now we see through a mirror dimly, but one day we will see Him face to face.

John 14:1,2 says, 'Let not your heart be troubled; you believe in God, believe also in Me. In My Father's house are many mansions; if it were not so, I would have told you. I go and prepare a place for you.'

21 FEBRUARY

Be united with all people

'I looked, and behold, a great multitude which no one could number...'
Revelation 7:9

RECOMMENDED READING: Revelation 5:9–14

I received from our daughter a video clip of a lady in South Africa. She lives in a township among hundreds of homes crammed so close together that people can hardly move between them. A reporter was invited inside her one-room shack. She lives there with her three children. It was not much larger than a garage. There was no hot water, and the family showered in a large bowl which was placed in the centre of the room. This was one of the larger homes, yet it was so small. She had a small garden in a corner of the home, which consisted of one flower in a small plant pot. When interviewed, she spoke most movingly of her Christian faith and was so thankful to God for all she possessed. She said, 'God's economy is always good.'

I was truly humbled to hear her and to experience the great joy she possessed. We have been thinking of our future home during the past few days. Well, this lady knew where her treasures were stored, and it wasn't down here! At the end of the clip, I cast my thoughts to heaven once again, and I look forward to one day meeting this lady in her eternal home and thank her for challenging me on earth.

Charles Haddon Spurgeon shared similar thoughts to the following in one of his sermons: When the church of Jesus Christ is complete, and all His people are gathered together, we will be among people of all nations, tribes and tongues. They will come from the north, south, east and west.

We will see souls of all ages, from the unborn and those innocent ones who have been murdered in the womb, to those dear saints who suffered from dementia during their old age.

We will see people from all levels in society—from godly rulers to those who pulled the oars as galley slaves.

We will see those who showed great patience during long periods of infirmity, enduring much pain. Alongside them will be those who suffered and died in agony at the stake and in labour camps, of whom the world was not worthy.

We will see the monk who rattled the world and made false doctrine pure again. Beside him will be translators of Scripture, who died in flames to give us this precious book in our own mother tongue.

Yes, they will all be there. Only Almighty God knows how many His Son has redeemed from every kindred, tongue, tribe and nation. I trust you will be among them!

22 FEBRUARY

The hand of the Lord had done it

'The hand of the Lord was against the city with a very great destruction.'
1 Samuel 5:9

RECOMMENDED READING: 1 Samuel 5

During the next week we will be considering the hand. We use our hands daily and without them life would be a struggle. Those who have lost one or both hands, through accident, illness or war, know how valuable they had been to them.

We take so much for granted, and so quickly forget God's goodness to us. We will be considering the hand of God; our own hands; and the hands of the Lord Jesus. Today we will begin to consider the hand of Almighty God.

1. The hand of justice. I was reading through 1 Samuel chapters 4 and 5, which record the capture of the ark of God by the Philistines. This was a very sad time for the Israelites, as not only was the ark of God captured, but Eli, the aged priest, and his two sons Hophni and Phinehas had also died. The Israelites were in deep mourning.

The ark of God was brought to Ashdod, and placed alongside the god, Dagon. The following morning, the Philistines found their god on its face before the ark of the Lord (1 Samuel 5:3). After being put back in its place, the following morning they found Dagon with its head and hands broken (1 Samuel 5:4).

This was no accident; the hand of the Lord had done this.

Almighty God will not share His glory with another and in His good time all who try to usurp His authority will eventually go the same way as Dagon.

Another incident is found in 2 Samuel 6, when David was bringing the ark back to Jerusalem. The ark was set upon a new cart, but on the journey the oxen stumbled. Uzzah put out his hand to steady the ark of God, but God struck Uzzah for His error and he died.

God had made it abundantly clear that the ark must be carried by the priests only and that day the hand of God was made evident because of disobedience.

God must be obeyed before anything or anyone. This event is a stark warning to us all. His justice will be carried out sooner or later. Any rival, such as Dagon, will displease Him. Disobedience will be repaid. He must have the pre-eminence at all times and all occasions.

Obedience will always bring His blessing, for His hand is gentle on all those who obey Him.

23 FEBRUARY

Authority in His finger

'The Lord delivered to me two tablets of stone, written with the finger of God.' Deuteronomy 9:10

RECOMMENDED READING: Exodus 20

Yesterday we saw how God's hand of justice was placed upon the Philistine god, Dagon. The result was clear for all to see. Dagon had fallen off his shelf with his head and hands broken. God also demonstrated His justice upon Uzzah for placing his hands on the Ark of the Covenant. Today we see God's hand of instruction and His hand of deliverance.

2. Hand of instruction. In Exodus 20, we have before us the receiving of the Ten Commandments. These are not a set of requests from God; these are commands; words of instruction for our good. They were given to His people, not to be a burden but to be a blessing.

The first three commandments point to our relationship with God. The final six direct our relationship to each other. The fourth is the vital link between the two, pointing to our relationship with God, and the concern we have for others.

The keeping of these commandments cannot save us, but they are the tutor to lead us to the One who can—the Lord Jesus Christ.

As we cannot keep them perfectly due to our sin, no matter how hard we may try, we must thank God that Jesus did.

These commandments were not only spoken by God, but they were, as Deuteronomy 9:10 tells us, '… written with the finger of God'. He had His hand upon them.

3. Hand of deliverance. In Exodus 3, God gave Moses instructions regarding the deliverance of his people from bondage in Egypt. In v.20 He says, 'I will stretch out My hand and strike Egypt with all My wonders which I will do in its midst, and after that he will let you go.' And God kept His word!

Throughout the Bible we have numerous instances of God's amazing deliverances.

The greatest of all was our deliverance from the bondage of sin which held us firmly in its grasp. Then, just at the right time, God's Son, the Lord Jesus Christ, came to break the chains that held us and set us free.

There will never be a greater deliverance than our deliverance from sin.

24 FEBRUARY

The power of his hands

'Immediately Jesus stretched out His hand and caught him, and said to him, "O you of little faith, why did you doubt?"' Matthew 14:31

RECOMMENDED READING: Luke 24:36–53

Over the last two days we considered the hand of Almighty God: the hand of justice, the hand of instruction, and the hand of deliverance. Today, let us consider the hand of our Lord Jesus Christ.

1. The hand of power. Whenever we turn our thoughts to God, we see almighty power. When we consider our Lord Jesus Christ, we see that same power in human action.

(a) He had power over disease. In Mark 8:23 we read, 'He took the blind man by the hand and led him out of the town. And when He had spit on his eyes and put His hands on him, He asked him if he saw anything.'

Jesus has power to heal. There are many similar examples throughout the gospels. Those hands can still give healing and strength to those in need of His touch.

(b) He had power over death. We have in Mark 5 the account of the raising of the daughter of Jairus. In v.41 we read, 'He took the child by the hand and said… "Little girl, I say to you, arise."' He also raised the son of the widow of Nain (Luke 7).

One day every believer will experience that same power when we too will rise from the grave to be forever with the Lord.

(c) He had power over nature. One example of this is seen in the feeding of the 5,000 men, besides women and children. This miracle is the only one recorded in all four gospels. In Luke 9:16 we read, 'He took the five loaves and the two fish, and looking up to heaven, He blessed and broke them, and gave them to the disciples to set before the multitude.'

What He created, He can use for His purpose.

As people throughout the world have experienced, those hands can still perform miracles today. His touch has not lost its power.

25 FEBRUARY

He grips us tight

'*He had in His right hand seven stars.*' Revelation 1:16

RECOMMENDED READING: John 10:22–30

We are considering the hand of our Lord Jesus Christ. Yesterday we noted that it was the hand of power. Today we conclude with two further thoughts regarding His hand.

2. The hand of security. In Revelation 1, we have the beginning of John's vision during his time of exile on the island of Patmos. From v.13, he gives us a description of the Son of Man (the Lord Jesus Christ). In v.16 we are told that, 'He had in his right hand seven stars.' The seven stars are the churches, His own people, whom He redeemed by His own precious blood.

We who are His children are safe and secure in the palm of that right hand and no one can snatch us from His grasp.

In John 10:28 we are told that we are secure in Jesus' hand. Then, in v.29, He also says we are secure in the Father's hand. That double security should bring to us great comfort.

When I go for a walk with my wife Kathryn, I try to remember to hold her hand. If at any time she is off-balance or slips, I am there to grip her hand so she doesn't fall.

I am thankful that Jesus' grip on us is far stronger than my grip. The hymn, 'Guide me, O thou great Jehovah' by William Williams (1717–91), reminds us that, 'He holds us with His powerful hand'. Let us today be thankful that we are in His hand and that we are gripped tight.

3. The hands of salvation. I cannot fail to mention that 2,000 years ago, His hands were stretched out upon a cross on Calvary's hill to save us.

The hands that had blessed little children, healed the sick, raised the dead and fed the multitudes; those same kind, gentle, loving hands were cruelly nailed to a cross of rough wood.

The Lord Jesus hung on that cross in agonising pain and yet, at the same time, looked down upon us in love and compassion, only too willing to forgive if we turned to Him in repentance and faith.

If one day I may just hold those hands for a moment, that would mean so much to me.

May our hands be a blessing to others, just as His hands have been a blessing to us.

26 FEBRUARY

A useful not useless hand

'He said to the man, "Stretch out your hand."' Luke 6:10

RECOMMENDED READING: Mark 3:1–6

It was another Sabbath day. The people were in the synagogue and Jesus was about to teach. But on this particular Sabbath, there was a man present, whose right hand was withered (v.6). Jesus said to the man, 'Stretch out your hand.'

Who this man was, we do not know. He may have been a mason, a potter, a carpenter or a farmer. What we do know is that he was unable to fulfil his proper function in life, and he longed to be useful again.

Over the past four days we have been considering both God's hand and the hand of our Lord Jesus. Now we consider our hands.

1. The hand is for work. The hand is a symbol of usefulness. A withered hand is useless; it cannot work.

As Christians we are going to be judged for what we have accomplished through our lives. The Lord asked Cain a question, 'What have you done?' (Genesis 4:10). It is precisely that question which will be addressed to you and me on that great day. It is fruit that glorifies God. Remember that it was our Lord who cursed the barren fig tree because it had produced no fruit! We can be busy doing many things, but what have we to show for it? Are we seeing fruit?

If our hand is withered, then ask the Lord to heal it. Then put that hand to work, His work. There is a work for Jesus only you can do.

2. The hand is for warfare. It is with the hand that the soldier draws his sword and fights his battles. The believer uses the sword of the Spirit (Ephesians 6:17) with the strength of his hand. Remember the Bible is sharper than any two-edged sword.

But how often my hand is withered and the sword remains in its sheath. Sometimes I am not winning my own battles, nor contributing to the spiritual battle fought by the church of Jesus Christ.

Jesus says, Stretch out your hand.' That withered hand can be healed, and He has the power to do it.

27 FEBRUARY

A very important part of the body

'This is the day the Lord has made; we will rejoice and be glad in it.'
Psalm 118:24

RECOMMENDED READING: Psalm 122

During the past few days, we have looked at the hand of Almighty God and the hand of our Lord Jesus Christ. Now we conclude by looking at our own hands. We have considered the hand for work and for warfare. Today we look at the hand for welcome and for worship.

3. The hand is for welcome. The hand expresses the warmth of a human relationship. If there is one thing that I have missed during this time of lockdown it is welcoming people into the church with a warm handshake. I know some people shake like a wet cod whilst others grasp your hand like a clamp. Either way, it is a sign of welcome.

It is always sad when human relationships become cool and strained. It can often be through a clash of personalities, which can bring jealousy and friction.

We need to remember that it is through the cross that we have been brought together. If the hand of welcome is withered, then look to Jesus for healing.

I cannot wait to shake your hand again!

4. The hand is for worship. In 1 Timothy 2:8 we read: 'I desire therefore that the men pray everywhere, lifting up holy hands, without wrath and doubting.'

Is our hand withered? There are times when our worship has lost much of its joy. Our prayer life has become stale and we find the Bible dry.

Even though, at the present time, we are restricted to social media for our worship, may we still be able to say with the Psalmist, 'I was glad when they said to me, 'Let us go into the house of the Lord'" (Psalm 122:1).

For many of us, the house of the Lord may be our own front room or study, but we can still worship Him there. He is not tied down to time or even place.

So, if your hand is withered, and you find worship, prayer and reading God's Word difficult, then ask Him to heal it and He will.

God created us with two hands; let us use them for His glory and towards the growth of His kingdom.

28 FEBRUARY

Using your hands for God

'What is that in your hand?' Exodus 4:2

RECOMMENDED READING: Exodus 4:1–17

Edwin Van der Sar was born on 29 October 1970. He was a Dutch footballer who played as a goalkeeper for Manchester United. He appeared for his country on 130 occasions and won numerous awards. He is just over 6 feet 5 inches (almost 2 metres) tall and known as the safest hands in football.

On 18 February 2009, he set a world record for the longest time without an opponent scoring against him. His clean sheet lasted 1,311 minutes, or 21 hours 51 minutes of play without conceding a goal. With a total of 21 matches and no goal being scored against him, he won the Barclay Golden Glove award for that season. Those hands have earned him a lucrative and successful career.

Edwin Van der Sar used his hands to forge a successful career in football. The Christian uses his or her hands for the glory of God.

When we have stretched out our hand for healing, we can then put it to good use by putting something in it.

The Lord said to Moses, 'What is that in your hand?' (Exodus 4:2).

Moses had been commissioned by Almighty God to lead the children of Israel out of Egypt. But Moses was apprehensive about the reaction of the Egyptians, and also his own people.

'I'm not the person for this task! I'm not eloquent. I'm not gifted for such a challenge! Surely there are others more capable than I am!' (Exodus 4:10).

Earlier the Lord had said to Moses, 'What is in your hand?' He said, 'A rod.' (Exodus 4:2). Just a rod; a stick; a piece of wood.

Verse 17: 'You shall take this rod in your hand, with which you shall do signs.' The signs, performed through the rod, would be proof that God had sent him.

Great miracles were accomplished with that rod when Moses obeyed the Lord. It was insignificant in itself, but it became a powerful instrument when it was committed to the Lord.

It is amazing the things that can be accomplished when the tool in our hand is given to the Lord's work.

Tomorrow we shall consider some servants of the Lord whose hands were used in his service.

> 'Take my hands and let them move
> At the impulse of Thy love.'

Frances Ridley Havergal (1836–79)

29 FEBRUARY

Use the gift God gave you

'Then they set their hands to this good work.' Nehemiah 2:18

RECOMMENDED READING: Nehemiah 4

Yesterday we saw how a rod in the hand of Moses accomplished great things when God's servant used what God had given him.

Today we will look at a number of men in the Bible who accomplished great things when the tool in their hand was given to the Lord's work.

'What is that in your hand David? Only a sling?' But God used that sling to topple a giant named Goliath and give an unexpected victory to the Israelites over the Philistine army.

'What is that in your hand Joshua? Only a trumpet?' But God used those trumpets to bring down the walls of that strong, fortified city of Jericho.

'What is that in your hand Nehemiah? Only a trowel?' But with it, God used His people to rebuild the walls of Jerusalem in the amazing time of fifty-two days.

'What is that in your hand Peter? Only a net?' But God used it to catch fish—a multitude of them—when Jesus commanded him to cast it on the other side of the boat. Later, he would catch not fish but men.

'What is that in your hand Luke? Only bandages?' Yet with them God used Luke to heal the sick. He also travelled many miles with the apostle Paul taking care of his physical needs.

'What is that in your hand Paul? Only a pen? Then use it!' The apostle spent many hours writing to the churches, teaching, admonishing and encouraging.

John Bunyan only had a pen, but in Bedford prison he wrote the immortal 'Pilgrim's Progress' which has sold millions of copies in many languages throughout the world.

'What is that in your hand Ezra? Only a scroll? Written on that scroll is the law of God. Preach it!'

The Word of God has been preached for centuries and has pointed men and women to the Lord Jesus Christ, the only Saviour from sin. That message has transformed the lives of millions because pastors, evangelists and teachers have used what was in their hands—the Bible, God's Word.

What is in your hand? In our congregations there could be accountants, carpenters, gardeners, doctors, lawyers or engineers. Use the gift that God has given to you.

The Lord often uses small tools to perform large tasks. Use what God has put in your hand. If you don't, He could remove it. Now is the time to let your gifts be used.

1 MARCH

Getting to know God better

'The people who know their God shall be strong and carry out great exploits.'
Daniel 11:32

RECOMMENDED READING: Job 42:1–6

The attributes or characteristics of God is a subject that we need to be reminded of on a regular basis. Though it is a central aspect of our faith, I fear that it has become one of the most neglected. All our doctrine springs from, and rests upon, God's character. Therefore, we neglect His attributes at our peril.

Daniel 11:32 says, 'The people who know their God shall be strong and carry out great exploits.' Note carefully that it says, only those who know their God.

Having been involved in itinerant ministry for nearly 50 years, I must honestly say that one of the greatest weaknesses within the Christian church today is a spiritual one. This is due to the fact that we do not know our God as we should do.

Yet it is so important that as Christians we come to know Him as He really is, and not as we wish Him to be.

I believe this subject is vitally important, because if our knowledge of God is limited and flawed, then our understanding of doctrine is limited and flawed. That will immediately lead to unbalanced doctrine which can become a major problem within the church today.

There is an elderly gentleman called Ashley who lives in our village and used to come to our weekly lunch before lockdown. He has lived in the village all his life and he is most interesting to talk to. He told me about the village wheelwright whose job was to make and repair cartwheels.

He would take a block of hardwood and then, with a chisel and lathe, develop the hub of the wheel until it was perfectly balanced and round. He would then chisel the sockets for the spokes. If every spoke was in the right place and correctly spaced, and the spokes the same length, he had formed a perfect circle.

If one spoke was short or missing, when the wheel revolved it would come down heavily at certain points. If the hub is right, and the spokes are right, he has a perfectly balanced wheel.

God is in perfect balance. He is the hub, and the spokes are doctrine. If our knowledge of God is right, so will be our doctrine.

It is exactly the same when we consider our Lord Jesus Christ, for He is God in human form.

2 MARCH

Don't make our God too human

'You thought that I was altogether like you.' Psalm 50:21

RECOMMENDED READING: Psalm 33

Yesterday we began our introduction into the attributes of God. We concluded that if our knowledge of God is right, so will be our understanding of doctrine. As we begin to look at some of God's attributes, we must not over-emphasise one above the others, or we become unbalanced. Let me try and explain what I mean.

If we just speak about God's love, it can become too sentimental if not accompanied by His anger and justice. There is always the danger of over-stressing one aspect of God's character at the expense of neglecting, or totally ignoring, others. We need the various aspects of God's nature to be perfectly balanced. It is so important to see God as He really is, without Him being just some figment of our imagination.

Doctrine must be preached and taught without bias or overstress. Even the God of the pulpit can be far removed from the God of the Bible if we are not careful.

Think of a pendulum. Too far right, or too far left is dangerous. It must return to the point of balance.

During the time of the 'Toronto Blessing', the emphasis was clearly on the gifts of the Spirit, but little else. Some churches counteracted that by hardly referring to the Holy Spirit at all. Extremism from both ends is concerning.

Some say we must not get excited as others do. However, I find that in some places of worship we are so cold, even when the heaters are on in summer. The pendulum must be balanced; we must be balanced.

As we begin this series my prayer is Jeremiah 9:23–24: 'Thus says the Lord: "Let not the wise man boast in his wisdom, let not the mighty man boast in his might, let not the rich man boast in his riches, but let him who boasts boast in this, that he understands and knows me, that I am the Lord"' (ESV).

Linford Christie, the Olympic gold medal winning athlete, was once asked, 'Why were you successful?' He replied, 'I was hungry for success.' Over these next few days, may we be hungry for God!

Our plumb line cannot sound the depths. Our eyes cannot reach the summit. But may God's Word teach us humility, caution and, above all, reverence.

3 MARCH

He speaks and it is done

'But the thunder of His power who can understand?' Job 26:14

RECOMMENDED READING: Habakkuk 3:1–6

Today we begin to consider our first attribute of God.

1. **The power of God.** During the next few days, I want us to look at the power of God in creation, the power of God in Christ and, finally, the power of God in His people.

In preparing these thoughts, I have come to the conclusion that it is an impossibility to describe the power of God. However, I did come across this statement, from an unknown author, which may help us. 'The power of God is the strength and ability He has to bring to pass all He commands and desires.' If He could not do this, He would cease to be God. God's power gives life and action to every aspect of His nature.

Mercy would be nothing more than feeble pity without His power. Promises would be nothing more than empty words without His power to fulfil them. Predictions concerning judgement would be nothing more than an empty scare without His awesome power.

Let us just consider the voice of God for a moment. Psalm 62:11 says, 'God has spoken once, twice I have heard this: that power belongs to God.' The verse tells us that God spoke once; with God that is all He has to do; it is enough!

We tend to speak so often, and we are so repetitive in what we say. My wife, Kathryn, will say to me, 'You've already said that, and I got the message first time,' or, 'You told that joke before, and I didn't find it funny then.'

In high official places, people love to hear their own voices and are continually saying the same things. After every murder that is committed or following every terrorist attack or injustice, leading politicians will come up with the same words. You can nearly repeat them in your sleep. 'They will be brought to justice; we will conquer terrorism; we will learn from our mistakes.' They keep repeating the same words because they keep making the same mistakes.

But it is not so with God. He speaks once and makes no mistakes. His Son, our Lord Jesus Christ, is the exact image of His Father both in word and action. We, therefore, need to listen and look.

4 MARCH

He is truly awesome

'God has power to help and to overthrow.' 2 Chronicles 25:8

RECOMMENDED READING: Job 38:1–11

We continue to consider the power of God. Within that attribute we thought about the voice of God. Today we turn our attention to the actions of God. Daniel 4:35 says, 'He does according to His will among the hosts of heaven and among the inhabitants of the earth; and none can stay His hand or say to Him, "What have You done?"' (ESV)

God is the beginning of all forms of power. You don't have to turn to somebody else or look somewhere else.

His power is seen in the wind. His power is seen in water. His power is seen in the sun. His power is all around us.

We also see His power in the governments of the world. As we look back through history, empires have risen and during their time of existence they seemed unshakeable and immoveable. You read of the Assyrian, the Babylonian, the Persian, the Greek, the Roman and, dare I say, even the British Empires. But where are they now? Their remains are found in museums.

All governments of the world and their leaders submit to God's authority and power—if they only realised it. By his power they rise, and by His power they fall. All authority is ordained by God. He is the creator of all power.

Let me also remind you that God's power is never overtaxed, and that same power will never exhaust itself.

Job 26:14 says, 'Who then can understand the thunder of His power?' (NIV). God's power is unending and eternal.

Habakkuk 3:4 says, 'His brightness was like the light; He had rays flashing from His hand, and there His power was hidden.' That last phrase reminds me that God's power hides more than it reveals.

We have an amazing and awesome God. We will never understand or grasp the immensity of His power. Our puny minds do not have the ability to fathom it.

However, what is the most amazing truth of all is that this great, powerful God, who controls all that is in the heavens above and on this earth below, is our Father and we are His children. Get your head around that! It's enough to blow the mind!

5 MARCH

God spoke and it happened

'In the beginning God created the heavens and the earth.' Genesis 1:1

RECOMMENDED READING: Job 38:1–11

Today we continue considering the first attribute of God—His power.

(a) The power of God in creation. In 2019, NASA astronaut, Jeffrey Williams concluded his fourth space mission. He broke the United States record for the most days in space, returning to earth after 538 days. When interviewed he said, 'Up there you see the design; you see the beauty; you see the purpose; you see order in every detail. That's what I see when I look out of my window.'

Psalm 89:11 says, 'The heavens are Yours; the earth also is Yours; the world and all its fullness. You have founded them.'

When God spoke, a beautiful world was brought into existence over six days, and we are privileged to live in it and see it.

Whether we look into the night sky to see the billions of stars, dive into the world's oceans and see the remarkable creatures that live there with their beautiful colours and designs, or view the magnificent mountain ranges and all the wonder of God's nature, not in black and white, but in technicolour, we begin to realise what a great and almighty God we worship.

Then I look at ourselves, for we are fearfully and wonderfully made. We have sight, hearing, taste, speech and a brain more intricate than any modern computer system. We have a heart, lungs, liver, and kidneys to name a few, all enclosed within an amazing skeleton to protect them.

Don't let evolutionists deceive you. There is a great designer who created all these things, and He upholds them by His mighty power. I do not have the vocabulary to describe Him. I am just lost in wonder, love and praise.

I say with the Psalmist in 8:4 'What is man?' We are nothing more than a tiny speck that becomes a part of history. While we are on this planet, we become so ambitious and proud of our achievements. Get real! We are not as clever as we think we are.

Yet, despite our insignificance, God knows each of us by name and loves us more than we will ever know. That love was so great that He sent His Son to give His life for us on Calvary's cross, to fit us for heaven to live with him there.

6 MARCH

God's power in Christ

'He is the image of the invisible God, the firstborn over all creation.'
Colossians 1:15

RECOMMENDED READING: Hebrews 1

Yesterday we considered the power of God in creation. Today I want to turn our thoughts to:

(b) The power of God in Christ. When we turn our thoughts toward God, we see almighty power. When we consider our Lord Jesus Christ, we see that same power, but this time in human action. We see:

- *Power in His life*. When I look at the Lord Jesus, I see a man living in the same world that I live in. He knew hunger and thirst, physical weakness and fatigue. He knew what it was to be disappointed with people, and let down by people, even his own followers. Yet, He stood against everything the evil one was able to throw at Him.

- *Power in His miracles*. Here is One who commanded even the demons and they obeyed Him. He had power over disease. Nothing was beyond His ability to heal. The blind were able to see, the deaf could hear, the dumb could speak, the lame could walk, the lepers were cleansed.

- *His power over nature*. The hungry were fed; the sea was calmed; the fig tree died; the multitude of fish were caught. He walked on water and turned water into wine. Nothing was beyond the power of our Lord Jesus Christ.

- *Power in His cross*. When we turn our thoughts to the cross, we see a remarkable paradox. From a human point of view, we see a man dying in weakness. But, when we look more closely, it is not weakness we see but amazing strength. We see on the cross the power of God.

The weakness of Christ was meant to reveal the power of the devil, but God, as He often does, turned the tables. Instead, we see the power of Christ and the weakness of the devil. The cross was a powerful victory.

2 Corinthians 13:4 says, 'He was crucified in weakness, yet He lives by the power of God.'

When we turn our thoughts to the resurrection, we see our Lord Jesus victorious over the last enemy—death. He defeats all the powers set against Him. He conquers sin, death and hell. The devil is defeated and Christ rises triumphant.

Our Lord Jesus is almighty and victorious, and to Him alone be all honour and glory and power both now and forever.

7 MARCH

God's power in us

'The God of Israel is He who gives strength and power to His people.'
Psalm 68:35

RECOMMENDED READING: Acts 6

We have considered the power of God in creation and the power of God in Christ. Now our thoughts become more personal.

(c) The power of God in us. I will be looking at two areas today and conclude with two other areas tomorrow.

- *We are created by His power.* Genesis 1:27 makes it abundantly clear that, 'God created man in His own image; in the image of God, He created him; male and female He created them.' The Bible is very clear on this. Gender is not fluid.

God must have known the problem sinful human nature would have over this issue, so in just one verse He emphasised it three times.

Throughout Scripture, the prophets, the psalmist, and the apostles all testify that we were created from the dust of the earth by an all-powerful Creator. Every part of our body was placed by Almighty God in the appropriate place so that we could function as God intended.

We are fearfully and wonderfully made by a master designer who is Almighty God. If we deny this, we seek to rob God of His glory.

- *We are saved by His power.* From that day when we rebelled against God in the Garden of Eden, we became spiritually dead. We were without God and without hope in this world.

We cannot rescue ourselves from this lifeless condition as we do not possess the power to do so. Neither can anyone else rescue us. Only Almighty God can give us spiritual life.

Read what Paul says in Ephesians 2:4,5: 'But God, who is rich in mercy, because of His great love with which He loved us, even when we were dead in trespasses, made us alive together with Christ.'

Again, I have to remind us that only God gives to us spiritual life. Why am I so sure of this? Because it takes power—Almighty power—to accomplish it. If God had not released His power upon us, and within us, we would still be in our sins facing eternity without Him.

Let us thank God today, and every day, for the gift of His Son, who not only died for our sins, but also rose again from the dead and lives for evermore.

Kept and changed

'Those whom You gave me I have kept.' John 17:12

RECOMMENDED READING: Ephesians 2

We have been looking at the power of God in us. We have seen that we have been created by his power and saved by that same power. Today we turn our attention to being kept and changed by God's power.

• *We are kept by His power.* In the Great High Priestly prayer in John 17, Jesus says in v.11, 'Holy Father, keep through Your name those whom You have given Me.'

Christians are very much aware that they are constantly facing a spiritual adversary. He is a deceiver, a liar, a cheat, and a murderer. He will do everything possible to bring us down, and by doing so cause damage to the cause of our Lord, His Church.

If we were left to ourselves, we would fail and fall. Therefore, we are to be strong in the Lord and in His mighty power. We cannot keep ourselves, but let us thank God, today and every day, that we are being kept by Jesus Christ.

The words of the old hymn say, 'Moment by moment we are kept in His love' (Daniel W. Whittle 1840–1901).

• *We are changed by His power.* If we look back to the days before our conversion, we should notice that a significant change has taken place in every area of our life. If there isn't a change to be seen, then there should be much cause for concern.

The good news is that this change is continuing. God's power is constantly at work in our lives, transforming us into the image of our Lord Jesus Christ.

One day we will be completely transformed by his power and we will become like Him.

The message throughout Paul's letters is clear: we once were … we now are … one day we will be. It is God's power at work within us.

We have been changed; we are being changed; we will be changed. That change is brought about by the power of God.

Thanks be to God who gives us the victory through our Lord Jesus Christ.

So, wherever we look, we see God's power. It is there in creation; we see it in Christ as we read the Scriptures; we see it in us as He graciously and patiently transforms us into His likeness and image.

9 MARCH

His supreme title of honour

'Holy, holy, holy is the Lord of hosts; the whole earth is full of His glory.'
Isaiah 6:3

RECOMMENDED READING: Psalm 99

During the past few days, we have been considering the power of God. We have seen it in creation, in our Lord Jesus Christ and also in us. Today we turn our attention to another attribute of God.

2. The holiness of God. I have said before, and will say it as long as I am able, that we will never fully understand the doctrines contained in the Bible if we do not know our God.

We now come to *the attribute of all attributes* because everything we read or study in the Bible must be set against the holiness of God.

Before we even consider our own spiritual life, we need to look at the standard before us. Exodus 15:11 asks, 'Who is like you, glorious in holiness?'

The phrase, 'the Holy One' is often repeated in the Bible (2 Kings 19:22). That is because God is the source of holiness. He is the only standard of perfection before us.

As you read the Bible, you will find that the main emphasis throughout is holiness, particularly when it refers to Almighty God.

Where do you hear of His wise name? Yet wisdom comes from God. Where do you hear of His good name? Yet God is good. Where do you hear of His love name? Yet love is at the very heart of God; it is His nature to demonstrate love.

But constantly throughout the Bible we read of His holy name. Let's call it His supreme title of honour.

In Isaiah 6, the prophet has this amazing vision in the temple. We are told in v.3 that seraphim cried to each other saying, 'Holy, holy, holy is the Lord of hosts.'

We see holiness revealed throughout His entire being. His wisdom is holy. His justice is holy. His power is holy. His truth is holy. His love is holy. And so we could go on. This is why holiness is *the attribute of all attributes*. It is intertwined throughout them all.

> 'Holy, holy, holy, Lord God Almighty!
> All Thy works shall praise Thy name,
> in earth and sky and sea:
> Holy, holy, holy; merciful and mighty,
> God in three Persons, blessed Trinity!'
>
> Reginald Heber (1783–1826)

10 MARCH

Holy in all His ways

'Oh, worship the Lord in the beauty of holiness!' 1 Chronicles 16:29

RECOMMENDED READING: Psalm 29

Today we continue our consideration of the holiness of God. This attribute is at the heart of His whole being.

I want to mention three areas where His holiness is clearly evident but concentrating most of our thoughts on the last.

(a) We see holiness in His works. Psalm 145:17 says, 'The Lord is righteous in all His ways, and holy in all His works.'(AV). From the creation of the universe and everything in it, we can see holiness stamped with His authority. Every action God performs has holiness shining through. We not only see holiness in His actions, but His thoughts are pure and holy. He cannot think evil because His very nature is holy. Every word God utters bears the marks of holiness. He expects us to listen and obey.

'Holy, holy, holy is the Lord of hosts' (Isaiah 6:3).

(b) We see holiness in His law. Romans 7:12 says, 'The law is holy, and the commandment holy.' When we read the Ten Commandments in Exodus 20, we become aware of God's holiness shining through His character. The words express to us who He is and what He expects from us—His creatures.

We cannot ignore His law, neither can we take it lightly, for God is conveying to us who He is. It is therefore incumbent upon us to take His commandments seriously.

(c) We see holiness in the cross. Nowhere in the Bible is the holiness of God more vividly displayed than at Calvary. God's hatred for sin was clearly shown to all. Matthew 27:46 says, 'My God, My God, why have You forsaken Me?' The answer is surely because God is holy.

When we turn our eyes to the cross we see love clearly displayed before us. But we see more than love, we see holiness. God forgives sinners but hates our sin. He judges sin. On the cross our Saviour bore all the anger of God against our sin. Why? Because God is holy.

When you think about it carefully, there is no difference between Calvary and Hell as far as God's anger is concerned. I thank God today that He justifies the sinner at Calvary.

As we conclude there is a massive challenge before us: 'Be holy, for I am holy' (1 Peter 1:16), says the Lord. You will be saying that is an impossibility while I live on this earth. Nevertheless, that should be our aim and our goal.

11 MARCH

Conquering the gremlins

'You shall be holy, for I the Lord your God am holy.' Leviticus 19:2

RECOMMENDED READING: Ephesians 4:17–30

During the past few days, we have been considering the holiness of God and the standard He has set before us. Today I want us to consider how we measure up to that standard. I have found this subject a personal challenge, but we must press on and let God speak to us. We have thought about the principle and God, and now we turn our attention to the practical and us.

The main thrust of Paul's message from Ephesians 4 is the apostle wanting to show that a revolutionary change has taken place in the Christian's way of living.

Holiness is not an option; it's a standard that every Christian should live by. He was writing to young believers who were now 'in Christ Jesus' (Ephesians 2:6,7). Their life should now reflect that change.

They were in darkness; now they are in the light. They were once dead in sins; now they are alive in Christ. They were once blind to spiritual truths; now they can see. They were once deaf to the voice of God; now they can hear.

A spiritual transformation has taken place and life will never be the same again.

As we look at our conduct as believers, God doesn't want us to look for gremlins in each other. He wants us to look for gremlins in ourselves. So, let us look into the mirror and see ourselves as God sees us: then ask Him to help us in our Christian growth. I just want to look at three areas where His help is needed. We will turn to one of these areas today and the remainder tomorrow.

(a) Speak the truth. In Ephesians 4:25 it says, 'Therefore putting away lying … speak truth.' Lying and truth are exact opposites. Lying involves anything that has any degree of falsehood in it, such as deception, half-truths, or exaggeration. A necessity in human relationship is truth, particularly among God's people.

When I became a Christian, I had to realise that lying is one of the filthy garments of our former life. Our adversary, the devil, is the father of lies.

But our Lord Jesus Christ described Himself as 'the truth' (John 14:6). We must therefore speak the truth, whatever the cost.

Watching your steps

'Blessed are the pure in heart, for they shall see God.' Matthew 5:8

RECOMMENDED READING: Matthew 5

We continue to see how close we live up to God's standard of holiness. Yesterday we considered, 'speaking the truth'. Today we look at two more areas where God's help is needed.

(b) Curb your anger. Ephesians 4:26 says, 'Be angry and do not sin.' Anger is so common. It can involve resentment, emotion and bad temper. But Paul indicates that sometimes anger is not sin. Our Lord was angry on more than one occasion, but He did not sin in His anger.

When I hear of innocent people being deliberately murdered in bomb attacks—I'm angry! When I read of millions of people left homeless through war—I'm angry! When I see millions dying of starvation, and we throw tons of good food away—I'm angry! When I read of 200,000 abortions taking place in the UK each year—I'm angry!

Are you not angry? But this isn't sin. We sin in anger when the root is self. Ruth Paxson (1889–1949), who was a missionary, said, 'To be angry and sin not, we must be angry at nothing but sin.'[9]

We are told in v.26, 'not to let the sun go down while we are still angry'. If there is anger within our hearts, let us check it out before the day is over to see whether it has been sinful or not. If it has, let it be confessed to God and, if possible, put right. This is particularly so if it involves a member of the family. I'll guarantee one thing: your sleep will be much sweeter.

(c) No more stealing. Ephesians 4:28 says, 'Let him who stole steal no longer.' Lying, anger and stealing are the most common sins of all. I am sure we would agree that to take possessions that belong to another person without permission is stealing, but God's standards go much further. Gambling, refusing to pay our debts on time, misuse of funds or trying to dodge paying taxes, and wasting time on social networks during working hours are all forms of stealing which the Christian should avoid.

However, stealing is also withholding from God that which should be given to Him (Malachi 3:8). We all need to honestly answer that question.

The standard God has set for a walk in holiness is very high, but it is not unreasonable. We all should endeavour, with God's help, to develop this characteristic in every area of our life. Be encouraged for one day it will be perfected (Psalm 17:15).

13 MARCH

God knows everything

'Such knowledge is too wonderful for me; it is high, I cannot attain it.'
Psalm 139:6

RECOMMENDED READING: Psalm 139:1–18

3. The knowledge of God. A white missionary was speaking to a large congregation of dark Africans. In his message, he used a large number of childish illustrations to get his point across. At the close of the meeting, one of the African leaders approached him and said, 'No good man! You didn't make your God big enough.'

Our message must be understandable and relevant to those to whom we speak, but never at the expense of belittling the Almighty One. Psalm 147:5 says, 'Great is our Lord, and mighty in power; His understanding is infinite.'

The theological term for the knowledge of God is 'omniscience', or to put it more simply, 'very great and expansive knowledge'.

There are two ways by which we can develop and expand our knowledge:

(a) Through much study. That means putting all those little grey cells to work. A favourite programme of mine is *University Challenge*. No, I can't answer the questions, unless they are on Yorkshire cricket! However, I am amazed at the knowledge young people possess who are only in their early 20s.

(b) By way of experience. As we go through life, we often find this is a great teacher. No matter how much we learn, we cannot compare the knowledge of the Creator with those whom He has created. God does not acquire knowledge or increase in knowledge. To put it as clearly as possible, God knows everything!

He knows the past, present and future. He knows you and me intimately. We can hide nothing from his all-seeing eye. Hebrews 4:13 says, 'There is no creature hidden from his sight.'

God's knowledge is perfect. He never imagines, exaggerates or overlooks anything. Psalm 139:6 says, 'Such knowledge is too wonderful for me; it is high, I cannot attain it.'

Even though His knowledge is daunting and often frightening to those who are strangers to Him, it brings great peace to those who are his people— whose sins have been forgiven by the blood of the Lord Jesus.

The realisation that He knows our worries and concerns as well as our weaknesses and limitations, brings great comfort to every child of God. To be aware that this great, omniscient God is our heavenly Father, who meets our needs because He knows them, gives us much strength as we face another day.

14 MARCH

The knowledge of God

'O Lord, You have searched me and known me.' Psalm 139:1

RECOMMENDED READING: Psalm 147:1–5

Just spend a few moments pondering upon the opening verses of Psalm 139. One thing becomes clear; God knows everything.

Ezekiel 11:5 says, 'For I [the Lord] know the things that come into your mind'—every one of them.

When Adam and Eve sinned in the garden, they tried to hide among the trees. But God knew.

No one saw Cain commit the first murder by killing his brother Abel. But God knew.

David did all he could to hide his wicked act of killing Uriah the Hittite in battle following his adultery with Bathsheba. But God knew.

The prophet Jonah tried to hide from God when he disobeyed God's instructions to go to Nineveh. But God knew.

If people could take away just one attribute from Almighty God it would probably be His infinite knowledge. To carry on their lives without God's knowledge would make things so much more comfortable. But, no matter how we may wish and try, God cannot and will not change his character.

I have spoken to many Christians over recent days who have expressed their concern to me about the present state of the world and the future.

Although we live in days of uncertainty, and COVID-19 has definitely emphasised that truth in many people's minds, God knew this was coming, and He knows how and when it will end.

The destiny of people and nations is not in the hands of Putin, Johnson, Biden, or any other world leader; it is in God's hands.

If you think the future is under your personal control, I ask you to think again. It never has been and never will be.

Proverbs 15:3 says, 'The eyes of the Lord are in every place, keeping watch on the evil and the good.'

Does that mean that God knows and sees all my sins? Will He remember them? If you are a Christian let me bring you some comfort. Jeremiah 31:34 says, 'I will forgive their iniquity, and their sin I will remember no more.'

On the cross, the Lord Jesus Christ carried our sins and endured God's anger because of those sins. Jesus became our substitute and freely gave His life and died in our place. Our sins are forgotten and remembered no more. Step out today with that assurance ringing loudly in your ears.

15 MARCH

Faithful at all times—the faithfulness of God

'Therefore know that the Lord your God, He is God, the faithful God.'
Deuteronomy 7:9

RECOMMENDED READING: Psalm 89:1–33

4. The faithfulness of God. God's faithfulness is one of the most comforting attributes that God possesses. When difficulties and disappointments come our way, as sure they will, we can rest with confidence on the knowledge that God will remain faithful to His people. We can always depend upon Him, and count on Him to be true to every word He has spoken, for Hebrews 10:23 assures us that, 'He who promised is faithful.' He cannot deny His word or betray His character.

When we look across the world today, people are so unreliable and often disappoint us. Their word is not kept and their promises are often broken. Unfaithful is a good word to describe them.

We see it in human relationships. Marital breakdowns affect Royalty and celebrities as well as the general public. What is of greatest concern is to see Christian couples being unfaithful towards one another.

But we also see it in politics and no party can plead their innocence. Promises that are declared in their election manifestos are not kept. In fact, anything becomes permissible if it gets them into power. We can extend this to international affairs as nations do not trust each other. Look over the history of the word and broken treaties are scattered everywhere. When you do not trust one another, it breeds fear and conflict.

The gravest of all is when it creeps into religion. My heart sinks when I meet or hear of people who say they believe the Bible yet reject large sections of it. Some preach, yet reject the Bibles vital message, while some seemingly good men have not only drifted, but now even deny its truths and, worse still, even attack them.

Wherever you turn your eyes in the world today, unfaithfulness is so evident.

How gratifying it is to look to the One who is faithful at all times and who doesn't break His covenant.

For God to be unfaithful is an impossibility. 2 Timothy 2:13 says, 'If we are faithless, He remains faithful.'

Always remember that through the changing scenes of life, in trouble or in joy, God is faithful. He will never let us down or fail us.

I cannot conclude without mentioning God's faithfulness in keeping His promise to send His Son. Those promises in the Old Testament were kept when Jesus came to earth to be our promised Saviour.

16 MARCH

Only God is good—the goodness of God

'You are good and do good.' Psalm 119:68

RECOMMENDED READING: Psalm 107:1–15

5. The goodness of God. To say that God is good seems so inadequate compared to some of His other attributes. Yet He is good and does good.

Let's turn to Genesis 1.

(a) We see God's goodness in creation. After nearly every day of creation (vv.4, 9, 11, 18, 21, 25) we read, 'God saw that it was good.' Then in v.31 we read, 'Then God saw everything that He had made, and indeed it was very good.'

Even today, thousands of years later, with sin rampant and ungodliness all around us, the words of Psalm 33:5 are still relevant to us: 'The earth is full of the goodness of the LORD.' We have so much beauty within a short distance from our homes, yet we often take it for granted with little thought for the One who gave it all to us.

A 93-year-old man in Italy was so encouraged when his health improved, after being cared for in hospital. When a doctor came round to see him, he told the old man that he would have to pay for the use of the ventilator for one day. The old man began to cry. The doctor advised him not to worry over the bill as he would receive help. The old man said:

> I don't cry because of the money I have to pay. I can pay all the money. I cry because I have breathed God's air for 93 years. And I never had to pay anything for it. But for using the ventilator for just one day I have to pay 5,000 Euros. I realise now how much I owe God, and never thanked Him for it.

Oh, that all people would praise the Lord for his goodness.

(b) We see God's goodness in salvation. Despite the fact that all receive some measure of God's goodness and love, yet His goodness in grace is something very special, because it is only known to the Christian.

Remember that we are all children of wrath. We are no different from other men and women. But through God's goodness we have been chosen to become recipients of His grace.

In His goodness, God sent His only Son, the Lord Jesus Christ, to give His life for us by shedding His blood on Calvary's cross. What we owe Him can never be repaid. He gave us what we didn't deserve: forgiveness of our sins and eternal life.

Oh, that Christians would praise the Lord for His goodness!

17 MARCH

Our faithful unchangeable Friend—the unchanging God

'I am the Lord, I do not change.' Malachi 3:6

RECOMMENDED READING: Hebrews 1

6. The unchanging God. The theological term is 'immutability'. It means that God is not susceptible to change; He is always the same. It is this attribute that makes Him so different from those He has created.

As we look around the world today, we are surrounded by turbulence and change, but, despite this, God does not change His character or conduct. We can be confident that His power will not diminish, nor will His glory fade. He will remain the same for ever.

His wisdom will not change; His Word will never pass away; His love is everlasting; His knowledge will never be surpassed. Nothing needs to be added to him and nothing can be taken away.

Isaiah 46:11 says, 'I have spoken it; I will also bring it to pass. I have purposed it; I will also do it.'

He purposed the creation of the world; it came into being. He purposed the sending of His Son; from heaven He came. He purposed the salvation of His people; He is doing it. He purposed judgement; it will come.

From the beginning of Genesis to the end of Revelation, God has a plan and purpose, and He will not be blown off course. He knows where He is going and the route to get there and both are under His powerful control.

God is so different from the world's leaders who so often haven't the faintest clue where they are going or how to get there. They need the wisdom of the Almighty One, but sadly they are often too proud to seek it. We are so unstable, unchangeable and unreliable.

Throughout my life I have witnessed much change in many areas of our national life, and not all for good. But what concerns me most of all is the changes in behaviour, morals and standards. However, I thank God today that His Son, the Lord Jesus Christ has not changed: He is 'the same yesterday, today and forever' (Hebrews 13:8). In this I rejoice!

The hymn writer, Henry Lyte (1793–1847) was spot on when he wrote these words, 'Change and decay in all around I see; O Thou who changest not, abide with me.'

So, as we journey through this day and every day, let us be thankful that His Word, His power, His love, His wisdom and His truth are unchanging, because He is forever the same.

18 MARCH

Harder to be patient than to act—the patience of God

'Now may the God of patience and comfort grant you to be like-minded toward one another, according to Christ Jesus.' Romans 15:5

RECOMMENDED READING: 2 Peter 3:1–9

7. The patience of God. Today we will turn our attention to the patience of God. Another word that is similar in meaning is longsuffering. Numbers 14:18 says, 'The LORD is longsuffering and abundant in mercy.' The words 'slow to anger' are another definition of patience. Psalm 145:8 says, 'The Lord is gracious and full of compassion, slow to anger and great in mercy.'

So how do we describe patience? Let me assure you that patience is not a sign of weakness. Just speak to parents who have to control very difficult children. It is sometimes much easier to act than to show patience. When you are dealing with difficult adults over sensitive issues, it is easier to express your frustration than to remain cool and collected.

When we turn our thoughts on this matter to Almighty God, we see He is able to control all His actions and reactions when dealing with His disobedient children. Nahum 1:3 says, 'The Lord is slow to anger and great in power.'

People who hold great power in society are often people of swift passion which shows us why patience is so rare, whatever your status in life may be.

God is altogether so different from us. He possesses great power, but at the same time is slow to demonstrate His anger. Nehemiah 9:17 says, 'You are God, ready to pardon, gracious and merciful, slow to anger.'

When we come to Genesis 6 it is clear to see that the people had become corrupt. What is amazing is that God did not bring the flood until the people had been warned. 1 Peter 3:20 says, 'The longsuffering of God waited in the days of Noah.' (AV).

Noah preached and warned the people for 120 years. During this time God demonstrated His patience and withheld His hand from destruction.

Throughout the wanderings in the wilderness His people rebelled against His servant Moses, even to the extent that they made for themselves idols to worship.

They turned their backs on Him constantly, but He showed much patience toward them.

We also see His patience as we read through the New Testament, especially with his disciples.

Let us thank God today that His patience has not declined, even in our generation. He showed patience with us before we became Christians and that patience is clear, even after we committed our lives to him. We are here because of His patience.

19 MARCH

God be merciful to me, a sinner

'But God who is rich in mercy.' Ephesians 2:4

RECOMMENDED READING: Psalm 136:1–9

When we consider the attributes of God, there is one area where confusion becomes evident; that is distinguishing between the mercy, love and grace of God. The danger is to lump them all together, and not be aware of the clear differences between them. Because of this, great care needs to be taken. Therefore, we are going to consider each one independently. There will be similarities, but also major differences.

We will begin by looking at *the mercy of God*. In Psalm 136, the words, 'for His mercy endures forever', are recorded 26 times. Mercy is clearly one of God's attributes; therefore, it must endure forever. As we look at this part of God's character, there are three distinct aspects of mercy that we need to consider.

1. General mercy. Psalm 145:9 says, 'The Lord is good to all, and His tender mercies are over all His works.' When we reflect upon God's mercy, we notice that it covers all of His creation, which includes believers and unbelievers.

Matthew 5:45 says, 'He makes His sun rise on the evil and on the good, and sends rain on the just and on the unjust.' Everyone is included, whether they are deserving of it or not.

I have just been preparing a message on the fall in Genesis 3. Some people may ask, 'why was creation not completely destroyed after the fall as everything was affected by the sin of Adam and Eve?' There can be only one answer: the mercy of God.

When Almighty God looks upon the world and sees such evil practices being carried out by those He has created, why doesn't He step in and destroy and eradicate the sin that is so rampant in every area of life? There can be only one answer to the question; because of His great mercy toward us.

When you read Ephesians 2 very carefully, you find that mercy is always seen in the context of sin. Let us thank God today and every day that He is rich in mercy and doesn't want to see any perish but come to repentance.

20 MARCH

God's mercy sent Jesus

'Oh, give thanks to the Lord, for He is good! For His mercy endures for ever.'
1 Chronicles 16:34

RECOMMENDED READING: Psalm 136:10–26

Yesterday we began to look at the mercy of God and His general mercy. Today we turn our attention to two more aspects of God's mercy.

2. Special mercy. Unbelieving people can experience God's special mercy. My father was very much involved with the British Army during the Second World War. I found it most interesting to hear testimonies of men and women who lived and fought during those dangerous years. I believe we witnessed God's mercy at places such as Dunkirk, when the clouds were low and the sea was like glass, which enabled us to bring thousands of men back to our shores. They tell of remarkable escapes from hopeless and sometimes impossible situations. When the danger was at its height, even unbelievers prayed. God showed mercy to them in their time of trial. Robin Knox-Johnston, who was a round-the-world sailor, said: 'There is no such thing as an atheist in the Southern Ocean.'[10]

How many people, even in peacetime, tell of miraculous escapes from potentially fatal accidents—on the road, in the air, on the sea and in places of employment. Why? It has to be God's special mercy to them.

3. Sovereign mercy. The mercies which God shows to unbelievers are only temporary: they are for this life only. There is no mercy beyond the grave. This is another reason why evangelism is so important. However, sovereign mercy is extended to all those who have received God's salvation and this mercy endures for ever. Why? Because mercy is a characteristic of our eternal God. Christ did not bring to us God's mercy; God's mercy brought Christ. We must thank God today, and every day, that He who is rich in mercy, sent His only begotten Son to this earth to save sinners from hell, and open the gate of heaven to people such as you and me. So, while general and special mercies are shown to all creation, His sovereign mercy is only extended to those who are His children, bought by the precious blood that was shed by his Son on Calvary's cross. 'But God, who is rich in mercy, because of His great love with which He loved us, even when we were dead in trespasses, made us alive together with Christ' (Ephesians 2:4,5).

> 'Through this vain world he guides our feet, and leads us to his heavenly seat:
> His mercies ever shall endure, when this vain world shall be no more.'
>
> Isaac Watts (1674–1748)

21 MARCH

He is love and He loves

'He who does not love does not know God, for God is love.' 1 John 4:8

RECOMMENDED READING: 1 John 4:7–21

So often we become confused over God's mercy, love, and grace. There are similarities but they are all distinct from each other. Yesterday we considered the mercy of God. Today we turn our thoughts to *the love of God*.

God loves. We have experienced that on many occasions throughout our Christian life. But 1 John 4:8 goes much further when it states that 'God is love'. This is true, not only in His actions, but in His very nature.

I find that people talk quite casually about the love of God, but these same people are total strangers to the God of love and there is a great gulf between the two. It is the same when people talk about the peace of God; yet know nothing of the God of peace.

When we think of God, our human nature often kicks in and we think of human love which rules our emotions. We mustn't go in that direction. So, what does the Bible teach us about the love of God?

1. The love of God is holy. Although God is love, we need to recognise the fact that He will never ignore sin whether it is in the world or in the lives of His children. His love was clearly demonstrated at Calvary. It is here that He forgives the sinner but deals severely with sin.

People who intentionally turn their backs upon God will never understand the immensity of His love. Sin has to be dealt with because God is holy. At the cross Jesus carried the full weight of our sin alone, so that we would be spared God's wrath and face no condemnation.

Love is holy. God is holy. God is love. Notice how the characteristics of God intertwine with each other, yet maintain their own identity. The unbeliever will never grasp or understand this but, for those who are Christians, the wonder of it continues to amaze us, and stands before us as a glorious truth.

God's love is truly amazing and divine and demands our soul, our life, our all.

He loved me and gave Himself for me

'If anyone loves Me, he will keep My word; and My Father will love Him, and We will come to him and make Our home with him.' John 14:23

RECOMMENDED READING: Romans 5:1–11

We continue to explore the love of God. We have already seen that the love of God is holy. There are two further points to mention.

2. The love of God is not affected by situations that occur in our lives. I have used this illustration before, but it is so appropriate to our subject today. C. H. Spurgeon was talking to a farmer who had recently erected a weathervane on his barn. On the arrow he had inscribed the words, 'God is love.' He said to the farmer, 'What do you mean by having those words? Do you think God's love is changeable; that it veers about as the arrow turns in the wind?' The farmer replied, 'Oh No! I mean that whichever way the wind blows, God is still love.'

Events in our life will never change that fact.

Just spend some time reading the history of His people Israel. Deuteronomy 7:7 says, 'The Lord did not set His love on you nor choose you because you were more in number than any other people, for you were the least of all peoples.' There was nothing at all to attract God to Israel—in fact, just the opposite. He chose Israel because He loved them. There can be no other reason.

Have you ever asked why God chose you? What is there in us to attract God to us? There is more to repel Him! There is only one answer to that question: He loved us. We love Him because He first loved us.

3. The love of God is everlasting. Why? Because God is eternal. He is love and can never change His character.

Whatever concerns you today, whether it be health issues, bereavement, unemployment, family concerns, or even death itself, you are loved with an everlasting love. Jeremiah 31:3 says, 'Yes, I have loved you with an everlasting love; therefore, with lovingkindness I have drawn you.'

You will never find the beginning of God's love, because there isn't one. Neither will you come to an end of God's love, because there isn't one. It has always been there and will always remain there. It is eternal.

Let us rejoice that we are safe and secure in the arms of Sovereign love, and we shall remain there forever.

'In a love which cannot cease, I am His and He is mine.'

George W. Robinson (1838–77)

23 MARCH

Grace is truly amazing

'For the law was given through Moses, but grace and truth came through Jesus Christ.' John 1:17

RECOMMENDED READING: Ephesians 2:1–10

We have been looking into some of the many attributes of God. I want to conclude by turning our attention to one of the most beautiful words in the Bible—*grace*.

God has shown His mercy to those who are sinners. He has poured His love upon those who are unworthy of it. But salvation is through grace alone. I came across this statement, by an unknown author, which brings together all these wonderful attributes. 'Grace is God's sovereign love to those who receive His mercy.'

Grace is totally unmerited, unearned, undeserved and unsought. We cannot buy it; we cannot work for it; and neither can we win it. If we could do these things, it would no longer be grace. Almighty God reaches down to hopeless sinners and rescues them from total disaster.

The slave trader John Newton (1725–1807) understood the wonder of all this when He wrote, 'Amazing grace, how sweet the sound that saved a wretch like me.'

One of the clearest verses dealing with God's grace is given by the apostle Paul in Romans 11:6 where he says, 'If by grace, then it is no longer of works; otherwise, grace is no longer grace.' He then goes on to say in Ephesians 2:8, 'By grace you have been saved through faith, and that not of yourselves; it is the gift of God.' Verse 9 adds, 'not of works, lest anyone should boast'. The Bible cannot be clearer, for salvation is by grace alone.

I often wonder why these verses fail to grab us as they should. Unfortunately, familiar verses do tend to breed complacency. They become so common to us because we know them well. It is so encouraging to see the reaction on the faces of young believers when they first begin to grasp these truths.

No matter how long you have been a believer, or how young in the faith you are, never lose the thrill of these amazing truths. May they excite us every time we focus our minds upon them. If our hearts are cold, may the Holy Spirit warm them and bring them to life.

I warmly recommend a book written entitled *Grace, Amazing Grace*, by Brian Edwards and published by Day One.[11] It will thrill your soul. It is well worth setting aside the time to read it.

24 MARCH

The price has been paid

'Paul and Barnabas ... persuaded them to continue in the grace of God.' Acts 13:43

RECOMMENDED READING: Colossians 1:1–14

Over the past few days, we have been looking at the Mercy, Love and Grace of God. I want to spend one more day considering *the grace of God* with two more aspects of this attribute.

1. Grace is free. Romans 3:24 says, '... being justified freely by His grace through the redemption that is in Christ Jesus'. No one has ever or will ever be able to purchase it. It is free grace. It cost us absolutely nothing but cost God His son. No wonder the grace of God amazes us; and so it should!

A number of years ago I came across the following words from Pastor Molland, who was a minister in Devon:

Wordsworth could take a worthless sheet of paper, write a poem on it and make it worth thousands. That's genius.

Rockefeller could sign his name on a piece of paper and immediately make it worth millions. That's capital.

The Bank of England can take gold, stamp a lion on it and make it worth a fortune. That's money.

An artist can take material that is worth practically nothing and make it worth millions. That's art.

Almighty God can take a worthless, sinful life; cleanse it in the precious blood of Christ; put His Spirit in it; and make it a blessing to the human race. That's free grace.

2. Grace is sovereign. The Bible speaks about the throne of grace. It is a term we often us in prayer. On that throne sits the King of kings, our Lord Jesus Christ. But that throne is only accessible to those who have sought forgiveness of sins and placed their faith in Christ for salvation.

A reformer wrote the following words:

'Grace is a provision for men who are so fallen that they can never rise; so corrupt that they can never change; so blind that they can never see; so deaf that they cannot hear; so dead that God alone must open their graves and lift them to resurrection.'[12]

John Kent (1805–1886) wrote nearly 300 hymns, most on the theme of God's sovereign grace. One of his greatest and well-known hymns was 'Sovereign grace o'er sin abounding.'

His dying words were, 'I'm accepted, no merits of mine. I have nothing to boast without or within. It is of His grace I am what I am.'

25 MARCH

Unexpected surprises around the corner

'Behold I bring you good tidings of great joy.' Luke 2:10

RECOMMENDED READING: Acts 1:1–14

At a recent prayer meeting, a member of our fellowship said she had found the word, 'Behold', to be a great blessing to her, especially during this difficult time.

During the next few days, I want to take a journey through the Acts of the Apostles and consider some of God's unexpected surprises that begin with the word, 'Behold'.

As the disciples continued their work for the Lord, these surprises were a regular occurrence. We also must be alert and keep watching for them.

1. Encouragement from heaven during a time of bewilderment. 'Behold, two men stood by them in white apparel' (Acts 1:10).

The past few weeks had been like a roller-coaster ride for the disciples. They had been on the mountain top but had also experienced the deep valley. They just couldn't make sense of it all. What was happening?

They had just seen their Master taken from them. The One who had been their support and inspiration was no longer in their midst. They stood on the Mount of Olives in a state of utter bewilderment. But God didn't leave them in that condition for long. What a surprise to find two heavenly messengers standing beside them.

There are times in our lives when we also face bewilderment. We cannot understand God's plans and purposes for us. Many are struggling to come to terms with this pandemic. What is God saying to us through this? Why have I become so uncertain and bewildered over it? Why can't I understand Him?

Let me try and lift your spirit just a little. Remember how often, in times of bewilderment, God in his mercy comes into our midst with words of encouragement and cheer. It may be a verse or passage of scripture you have read. You may receive a phone call from a friend at the church, or a thoughtful gesture from a neighbour. Then an unexpected letter comes through the post, or an email online, which lifts your spirit. They are only small things, but just what you needed at that time.

One problem we do have is that we just don't listen to what God wants to say to us, or we are looking in the wrong direction for comfort.

Be of good cheer my friend; He is still in the midst of His people and hasn't forgotten you. Always remember this: with Jesus there will always be better times ahead.

26 MARCH

Keep looking upwards

'God is our refuge and strength, a very present help in trouble.' Psalm 46:1

RECOMMENDED READING: Psalm 121

We are looking at some of God's unexpected surprises in Acts which were an encouragement to the Lord's people in times of trial.

2. Help from heaven in times of opposition. 'Behold, I see the heavens opened' (Acts 7:56, ESV).

Stephen was on trial before the council of the Sanhedrin. In chapter 7 he was given the opportunity to present his case before the members. Although it is a long chapter, it is important to read it, as this was such a powerful and convincing address that Stephen gave. At the end, the members were cut to the heart and anger welled up within them (v.54).

It was in the midst of fierce, unrelenting opposition that Stephen looked up and was immediately assured of support from the throne of heaven. God had been listening and watching, and now He would act. Although the opposition was intense, Stephen was not alone; heaven had come to support him during his trial.

An important thing to learn regarding Stephen is that he adopted the right attitude; he looked upwards. If he had been looking at his enemies, he would have missed the heavenly vision.

There are occasions when we too face opposition, sometimes from the most unlikely sources and the most unlikely people. It may not be physical, as was the case with Stephen, but verbal, often couched in hurtful language. It is at times such as these that we, like Stephen, look upward to the place from where our help comes.

All the giants of the faith were conscious in times of opposition of their own weakness, but they knew where to look for spiritual strength and support. If you read church history, there have been times of great persecution when both men and women were burnt at the stake and faced many other terrible forms of torture, but they fixed their eyes heavenwards.

Throughout the world today, many of the Lord's people suffer greatly for their faith, both physically and mentally but, like Stephen, their eyes are fixed upward towards their future destiny.

May we ask Almighty God to give us spiritual strength whenever we speak out in defence of the gospel whatever the consequences may be. If we have to suffer for the cause of Christ, let us keep our eyes heavenwards, and, who knows, an unexpected surprise might be awaiting us. It did for Stephen; may it be the same for us.

27 MARCH

Obedience brings God's blessing

'Behold a man of Ethiopia.' Acts 8:27

RECOMMENDED READING: Acts 8:28–40

We continue our journey through the Acts of the Apostles looking at occasions when we come across the word 'Behold'.

3. Clear instructions for every step of the journey. Today we turn our thoughts to a third unexpected surprise, and, on this occasion, it involves Philip the evangelist.

God's servant was instructed by God to minister to multitudes of people in Samaria. Remarkable things were happening in the northern city with many people turning to the Lord in repentance and faith. Although Philip and others were very busy instructing the people, he also recognised and rejoiced that God was so powerfully at work among the nation.

It therefore may have come as a surprise to Philip to hear God instructing him to leave the work in Samaria and take a long journey into the desert region as there was someone of great importance that He wanted Philip to meet.

Although Philip may not have been fully aware of the reason for the journey; nevertheless, God's servant responds immediately (v.27).

What an encouragement he receives when he arrives there. To meet this man who was a representative of Candace, the queen of the Ethiopians, must have been a great honour to Philip. But a greater thrill was to come when he not only led him to the Lord, but also baptised him. Can there be a greater delight than to lead a lost soul to the Saviour?

Evangelists and pastors love to minister to a large congregation, which is a natural desire, but there are occasions when smaller fellowships need us the most. Jesus set us a great example, not only by ministering to vast crowds, but also giving His time to meet the needs of individuals who sought the salvation that only He could give.

There are occasions when God leads us unexpectedly into strange places and unlikely situations to win a convert for Christ. Never be surprised where God leads you, or to whom He leads you. Just be obedient to His direction. Whatever He says to you, do it. He will clearly guide us in the path of obedience if only we give time to listen carefully to His instructions.

28 MARCH

Always be ready for a surprise

'Regard the prayer of your servant.' 1 Kings 8:28

RECOMMENDED READING: 1 Samuel 1

We continue to look for more of God's sudden, unexpected surprises as we make our way through the Acts of the Apostles.

4. Unexpected converts in unexpected places. 'Behold, he is praying' (Acts 9:11). If anyone had approached Ananias and asked him, 'Who was the most unlikely person in Israel or Syria to be a convert to Christianity?' he would have probably said, 'Saul of Tarsus'. Who would have thought that Saul, who was responsible for the persecution and death of many Christian believers, would be found praying? Yet that is exactly how Ananias found this unlikely convert. Saul had just had an encounter with the risen Christ on his way to Damascus and was now in communion with his Saviour.

God is still the God of surprises. He still continues to call unlikely converts from unlikely places to be His followers. We need to pray more earnestly for the unlikely ones, because nothing is beyond the power of our omnipotent Lord.

God's power to transform lives is not in doubt. It is our weak faith to believe that is questionable. We need to pray more fervently for those who have spiritually sunk to the lowest depths. Some of them may be members of our own family, who at this moment are total strangers to God's love and grace.

A number of years ago I met a lady whose husband was an alcoholic, blasphemer and wife-beater. For forty years she endured his drunken assaults, which on occasions meant she had to being taken to hospital with broken bones. Despite friends advising her to leave him, she remained faithful. She prayed for him every day throughout their married life and, after forty years, a miracle of God's grace took place. He became a completely transformed man. Even the hopeless can have hope when God steps in.

There may be some reading this who have members of their own family who are strangers to God's grace. It may be a husband, a wife, a son or daughter and you are full of concern for them. Perhaps they were once involved in church life but over recent years have fallen back into worldly ways. You have been praying for them for many years but there seems no change.

Can I encourage you to keep on praying, even when the lamp of hope burns low? Always be ready for that sudden unexpected surprise that could be waiting for you.

29 MARCH

God can solve every problem

'Trust in the Lord with all your heart and lean not on your own understanding; in all your ways acknowledge Him, and He shall direct your paths.'
Proverbs 3:5-6

RECOMMENDED READING: Acts 10

As we continue to look for God's unexpected surprises, I want to consider two occasions in Acts 10 where we come across the word 'Behold'. Both have a relevant message to us.

5. Solution to problems in times of doubt. 'Behold, three men are seeking you' (Acts 10:19).

The entire chapter is centred upon a man called Cornelius who was a centurion in the Italian regiment (v.1). He had a clear vision of an angel of God, who said to him: 'Send men to Joppa, and send for Simon whose surname is Peter ... He will tell you what you must do' (vv.5–6).

As the messengers approached Joppa, Peter went up on the housetop to pray. Verses 11–16 describe the vision that he experienced. The vision was a great problem to Peter; he was unsure and uncertain as to what it all meant (v.27). He wondered what God was saying to him.

As he pondered this unsolvable problem, the men sent by Cornelius arrived at the house of Simon the tanner, where Peter was staying.

I believe there is a clear lesson that should be a great encouragement to us. When we are faced with doubt and uncertainty—when problems stare us in the face and we find a solution impossible—then we must wait upon God in believing prayer.

Perhaps God's answer is already waiting for us. He is always ahead of us, preparing the way.

6. Christian friends that God brings to us. 'Behold, I am he whom ye seek' (Acts 10:21, AV).

This conveniently follows from our previous point.

As the men from Cornelius searched for Peter, they were probably wondering how they could persuade him, a Jew, to return with them. In v.21 he presents himself to them. The following day he goes with them to Caesarea.

This event gives further encouragement to us. God can and does bring friends to us when we need them. If only we could trust Him more.

In my own life, during times of difficulty and uncertainty as to the way forward, God has sent someone to give wisdom and encouragement, or to say, 'I am he whom you seek.'

30 MARCH

He watches over us

'Do not fear, for those who are with us are more than those who are with them.' 2 Kings 6:16

RECOMMENDED READING: Psalm 9

We continue to look at occasions in the Acts of the Apostles where we read of God's unexpected surprises which are ushered in with the word, 'Behold'.

7. Deliverance from danger by a miraculous intervention. 'Behold, an angel of the Lord stood by him, and a light shone in the prison' (Acts 12:7).

James had been killed by Herod, who was causing much concern among God's people. Now Peter had been arrested and imprisoned. He was, to all human appearance, in a perilous position and his death seemed inevitable. To lose one leader was a great concern, but to lose two leaders—with one of those being Peter—would be a major blow to the morale of this young church.

The disciples had one option before them and that was to engage in prayer for the safety of their leader. However, they did so with seemingly little faith that their prayers would be answered, since they could not believe the answer when it came.

Peter was sleeping calmly, though his execution was set for the following day. In fact, he was sleeping so soundly that the angel had to strike him to awaken him out of his deep sleep. When he awoke, deliverance was at hand.

How often, as we look back over our life, have we been delivered from dangerous circumstances by God's intervention, often being completely unaware at the time? We will also never know how many times God has delivered us without ever realising it.

Most of us will take journeys by car on our roads that are often busy and dangerous. Despite driving carefully, there are sadly others who show little regard for the lives of other people. It is always good to commit our journeys to the Lord before we set off, asking Him for safety and protection against dangers seen and unseen. This should also apply to journeys by sea or air.

How comforting it is to know that in all situations in our life God is our shield and protector, and that He is always watching over His children whatever we do and wherever we may go. His eye misses nothing.

31 MARCH

God never sees a crisis

'Behold a certain disciple was there.' Acts 16:1

RECOMMENDED READING: Acts 15:36–41

8. Fellow workers raised up in time of need. Paul and Barnabas had a sharp disagreement over a young disciple called John Mark. He had joined them on a missionary tour but proved to be a disappointment to Paul. He returned home before the tour was completed.

Sometime later Barnabas wanted to give Mark a second opportunity to go with them but Paul was having none of it. He was not going to take another risk, hence the disagreement, resulting in Barnabas and Paul going separate ways.

Paul's heart was naturally sore with the loss of his good friend, as he was the one who had introduced him to the church in Jerusalem, shortly after his conversion on the Damascus road. He had also laboured with him in places such as Antioch. Nevertheless, he continued his work but with a very heavy heart.

It is important to mention that when Paul was in prison in Rome, shortly before his death, one of the men he especially asked to see was Mark. In 2 Timothy 4:11, we have these words, 'Get Mark and bring him with you, for he is useful to me for ministry.'

Eventually Paul arrived at Lystra where God had prepared a disciple to meet him; his name was Timothy. What a joy this young man became to Paul in his future ministry.

So, Timothy replaced Barnabas (Acts 16:1), and Mark went with Barnabas to Cyprus (Acts 15:39). How often God replaces an 'Elijah' with an 'Elisha'. When one man's work is completed, God raises up another to take his place.

We often wonder how the church can cope without a long-standing leading figure. The graveyard is full of indispensable people. God often raises up when we are bowed down. Therefore, we should never be over concerned when an apparent crisis comes our way, for God always knows what He is doing.

We must not forget that God never sees a time of crisis: He already has the answer for each particular situation.

So, the lesson for us is very clear: never become too despondent in a crisis. God will always have the right person for the right job at the right time. He will never cause His work to suffer.

1 APRIL

All guilty

'There they crucified him.' Luke 23:33

RECOMMENDED READING: Isaiah 53

We come to the time of the year when our thoughts have been, or are being, directed to the greatest sacrifice that has ever been made since the creation of the world. On that day, the Lord Jesus Christ, the Son of God, freely gave His life upon a cross outside the city walls of Jerusalem to save sinners from hell and offer them everlasting life in heaven.

During the coming days, our thoughts will be centred upon the passion of our Lord. I want to begin by considering these four words from Luke 23:33.

1. **'There' signifies a place.** The country of Israel is very similar in size to Wales. Though relatively small, a vast amount of biblical history is centred upon this familiar strip of land. In 2017 Israel had a population of nearly 9 million people, even smaller than London. The city of Jerusalem has only 874,000 inhabitants, yet millions of people from countries around the world visit its sites. The reason many come is that just over 2,000 years ago an event took place outside the city walls that has transformed the lives of countless numbers of people.

2. **'They' signifies the people.** A question that many have asked since that event took place is, 'Who really was responsible for that horrific act of injustice?'

It is clear that the religious leaders of that day carry a heavy responsibility. The people, encouraged by the priests, also had a significant part to play. Then there was Pilate who was pressurised by crowds who would not be silenced. We must not forget the soldiers who carried out this brutal deed.

But what about you and me? We too must hold up our hands and cry, 'Guilty!' Yes, we are involved, because it was for us, He hung and suffered there. In fact, the whole world stands guilty, because it was our sin that held him there.

Did God have any part to play in all this? Yes, a major part. It was He who was willing to send His Son to Calvary to save his people from their sins. Isaiah 53:10 is a verse that constantly amazes me: 'It pleased the Lord to bruise Him; He has put Him to grief.' Ponder upon those words over the coming days.

We will look at the third word tomorrow in more detail and see how much He was willing to suffer for us.

2 APRIL

What pains He had to bear

'There they crucified him.' Luke 23:33

RECOMMENDED READING: Isaiah 50:4–9

Yesterday we considered the first two words of v.33. Today we turn our thoughts to the third word.

3. 'Crucified' signifies the action. Have we ever paused long enough to consider the depth of suffering that Christ endured for us? According to a surgeon, wounds can be classified in a number of ways, and the Lord suffered them all for us.

Contused. This means the wounds are inflicted by a blunt instrument, such as a blow by a rod. The prophet Micah prophesied in chapter 5:1, 'They will strike the judge of Israel with a rod on the cheek.' This was fulfilled in the words of Matthew 26:67: 'Then they spat in His face and beat him.'

Lacerated. This means they are inflicted by a tearing instrument—the result of scourging. This had become a fine art among the Romans. The many-tailed lash, which was often made from the sinews of an ox, had sharp metal or ivory attached to the tip of each strip. In the hands of a cruel expert, Psalm 129:3 becomes very meaningful: 'The plowers plowed on my back; they made their furrows long.'

The torture and lacerations, with the consequent loss of blood, often resulted in the death of the victim, but it was not the means of our Lord's death. Isaiah 50:6 says, 'I gave My back to those who struck Me, and My cheeks to those who plucked out the beard.' These words were fulfilled in John 19:1: 'Then Pilate took Jesus and scourged Him.' Also remember that upon that lacerated back His cross was laid.

Penetrating. This means they were inflicted by a sharp pointed instrument—the crown of thorns. The Jerusalem thorn, from which the victor's crown was made, had spikes up to 4 inches (10cm) long. As the crown was placed upon His head (Matthew 27:29; John 19:2) the result was a circle of wounds which were deepened by the blow of the reed upon His head (Matthew 27:30). This alone would be an agonising experience.

> 'See, from His head, His hands, His feet,
> Sorrow and love flow mingled down;
> Did e'er such love and sorrow meet,
> Or thorns compose so rich a crown?'
>
> Isaac Watts (1674–1748)

Tomorrow we will conclude our thoughts on this important verse.

3 APRIL

The power of the cross

'For unto us a child is born, unto us a son is given; and the government will be upon his shoulder, and his name will be called Wonderful Counsellor, Mighty God, Everlasting Father, Prince of Peace.' Isaiah 9:6

RECOMMENDED READING: Psalm 22

We have been considering the four words found in Luke 23:33: 'There they crucified Him.' We have seen the place where it happened. We have looked at the people who were involved. We have considered the depth of suffering that He endured. In doing so, we have pondered on the wounds that were inflicted upon Him; contused; lacerated and penetrating. I want to consider two more before we come to our final word.

Perforating. This comes from the Latin word, 'to pierce through'. Psalm 22:16b says, 'They pierced My hands and My feet.' The iron spikes, which were used by the Roman soldiers, would have been driven between the bones so they did not break them. This was so that prophecy was fulfilled. God foreknew the painful death that his Son would have to endure, and it would have been an agonising death. Yet He permitted it to be so, because of His love for us.

Incised. This wound involves a cut by a sharp-edged instrument. John 19:34 says, 'But one of the soldiers pierced His side with a spear, and immediately blood and water came out.' This act was to ensure that if any life remained, it would be extinguished. Whilst it did not cause death in the case of Jesus, it was a guarantee that death had occurred. John saw it and recorded that it was true.

4. **'Him' signifies the person.** We have thought in some depth upon the suffering of our Lord, but as we conclude let us ask, 'Who was He?' Who was this man who endured so much, yet was innocent of all charges? Isaiah 9:6 tells us who He was. God tells us who He was. 'This is my beloved Son, in whom I am well pleased' (Matthew 3:17). The Son of God carried all my sin upon that tree. He became sin who knew no sin.

As I conclude these thoughts today, say quietly in your own heart these wonderful words: 'He loved ME and gave Himself for ME.'

'Hallelujah! What a Saviour!

> 'Upon that cross of Jesus my eye at times can see
> The very dying form of one who suffered there for me;
> And from my broken heart with tears, two wonders I confess;
> The wonders of His glorious love, and my own worthlessness.'
>
> Elizabeth C. Clephane (1830–69)

4 APRIL

Never walk with Jesus at a distance

'But go and tell His disciples—and Peter—that he is going before you into Galilee; there you will see Him, as He said to you.' Mark 16:7

RECOMMENDED READING: Psalm 51

Jesus had just been crucified. The events were still raw in the hearts and minds of the disciples. Now He lies in a cold, dark, borrowed tomb close to the scene of His crucifixion. People were left with just their thoughts about what had happened. Would they ever get over this tragic loss of such a close friend? Only time would tell. The crucifixion of our Lord affected the lives of many people that day, from Pontius Pilate who finally succumbed to the pressure, which was exerted upon him, to the Roman centurion who, as he watched Jesus die, acknowledged Him to be the Son of God. But all the followers of Jesus were affected by what had taken place in the city of Jerusalem just a short time ago.

During the next two days I want to consider the experience of just one man, Peter, whose thoughts would be like a tumble dryer, going backwards and forwards continually, with nobody to press the off switch. This would be a day he would gladly forget and put behind him, but he was too involved to cast the events from his mind. Yesterday, he could only be described as a miserable backslider. Mark 14:54 tells us that Peter followed Jesus at a distance. Following Jesus from the Garden of Gethsemane, he soon found himself in the wrong company (Mark 14:66). Though given the opportunity, he failed to reprove their sin. He failed the witness test. Silence is not always golden.

The believer who is not angry at sin may soon be a participant in it. It was not long after this that Peter flatly denied His Lord (Mark 14:68,70,71).

The steps of a backslider are progressive. One step eventually leads to another. Peter's three steps can often be repeated. We all need to take careful heed because the cock can crow very loudly and it is hard to shut our ears from the noise. The backslider is a disappointment to God and to their fellow Christians, but also to themselves.

On this Saturday, which would have been the Jewish Sabbath, all was now calm outside, but it was turmoil in Peter's mind.

Tomorrow I want us to try and consider what would be circling through Peter's mind. He had promised so much—why didn't he deliver?

Two attributes of God will come out clearly: His mercy and forgiveness.

> 'Ask the Saviour to help you, Comfort, strengthen and keep you;
> He is willing to aid you, He will carry you through.'
>
> Horatio R Palmer (1834–1907)

5 APRIL

From turmoil to triumph

'But go and tell his disciples—and Peter—that He is going before you into Galilee.' Mark 16:7

RECOMMENDED READING: Mark 16:1–7

We are considering the life of Peter immediately following our Lord's crucifixion. What was running through his mind following his denial?

1. He must have thought about the past. Peter was the first to declare Jesus as the Christ (Matthew 16:16). He was the first to prove his faith on the waves (Matthew 14:28). He was the first to defend his Lord (Mark 14:47). Now he is the first to deny Him.

2. He must have thought of his own loss of peace. He remembered his call on the shores of Galilee. He had witnessed numerous miracles and heard unforgettable parables. He had walked with Jesus through the pleasant lanes of Galilee, conversing with Him. He had never been happier than those times when he had been with his Master.

> 'What peaceful hours I once enjoyed, how sweet their memory still.
> Yet they have left an aching void the world can never fill'
> William Cowper (1731–1800).

3. He must have thought of the special favours Jesus had given him.

The Transfiguration—to have witnessed with James and John this remarkable event that had left such an impression upon him (2 Peter 1:16–18); to have been with Moses and Elijah; to have beheld the glory of Jesus and heard the voice of God was unforgettable.

Gethsemane—to have been in the garden when Jesus battled with temptation, and again gained the victory.

Yet he had failed miserably. He had failed when Jesus needed his support the most. 'And when he thought about it, he wept' (Mark 14:72). Peter was a broken, defeated man. He knew it; God knew it. But God had not forgotten Peter! In Mark 14:72, we see tears of repentance. In chapter 16:7, we hear words of forgiveness. 'Tell His disciples—and Peter', especially Peter—you must not forget Peter. It takes only one word to turn weeping into rejoicing.

For Peter, the coming days will mean forgiveness, joy, victory and a transformed life. That one mention of his name specifically in Mark 16:7 will turn cowardice into bravery and defeat into victory.

Spend some time reading from Acts 2 and see how Peter atoned for his backsliding; from powerless to powerful; from faithless to faithful.

6 APRIL

He lives who one was dead

'Thanks be to God who gives us the victory through our Lord Jesus Christ.'
1 Corinthians 15:57

RECOMMENDED READING: Job 19:23–26

A verse of scripture that has meant a great deal to me is John 19:41: 'Now in the place where He was crucified there was a garden, and in the garden a new tomb in which no one had yet been laid.' It was a great privilege to lead my first tour to Israel in 1982. I remember standing in a garden gazing at 'the place of a skull' and thanking God for the sacrifice of His Son upon a rugged cross. I then turned my eyes towards an empty tomb and, with a heart filled with emotion, thanked Him again for a living Saviour.

Why is the resurrection so important? Why does the Christian church place so much emphasis upon an event that took place over 2,000 years ago? During the next two days I want to give four reasons why the resurrection is at the heart of the Christian message and relevant for these challenging days in which we are living.

1. The resurrection conquers fear. The disciples of Jesus had been on an amazing adventure during the previous three years. They had seen some remarkable events and heard mind-blowing teaching, which they would never forget. But the adventure had come to an abrupt end; it was now over, and fear was filling their hearts and minds (John 20:19).

But the message of the resurrection was 'Fear not!' Matthew 28:5 says, 'Do not be afraid.' Mark 16:6 says, 'Do not be alarmed.'

Nearly 2,000 years later, fear still controls the hearts and minds of people. We meet it at the cradle and it remains with us to the grave. We face fear of the unknown, fear of unemployment, concerns over finance, anxiety about our family, health issues. Obviously of particular concern for millions, as I write, is the coronavirus pandemic. But the greatest fear for most people is the fear of death.

However, throughout the Bible the message is abundantly clear: 'Do not fear, nor be afraid' (Isaiah 44:8). We can go forward this day in the knowledge that He who was crucified and buried, is now risen, ascended and glorified, and one day He will come again in power and glory.

Tomorrow we will continue considering the importance of this great event which is unique to Christianity.

> 'I know that my Redeemer lives: What comfort this sweet sentence gives!
> He lives, he lives who once was dead, He lives, my ever-living head.'
>
> Samuel Medley (1738–99)

7 APRIL

He lives who once was dead

'He is not here, for he has risen.' Matthew 28:6

RECOMMENDED READING: Luke 24:1–12

We continue to see why the resurrection is such an important event for the Christian church.

2. The resurrection brings great joy. John 20:20 says, 'Then the disciples were glad when they saw the Lord.' Fear was only brought under control when they met the Lord following His resurrection. In the place of fear there came joy. Luke 24:52 says, 'They ... returned to Jerusalem with great joy.'

I am always challenged by the life of the apostle Paul. He was stoned, shipwrecked, beaten on numerous occasions, imprisoned, and even left for dead. Yet he could say to the believers at Philippi, 'Rejoice in the Lord always. Again I will say, rejoice!' (Philippians 4:4). We can rejoice if we are Christians because our names are written in heaven.

3. The resurrection defeats sin. 1 Corinthians 15:17 says, 'And if Christ is not risen, your faith is futile, you are still in your sins!' Because Christ is risen, our sins can be forgiven. 1 John 1:9, 'If we confess our sins, He is faithful and just to forgive us our sins and to cleanse us from all unrighteousness.'

In Genesis 3, sin became a reality. We need to acknowledge that fact, for its effects are all around us, even within us. Sin is also a tragedy. Lives are ruined by sin. Families are broken through sin. We hear of it; we read about it. Its results are everywhere. But God has provided a remedy in the death and resurrection of His Son.

4. The resurrection conquers death. Jesus said, 'Because I live you will live also' (John 14:19b). When our sins are forgiven, death has lost its sting. We then have a real, sure, hope of heaven and eternal life.

Heaven is not some figment of our imagination. Just as earth is a real place where we now have our existence for a very brief time, so heaven is a real place where we will reside for evermore.

It is a place God has prepared for those who have turned from their sins and have faith in the Lord Jesus, who died, yet rose again from the dead.

The resurrection is truly a message of hope. 1 Corinthians 15:20: 'But now Christ is risen from the dead.' 1 Corinthians 15:57: 'But thanks be to God, who gives us the victory through our Lord Jesus Christ.'

> 'He lives and grants me daily breath; He lives and I shall conquer death:
> He lives my mansion to prepare; He lives to bring me safely there.'
>
> Samuel Medley (1738–99)

8 APRIL

A peace the world cannot give

'The same day at evening, being the first day of the week ... Jesus came.'
John 20:19

RECOMMENDED READING: Matthew 28:16–20

The disciples were gathered together and the doors were firmly locked for fear of the Jews. Then suddenly, Jesus revealed Himself. Jesus made eight appearances within the first week of His resurrection, and all were on the Lord's Day, the first day of the week. Today, we look at the words spoken by Jesus. Tomorrow we will look at the actions of Jesus.

He brings a message of peace: 'Peace be with you' (John 20:19, 21). Peace is a commodity that is so difficult to find in this world, and therefore is absent in the lives of so many people today. However, we should still be searching and longing for its presence. There are three areas where our search should be directed.

(a) Peace with God (Romans 5:1). This can only be obtained when we receive forgiveness of our sins. Forgiveness only comes when we acknowledge that we are sinners in the sight of a holy God. We then turn our thoughts to Jesus, who alone rescues us from our sin by giving His life on the cross at Calvary. He died that we might be forgiven. He died that we might have peace with God.

(b) Peace with ourselves. In John 14:27 Jesus says, 'Peace I leave with you.' This world is turbulent. Our leaders are spiritually clueless as to how to solve the serious state in which we find ourselves. Yet, despite the tremors outside, the Christian possesses a peace that passes all human understanding. It is a peace that the world cannot give and, thankfully, a peace that the world cannot take away.

(c) Peace with each other. In his letter to the church at Thessalonica Paul says, 'Be at peace among yourselves' (1 Thessalonians 5:13). How easily tensions can arise, even among fellow Christians. Unkind words can then soon follow. Relationships become strained and sometimes broken. This should not be so. Again, in that fifth chapter, Paul says in v.15, 'Seek to do good to one another and to everyone' (ESV). That includes 'peace.'

Jesus says to His disciples in Mark 9:50, 'Have peace with one another.'

Throughout our Christian life let us, if at all possible, live peaceably with all people. By doing so God is glorified, and His Name is honoured.

> 'Peace, perfect peace, In this dark world of sin?
> The blood of Jesus gives us peace within.'
>
> Edward H. Bickersteth (1825–1906)

9 APRIL

He is always in the midst

'Jesus came and stood in the midst.' John 20:19

RECOMMENDED READING: John 20:11–18

Yesterday we considered the words of our Lord Jesus when He said to His disciples, 'Peace be with you' (John 20:19). Today I want us to think about what He did that evening. We read in v.19: 'Jesus came and stood in the midst.' That, after all, is His rightful place. He must always be there.

All Christians can rejoice today because He is still in the midst bringing a message of peace to troubled hearts. While this brings great comfort, it also presents a great challenge to us.

1. He is in the midst of His Church. In Revelation 2:1 we read, '… who walks in the midst of the seven golden lampstands.' He walks among the churches, His people. As He does so, He hears every word and sees every action. As he speaks to all the churches, there is one phrase that is repeated to each one. Verse 2 says, 'I know your works.' In other words, 'I know what you have done.' This thought should be a challenge to us all, both young and old. Think before you speak. Pause before you act. Be careful in all things. Jesus misses nothing!

2. He is in the midst of the home. When I was growing up as a young lad, my parents had a plaque that stood intentionally in a most prominent place in the lounge. It had these words inscribed on it: 'Christ is the Head of this house; The unseen guest at every meal; The silent listener to every conversation.' Isn't that a challenging thought for every Christian family? If we read those thought-provoking words every morning, it could, and should, make a significant difference to our conduct throughout the day.

3. He is in the midst of our life. Jesus must direct all our affairs: our time, our finance, and our activities. May we see nothing and read nothing that would displease Him. He should control our character, our conduct and our conversation. We should never take one step, or make one decision, without consulting Him. A verse that has meant a great deal to me over many years has been Proverbs 3:5–6: 'Trust in the Lord with all your heart and lean not on your own understanding. In all your ways acknowledge Him, and He shall direct your paths.'

Let us ensure that Jesus is in the midst at all times.

> 'Jesus stand among us In your risen power;
> Let this time of worship Be a hallowed hour.'
>
> William Pennefather (1816–73)

10 APRIL

Risen indeed!

'But now Christ is risen from the dead.' 1 Corinthians 15:20

RECOMMENDED READING: 1 Corinthians 15:12–26

The whole structure of Christianity rests upon the resurrection of our Lord Jesus Christ. The doctrines that we believe are dependent upon the fact that Jesus died for our sins and has now risen from the dead.

1. The deity of Christ is proved by His resurrection. Romans 1:4 says Jesus Christ was '… declared to be the Son of God with power according to the Spirit of holiness by the resurrection of the dead.' If Christ had not risen, His deity would have to be questioned. Throughout the Gospels, Jesus clearly stated that He was the Son of God. This was one of the reasons why the synagogue rulers put Him to death. The resurrection assures us that His words could be relied upon because they were true. There is no doubt whatsoever that He was and is the Son of God.

2. The sovereignty of Christ is dependent on His resurrection. Romans 14:9 says, 'For to this end Christ died and rose and lived again, that He might be Lord of both the dead and the living.' Jesus is Lord over all creation. All people and events are under His sovereign control. Nothing occurs without His knowledge and permission. We seem to have little problem in accepting that fact when things go well. However, it is just as important to believe that truth in times of pain and helplessness.

3. Our justification stands upon the resurrection. Romans 4:25 says, '…who was delivered up because of our offences, and was raised because of our justification.' The apostle Paul has no doubt in saying that if Christ had not risen our faith would be of no value at all. That also is applicable to our salvation, our redemption, our adoption as well as our justification. This applies to every believer throughout the history of the world.

4. Our own resurrection is totally dependent on the truth of his resurrection. Romans 8:11b says, 'He who raised Christ from the dead will also give life to your mortal bodies through His Spirit who dwells in you.' The truth is clear and easy to be understood. If Christ is not risen, then we shall not rise. If He is risen, then we too shall rise to be with Him. Throughout the history of the church, the message which has been preached and believed is that 'Christ is risen from the dead' (1 Corinthians 15:20). Jesus said, 'Because I live, you shall live also' (John 14:19).

'He arose! He arose! Hallelujah Christ arose!'   Robert Lowry (1826–1899)

11 APRIL

We should be selfless not selfish

'Let each of you look out not only for his own interests, but also for the interests of others.' Philippians 2:4

RECOMMENDED READING: Philippians 2:1–16

Just a short climb from our home, you see a beautiful view into the county of Worcestershire and the Malvern Hills. I try to take this walk most mornings to enjoy looking at God's amazing creation.

We should thank Him daily for our physical eyes, but even more for spiritual eyesight so that we can understand more of His character and love for us.

This prompted me to consider for the next few days the words 'look' and 'looking.' The first I want us to think of should be a clear warning to us all.

1. The selfish look. In chapter 56 of his prophecy, Isaiah is dealing with Israel's irresponsible leaders. In v.11 he says, 'Yes, they are greedy dogs which never have enough. And they are shepherds who cannot understand; they all look to their own way, every one for his own gain.'

We are living in a materialistic society, and even Christians are in danger of being caught up in it. The number one concern for most people is 'I'. We have iPads, iPhones, iPods, iTunes, iPlayer and much more.

There are those who keep their eyes focused daily on the stock market to see how their shares are performing. We listen to the budgets or financial statements to see how it will affect our bank account; hoping all the time that our lifestyle will be maintained or, better still, improved.

Despite the economic uncertainty at the present time, most people in the UK and the West still live comfortably compared with many throughout the world.

The selfish look should concern us because when we are rich in material things, we are often poor in our relationship with God.

Remember that the man, who gains the world but loses his soul, has made a miserable bargain. A Christian is one who doesn't have to consult his bank account to see how wealthy he really is.

Philippians 2:4 says, 'Let each of you look out not only for his own interests, but also for the interests of others.' There was one perfect example who always looked out for the interests of others, ignoring His own; it was the Lord Jesus Christ.

As we seek to follow His example, let Philippians 2:5 be our constant guide, 'Let this mind be in you which was also in Christ Jesus.'

12 APRIL

Keep your eyes from looking back

'Do not look behind you.' Genesis 19:17

RECOMMENDED READING: Exodus 14

Yesterday we began to consider the words 'look' or 'looking'. We were warned about the selfish look and to bear in mind the concerns of others, just as our Lord showed His concern for those in need of His help. Today we turn our thoughts to the backward look.

2. The backward look. God was about to destroy the cities of Sodom and Gomorrah. Before He did so, He urged Lot and his family to leave urgently and not to look back at the blazing cities.

However, in Genesis 19:26 we read, 'His wife looked back.' God's judgement for disobedience came upon her and she became a pillar of salt. She stood that day on the plain as a graveyard memorial to all those who are disobedient to God's instructions.

When God brought His people out of bondage in Egypt, there were times when they wanted to return to the land of oppression. Due to their constant disobedience and desire to go back, God's patience eventually ran out and that generation died in the wilderness.

Throughout the Bible we have numerous examples of people who thought they knew best and turned their backs upon God's divine instructions. Disobedience will always result in God's displeasure, and in some instances His divine anger.

There is, however, a second warning in looking back. We would do well to heed its lesson.

If you turn to Luke 9:62, we have the following words: 'No one, having put his hand to the plow, and looking back, is fit for the kingdom of God.' What a clear warning that is from our Lord!

When we commit our lives to the Lord Jesus Christ and promise to follow and serve Him to the end of our days, we are to press on regardless of the cost, whether human or financial. We must never deviate from or lose sight of our heavenly calling. His work must always come first, over and above anything else. To turn back from the road that we are travelling on will only result in heartbreak. Even if the journey is difficult, He will be beside us if we keep our eyes ahead.

13 APRIL

Keep your eyes on the road ahead

'Let us run with endurance the race that is set before us.' Hebrews 12:1

RECOMMENDED READING: Ruth 1

We continue our consideration of the words 'look' or 'looking'. We have thought about the selfish look and the backward look. We now fix our eyes to what is ahead.

3. The forward look. In Exodus 14, the Israelites, having left the land of their captivity in Egypt, soon found themselves in a cul-de-sac. If they turned back, they would find themselves retreating into the hands of Pharaoh and his army (v.12). If they stood still, they would eventually be engulfed by them. There was no alternative but to obey the command of the Lord (v.15).

In our Christian pilgrimage we must never retreat. Yes, there is a time to pause, weigh up the situation and seek God's will and direction for us, but we cannot, and must not, stand still indefinitely. The church must keep pressing forward, and so must we as individual believers.

As with the Israelites at the Red Sea, we need a strong faith, not only to step out, but to step in, and to step through. In Proverbs 4:25 Solomon said, 'Let your eyes look straight ahead.'

We must never be tempted to stray from the path God has set for us. If we do, it can be a difficult journey finding our way back to the right path.

In every generation Christians must be alert to the fact that they are in a spiritual warfare. God did not intend life to be a picnic. It is an intense battle with an enemy who never plays to the rules. Satan is a cheat, a deceiver, a liar and a murderer. Despite this, we must press on with our eyes fixed upon our commander-in-chief, the Lord Jesus Christ, knowing that in the end victory is secure.

Sabine Baring-Gould (1834–1924), during his time as rector in Horbury, West Yorkshire, wrote what became a very well-known hymn. The chorus reads:

> 'Onward! Christian soldiers, marching as to war,
> With the cross of Jesus going on before.'

We must keep looking ahead. The road will be rough at times and it may be steep in places. There will be people who will try to obstruct our journey and discourage us. But we must always maintain that forward look.

14 APRIL

Look and live

'Look to Me, and be saved.' Isaiah 45:22

RECOMMENDED READING: Romans 5

The message today is based on the testimony of a young man who became one of this nation's greatest preachers.

4. The saving look. It was Sunday 6 January 1850. The weather was cold and a heavy snowfall made travelling very difficult. The skies had a sombre look, as did the face of this unhappy teenager from the town of Colchester.

He was from a Christian family and Sunday was the day to attend the House of God. Despite the conditions, he was determined to trudge through the snow and attend the morning service.

As the weather deteriorated even further, he decided to turn down Artillery Street and attend a small Primitive Methodist Chapel. The inclement weather had kept many away and only twelve to fifteen people were in attendance. He decided to sit at the back under the gallery. He had heard that the Primitive Methodists sing so loudly that it gave people a headache, but he would put up with that inconvenience.

Not only had the weather affected the number in the congregation, but the minister was also unable to come. Eventually, a thin looking man climbed the steps and entered the pulpit. He was a labourer who worked on the land.

The young man in his testimony states that the preacher wasn't instructed or articulate. In fact, he was really stupid. He had to stick to his text because he had nothing else to say that was worthwhile. He didn't even pronounce his words correctly.

He spun his message out for ten minutes. Then he recalls that the preacher 'saw me under the gallery and knew I was a stranger. He fixed his eyes upon me and said, "Young man, you look very miserable, and you always will be if you do not obey my text."' [13]

Then, lifting up his hands, he shouted, 'Young man, look to Jesus, look, look, look!' The young man said, 'I immediately looked and the cloud was gone; the darkness rolled away and I saw the sun. I saw Jesus dying for me as my Saviour.'

The young man was Charles Haddon Spurgeon, England's 'Prince of Preachers', who, in his early 20s, was preaching to 6,000 people, morning and evening at the Metropolitan Tabernacle in the city of London.

I urge you today to look to Jesus, for He is willing to forgive the sins of all who turn to Him in repentance and faith. Look and live!

15 APRIL

The best is to come

'Looking for the blessed hope and glorious appearing of our great God and Saviour Jesus Christ.' Titus 2:13

RECOMMENDED READING: 2 Peter 3

We have been considering the word 'look' during these past few days. Today we conclude with:

5. The expected look. What a wonderful prospect awaits the Christian! A day is coming when our Lord and Saviour, Jesus Christ, will return to this earth in power and glory and every eye will see Him. Until that day, we continue looking and waiting with great expectation.

I find that there are two subjects that we hear very little about. They are rarely preached upon and only occasionally do we have conversation about them. They are the 'Return of Christ' and 'Heaven', our future destiny. I have often asked why. I fear we are far too comfortable down here on this earth. We have beautiful homes with familiar things around us and seem reluctant to let them slip from our grasp. We are comfortable and content with our lot and unwilling to give up our lifestyle and its familiarity.

But the Bible tells us that this world is not our home: we are just pilgrims here until we reach our future home which God has prepared for us. Our true citizenship is not here, but in heaven.

The persecuted church which is scattered throughout many parts of the world, such as North Korea, China, North Africa, Asia and the Middle East, don't have our problem. They have very little to leave and can't wait to do so. The return of our Lord and heaven dominates their conversations. For them, the sooner the better.

When the apostle Peter wrote to the persecuted church, he said in 2 Peter 3:13–14, 'Nevertheless we, according to His promise, look for the new heavens and a new earth in which righteousness dwells. Therefore, beloved, looking forward to these things, be diligent to be found by him in peace, without spot and blameless.'

Paul, writing to the Philippians in 3:20 said, 'For our citizenship is in heaven, from which we also eagerly wait for the Saviour, the Lord Jesus Christ.'

God has given to us a pair of eyes so that we can look. He has also given to us spiritual eyes so that we can look inward, backward, forward and upward. But those eyes should be looking onward to the time when we shall be with our Lord and Saviour for ever.

Until that day may we be constantly looking for His glorious appearing.

16 APRIL

The Bible, our reliable guide

'Your word is a lamp to my feet and a light to my path.' Psalm 119:105

RECOMMENDED READING: 2 Timothy 3:14 – 4:5

During this period of lockdown, it seems very strange looking outside and seeing the car standing idle with nowhere to go. Travelling has been a large part of my life for more than fifty years. My wife has often accompanied me on my travels, along with my set of road maps. Although I now have satnav, I still keep my map book.

Even today you can visit major stationers or online stores and come across a section entitled MAPS. The mind boggles at the large selection before you. There are maps of towns and cities, counties and countries. You will find maps for walkers, survey maps, maps of underground and railway networks and maps of the world. There are maps for every requirement the traveller may have.

So why are maps still important for people today? There are many reasons, but I will just mention two:

- To point the way and help us to reach our destination.
- To prevent wandering into danger and unforeseen pitfalls.

This is exactly what the Bible does for people such as you and me.

Psalm 119:1,3 tells us that if we walk in the way of the Lord we will be blessed. The word 'blessed' means experiencing God's divine favour.

Psalm 119:10 asks that we do not wander from God's commandments. Walk in His way and we are safe, but disobedience to His instructions will eventually result in our downfall.

During the coming days I want to look at a number of comparisons between a road map and God's Word, the Bible. To help me do so, I want to use some one-word headings that I came across a number of years ago, and all begin with the letter 'C'.

May God's word prove to be for us a lamp to our feet and a light to our path.

> 'O may these heavenly pages be
> My ever dear delight;
> And still new beauties may I see,
> And still increasing light!'
>
> Anne Steele (1717–78)

17 APRIL

Do not add or take away from the Bible

'All scripture is given by inspiration of God … that the man of God may be complete, thoroughly equipped for every good work.' 2 Timothy 3:16,17

RECOMMENDED READING: Revelation 22

Following on from yesterday, I would like to go through a number of comparisons between a road map and God's word, the Bible.

1. Complete. A road map with sections missing is incomplete and of little value to the traveller. Imagine purchasing a map book of England with the County of Yorkshire missing. The thought of it is horrendous and sends a shudder down my spine!

Or imagine buying a *London A–Z* and when you turn to the West End you find the pages blank. The book would be practically worthless.

When I turn to the Bible, I have in my hands a book that is complete. There is nothing missing and we need nothing extra to add to it. In Proverbs 30:6 we have a clear warning from God. It says, 'Do not add to His words, lest He rebuke you, and you be found a liar.'

Revelation is the last book in the Bible, and in 22:18–19 God has clear warnings to give us. We are not to add to His words, neither are we to take anything away.

Psalm 119 consists of 176 verses and nearly all of them refer to the importance of God's Word, His statutes, His laws and His commandments.

When the Bible was compiled, all sixty-six books made it complete. In Genesis we read of the fall of man through disobedience. Through the Old Testament we read of God's dealings with His chosen people, Israel, from bondage in Egypt to the Promised Land. We have accounts of the message that faithful prophets proclaimed to them before they were taken into captivity and then, after 70 years, returned to their homeland.

The New Testament begins with the life of Jesus recorded in the four Gospels, culminating in His death and glorious resurrection, and finally followed by His ascension.

We then have the account of the birth and growth of the early church in Acts, and the letters the apostle Paul wrote to the churches and individual believers. We also have letters written by James, Peter, John and Jude. Finally, we come to the Revelation of John to the churches in Asia concluding with a glimpse into our future destiny.

In this great book we have all we need to find salvation in Christ and a safe journey to the Promised Land. It is the most reliable guide.

18 APRIL

It is accurate and trustworthy

'The entirety of Your word is truth.' Psalm 119:160

RECOMMENDED READING: Hosea 14

Yesterday we began to consider a number of comparisons between a road map and God's Word, the Bible. We commenced with the word, complete. Today we turn to our second word:

2. Correct. A road map needs not only to be complete with all the details you require for the journey, but it also must be accurate. If it contains errors, then you could be facing great problems along the way.

Just imagine you are travelling down a one-way street in the wrong direction all because the arrows on your map/satnav had been printed or programmed incorrectly.

Or you are travelling down the motorway intending to exit at the next junction. When you arrive there, you discover it is for traffic joining the motorway only. The map had again been printed incorrectly.

Our verse today from Psalm 119:160 says, 'The entirety of Your word is truth.' The Bible is correct from beginning to end. There are no errors or mistakes.

In Genesis 3, the evil one put doubt into the mind of Eve in the Garden of Eden. In v.1 he said, 'Has God indeed said, " You shall not eat of every tree of the garden?"' The evil one caused Eve to question God's authority, then, in v.4, to deny it.

We can be totally assured that God's Word is reliable, dependable, trustworthy and flawless. God has guaranteed it to be so. You can therefore read its pages with total confidence. Every promise has a guarantee attached to it. God never breaks His word. He is always true to His covenant with us. God never does U-turns or leads us up a blind alley. He has a plan that was conceived in eternity past and will never deviate from it.

Psalm 119:142 says, 'Your law is truth.' God is always faithful to His word and sticks to it. You can depend upon it. Proverbs 30:5 says, 'Every word of God is pure.'

In these days, mistakes are commonplace in our society. We see it in government, local and national; we even see it in our Courts of Justice.

How reassuring to turn our eyes to a book that is trustworthy. The Bible will never let you down or lead you astray.

19 APRIL

Gossip the gospel

'Speak, Lord, for Your servant hears.' 1 Samuel 3:9

RECOMMENDED READING: 1 Samuel 3:1–10

As we continue to look at comparisons between a road map and the Bible, we turn to our third word.

3. Communicates. Have you ever travelled on a particular road and reached a point on the journey that has become so complex that you find it difficult to negotiate your way through? If that has not been your experience, then can I suggest trying Milton Keynes.

The satnav is sending you round in circles, so you stop and study your map carefully, but it doesn't help at all. You eventually, in intense frustration, ask someone to help you get to your destination. You show them your map and they explain the easiest route. It then becomes abundantly clear.

God spoke to Samuel when he was a young boy in the temple at Shiloh. He then had to communicate that message to Eli.

When God has spoken and brought salvation to us, then we must fulfil our responsibility and communicate it to others.

Psalm 119:46 says, 'I will speak of your testimonies … and will not be ashamed.'

That particular verse reminded me of a visit I made to the Home Office with a former chairman of Day One Christian Ministries.

As we were walking through the city of London, a young man approached us and asked the way to a certain part of the city. My colleague immediately replied, 'Yes, I know exactly where you need to go but, before I give you directions to your destination, let me give you even more important directions.' There on a busy London street he communicated the gospel to him without any sign of embarrassment in doing so. It was as natural as sitting down for your evening meal.

We can be so slow in taking opportunities to communicate the gospel to others, even when the opportunity is served on a plate for us.

Our task is to communicate the gospel to those who are confused and have lost their way in life. We must never be ashamed to talk to people about the Bible's message and its author.

Let us use the opportunities that God gives to us, and if possible, make opportunities. Perhaps a word from us may be just the beginning of some lost soul being set in the right direction.

20 APRIL

Old but forever new

'The entrance of Your words gives light; it gives understanding to the simple.'
Psalm 119:130

RECOMMENDED READING: Matthew 5:1–20

I want to conclude our comparisons between a road map and the Bible by considering two more similarities.

4. Contemporary. If you use a road map or a satnav, it must be up to date. All new roads must be included, whether they are motorways or minor roads.

How many times have you looked at your map before setting out and, on your journey, you meet a sign which says, 'New Road Layout Ahead'? In frustration you exclaim, 'I didn't expect this: it wasn't on my map!' Then, to your dismay, you discover your map book was printed in 1994.

The Bible, however, is contemporary; it is not dated. Though written centuries ago, it is as relevant as tomorrow's newspaper. A map book has to be continually updated to be relevant. The message of the Bible remains the same throughout each generation and never needs updating to be relevant.

Psalm 119:89 says, 'Forever, O LORD, Your word is settled in heaven.'

The Bible reminds us that from the dawn of history, man is the same; his needs are the same; and God's word to him is also the same.

Preaching God's word also must be contemporary and relevant to man's need and the situation in which he finds himself. However, always remember that preaching is based on a message that is unchanging.

5. Clear. Some maps need a magnifying glass or a very large zoom capacity. There is too much detail in too small a space. It's cluttered and unclear.

On some occasions the pages are not aligned correctly, so roads do not join at the correct place. It becomes frustrating and bewildering. The message of the Bible however is very clear. Psalm 119:105 says, 'Your word is a lamp to my feet and a light to my path.' We do not need to remain in darkness. If we are in a fog, the Bible brings light.

- It tells us about ourselves; we are sinners.
- It tells us we need a Saviour; His name is Jesus.
- It tells us how to live and how to die.

It is clear. We will have no excuses.

I have been very thankful for maps over many years of travelling. I am now grateful for my satnav, despite what other people may say. I am, however, far more thankful for my Bible. It points the way and prevents me wandering astray into dangerous areas. It will do the same for you.

21 APRIL

From darkness to light

'I have come as a light into the world, that whoever believes in Me should not abide in darkness.' John 12:46

RECOMMENDED READING: 1 John 1

As we journey through life, we see many contrasts. During the next few days, I want to consider some contrasts that can be found in the Bible. As we do, we will be able to see what God, in His mercy, has delivered us from and what He has called us to. We begin by looking at darkness and light.

Let us first consider **darkness**.

1 Peter 2:9 reminds us that, the Lord has '… called you out of darkness into His marvellous light'.

Ephesians 6:12 reminds us that we are confronted by Satan and his agents who are rulers of darkness. The devil is no myth. Neither is he just a powerful force; he has a real personality. He is the enemy of God and all that God seeks to promote, protect and uphold. The devil is engaged in an unseen battle for the soul of man, which involves you and me.

In Luke 22:53, Jesus spoke of this '… power of darkness'. We should all be aware of our enemy's character. He is a thief, a liar, a deceiver, a cheat and a murderer. He wants your spirit so he can control and manipulate you for his evil ends. The consequences of submitting to him are death and hell.

He loves darkness because that is where we stumble and fall. He is the prince and ruler of darkness. In the dark we are unsure of the way forward, fearful of taking the wrong direction. Without a hand to trust we go completely astray.

Now let us consider **light**.

1 John 1:5 says, 'God is light and in Him is no darkness at all.' In Christ we have been delivered from the power of darkness.

Jesus said in John 8:12, 'I am the light of the world. He who follows Me shall not walk in darkness, but have the light of life.'

When you are in the light you don't stumble. We not only have our Lord's hand to hold or His arms to carry us, but we have the Bible as our compass and guide.

Who wants to walk in darkness when you can have the light of life beside you? Why walk in the light alone when you can have fellowship with others on the journey?

No Christian should be isolated as we journey to heaven. To have company with those of the same mind makes the journey pleasant and much more enjoyable.

22 APRIL

I want to trust you

'You shall know the truth, and the truth shall make you free.' John 8:32

RECOMMENDED READING: Zechariah 8:1–17

Yesterday we began looking at contrasts we find in the Bible. Our first was darkness and light. Today we turn our attention to deception and truth.

First, we consider ***deception***.

Human nature is constantly in search of truth and reality. But Satan, the great deceiver, falsely poses as an angel of light and truth. We need to be constantly alert to this crafty chameleon that changes his image and redirects his attack in an instant. Even the strongest of believers must not at any time drop their guard.

The first attack came in Genesis 3:1 when he caused Eve to question God's authority: 'Has God indeed said, "You shall not eat of every tree in the garden?"' He implants doubt into the mind and we become uncertain of God's instructions to us. He then causes us to deny God's authority. Despite God's clear instructions (vv.2,3), in v.4 the devil said to Eve, 'You will not surely die.' Clearly a deception and lie.

Sadly, there are sections of the church today where questioning God's authority is commonplace. This has led to those in leadership even denying His authority and the great doctrines of the faith. Like the serpent some speak with forked tongue.

The devil's aim is to deceive and keep us from knowing God. As long as we keep a good distance from the truth, he achieves his purpose.

Let us now consider ***truth***.

Are you searching for truth about God, about yourself, and about your future destiny? It is here that the Bible comes to your aid.

John 17:3 says, 'And this is eternal life, that they may know You, the only true God, and Jesus Christ whom You have sent.' Jesus came to reveal the truth about God. When man looked at Christ, he saw himself in his true nature and it was far from a pretty sight.

John 8:32 tells us that the truth is not hidden from us. We can know the truth because Jesus Christ is truth '… and the truth shall make you free'.

The search for reality is a search for truth, substance and permanence. When the light of Christ enters the heart, God gives His Holy Spirit to guide us into truth. Let Christ control every area of your life and your search for truth will be rewarded. Why live life being constantly deceived by one who is a liar from the beginning? It can only bring you untold misery, especially when you can know and live in the truth.

23 APRIL

Clean hands and pure hearts

'Blessed are the pure in heart, for they shall see God.' Matthew 5:8

RECOMMENDED READING: Philippians 4:4–13

We are looking at contrasts that are found in the Bible. For today:

First let us consider ***sin***.

Unfortunately, most people do not realise the seriousness of this disease and it can and does spread quickly. What is serious is that people ignore it, and the media popularise it. Sin is a reality that originated in the Garden of Eden when our first parents disobeyed God's instructions. It is not only a reality; it is also a tragedy. It can be described as a growing cancer that can, if not dealt with, bring devastating consequences resulting in death.

God knows the heart of man is desperately wicked, rebellious, self-willed and corrupt. John 3:19 makes that very clear: 'And this is the condemnation, that the light has come into the world, and men loved darkness rather than light, because their deeds were evil.' We are desperately sick and in need of the great Physician.

Now let us consider ***purity***.

In a corrupt and polluted world, purity is a rare quality which we can never attain by ourselves no matter how hard we may try. If we are totally honest, society has everything geared up so that we are kept at a distance from purity. From childhood to adulthood, the pressure to conform to this world and its ways has rarely been greater.

Children disobedient to parents; men and women sleeping around with different partners, even among professing Christians; broken marriages in alarming numbers; gender-based violence; over 200,000 abortions in the UK alone in just one year; and we could go on.

Yet God created us in His own image and for His glory, but we fail to reflect it in our lives. The world seeks to conform us into its image, whilst God is seeking to conform us into the image of His Son.

In order that we might achieve God's purpose, God sent His own perfect and sinless Son to forgive and remove our sin and make us pure. Ephesians 1:4 reminds us that He chose us so 'that we should be holy and without blame'. God is gradually bringing the Christian back to the image that was originally there before the fall.

Christian, we are far from perfect, but let us grow in purity and holiness, hating even the very thought of sin in our lives. Let us be thankful that when God looks at the Christian, He sees no stain of sin. He sees in the believer His Son; perfect, sinless and pure.

24 APRIL

Death is never the end

'Be faithful unto death, and I will give you the crown of life.' Revelation 2:10

RECOMMENDED READING: Romans 6

We have been looking at some of the main contrasts in the Bible. Today we conclude with death and life.

Let us first consider ***death***.

The fall in Genesis 3 was the result of disobedience to God's instructions. This did not just apply to Adam and Eve, but to the whole human race.

Death was Satan's objective, but it is not the end. Hebrews 9:27 reminds us that we are all accountable to God on the day of judgement after we die.

I share with you three statements: the first from an atheist and the other two from Christians.

Christopher Hitchens said, 'I feel a sense of waste about it [dying] because I'm not ready.' [14]

Carey Francis of Kenya said, 'When I go, I want God to find my letters answered, my work up-to-date, and me still hard at it.' [15]

John Wesley said, 'I want to live this day as if it's my last.' [16]

Death is something we will all face sometime. We are all made aware of the loss of a loved one, or a close friend, but a time will come when we also will find ourselves, as the late Derek Prime put it, 'in the departure lounge'. For the unbeliever this will be a horrendous prospect that should fill them with dread. Yet now they seem oblivious to it. But there is an alternative to consider.

Let us now consider ***life***.

The life that God offers is eternal. Jesus broke the power of sin and the stranglehold of Satan by conquering death. When our Saviour died, three days later He rose again from the dead.

John 5:24 says, 'He who hears My word and believes in Him who sent Me has everlasting life, and shall not come into judgement, but has passed from death into life.'

Life consists of decisions that can change the course and direction of ourselves and others.

Deuteronomy 30:19 says, 'I have set before you life and death, blessing and cursing; therefore, choose life, that both you and your descendants may live.'

From darkness to life … from gloom to glory … from death to life—this is what has happened to every Christian. This is what can happen to you.

I conclude with a quote from George Standing, who was a preacher in the UK: 'Death is certain—but for the Christian it is just a translation from a world that is not his friend, to a world where his best friend awaits him.'

25 APRIL

Human effort to reach God

'Come, let us build ourselves a city, and a tower whose top is in the heavens.'
Genesis 11:4

RECOMMENDED READING: Genesis 11:1–9

During the next three days we will be looking at the construction of the Tower at Babel.

Following the flood (chapters 6–8), God tells Noah and his family in Genesis 9:1, 'Be fruitful and multiply, and fill the earth.' It wasn't long before tribes were formed and settled in their allotted place. But there was one group who were reluctant to spread too far and decided that it would be more secure if they all settled together in the land of Shinar which was in Babylon.

They chose Shinar because the land was fertile with good open spaces and this would meet the needs of a growing tribe.

1. **The time had come for action.** We are told in v.4 that they decided to build a city, and a tower whose top would be in the heavens. They wanted to be recognised for this great construction. They were proud and ambitious of their plans and nothing would stop them achieving their aim.

'Hey ho! Hey ho! It's off to work we go.' One thing they failed to consider was that in God's sight these men of Babel were mere 'dwarfs'.

It's interesting to note that we have the names of those who were responsible for building the tabernacle in the wilderness and the temple in Jerusalem, but no record is left of anyone involved in the building of this tower.

These people tried to reach heaven by their own means, but heaven is God's domain, not ours. We go there by grace alone, not by our own personal achievement. These people at Shinar were building for their own glory, not God's. Although we are not told, I wonder if Nimrod had some involvement in this project. He certainly had personal ambition with the intention of becoming a distinguished leader.

Luke 1:51,52 tells us that God scatters the proud, and brings down the mighty. He accomplished both to the men of Babel.

So, the work to build this tower commenced, but what lessons are there to be understood from this story? The first is that these proud people would be the ones to fail as the city was never completed (Genesis 11:8).

But second and most important of all is that God will not share His glory with another. God's purpose is to exalt the name of His Son, and we should never lose sight of that important fact.

Look what I can do!

'Let us make a name for ourselves.' Genesis 11:4

RECOMMENDED READING: 2 Chronicles 2:1–10

Yesterday we turned our thoughts to the story of Babel and the people's aim to build a tower to reach the heavens. Today I want to continue with the same theme.

2. Their personal ambition. Despite their intention to build a city and tower to reach the heavens, there was one major problem facing them. The materials for building were far from adequate. Genesis 11:3 says, 'They had brick for stone, and they had asphalt for mortar.' The materials were sub-standard for the task before them, so they had to use what was available.

Despite the drawbacks, it clearly didn't quash their eagerness to get the task completed. They were clearly up for the challenge!

Throughout history, we have developed the ability to invent skills in medicine, exploration, construction, and numerous forms of technology, which has proved to be a great blessing to many. However, it has also brought much concern too. It is a fact that, from good intentions can spring much evil. The world is full of good people who do bad things.

Now I don't want to ignore the achievements of many inventors who have improved the lives of many people. We also need to be aware of the fact that many great scientists have been Christians, as is the case today. Without doubt, over the years we have seen great advancement in medicine and technology, but that can also create another problem. Ambition has resulted in pride. Someone said, 'What we can do leads to what we may do and concludes with what we will do.'

If we make it, we can get rid of it, and that leaves God right out of the thinking and planning. Human ambition has become the norm and biblical principles have been totally ignored.

The people in Shinar had lost contact with their Creator and that is what has happened to our generation. Man's progress has left God right out of the picture. 'Let us build ourselves … let us make a name for ourselves' (Genesis 11:4). Is this not a clear warning to all the world's leaders?

Despite the greatness of our Lord Jesus Christ, He humbled Himself, even to the humiliating death upon a cross.

The proud will be humbled, as happened to the men of Babel. That will also happen to our proud leaders today, whether they be in politics, business or science.

God will not share His glory with another. Babel still speaks today!

27 APRIL

God steps in to frustrate men's actions

'The Lord came down to see the city and the tower which the sons of men had built.' Genesis 11:5

RECOMMENDED READING: Genesis 3:8–24

We have been considering the construction of the tower of Babel. We have seen the sin of the people in making a name for themselves. However, at the same time, we notice their intentions were tinged with a feeling of anxiety, due to insecurity. Genesis 11:4 says, '… lest we be scattered'.

It is when we come to v.5 that we see an important change of direction in the whole story. God steps in to frustrate their plans.

How similar is this story to the events in Genesis 3 where, in v.5, Eve's desire is to be as God. In v.8 God visits the garden to bring judgement. But despite their disobedience and fall, God responds by bringing them hope. Verse 21 tells us, 'The Lord God made tunics of skin and clothed them.' God still cared and loved them.

In returning to chapter 11, we see in v.7 God bringing judgement upon the people and in the following verse He carries it out. The Lord comes down; the people are scattered; the city remains unfinished.

Yet throughout the Bible there is a message of hope. Turn to the next chapter and we see a new nation coming into being through the family of Abraham.

The message of the gospel is that no one can attain heaven outside of Jesus. God came down to enable us to go up. That is the gospel we must proclaim. It is not our work, it is His alone. There is no hope for sinners without God's grace. We all deserve God's judgement for building our own towers.

I am so thankful today that God came down. He came down to a town called Bethlehem, not to a glittering palace, but into a filthy stable (Luke 2). In the manger lay the Son of God, who came to reveal to us the character of God, and to pour out His life blood on a cruel cross. He died carrying our sin, and took upon Himself God's wrath, so our iniquity would be totally erased and we would experience peace with God.

If you have never experienced His peace and forgiveness, then I ask you to tear down those towers you are building and look to Jesus; turn your eyes towards the cross and see what love was shown to rebellious sinners. There is hope, but it will not be found in you; it is in Christ alone.

28 APRIL

Meeting with the living God

'He took one of the stones of that place and put it at his head, and he lay down in that place to sleep.' Genesis 28:11

RECOMMENDED READING: Matthew 1:18–25

Today we turn to Genesis 28 to consider the stairway that God had constructed at Bethel. This experience would transform Jacob's life.

How often do you dream? Do you remember them or do they quickly fade from your memory? Are they pleasant, or do they turn into nightmares?

The dream Jacob had on his way to Padan Aram would never be forgotten. In this barren, deserted place, he met with the Living God. During the next few days we will consider this amazing dream.

In Genesis 27, Jacob had deceived his father, Isaac, by pretending to be his brother Esau. Through this deception, he had stolen the blessing which was due to his brother. Now his life was in danger as Esau had threatened to kill Jacob as soon as the time of mourning for his father had passed (Genesis 27:41). Jacob had to flee for his life. His escape was made easier when his father instructed him to find a wife from the daughters of Laban, his mother's brother.

So, the eventful journey began. He was about 50 miles from home and the sun was beginning to set. He settled down for probably his second night under the stars. He selected a smooth stone and used it for a pillow. Not the most comfortable object for your head after a weary journey, but who cares if you are going to have a dream that will transform your life.

Remember that Jacob was in no spiritual condition to be searching for God, but God, in His great mercy, was looking for a meeting with Jacob.

The apostle Paul was another man who was in no condition to be seeking after God, but on the road to Damascus God met with Paul, and that meeting changed his whole life and future.

When a person encounters God, he will never be the same again. How many of us sought after God? We were spiritually deaf, blind and dead with no desire whatsoever to welcome His presence into our lives.

But thank God a day came when God sought and found us, and we could not resist His overwhelming love and grace, which He demonstrated toward us.

Thank God for that day when He lifted us from the deep, slimy pit that we had sunk into, and set our feet upon the Rock, and pointed us in a new direction.

29 APRIL

A glorious vision

'He dreamed, and behold, a ladder was set up on the earth, and its top reached to heaven.' Genesis 28:12

RECOMMENDED READING: Matthew 2:1–15

Yesterday we travelled with Jacob to Padan Aram where he stopped for the night at Bethel. During the night he had an amazing dream that he would never forget.

1. **Behold a ladder.** When we come to the word 'Behold', what follows is another of God's sudden, unexpected surprises. The last thing Jacob expected to see was a ladder. This was the longest ladder he had ever seen. It was set on the earth and its top reached to heaven.

There has always been great competition to build the tallest structure in the world. When I was young, it was the Empire State Building in New York. Today, it is dwarfed by the Burj Khalifa in Dubai. It is 2717 feet (828 metres not including the antenna) from the ground, which is just over half a mile. Buildings such as these are remarkable achievements and take years to construct.

However, within seconds, God shows Jacob a ladder far higher than any human structure. It is a ladder with its top in heaven. This conveys a wonderful message to us. We mere humans on earth can have direct access to God's throne in heaven, but only through His Son, the Lord Jesus Christ.

But now this dream becomes even more amazing.

2. **Behold God's angels.** We read in v.12 that angels were ascending and descending on this ladder. In the early chapters of Genesis, prior to this event, I can find only three instances of humans encountering angels.

The first is in Genesis 16:7 when an Angel of the Lord found Hagar in the wilderness. The second is in Genesis 19:1 when two angels arrive in the city of Sodom. The third is in Genesis 22:11 when the Angel of the Lord prevented Abraham from sacrificing his son Isaac. Now Jacob sees not one or two, but a whole company of angels.

But there was even more in this dream.

3. **Behold the Lord (v.13).** It's not angels we long to see for they are just God's servants. It is the Lord we desire to set our eyes upon. Angels haven't rescued us; angels haven't saved us from sin and hell. It is the Lord and He only who is our salvation. He alone is the giver of eternal life.

What a glorious vision this was to behold.

30 APRIL

The voice of God

'Behold, the Lord stood above it.' Genesis 28:13

RECOMMENDED READING: Genesis 28:13–15

Following the vision, Jacob now hears the voice of Almighty God.

1. God reminds Jacob of who He is. In v.13 He says to Jacob, 'I am the Lord God.' You cannot be clearer than that! He is not an unknown God, but a God who reveals Himself. He had done this to his grandfather Abraham and to his father Isaac. Now He is speaking to you Jacob. It would be wise to listen to all He has to say to you.

2. He reminds Jacob of His generosity. In v.13 He says, 'The land on which you lie I will give to you and your descendants.' We have a rich provider who gives to us far more than we deserve. He gives all that we need, but He can also withhold. He gives because of His unfailing goodness to us.

3. God reminds Jacob of his presence with him. In v.15 He said to Jacob, 'I am with you.' What a comforting assurance this was to His child. In the midst of this barren wilderness, God was there with him. God will never leave us, not forsake us—ever. As we journey through our wilderness, He is with us every step of the way.

4. God reminds Jacob of His constant protection. In v.15 He told Jacob, 'I will keep you'—keep you from evil, keep you from falling, keep you through dangers seen and unseen. He walks beside us; He walks behind us; He walks before us; He is beneath us; He is over us; He is within us; and He encircles us. That is what I call protection. He promised Jacob, 'I will keep you wherever you go.' That same assurance applies to all God's people.

5. God reminds Jacob of His promises. In v.15 He told Jacob, 'I will not leave you'—now or at any time in the future. 'I am with you always, even to the end of the age' (Matthew 28:20).

6. God reminds Jacob of His plans for him. In Genesis 28:15 God said to Jacob, '… until I have done what I have spoken to you'.

All the points I have shared with you are God's guarantees. They were for Jacob, but also for us too. God had a plan for Jacob's life. God has a purpose for our life too, and He will fulfil it.

> 'Guide me O Thou great Jehovah, Pilgrim through this barren land,
> I am weak but Thou art mighty, Hold me with Thy pow'rful hand.'
>
> William Williams (1717–1781)

1 MAY

Jacob responds to this dream

'Then Jacob awoke from his sleep and said, "Surely the Lord is in this place, and I did not know it."' Genesis 28:16

RECOMMENDED READING: Genesis 28:16–22

Jacob had seen with his eyes an amazing vision. He had also heard the voice of Almighty God with his own ears. Now had come the time for him to respond to what he had seen and heard. He responded to all that had happened in two ways:

1. **He makes a confession.** In v.16, after he woke from his sleep, he said, 'Surely the Lord is in this place, and I did not know it.' He wasn't the only one to have such an experience.

It was the evening of our Lord's resurrection (Luke 24:13–35). Cleopas and his companion were walking on the road leading to the village of Emmaus, about seven miles from Jerusalem. On the journey a stranger joined them and entered into conversation about the amazing events that had occurred that day, but they were totally unaware who this stranger was. Jesus could not have been nearer, yet they were ignorant as to His identity. God is often least where we expect him to be.

Back in Genesis 28:17 Jacob said, 'How awesome is this place! This is none other than the house of God, and this is the gate of heaven!' It is always awesome when God is there. When Jacob became aware of God's presence, the pillow for his head became a pillar for worship (verse 18).

2. **Jacob responds with a commitment (vv.20–22).** In yesterday's thoughts we saw how God gave Jacob a number of assurances (vv.13–15). Jacob was now responding with a commitment that the Lord, who gave these promises, would be his God (v.21).

This encounter at Bethel was an experience Jacob would never forget. The meeting with God would spur him on and encourage him in the many trials he would face later in his life.

May our encounters with Almighty God be a great encouragement to us as we journey through this life. We may not have such a striking vision as Jacob had, but God still speaks to His children through his precious Word. When He speaks, we must respond in obedience to Him.

2 MAY

Jesus is the only way to heaven

'And he called the name of that place Bethel.' Genesis 28:19

RECOMMENDED READING: John 1:43–51

Jacob's night began with an amazing vision. He then heard the voice of God speaking personally to him. He responded with a commitment that the Lord would be his God. Today we conclude our visit to Bethel.

We have looked at this event as it unfolded, but there is one important question we must ask before we move on. This story centres upon God, angels and a ladder. But where is Jesus in all this?

If you turn again to John's Gospel and the first chapter there is something very important to note. Towards the end of the chapter, we read of God's encounter with Nathaniel from v.45. Note especially v.51: 'Most assuredly, I say to you, hereafter you shall see heaven open, and the angels of God ascending and descending upon the Son of Man.' This clearly depicts Jesus as the ladder.

It is drawing our attention to the fact that Jesus, and He only, is the link between earth and heaven. To make the link possible, we turn our eyes to the cross where God met the deepest needs of man. Sin had to be dealt with, and Jesus dealt with it by dying in our place and taking the punishment that we deserved.

No one can approach the Father except through the Lord Jesus Christ. He is the only way to heaven. This separates Christianity from every other religion in the world. Christianity is unique because of Jesus.

There may be some reading this who have only recently stepped upon the first rungs of the ladder. May I encourage you to keep climbing and never look back. As you climb, earth becomes more distant and heaven more near.

There may be others who are more than halfway in their climb. Yes, it may be getting difficult at times, but keep pressing on the upward way, for you are gaining new heights every day. The Saviour will hold you and help you on the journey.

But, for others, the summit is in sight. Your climb may be a little slower now, but the saints and angels are encouraging you. More than that, the Father is there reaching out His hand. Just grasp it; it will make the last steps much easier.

Oh! What joy awaits you!

3 MAY

On the isle but in the Spirit

'"I am the Alpha and the Omega, the Beginning and the End," says the Lord.'
Revelation 1:8

RECOMMENDED READING: Revelation 1:1–9

John, the apostle, was in his nineties and had been banished to the penal colony of Patmos. It is a small island eight miles by four miles, off the coast of Greece.

Today, Patmos is a holiday island visited by many tourists, but that was not the case when John was there. During his time on the island, he experienced persecution and loneliness and knew what it was to suffer for the Word of God and the testimony of Jesus Christ. Yet, though he was on the island (v.9), he knew what it was to be in the Spirit (v.10).

Dr W. E. Sangster was one of Methodism's finest ministers and spent many years at Westminster Central Hall in London. On a Sunday he would preach to a congregation of up to 3,000 people, both morning and evening. It was while he was in the full bloom of his ministry that he developed progressive muscular atrophy, which greatly affected his speech. In the end he had to step down from preaching the gospel that he so loved to declare.

The following Easter Sunday, after he had stepped down, he was making his way to the Central Hall when a lady stopped him and expressed her sadness over his illness. She shared his disappointment at not being able to climb those pulpit steps and shout, 'Hallelujah, Christ is risen!' He turned to her and said in a croaky voice, 'Yes, I am sad not to be able to shout those words from the pulpit this morning, but it would be far worse if I didn't feel like shouting them.'[17]

William Sangster was on the island, but he was in the Spirit. He died in 1959 at the age of 60.

There may be some today who are reading this, and they know only too well what it is like to be on the island. It may be ill-health; unemployment; being part of a dysfunctional family; bereavement; battling mental health; or the need to isolate due to COVID-19.

Whatever your physical island may be, I trust you will know what it is to be in the Spirit.

Though on the island, John was in the Spirit and saw one like the Son of Man (v.13). A day is coming when it will be a reality for us to see Jesus face to face.

4 MAY

Jesus, the King and Great High Priest

'I saw seven golden lampstands, and in the midst of the seven lampstands One like the Son of Man.' Revelation 1:12,13

RECOMMENDED READING: Matthew 17:1–9

Yesterday we began to look at the amazing vision John, the apostle, had when he was banished to the island of Patmos. Though it was a place of suffering and loneliness, it was also a time when he was in the Spirit and saw a vision of the Lord.

In this vision John saw and recorded for us three things.
- Christ's apparel
- Christ's appearance
- Christ's authority

During the coming days we will be looking at each of these with particular emphasis on the second—Christ's appearance. First of all, we consider:

His apparel. In v.13 we are told that he was, '... clothed with a garment down to the feet and girded about the chest with a golden band'. Clothes were very significant in ancient society. You could often tell a person's rank and authority from his or her clothing. In v.13 John notices two important aspects of the clothing Jesus wore.

1. *The full-length robe.* Generally, the longer the robe, the higher the social standing. Here the robe reaches down to the feet. In Mark 16:5, on the morning of the resurrection, women entered the tomb where Jesus was laid following His crucifixion. They saw a young man clothed in a long white robe. In Isaiah 6:1, the prophet '... saw the Lord sitting on a throne, high and lifted up, and the train of His robe filled the temple'. Note the specific details regarding the robe in both events.

2. *The golden sash.* The golden sash, or band, speaks of nobility. When the wearer was working, the sash secured the clothing around the waist. When he was resting the sash was worn across the chest. The material and style speak of royalty. In Exodus 28, the high priest, Aaron, wore a beautiful sash of gold.

Our Lord Jesus Christ is not only our King, but our Great High Priest who constantly intercedes on our behalf.

5 MAY

Jesus misses nothing

'His head and hair were white like wool, as white as snow, and His eyes like a flame of fire.' Revelation 1:14

RECOMMENDED READING: Psalm 139:1–12

We continue to look at the amazing vision of our Lord which John the apostle had, as recorded in Revelation 1. Yesterday we viewed our Lord's apparel. Today we turn to:

His appearance. We are told in v.13 that John saw One like the Son of Man. The title, Son of Man, is used 100 times in the prophecy of Ezekiel. It was also Jesus' favourite name for Himself and he used it over 80 times. From verses 14 to 16 of Revelation we have seven descriptions of the Son of Man. Today we will consider two of these.

1. 'His head and hair were white like wool, as white as snow' (v.14). Here is a sign of maturity. Whiteness of hair signifies to us someone who has matured in age or possesses much experience that can be passed on to others. As far as human nature is concerned, age and maturity do not always go together. When they do, what a blessing they can be to those who are younger.

With regard to our Lord, He possessed maturity, wisdom, and purity to the full. He is also described as the Ancient of Days, for He is the Eternal One (v.8).

When you are on the island, who do you go to? You go to someone with experience who understands what you are going through—a friend who is mature, experienced and wise. There is no one better than your Saviour.

2. 'His eyes like a flame of fire' (v.14). Here is a sign of scrutiny. I see here a picture of searching eyes. There is nothing in our lives that is hidden from the Lord. He even searches out the very thoughts of our heart. Man looks on the outward appearance; Jesus looks upon the heart. He sees all and knows all.

A passage of Scripture I turn to is Psalm 139. It always challenges me to realise that He knows, sees, and hears everything. We must never think we can hide anything from Him.

But I always find it comforting to know that His eyes are upon the righteous and His ears are open to their cry. May that thought be reassuring for you at all times.

6 MAY

God demands our time and energy

'We beheld His glory, the glory as of the only begotten of the Father, full of grace and truth.' John 1:14

RECOMMENDED READING: 2 Peter 1:12–18

We continue looking at John's vision on the island of Patmos. Yesterday we considered two aspects of Jesus' appearance in Revelation 1:14. Today we turn our thoughts to v.15.

3. *'His feet were like fine brass, as if refined in a furnace' (v.15)*. Here we have a sign of activity. When Jesus was here on earth, He knew the urgency of the message God had given Him. He didn't waste a moment's time. He had only three years to fulfil His ministry; time was limited and very precious. He covered every part of the land of Israel, and beyond, fulfilling the task He had been given to do.

What about ourselves? Are we as active for the Lord as we should be? Do our feet burn with energy and enthusiasm? In Yorkshire we say, 'Some will work and some will let them!'

In 1 Corinthians 15:58, Paul urged the Corinthian believers to be, '… always abounding in the work of the Lord'.

We must never forget that our time is also limited. We only have this life to declare the gospel. There will be no evangelism in heaven. Let us use our days wisely so that we also finish the work God has given us to do.

4. *'His voice as the sound of many waters' (v.15)*. Here we have a sign of adaptability. It is so comforting to sit beside a gentle stream and hear the ripple as its waters pass by. The voice of Jesus could be just like the gentle ripple of a stream. 'My peace I give to you,' and 'Let not your heart be troubled' (John 14:27).

But when He challenged the scribes and Pharisees, His voice was like the billow of a mighty ocean during a storm. It was not always gentle Jesus, meek and mild.

Preachers have a clear example to follow. There are occasions when we need to bring a word of encouragement and comfort to broken hearts. But there are times when we need to shake the dead and warn people of judgement to come.

Whether we are ministering to large numbers of people or evangelising to individuals, may our voice be as the sound of many waters.

7 MAY

We are held in His hand

'For the Lord upholds him with His hand.' Psalm 37:24

RECOMMENDED READING: Psalm 37:23–40

We continue with the vision of our Lord that John saw during his time on the isle of Patmos. Our attention has been drawn to the head, the eyes, the feet and the voice of our Lord. Now we turn to His hand.

5. *'He had in his right hand seven stars'* (v.16). Here we have a sign of security. The seven stars that John refers to are the angels of the seven churches, His own people. He who upholds this great universe which He created has a special care for His people.

In the late 1970's, three months after I became General Secretary of what is now Day One Christian Ministries, I was invited to Northern Ireland for a seventeen-day preaching tour. This was my first visit to the province.

As this was during the height of the troubles, security was a major issue. A member of our Northern Ireland Committee would be driving me to my meetings, which covered many parts of the province. When we visited churches near the border, a good friend agreed to accompany us. I was somewhat taken aback to discover that he held a high position in the Ulster Constabulary.

As with many at that time, he was on the wanted list of the IRA, so this was a big decision for him to leave the security of Belfast. As we began the journey, I began to express my appreciation at his willingness to do this for our ministry.

He turned to me in the back of the car and said, 'I am taking no risk when I am helping to further the Lord's work. Thirty years ago, I committed my life to the Lord Jesus and placed it in His capable and secure hands. I know that no one can touch a hair of my head unless my God permits it.' I will never forget his words as long as I live.

It is so comforting and reassuring to know that we too are in His right hand, safe and secure and no one can pluck us out. We are held and gripped tight. Nothing and no one can harm us when we are there.

'Loving Shepherd of your sheep,
keep me Lord, in safety keep;
Nothing can your power withstand,
none can snatch me from your hand.'

Jane E. Leeson (1809–81)

Do not add or take away from the Bible

'I watched till thrones were put in place, and the Ancient of Days was seated; His garment was white as snow, and the hair of His head was like pure wool.'
Daniel 7:9

RECOMMENDED READING: Daniel 10:4–7

Today we conclude John's revelation of the appearance of our Lord with two more signs.

6. ***'Out of His mouth went a sharp two-edged sword' (Revelation 1:16).*** Here we have a sign of authority. Hebrews 4:12 tells us, 'The word of God is living and powerful, and sharper than any two-edged sword.' When our Lord Jesus Christ speaks, it is with unrivalled authority. It is, therefore, wise to listen to everything He has to say to us.

There are some people who say that the church is our authority. I completely disagree! We have one authority and that is the Word of God.

How sad it is to be aware of many, even in positions of leadership within the church, who question and undermine its authority. Is this one reason why we are so ineffective among people today?

Paul told young Timothy to, 'Preach the Word!' (2 Timothy 4:2). This we must continue to do faithfully, and to God's glory.

7. ***His countenance was like the sun shining in its strength (v.16).*** Here we have a sign of holiness. When John saw the appearance of Jesus, he '… fell at His feet as dead' (v.17).

In Matthew 17 we are taken to the Mount of Transfiguration. Jesus was there with Peter, James and John. As they gazed at their Master, 'He was transfigured before them. His face shone like the sun' (v.2).

Today we look through a mirror dimly, but one day we shall see our Lord face to face in all His beauty and purity. According to Matthew 5:8, it is the pure in heart that shall see God. What is wonderful for us is that we shall have every stain of sin removed from us, and we shall be like Him.

> 'Take time to be holy, the world rushes on;
> Spend much time in secret with Jesus alone.
> By looking to Jesus like Him thou shalt be;
> Thy friends, in thy conduct, His likeness shall see.'
>
> William Dunn Longstaff (1822–94)

Christ's authority

'All authority has been given to Me in heaven and on earth.' Matthew 28:18

RECOMMENDED READING: Hebrews 1

We have noted our Lord's apparel and considered His appearance; we now conclude by being reminded of:

His authority. The unrivalled authority of Christ is declared in the three claims that He made:

1. I am the first and the last. We have these words recorded in Revelation 1:17 and 2:8. It is equivalent of the Alpha and Omega. This title is only used three times elsewhere. You will find it in Isaiah 41:4, 44:6 and 48:12.

He is the author of our faith. He is the finisher of our faith. In other words, He is the Eternal One without beginning and without end.

2. I am the Living One. In Revelation 1:18 we read, 'I am He who lives, and was dead, and behold, I am alive forevermore.' In chapter 2:8 we read in the message to the church at Smyrna that he '... was dead, and came to life'.

We must always remember that no one took His life; He freely gave it up for His people. Three days later, He broke the chains of sin, the grave, death and hell, and is now alive for evermore.

Because He lives, we can be assured that we shall also live with him throughout eternity.

3. I am the Sovereign Lord. Revelation 1:18 says, 'I have the keys of Hades and of Death.' Here is absolute authority. No one can challenge it.

At Caesarea Philippi, John heard Jesus promise that the gates of hades would not overcome His church (Matthew 16:18). Now the issue is even surer. Those very gates will be locked upon the author of evil himself and the Lord will lock them.

What an experience this must have been for John! He was on the island, but in the Spirit, and it all took place on the Lord's Day. If you ever feel that you are on the island, suffering and lonely, may you know the experience of being in the Spirit.

Today may we feel the presence of the Triune God as we have never experienced Him before. May His presence be among us, not only in times of worship and conversation with others, but also in the quietness of our own homes as we meditate upon His Word.

10 MAY

To forgive and be forgiven

'You shall say to Joseph: "I beg you, please forgive the trespass of your brothers and their sin."' Genesis 50:17

RECOMMENDED READING: Genesis 50:15–22

In reading the concluding verses of chapter 50, I was struck by the way Joseph was willing to forgive, and then put behind him the evil actions of his brothers.

Although Joseph showed a lack of wisdom towards his brothers, they showed evil intent towards him on more than one occasion. Most people would look for revenge when they have been mistreated, but Joseph believed this was God's plan and purpose for his life.

I want to think about the word forgiveness. It is a huge subject that demands our consideration.

1. **To forgive can be difficult.** Pride is often a barrier to forgiveness. We find it hard to acknowledge that we have done wrong, even when it is so obvious to others.

For some people the most difficult word in our vocabulary is 'sorry'. But true forgiveness can only be given when the one who has offended you seeks your forgiveness with total sincerity.

It can be difficult to ask for forgiveness, and equally difficult to forgive, but both must be done. Never hold a grudge. Hatred can make you feel strong but harbouring it can be corrosive and destructive.

It can cost to seek forgiveness, and to grant it.

2. **To be forgiven is precious.** Jacob was terrified at the prospect of meeting his brother Esau. After stealing his brother's blessing in such a deceitful way, Genesis 27:41 tells us that Esau threatened to take Jacob's life. Therefore, it must have been a complete surprise when, on his return home, 'Esau ran to meet him, and embraced him, and fell on his neck and kissed him' (Genesis 33:4).

A similar reaction is seen with Joseph and his brothers (Genesis 45:15).

Someone once said, 'He who cannot forgive others, burns the bridges over which he himself must pass.'

The believer's greatest weapon is forgiveness. Satan cannot understand it, or handle it.

To forgive and be forgiven is an experience we should treasure and receive with gratitude.

Tomorrow we conclude by thinking of God's forgiveness to sinners such as us.

11 MAY

Total forgiveness in Christ

'... who forgives all your iniquities.' Psalm 103:3

RECOMMENDED READING: Psalm 32

We have been looking at the subject of forgiveness. We have seen how difficult it can be to forgive, but also how precious it is to be forgiven. We conclude with the greatest experience of all:

3. To know God's forgiveness for all our sin. We can read of a number of examples in the Old Testament of people who have experienced forgiveness. Joseph's brothers were forgiven after they disguised his death and sold him to Midianites, knowing full well he would become a slave in Egypt. Another example is the story of Esau who forgave his brother after Jacob stole the blessing from his father Isaac.

But the clearest example of forgiveness is seen in God's Son, the Lord Jesus Christ. Because of our sin against Him, it would have been just for God to punish us and banish us to hell. However, there was one alternative, and that was for God to forgive and bear the pain Himself.

Writer Rita Snowden (1907–1999) said, 'Forgiveness ... is the wonder of being trusted again by God in the place where I disgraced Him.'[18]

The New Testament also tells of two men who experienced God's power of forgiveness and then went on to serve Him faithfully to the end of their earthly days. One was the apostle Peter who, just before the crucifixion of his Lord, denied that he ever knew Him. The other was Saul of Tarsus, who later became the apostle Paul. He was responsible for the imprisonment, and in some cases the deaths, of many of the Lord's people before his conversion.

Both men knew the truth of Psalm 32:1: 'Blessed is he whose transgression is forgiven, whose sin is covered.'

I am thankful today that our sin is also covered by the blood of the Lord Jesus, which was poured out for us on Calvary's cross. There is no forgiveness of our sin without the shedding of His blood.

As we read these words, let us rejoice that we worship a God who has forgiven, not some of our sin, not most of our sin, but all of our sin. That includes our past, present and future transgressions.

This fact should melt our hearts and enable us to forgive all those who have sinned against us.

> 'When I survey the wondrous cross
> On which the Prince of glory died,
> My richest gain I count but loss
> And pour contempt on all my pride.'
>
> Isaac Watts (1674–1748)

12 MAY

Be thankful for sleep

'Come aside by yourselves ... and rest a while.' Mark 6:31

RECOMMENDED READING: Mark 6:1–13, 30–46

Do you ever feel like the disciples? So much is happening, and you are trying to do a multitude of things, with no time even for a cuppa. I suggest you are in good company.

At the dawn of history God instituted rest. He knows how we are made, and how important it is for us to find time to rest.

1. During the day. From our childhood, rest was an important part of our growing up. Children and even adults get grumpy when they are overtired, so rest is essential.

Even in employment, most work is structured so that we have tea breaks and lunch breaks. As you get older, the tea breaks get a little longer, as do the lunch breaks.

However, that is nothing compared to when you retire. A pleasant hour of sleep after lunch becomes routine, and you don't feel even a tiny bit guilty for it.

In Mark 6, the disciples had been very busy, and the rest of the day looked to have a hectic schedule. So, Jesus wisely advised them to come apart from the crowds and have a well-earned rest.

2. Every night. How thankful we should be for sleep. It's the best prescription I know of. It is a gift that God has given to all human beings, whatever their race or status in life. After toil comes a night's rest.

Psalm 127:2 says, 'He gives His beloved sleep.'

Every night, when we put our head on the pillow after a busy day of work, we should thank God for the gift of sleep. The time when you value the blessing of sleep is when you can't sleep.

When our son was a baby, he was fed and he slept. His wife says the routine hasn't changed. I couldn't understand parents complaining about lack of sleep. As far as I was concerned, parenting was a doddle: eat and sleep—simple.

Then we had our daughter. After rocking the pram at 4am, then off to work at 7am, my opinion quickly changed. How much we appreciated our first undisturbed night of sleep.

Sleep is a gift from God, a most precious gift—one that cannot be truly valued until it is taken away from you.

13 MAY

A vital part of life

'The Son of Man is also Lord of the Sabbath.' Mark 2:28

RECOMMENDED READING: Deuteronomy 5:1–22

Yesterday we looked at God's gifts of rest and sleep. We need times for relaxation during the day and each night we appreciate the blessing of sleep.

However, there is one more aspect of rest that we often overlook. It is the need for a day of rest each week.

When God created this beautiful world in six days, He rested on the seventh. He was setting us an example, so that after six days of labour, we too should set aside a day to rest and remember our Creator in worship to Him.

Now God could have created the world and everything in it in six weeks, or in six months, or even six seconds. We must never limit the power of Almighty God. However, He chose to do it in six days. There was a deliberate purpose in doing so. God was setting a pattern: six days of work to be followed by a day of rest.

This day is not a temporary Jewish ordinance, but a God-given gift for the benefit of all people and for all time. The example of a day of rest after six days of work was given before the Jewish nation ever came into being. If a perfect man, such as Adam, needed a day of rest, how much more do we, who are fallen creatures, need the benefits of this precious gift from God.

God looked upon this day with such importance that He included it into His moral law, which was given to Moses in the form of the Ten Commandments. If it is this important to God, it also should be important to us.

If God had not given a day of rest, it would have been necessary for someone to have invented it. In the busy and pressurised world in which we all live, this day is necessary for us all.

It is possible that if we neglect this day of rest, illness can be the consequence. That is why some illnesses need enforced rest.

Let us not take rest and sleep for granted, whether it is during the day, during the night or on each Sunday.

God knows what we need—after all He created us. So let us thank Him for this precious gift and make good use of it.

I think it's time for a little shut-eye. See you tomorrow! Zzzzzzz

14 MAY

The victory belongs to God

'Arise, for the Lord has delivered the camp of Midian into your hand.'
Judges 7:15

RECOMMENDED READING: Judges 7

It was Sunday 22 March when the country went into lockdown and we commenced sending these daily messages. We never expected three months later to have reached one hundred days.

From my early teens I loved playing and watching cricket. My dream was to play for Yorkshire and England. Alas! It was only a dream. However, I do remember an opening batsman by the name of Geoffrey Boycott who, on 11 August 1977, was the first man to score his one hundredth hundred in a test match against Australia at Leeds.

In the Bible there are a number of events that involve the number one hundred. During the next two days I want to consider three where the number played an important part in the story.

1. Gideon and his three hundred men. In Judges 7, Gideon was preparing to do battle with the Midianites and Amalekites. He had thirty-two thousand people supporting him. However, God clearly told him that number was far too many lest Israel claim the glory and boast over their victory.

We read that twenty-two thousand returned as they were fearful and afraid. That left just ten thousand to go into battle. But that was still too many, so God gave them another test (vv.5,6) which left just three hundred to fight against an army as numerous as locusts (v.12).

Gideon divided them into three companies, with one hundred in each. With torches, pitchers and trumpets, God brought victory to Israel. The glory was God's alone.

The Christian church is numerically small compared with the enemies of God. Our resources are also limited. Yet despite that, God has assured His people of victory as we battle against the forces of evil, which are so prevalent in the world today.

Whenever we see God at work, we must never claim the victory for ourselves, as without Him we would certainly fail and fall. We also need to be reminded that He will not share His glory with another.

We must acknowledge that any victory is His alone, and to Him be all the praise and glory.

15 MAY

Concern for the hundred

'There will be more joy in heaven over one sinner who repents than over ninety-nine just persons who need no repentance.' Luke 15:7

RECOMMENDED READING: 1 Kings 18:1–16

In the Bible there are a number of events that refer to the number one hundred. We looked at the story of Gideon yesterday. We conclude with two more where the number one hundred is significant.

2. Obadiah and the hundred prophets. We read in 1 Kings 18 that God, in His providential mercy, placed Obadiah in the palace of King Ahab and was in charge of the king's household. We are also told in v.3 that '… he feared the Lord greatly'.

Ahab and his notorious wife Jezebel had slaughtered many of the Lord's prophets. Obadiah, realising he was called to the palace for a purpose, showed great bravery by taking one hundred prophets, hiding them in two caves, and sustaining them with bread and water.

Almighty God always has His people in the right place for the right time ready to follow His instructions. Both Nehemiah and Esther were in the court of Persia just when they were needed to be of service for God.

Today, both in the Royal Household and in Parliament, God has His own people to stand and testify for Him. He will never be left without witnesses, even in the corridors of power.

Each of us has been called by God to serve Him just where He has placed us. All we have to do is to be faithful and obedient.

3. The shepherd and his one hundred sheep. Sheep are a common sight in the land of Israel. The shepherd knows his sheep because he spends time with them. The sheep also know the shepherd, which is why they follow him.

In Luke 15, we read that one was lost in the wilderness, which can be a dangerous place for a lone animal. Why take a risk for just one lone sheep when you already have ninety-nine? The answer is simple: the shepherd loved that one sheep as much as the other ninety-nine.

What if God should say, 'I have my chosen ones; My church is complete apart from that one stubborn, awkward soul who should have known better?'

God's love is so great that He would search for that one errant soul who was in danger from the enemy. If that soul was you, aren't you thankful that He searched for you until He found you and brought you back rejoicing to the safety of the fold? God is concerned for the safety of the entire flock.

16 MAY

Our eternal destiny

'Between us and you there is a great gulf fixed, so that those who want to pass from here to you cannot, nor can those from there pass to us.' Luke 16:26

RECOMMENDED READING: Luke 16:19–31

A few weeks ago, I wrote a brief series on the subject of contrasts. I strongly felt that I should have done one more but, as it was a difficult subject, I left it alone. My conscience has troubled me ever since, so I retrace my steps to cover the subject of heaven and hell. I want to consider three contrasts.

1. There is no rest in hell. Hell will give no peace, no times of quiet and no calm. When you go through a period of illness, most times you do have occasions of respite and ease from your distress. There will be no relief in hell. The troubled will find no rest.

Heaven is perfect peace and rest.

In this life the Christian will labour for their Lord and face the trials and challenges that come with it. We are often tired and weary in the work, but never tired of it. We labour on and spend our time and energy on gospel work. When we die, we then rest from our labours, and relish in the peace and tranquillity of heaven and all the good things that it offers us. Then our work is done!

2. There is no joy in hell. In this life we have times of pleasure, but it is interspersed with grief and sadness. Hell will be a place of unending grief. Joy and happiness will be absent (Luke 13:28). If you are not a Christian, you can avoid this place of misery and pain, and find the joy that only Christ can bring.

Heaven is a place of joy.

In heaven there will be no sadness or grief. We will have the joy of experiencing the sights of heaven; the thrill of fellowship with the saints we have read about; and above all, relish those precious moments in the presence of our Saviour.

3. There is no communion with God in hell. The unbeliever will spend eternity with the words, 'if only' on their lips. I beg of you, do not die with regrets. While you have breath, repent of your sin and look to Jesus.

Heaven is unending communion with God.

To look into His face and never sin again will be eternal bliss; to finally have an answer to all my unanswered questions will be so reassuring; to commune with my Creator and thank Him for all He has done will be such a privilege. I will have all eternity to do it.

17 MAY

The king calls upon God

'*And Jehoshaphat feared, and set himself to seek the* LORD.' *2 Chronicles 20:3*

RECOMMENDED READING: 1 Kings 22:41–50

The Moabites, Ammonites and Edomites are on the horizon ready to attack. Jehoshaphat is informed that this vast army was already at En Gedi, near the Dead Sea. This is a serious situation for Jehoshaphat and his army. What does he do? 2 Chronicles 20:3 tells us that he prayed. But notice the prayer carefully. It follows a similar pattern to other Old Testament prayers by great men such as Nehemiah, Daniel and Ezra. During the next three days we will consider his prayer and God's response to it.

1. He first acknowledges who God is (v.6). He is the God of his fathers, Abraham, Isaac and Jacob. He is the God of the lawgiver Moses. He is the God of the prophets and judges. He is also the God of the Psalmist and second king of Israel, David.

When we come before Him in prayer, let us remember who we are coming before. He is not a man like us. He is the eternal Creator of the universe. He is the Father of our Lord Jesus Christ. We should approach Him with reverence and godly fear, for there is none like Him.

2. He acknowledges where God is (v.6). His throne is in heaven. Here He is worshipped by the elders and every living creature. In the prayer which He taught His disciples, our Lord began with these words: 'Our Father in heaven.'

He dwells where there is no sin. It is a place that is pure and holy and where no unclean thing dwells; a place that knows no pain or sadness; a place that knows no darkness for all is light; a place that is totally secure, where no evil can enter; a place where all forgiven sinners can call home; a place that is beyond all human description—a land of pure delight and perfect bliss. That is where God dwells.

3. He acknowledges what God does (v.6). He rules over all the kingdoms of the world. Let us be grateful that no earthly ruler or political power controls this world. Let us rejoice that Almighty God rules over all things and all the people of the world. No one can withstand Him, no one can question Him, and no one can ever depose Him. He is God, the only God, the true God, and the Living God. There is no other.

If only our leaders, and those in authority would acknowledge this, the world would be a far better place in which to live.

18 MAY

When you are at your wits end

'O our God ... we have no power against this great multitude that is coming against us; nor do we know what to do, but our eyes are upon You.'
2 Chronicles 20:12

RECOMMENDED READING: 2 Chronicles 20:1–30

Jehoshaphat is facing a vast army bent on destruction and he does not know what to do. Yesterday we saw that he acknowledged who God is, where he dwells and what He does. Now he is totally honest with God. He holds nothing back but opens his heart to Him.

1. We are powerless (v.12). We do not have the manpower, the expertise or the equipment to defeat them. They are far stronger than we are. Do you feel like that? Does your fellowship feel like that? I am thankful that God doesn't feel like that! Yes, we are outnumbered. The press and media show their opposition to those things that are precious to us. The world constantly overwhelms us. Governments often despise us and ridicule our beliefs. The so called 'wise and clever people' belittle God's Word, and we are left demoralised and dejected. We are powerless without God.

2. We cannot see a solution (v.12). You can picture Jehoshaphat throwing his arms into the air in exasperation. 'We don't know what to do.' I find this can be the most dangerous situation to be in. You turn in desperation to use different tactics as there is nothing to lose. You are at your wits' end. Have you ever felt like this? We employ new methods with little, if any, success. We make things more appealing and shorten the length of the church service or reduce them to just the morning. We invite special guests, especially if they are famous. We purchase up-to-date technology, advertise on the internet and arrange new attractive programmes. We expend much effort, but it brings little results. Then we acknowledge with Jehoshaphat, 'We do not know what to do.'

3. Our eyes are upon You (v.12). Have our eyes been fixed far too long upon things, methods and presentation?

Let me be clear in saying that we should be the best that we can be and look as presentable as possible. I am not saying we should be opposed to new areas whereby we can reach the lost. What I am saying is that, from personal experience, we seem so reluctant to spend time with God in prayer. We prefer doing things than casting our eyes in God's direction.

We need to give time to the Lord and listen to Him. If we do, we might be surprised at what He has to say to us and stunned by the results.

19 MAY

God always knows what to do

'Thus says the LORD to you: "Do not be afraid nor dismayed because of this great multitude, for the battle is not yours, but God's."' 2 Chronicles 20:15

RECOMMENDED READING: Romans 8:31–39

King Jehoshaphat, who was facing a military crisis, has been speaking to Almighty God. Now God speaks to His servant words of comfort and reassurance.

1. Do not be afraid (v.15). How often we read these words in the Bible, especially at critical times. In the book of Joshua, God's servant is about to take on the great responsibility of leading the people of Israel across the river Jordan into Canaan. There are many battles to be fought, some against powerful opposition. In Joshua 1:9 God says to him, 'Be strong and of good courage; do not be afraid, nor be dismayed, for the LORD your God is with you wherever you go.'

God spoke the same words to shepherds in the fields around Bethlehem following 400 years of silence. He then announced to them the birth of the promised Messiah (Luke 2:10).

God also repeated these words to the women who came to the tomb. Then they made the amazing discovery that Jesus had risen from the dead (Mark 16:6).

He speaks the same words to pastors and leaders as they seek to serve the Lord in these challenging and difficult days in which we live. He says the same words to you and me when we see the vast and growing opposition to our message. 'Do not be afraid.'

2. Do not be dismayed (v.15). We often feel like Jonah and Elijah. We become dejected and downhearted in our Christian service.

There seems to be little growth in the fellowship despite the effort to encourage fellow believers. And where is the concern and enthusiasm among God's people in reaching the lost? You are dejected and discouraged because you think the growth of God's kingdom depends on you.

We all need to remember, as David did when he faced the Philistine giant, Goliath, in the valley of Elah. The battle is not yours, but the Lord's.

Jehoshaphat was told in v.17, 'You will not need to fight in this battle ... stand still and see the salvation of the LORD ... for the LORD is with you.' So, what did the people do? Verse 18 tells us they prayed and worshipped. What was the result? Moab was destroyed (vv.22–24). God's enemies were defeated (v.22).

So, when you don't know what to do, remember the One who does.

Jesus is precious

'Therefore, to you who believe, He is precious.' 1 Peter 2:7

RECOMMENDED READING: 1 Peter 2

The apostle Peter probably had little as far as this world was concerned, but when he wrote his two letters, he spoke of five things that were precious to him and should be to us also. Peter loved to use the word *precious*, so what did he count as precious?

1. Jesus is precious. In 1 Peter 2:7 he says, 'To you who believe, He is precious.'

There was a time in our lives when Jesus was nothing more than a name on paper, a person we read about, a person of history, but nothing more. We didn't give Him a second thought. Some believed He had special powers, such as healing. He was certainly an exceptional teacher and communicator. Others would go even further and state that He was the Son of God, who died and rose again from the dead.

Although we live in a secular age where people seem to be ignorant about Him, there are still those who are familiar with certain aspects of His life. However, there is a vast difference between knowing about someone, and knowing them in an intimate and personal way.

As far as Peter was concerned, Jesus was not some figment of his imagination. He was not just a character of history; he was a real person who had made a dramatic impact upon his life. Jesus had revolutionised him. He had made a sinner into a saint; a faint-hearted disciple into a brave-hearted apostle. Yes, Jesus was precious, not only to him, but to many of his friends also. He had totally transformed both him and them.

In 1 Peter 2:4 we read, 'Coming to Him as a living stone, rejected indeed by men, but chosen by God and precious.'

I am reliably informed that the world's most expensive diamond is the Cullinan which is valued at a mere 400 million dollars; a very suitable gift for a wedding anniversary. Well, I am sure it will give pleasure to some, if they could get hold of it. It sparkles, but it is a lifeless stone.

The Lord Jesus Christ is a living stone, a chief corner stone. The whole building holds together because of Him.

It is indeed sad that He is rejected by most people, even His own people, the Jews. But to those whose lives have been eternally affected by His presence, He is undoubtedly precious. Is He precious to you?

Blood means life

'You were not redeemed with corruptible things, like silver or gold ... but with the precious blood of Christ.' 1 Peter 1:18–19

RECOMMENDED READING: 1 Peter 1

Sometime during your life, you may have been given a gift that has become very precious to you. It may be an item of great value, or the person who gave it meant a great deal to you, such as a parent or very close friend. Some gifts are worth very little to other people, but they are very precious to you.

Yesterday we began looking into Peter's two letters, giving special attention to the word *precious*. Today we consider another occasion when Peter uses the word *precious*.

2. His blood is precious. A diamond can give some people a great deal of pleasure, but if it is lost or stolen, it can give them much grief. Despite its beauty, it is corruptible. Blood, however, is not only important to God, it is vital for us.

God's plan of redemption began with the taking of an animal's life to clothe Adam and Eve following their fall into sin. Blood was shed so that they would become acceptable in the sight of God.

To our first parents, blood meant life, forgiveness and hope. It was a sign of God's pardon for sin. The Bible reminds us that, 'without the shedding of blood, there is no forgiveness of sin' (Hebrews 9:22, ESV).

When Israel prepared to leave Egypt, there was one more plague to come over the land. All the firstborn in the land would die. God instructed His people to kill a lamb or goat and daub the blood on the doorposts and lintels of their houses so, when the Angel of death saw the blood, he would pass over.

Throughout the Old Testament, the blood of millions of bulls, goats and lambs were shed to satisfy God's anger over the sins of His people Israel. But this was a continuous process with no end in sight. Sin had to be dealt with because God is holy.

At the appropriate time, God stepped into history and sent His only begotten Son. Instead of an animal being the victim for our sin, Jesus Christ became our sacrifice so that our sins would be forgiven forever.

The sacrifice of Himself, was a one and only sacrifice, never needing to be repeated again. On the cross Jesus endured the full anger of God over our sin so that we might be spared.

It is the blood of Jesus that cleanses from all sin and gives us hope of eternal life.

22 MAY

The heart of our faith is Jesus

'... looking unto Jesus, the author and finisher of our faith.' Hebrews 12:2

RECOMMENDED READING: 2 Peter 1:1–8

In 1990, my wife, Kathryn, joined me on a deputation tour of the Western Isles of Scotland. We had a most encouraging time and came back with happy memories and new friendships established. Those feelings evaporated very quickly on our return when we discovered our house had been broken into during our absence. Many of my mother's belongings had been stolen, as she lived with us during the latter years of her life. Most had little value, but the grief on her face was unforgettable as they were very precious to her. Thankfully her faith remained strong and intact.

Peter loved to use the word *precious* in his two letters. He has told us clearly that both Jesus and His blood are precious. Today we turn our attention to the third occasion where he used this word.

3. Your faith is precious. In 2 Peter 1:1, the apostle is writing 'to those who have obtained like precious faith'. This faith only comes because of the work that God, His Son and the Holy Spirit have done in our lives.

With faith in Him, we can look ahead because of what has been accomplished in the past. Author Philip Yancey (1988) wrote, 'Faith means believing in advance what will only make sense in reverse.'[19] Old Testament believers looked ahead with faith to what one day would happen. Christians look back with thanksgiving at what has taken place.

Our faith is precious because it is centred upon the Lord Jesus Christ. Someone said that, 'Faith never goes beyond Christ; neither does it ever stop short of Christ.'

In that great eleventh chapter of Hebrews, we have the roll of honour of the faithful. It begins in v.1 by reminding us that, 'Faith is the substance of things hoped for, the evidence of things not seen.'

When we read 1 Peter 1:7, the apostle talks about faith being genuine. Let us ensure that it is so. We don't want anything fake about the faith of the Christian; it has to be real and clearly evident in our daily living. Above all, we must count our faith to be precious to us, and others must notice how precious it is.

23 MAY

Be aware of the outward appearance

'Let it be ... the incorruptible beauty of a gentle and quiet spirit, which is very precious in the sight of God.' 1 Peter 3:4

RECOMMENDED READING: 1 Peter 3:1–16

We have been considering the word *precious*—a word Peter loved to use in both of his letters. We continue with a further example of something that Peter counted precious.

4. Your gentle and quiet spirit is precious. Today Peter reminds us of the importance of possessing and cultivating a gentle and quiet spirit.

Today billions of pounds are spent by film and television celebrities trying to improve their image. It will include clothing, jewellery, hairstyles and, in some cases, even cosmetic surgery. However, beneath that beautiful exterior can be a very different interior.

Some of these famous faces come before the cameras and look beautiful, until they open their mouths.

Let us come down to earth and be completely honest. It is not the clothing you wear, the jewellery you possess, or the style of hair that brings beauty. It is the inward spirit that is the most important.

There are people who spend vast amounts of money taking their pets to a parlour for shampoo and beauty treatment. If you take a dog, it will still come out as a dog.

Humans can spend all they want on outward adornment, but inwardly they are still dirty sinners needing God's cleansing through the blood of the Lord Jesus Christ.

A gentle, quiet spirit is beautiful, incorruptible and above all, precious in the sight of God. This removes boasting, anger, jealousy, bad temper, grumbling and complaining. This is a message to the young as well as to older believers.

The young, in particular, face an internal battle for their soul. They are under enormous pressure to conform to the image of this world, through the media and advertising. Resist the urge to conform. God wants you to be conformed to the image of His Son.

Older believers also have a challenge facing them. It is to show young people how you can grow old gracefully and not grumpily.

We all need to realise that it is not the outward adornment that is important to God. What is precious to Him is a beautiful inward spirit. Let us strive for that which will give great pleasure to God.

24 MAY

God's precious promises

'... have been given to us exceedingly great and precious promises.' 2 Peter 1:4

RECOMMENDED READING: 2 Corinthians 1:15–24

During the past few days, we have been considering the word *precious*. It is a word that the apostle Peter used often in his two letters. We have seen that Jesus is precious; His blood is precious; our faith is precious; and a gentle and quiet spirit is precious. We conclude these thoughts with:

5. God's promises are precious. I have always been reluctant to make promises to my family and friends. It is never a good thing to go back on your word and break a promise. Today it seems a very easy thing for people to do, especially if it gets them out of a tricky situation. It is better not to make one than break one.

God's promises, however, are always reliable, dependable and trustworthy. When God makes a promise, you can be assured it will never be broken.

In 2 Peter 1:4, Peter describes God's promises. He reminds all believers that they are precious—far more precious than a large gem or a bulging bank account. In fact, he calls them, '... great and precious promises.'

Actually, he goes even further than that. Paul was renowned for his extravagant use of adjectives. Now Peter imitates the great apostle, for he calls them, '... exceedingly great and precious promises.' No number of adjectives can describe the extent of God's promises as they are beyond description and all are meant to be a blessing and encouragement to His people.

His promises have given us life. They have given us power. They have given us comfort. They have given us guidance. They have given us eternal life. And all these come to us because of Jesus, His beloved Son.

Cling to God's promises, cherish them in your memory and write them upon your heart, for we never know when we will need to recall them.

When I was growing up in Sunday school, we would sing a chorus that began with these words: 'Every promise in the book is mine; every chapter, every verse, every line.

All are blessings of His love divine; every promise in the book is mine.' (Author unknown)

As we finally gather our thoughts together under the word 'precious,' one thing becomes abundantly clear. The world's interpretation and the Christian's interpretation of the word are diametrically opposite.

The Christian should be able to say, 'I'm standing on the promises of God.' He is truly precious!

25 MAY

God keeps His promises

'I will certainly be with you.' Exodus 3:12

RECOMMENDED READING: Exodus 3:1–15

Friendship is very precious and something we should all value and treasure. To have someone with whom you can enjoy a meal, play sport, share a problem, or just to have a chat with, is one of life's great blessings.

But our friends have other responsibilities, so they cannot be with us all the time and neither should we expect them to be.

How about having a friend who is always with us—an ever-present companion? Think about having someone with whom you can share everything, no matter how personal and intimate it may be. Someone who knows all about us and is always ready and willing to help and listen to those things that worry and concern us.

In Exodus 3:12 God says, 'I will certainly be with you.' Here we have a promise, a guarantee, and assurance to all God's people. So, whatever our circumstances and whatever challenges we face, we can rest with total confidence in this promise.

1. **The Giver of the promise.** 'I...'. Yes, God said it! These are not the words of man; this is God who is speaking. He is the One who possesses all power in heaven and on earth. He is giving this guarantee to us and when God speaks, we should listen.

2. **The certainty of the promise.** 'I will certainly ...'. Humans have a tendency to go back on their word. We can even be let down by friends, who can cancel an appointment at the last minute or change plans that have been set.

But when God speaks, it is done. What God says can be completely relied upon. He has never broken his word and we can be confident He never will. We can always depend on His word for it is fully trustworthy.

3. **The recipients of the promise.** '... be with you'. At this moment in time, you may be going through a number of difficult trials and you don't know which way to turn or what steps to take. Things are beginning to weigh heavily upon you and they are gradually getting you down.

What an assurance this is from God! He has promised to be with you at all times, in all places, and in all circumstances. The great God of heaven, the Creator of the universe, is with us constantly.

What an honour and privilege, not just to know it, but also to experience it.

26 MAY

All round protection

'But Noah found grace in the eyes of the Lord.' Genesis 6:8

RECOMMENDED READING: Genesis 6

Yesterday we considered the words from Exodus 3:12: 'I will certainly be with you.' During the next few days, I want to turn our thoughts to three men in the Old Testament who both knew the truth of those words.

Today I want us to consider Noah. Almighty God had created a beautiful world for us to enjoy, but it was ruined by sin. This resulted in a great gulf between a holy God and sinful man and has affected every human being that has ever lived on this earth since.

When we come to Genesis 6, we see the reality and tragedy of the fall of man, but we also see God's response to it. He decided to destroy everything He had made. Only Noah and his family were spared.

It was 1656 years since the creation of the world, and the time had come for God to open the heavens with devastating effect and flood the entire world. Every living thing on the face of the earth would be destroyed.

There would be forty days and forty nights of constant rain which would cover the mountains and bring death to all creation, apart from those within the ark.

Eventually the waters would subside, Noah and his family would step out of the ark and life would begin again. God made a covenant with Noah and assured him that the world would never be destroyed by a flood ever again. He placed a rainbow in the sky to seal that promise.

Throughout this time God protected Noah's family from the dangers outside and also within the ark. He saved them from an evil world that had to be destroyed.

A time is coming when God will once again step into history with even greater devastation and destroy this world in which we live. Only those who are in Christ will be saved from this frightening event. As God protected Noah and his family from the evil around them, so God, in His great mercy, will protect us. As Noah found grace in the eyes of the Lord, so will we.

If we are His people, we have this great assurance that, 'I will certainly be with you' (Exodus 3:12).

As we journey through this life, He will watch over us and keep us from the evil one (John 17:15). We are safe and secure if we keep close to Him.

27 MAY

From prince to pauper

'Go, and I will be with your mouth and teach you what you shall say.'
Exodus 4:12

RECOMMENDED READING: Exodus 4

Yesterday we saw how God protected Noah during the great flood and assured him of His presence.

Today we turn our attention to Moses. Moses was an exceptional character. He was a man who saw the glory of God; who spoke personally with God; and who walked closely with God.

He lived for 120 years. The first 40 years were spent as a prince in Pharaoh's court. The next 40 years were spent as a shepherd in the desert seeking God's will for his life. The final 40 years were spent leading a multitude of Israelites from bondage in Egypt, through the wilderness, to the border of the Promised Land. Someone said that Moses spent 40 years thinking he was somebody, 40 years learning he was nobody, and 40 years learning what God can do with a nobody.

During the second 40 years of his life, he met Jethro who was to become his future father-in-law and a helpful advisor. He married Jethro's daughter, Zipporah, and had two sons, Gershom and Eliezer.

However, the most significant event was his encounter with God at Horeb when God spoke to him from a burning bush that was not consumed. This was another major turning point in his life, as God instructed him to return to Egypt and bring God's people out of bondage.

Moses was naturally filled with trepidation at the prospect of confronting Pharaoh, but God assured him that he would not return alone. Aaron, his brother, would accompany him. Most important of all, God would be with them, speak through them and protect them.

Moses would have given anything to opt out but being obedient to God was paramount. God's instructions must be obeyed.

Don't fight with God! You will be knocked over in the first round.

The message today is clear. If God calls you into His service, obey Him. To disobey will only bring His displeasure; to obey will always result in His blessing being upon you.

So, my advice is to never argue with God—you are bound to lose. Save your energy for the task in hand and be assured that He will certainly be with you, at all times, and in all places.

The old hymn says: 'What He says we will do, where He sends we will go—never fear, only trust and obey.' (J. H. Sammis, 1846–1919)

28 MAY

The son of Nun and leader of many

'No man shall be able to stand before you all the days of your life; as I was with Moses, so I will be with you.' Joshua 1:5

RECOMMENDED READING: Deuteronomy 34

We have considered the life of Noah and Moses who were assured of God's presence with them. Today I want to turn our thoughts to another man that needed, and received, the same assurance.

We consider the life of Joshua. Joshua was one of twelve leaders of Israel who went out to spy the land of Canaan. When they returned to Moses, Joshua, along with Caleb, encouraged the people to take possession of the land. Regretfully, ten of the spies brought back a negative report and the people believed them.

You often find that people tend to accept the worst situations when they have a negative attitude. Their unbelief resulted in forty more years of wandering through a cruel wilderness.

Eventually God brought His people back to the River Jordan, for the time had come to cross over into the land of Canaan. Moses, however, had completed the mission God had given to him and so God instructed him to climb Mount Nebo and be gathered to his people.

Joshua was now to take on the huge responsibility of leading God's people into the land He had promised them. He needed wisdom, a guiding hand, and, above all, the assurance of God's presence with him.

In Joshua 1:3 God assured His servant that He would give him every place he set his foot upon. He also assured him in v.5 that He would never leave him or forsake him.

He told Joshua to be strong and very courageous as he led this multitude into the land that flowed with milk and honey, for this would be their inheritance. The key words are in the heart of v.5. God said, 'As I was with Moses, so I will be with you.'

This is a message to us all, but particularly those who are in any position of Christian leadership, whether it is a pastor, an elder, a deacon, a youth worker, or a missionary. When God speaks, we act.

Whether we are taken through the dark and often painful valley, or journey beside the quiet waters, God is there guiding every step of the way until our work has been completed. So, press on! You are not alone.

29 MAY

Stop doubting and believe

'Jesus came and stood in the midst.' John 20:19

RECOMMENDED READING: John 20:19–31

We have been considering three men in the Old Testament, Noah, Moses and Joshua, who were assured of God's presence with them when they needed Him most.

Today I want to look at a man in the New Testament who was absent when he should have been present. We turn our thoughts to Thomas.

It was the day of our Lord's resurrection and Jesus had made a number of appearances during that day. Now it was evening and the disciples were gathered together with the door firmly locked in fear of the Jews. Suddenly Jesus appeared unexpectedly. He was in the midst of those He loved, but Thomas was missing.

Throughout the following week the disciples tried to convince Thomas that they had seen the Lord, but he could not believe.

The following Sunday, a week after the resurrection, the disciples were again together and this time Thomas was with them. Jesus again appeared unexpectedly. He looked at Thomas and showed him His hands, His feet and His side. He told Thomas to reach out and touch them, to stop doubting and believe (v.27).

It was just a mild rebuke, but it packed a mighty punch. Thomas could only reply by saying, 'My Lord and my God' (John 20:28).

There are times when we stand alongside Thomas. We have our doubts, we have our fears, and we forget God's promises to us. We forget the many past occasions when God has come to us with words of reassurance and comfort, bringing renewed hope during times of uncertainty and distress.

How many times has He said to us, 'I am with you'? Yet when the next crisis comes around, we are back to dejection, doubt and despair.

When will we ever learn to trust completely in his promises, and cling to His words of reassurance? Do not ever doubt His love for you, nor question His care over you. He always wants the very best for you and all things will be for your good.

As He was with His disciples in that upper room, and assured them of His continued presence with them, so today He comes to us in our need and says, 'I will be with you.'

Stop doubting and believe it with all your heart! He has never forsaken those who trust in Him, and He will not forsake you.

30 MAY

About turn! Quick march!

'Repent therefore and be converted, that your sins may be blotted out, so that times of refreshing may come from the presence of the Lord.' Acts 3:19

RECOMMENDED READING: Ezekiel 18:21–32

The sergeant major marched onto the parade ground, his company standing at ease. He immediately called them to attention. Then in his powerful commanding voice shouted, 'About turn, quick march!' At once they obeyed his instructions.

In Acts 3:19 we have two very important words of command; repent and be converted. Repentance is when we realise the evil that sin has brought to our lives. When we become aware of it, we resolve to take action and forsake it. However, without conversion, we have little realisation of the damage it is doing to us and the future danger we are facing.

To be converted is doing an about turn. It is a change of mind which results in loving that which once we hated and hating what we once loved. We turn from our sin and seek to live a life that is holy and pleasing to God. We turn from this world and set our affections on things above. We turn from feeding our selfish nature to pleasing and living for the Lord Jesus Christ.

These are two words that require action. C.H. Spurgeon used the illustration of a man possessed to emphasise the distinction between these two words. When the possessed man had the demons cast out of him, Spurgeon compared that to repentance. But, when he put on his clothes, was no longer filthy and naked, and was in his right mind, that was compared with conversion.[20]

Repentance is an important part of conversion; we could look at it as the door to a new beginning.

When the prodigal son was feeding the pigs after spending all his inheritance on riotous living, he suddenly began to consider how low he had sunk into sin. We are told that he came to himself; that is repentance. When he set out to return to his father's house, that was conversion.

Repentance never stands alone but always linked with a turning from sin. Sadly, there are some people who are sorry for their sin, but never turn from it. Christianity is more than saying sorry; it is doing something about it.

Have you repented and been converted? If not, in the name of Jesus I say to you, 'About turn and quick march!' March along the narrow road that leads to eternal life.

Breaking the barriers

'A certain man of Bethlehem, Judah, went to sojourn in the country of Moab, he and his wife and his two sons.' Ruth 1:1

RECOMMENDED READING: Ruth 1

From the dawn of history, men and women have had the urge to break the barrier. Records are there to be broken; frontiers are there to be crossed; mountains are there to be climbed; the impossible is to be made possible. The motto for the Olympic Games is 'Faster—Higher—Stronger'. Athletes will devote years of training to break records. Challenges in life also have to be faced, and we all have the desire within us to beat our personal best.

During the next few days, I want to turn our thoughts to a young woman in the Bible who broke a number of barriers and is fondly remembered thousands of years later for doing so. Her name was Ruth.

Ruth lived in the country of Moab at a time when the judges ruled a famine-stricken Israel. There has been long debate over which judge ruled at this particular time, as the Bible does not inform us. It may have been towards the beginning of their rule for Boaz, one of the heroes of this time, was born to Rahab. Rahab had rescued two Israelite spies from Jericho and was saved by them when the walls fell down and the city destroyed. You can read her story in Joshua 2–6, when Israel was still busy conquering their God-given land.

The story of Ruth may have taken place during the days of Gideon, because in, Judges 6:1–6, we read of a famine which occurred during the Midianite invasion. So, who were the Moabites? These people descended from Lot, the nephew of Abraham. By her father, his elder daughter had a son who was called Moab, and the nation became a sharp thorn in Israel's side for many years to come. The nation of Israel, which had known God's blessing, was going through very turbulent times. They were in an utter mess spiritually, morally and economically. A king didn't reign, but chaos did.

Due to this famine in the region of Bethlehem, Elimelech, his wife Naomi and their two sons, Mahlon and Chilion, decided to leave the turmoil behind and set up their home in the land of Moab. Elimelech died, and Naomi's two sons married women of Moab whose names were Orpah and Ruth. About ten years later, Mahlon and Chilion also died, which left three widows.

Naomi decided the time had come to return to Judah. Orpah and Ruth decided to accompany her to the border. In Ruth 1:8, Naomi encouraged them to return home, and Orpah did so. However, Ruth would not let Naomi return without her, and so they began a long and difficult journey back to Bethlehem (v.14). Before them lay an adventure that would change the course of history. God was in control every step of the way, as He also is in our lives.

1 JUNE

The generation barrier

'Ruth said, "Entreat me not to leave you, or to turn back from following after you."' Ruth 1:16

RECOMMENDED READING: Ruth 1

Yesterday we were reminded of the background to the story of Ruth. During the next few days, we will look at four important barriers that Ruth crossed.

1. **The generation barrier.** We are not told the age difference between Ruth and Naomi, but Ruth was a young widow, whereas Naomi, Ruth's mother-in-law, had been a widow for a good number of years (1:11). There clearly was a generation gap which could have been a significant barrier to them. For Ruth, here was a barrier to be broken, and she broke it.

In the New Testament we read of other generation barriers that were broken. Barnabas and Mark were different generations, but they worked together for the spread of the gospel. The same applied to Paul and his 'son in the faith', Timothy (1 Timothy 1:2).

Paul has much to say about the generation gap in 1 Timothy 5:1–8.

I am always impressed when I watch our Queen in a carriage procession through the streets of London and see how Her Majesty attracts both young and old, who pay their respects to her. Queen Elizabeth II is a lady who has broken the generation gap even in her mid-90s.

When I recall my teenage years, I am so grateful to God for the elderly believers, who were an inspiration to me as I embarked upon my Christian pilgrimage. Could I urge all young people who may be reading this, to learn from and respect older members of your congregation. Don't despise their age and experience; they have much to teach you.

But can I also say to our elderly friends: do not quench the enthusiasm of young believers. Just channel it in the right direction. Never look down on the young but encourage them on their journey in life.

They might talk differently—don't we all! Sometimes they may look differently but try to understand them and work with them. They are growing up in a very challenging and dangerous world and they need your help. In fact, you might learn something from them if you give them time.

When we turn to the Gospels, we read of a man who broke the generation barrier. Young children gathered around Him and He didn't turn them away. He also showed compassion on the elderly in their time of need. His name was Jesus. A good example to follow, don't you think?

2 JUNE

The social barrier

'Wherever you go, I will go; and wherever you lodge I will lodge.' Ruth 1:16

RECOMMENDED READING: James 2:1–9

We have turned our thoughts to a young woman called Ruth from the land of Moab who broke a number of barriers. The first we considered was the Generation Barrier. Now we look at:

2. **The social barrier.** There was great animosity between Israel and Moab. Moabite people were idol worshippers and, to Israel, they were outside the covenant as they were not direct descendants of Abraham, God's special people. Ruth, however, left the comfort and security of her people and crossed the social barrier.

We need to look carefully into our own lives and dismantle any barriers we have, even sub-consciously, erected. We need to reconsider again the words in James 2:1–9.

They may not look like you, they may not have wealth like you, they may not be educated like you, they may not be socially elite like you, but they need Christ—just like you. We need to be careful not to make swift judgements that could be regretted later.

A number of years ago I had a wake-up call. I was invited to preach at a church in a run-down area of south London. When I entered the pulpit, I noticed a young couple who stood out by their attire and inappropriate tattoos. When I started preaching, I thought this couple needed a spiritual transformation. I soon realised it was I who needed the transformation. Their eyes were fixed with open Bible and notebook.

Speaking to them afterwards, they were very young believers, but spiritually hungry. They told me they would love to get rid of their tattoos, but they were a permanent reminder of what they once were, and the barriers they had now crossed.

How would we react if a former prisoner came into our fellowship? Or a drug addict? Or a single parent with big problems? Would we shun them and wish they weren't here, or would we welcome them with open arms?

I think we need at times to be taken out of our comfort zone. We must never change our message for anyone, but we may need to change our thinking and cross the social barrier.

There are people out there who are very different to us, but they need to hear about the same Saviour who has loved us all and given Himself for us all.

3 JUNE

God has broken down every barrier

'Your people shall be my people, and your God, my God.' Ruth 1:16

RECOMMENDED READING: 1 Timothy 5:1–8

We have seen how Ruth crossed both the generation and social barriers. Today we conclude with two more barriers that were overcome.

3. The national barrier. Ruth is saying to Naomi, 'I will trust, though I don't fully see; I will travel with you, though I don't know where I am going; I will dwell with you, though I don't know where I will be staying; I will die with you, though I don't know where my final destiny will be; I will worship with you, though I don't fully know who your God is, or what He can do. I am leaving my gods of Moab behind. Help me to know the true God of Israel.'

Yes, for Ruth, this was the beginning of a new adventure. From now on she would be walking by faith, and not always by sight.

Ruth could not see what the future held for her, yet she was willing to cross the national barrier and make amazing discoveries. Israel was now before her; Moab was now behind her.

Hudson Taylor left his hometown of Barnsley (my hometown too—I had to get it in!) and made the dangerous journey to serve the Lord in inland China.

If Almighty God called you to leave your home and possessions to serve him in another part of the world, would you be willing to cross the national barrier?

4. The barrier of unbelief. Ruth could not see what the future held for her, yet she said to Naomi in v.16, 'Your people shall be my people, and your God my God.' In that one statement, both of today's barriers were crossed.

9 November 1989 was a momentous day in Berlin. The Berlin Wall had finally fallen and the twenty-eight-year barrier between West and East Germany had been broken.

But there was an even greater barrier that separated man from God. Two thousand years ago, that barrier was broken when the Lord Jesus shed His blood for sinners, then three days later rose again from the dead. Have you broken the barrier of unbelief? God will give you the faith to break down what you have erected.

Ruth travelled to Bethlehem with Naomi and, through God's providence, met and married Boaz. They had a son and named him Obed who became the father of Jesse, who became the father of David, king of Israel.

From that direct line came Jesus, the Son of God and Saviour of the world.

6 JUNE

Confession of sin must be sincere

'I have sinned.' Exodus 9:27

RECOMMENDED READING: Exodus 10:16–29

The Christian church is facing many challenges in the twenty-first century. However, one of the greatest is to ensure that we do not water down the message of the gospel to make it more palatable to unbelievers.

We are bending over backwards so that we do not cause offence to our congregations. We want visitors to our churches to enjoy the service and we want to ensure that the message is acceptable and easy on the mind. We are not to upset the people who come.

Now I want to be clear; we must not cause offence intentionally when we share the gospel with others, but we must remember that the gospel will be an offence if it is preached clearly and faithfully. The apostle Paul knew that only too well.

During the next few days, I want to consider two words that seem to be omitted from many pulpits. We will look into one of those words today and tomorrow. The word in question is sin.

There is no gospel without the acknowledgement of our sin. There must be a clear confession of our sins before God. I cannot find a promise of salvation anywhere in the Bible to any person who will not acknowledge their sin in the presence of a holy God. There are those who make a confession of sin, but it lacks sincerity, and therefore it is not genuine.

One such example can be found in the life of the Pharaoh at the time of Moses.

1. Pharaoh. Pharaoh's heart had become hardened despite the severe plagues that God brought upon the land of Egypt.

In Exodus 9:27, Pharaoh called Moses and Aaron and said to them, 'I have sinned … The Lord is righteous, and my people and I are wicked.'

In 10:16, Pharaoh once again makes the following confession: 'I have sinned against the LORD your God and against you.'

It means absolutely nothing to God to acknowledge that we have sinned when we face danger or a serious illness, and then forget it a short time afterwards.

True confession of sin is followed by repentance and a change of heart and mind. We must always be sincere and genuine. Remember, God loves the sinner, but hates our sin. It was our sin that Jesus carried on the cross to assure us of salvation and forgiveness.

7 JUNE

Confession must be genuine

'For I acknowledge my transgressions, and my sin is always before me.' Psalm 51:3

RECOMMENDED READING: Luke 15

The Bible teaches that there is no gospel without the acknowledgement of our sin. Yesterday we considered Pharaoh, whose confession lacked sincerity. Today we look at two more people who confessed their sin, but only one was truly genuine. We begin with the first king of Israel.

2. Saul. In 1 Samuel 15:3, God had clearly instructed Saul to kill the Amalekites and spare nothing. However, Saul took King Agag alive and the best of the sheep and cattle; he destroyed only that which was worthless. Even if we cannot comprehend the reasons for God's instructions, we must carry them out.

Due to Saul's disobedience, God regretted making him king. Samuel had to tell Saul of God's displeasure and that He had rejected him as king. In 1 Samuel 15:24 Saul says, 'I have sinned, for I have transgressed the commandment of the LORD.' He repeated similar words in v.30.

Sometime later he was chasing David through the mountains in the south of the country. David had the opportunity to kill Saul but he would not touch God's anointed one. Saul acknowledged his error and, yet again, said, 'I have sinned' (1 Samuel 26:21).

To say these words and not mean them is worthless. We must confess our sin with sincerity and make the words genuine. Then they must be followed with repentance and a change of heart and attitude.

Let us conclude with one young man who truly meant what he said.

3. The prodigal son. Here we have the genuine confession of a young man who left home with his inheritance. He spent it all in a far country in riotous living and finished up feeding swine to keep him alive. When he came to himself (and we all need to do that at times), he made his long journey home. He had prepared his speech for when he met his father but, when he was still some distance away, his father saw him, ran to meet him and embraced him.

Despite that welcome, he said in Luke 15:21, 'Father I have sinned against heaven and in your sight and am no longer worthy to be called your son.' His attitude and words proved beyond doubt that he was a changed person.

To experience God's forgiveness, we must acknowledge our sin with true sincerity. This must then result in a transformed character, for you cannot remain the same person.

8 JUNE

We are responsible for our own sin

'Without the shedding of blood there is no forgiveness of sins.'
Hebrews 9:22, ESV

RECOMMENDED READING: Exodus 12:1–27

Yesterday I said that the greatest challenge facing the church in the twenty-first century is to ensure that we do not water down the message of the gospel to make it more palatable to unbelievers. When we see numbers declining and the church facing ridicule, the temptation is to present the message in a consumer-friendly way without causing offence to the general public.

I also stated that there are two words which seem to be omitted from many pulpits. We have looked at the importance of sin, but now I want to look at the word blood.

So, where do we begin? The New Testament and Calvary? No. As a certain well-known song reminds us, we must start at the very beginning, a very good place to start.

1. **Eden.** Genesis 1:27 tells us that 'God created man in His own image.' He was perfect physically, morally and spiritually. He fitted well into a perfect creation.

When we come to chapter 3, we are introduced to the serpent who led Adam and Eve into sin. That perfect relationship with God was broken through a desire to be as God, and through disobedience to His clear instructions.

Verse 6 tells us how it all occurred. Eve saw; she took; she ate. And then she gave to her husband and he willingly became involved in her sin.

As soon as their eyes were opened, they knew that they were naked and sewed fig leaves to cover their nakedness. We cannot deal with our own sins; we cannot make ourselves respectable and acceptable to God no matter how hard we may try.

Then they tried to pass the buck for their sins onto others. Adam blamed Eve, who then blamed the serpent. The lesson is clear: we are each responsible for our own sin and we cannot pass the buck to someone else.

This is when God stepped in and showed mercy to those who didn't deserve it. Genesis 3:21 tells us that, 'God made tunics of skin and clothed them.' To do this, the blood of an animal had to be shed to make Adam and Eve acceptable to a holy God.

Tomorrow we travel to Egypt, and then to Jerusalem to see God's plan fulfilled in and through His Son, the Lord Jesus Christ.

9 JUNE

Forgiveness through the blood of Jesus

'… who Himself bore our sins in His own body on the tree.' 1 Peter 2:24

RECOMMENDED READING: John 19:14–35

Yesterday we saw God's act of mercy to Adam and Eve through the death of an animal to cover their nakedness and make them acceptable to Him. Today we travel to Egypt and finally Jerusalem.

2. Egypt. In Exodus 12:40 we are told that the children of Israel had spent 430 years in Egypt. Most of that time had been in bondage as slaves. Now the time had come for Moses to bring God's people out of the land of captivity and lead them to the Promised Land. Nine plagues had devastated the land of Egypt, but there was one more to come which would break the camel's back. A night was coming when all the firstborn of Egypt, including Pharaoh's household, would die.

To protect the children of Israel, the blood of a lamb had to be daubed upon the lintel and doorposts of each house. When the angel of death saw the blood, he would pass over and the people inside would be spared the horrific events of that night. A lamb would be killed and its blood would bring salvation to each Israelite home.

3. Jerusalem. Throughout the Old Testament, the blood of millions of bulls, sheep and goats was shed to provide forgiveness to God's people, Israel. This would continue indefinitely, as God's anger over His people's sin could never be satisfied.

However, a day was due to come when a remarkable event would take place. Outside the town of Bethlehem, an announcement would be made to shepherds that a baby had been born, who would become the Saviour of the world. God would come to this earth as a human baby. He would grow into manhood and, at the age of 33, be crucified outside the city walls of Jerusalem. No one could take His life, but He would freely give it up to save His people from their sin.

He would be called the Lamb of God who died to take away the sin of the world. It was the final and complete sacrifice. No further sacrifices would be necessary. He would pour out His blood so that we might know forgiveness of sins: past, present and future.

God was angry because of our sin, but Jesus took that anger upon himself so that we might escape the wrath of a holy God.

If you are a Christian, you have been redeemed with the '… precious blood of Christ' (1 Peter 1:19).

Hallelujah, what a Saviour!

10 JUNE

Opposites attract

'... has in these last days spoken to us by His Son, whom He has appointed heir of all things, through whom also He made the worlds.' Hebrews 1:2

RECOMMENDED READING: John 8:13–59

Let me take you back to your school days. Do you remember being taught in the physics lesson that opposites attract? A magnet has a north and a south. Two magnets will not come together if two norths are pointing towards each other; it needs a north and south being opposite to each other to attract.

It often happens that two people with totally different personalities become best friends.

When we turn to the Bible, we see how opposites attract and come together for good. We see this clearly in the life of our Lord.

1. **BC (Before Christ), yet AD (Anno Domini).** There are many professing Christians who sincerely believe that Jesus came into existence as a babe in Bethlehem about 2,000 years ago. He came to earth in the form of a human baby 2,000 years ago, but not into existence. John 1:2 tells us that, 'He was in the beginning with God.' Hebrews 1:10 supports that claim: 'You LORD, in the beginning laid the foundation of the earth, and the heavens are the work of Your hands.' This became a major problem to the Pharisees. Most of John 8 is given over to a discussion on this very issue. The Pharisees claimed that Abraham was their father, yet Jesus tells them plainly in v.58, 'Most assuredly, I say to you, before Abraham was, I AM.'

BC and AD come together like a magnet, as our Lord Jesus Christ is eternal with no beginning and no ending. He is 'the Alpha and the Omega, the Beginning and the End' (Revelation 1:8).

2. **God and Man.** One of the most important doctrines of our faith rests upon the deity of Jesus Christ. He is the Son of God, yet He also is the Son of Man.

As we read the four Gospels, we have clear accounts of the earthly life of our Lord. We see Him enduring every experience common to man, yet without sin. He faced temptation; He experienced suffering; He knew disappointment; He went through every negative emotion common to man. That is why He understands us.

But He is also the Son of God; human, yet divine. Read about His baptism in Matthew 3:17. Then read about His transfiguration in Matthew 17:5. His deity is clearly visible in both passages.

Throughout the Gospels these two opposites pull together. Jesus is the Son of Man, but also the Son of God.

11 JUNE

Opposites attract

'He [Jesus] poured water into a basin and began to wash the disciples' feet.'
John 13:5

RECOMMENDED READING: 1 Peter 5:5–11

Yesterday we used the illustration of a magnet to show how opposites attract. Two norths or two souths will repel. It needs north and south to be opposite each other to attract.

Today I want to conclude with two more opposites that came together for our good. Both can be seen in the life of our Lord.

3. Master, yet a servant. The clearest illustration to convey this message is found in John 13 when Jesus washes His disciples' feet. This was the most menial of tasks where slaves would wash the feet of weary travellers.

In this incident, the Son of God takes a towel, then pours water into a basin and performs this lowly task for the benefit and comfort of His disciples. God, the Creator of the universe, becomes a servant. The message is clear to us.

The Commander in Chief, George Washington, made an unexpected visit to inspect his soldiers. When he arrived, they were hard at work lifting a heavy piece of timber for a fortification. The corporal of the regiment was calling out to his men, 'Come on put your backs into it. Heave there!' He gave various instructions to the men to get those timbers in place.

Despite the large size of the corporal, Washington climbed down from his horse and said to him, 'What is the good of calling out to those men? Why don't you help them instead?'

The corporal straightened to his full height and said, 'Perhaps you are not aware to whom you are speaking sir! I am a corporal.'

'I beg your pardon,' replied Washington. 'You are a corporal, are you? I am sorry to have insulted you in that way.'

So, he took off his own coat and waistcoat and set to work helping the men to build the fortification. When he had finished, he said, 'Mr Corporal, I am truly sorry I insulted you, but when you have any more fortifications to get up, and your men are not pulling their weight and following your instructions, send for George Washington, Commander in Chief, and I will come and help them.' The corporal crept away totally ashamed of himself.[21]

Our Lord Jesus Christ may say: 'So you don't like helping the poor and caring for the sick? Then let your Commander in Chief do it.'

God knows just how to deal with the proud and the humble.

Follow the example of our Lord and be willing to be a servant to all.

12 JUNE

Shepherd yet a Lamb

'I am the good shepherd. The good shepherd gives His life for the sheep.'
John 10:11

RECOMMENDED READING: John 13:1–17

Through the illustration of a magnet, we have seen how opposites attract each other. We then turned to the Bible and considered BC and AD; the Son of God and Son of Man; and yesterday, Master and Servant. Today we look at our final pairing.

4. Shepherd, yet a Lamb. There are many passages of Scripture that we could turn to, but in John 10 we have a wonderful picture of our Lord Jesus Christ as the Good Shepherd.

If we turn to v.14, we are told that He knows His sheep, and v.3 reminds us that He calls His own sheep by name. This means that they are not just a number, but He has a personal interest in them.

We are also told in v.3 that He leads them out and goes before them. That is the exact opposite of sheep farming in the United Kingdom. Perhaps our sheep are not as intelligent as sheep in Israel! In this country the shepherd will follow the sheep with the help of a dog, or the dog will gather the sheep with the support of the shepherd. When you visit Israel, you will notice the shepherd goes before them and the sheep, without any encouragement or help, will follow. They know his voice.

We are His sheep and we follow Him for we know His voice, and He knows us by name. We avoid the false shepherds because their voice is unfamiliar to us. Our Shepherd has a personal interest in us and cares for all our needs. So much so that the Good Shepherd became the sacrificial Lamb. The Great High Priest became the sacrifice.

As Jesus began His ministry, John the Baptist said in John 1:29 'Behold! The Lamb of God who takes away the sin of the world!' In Isaiah 53:7 it says, 'He was led as a lamb to the slaughter.'

On the cross, the Lamb of God took our sins and made them His very own. He became sin who knew no sin so that we would not face condemnation when we stand before the Father.

It was at the cross on Calvary's hill that the Good Shepherd became the precious Lamb of God.

'Goodness and mercy shall follow me all the days of my life, and I will dwell in the house of the Lord forever' (Psalm 23:6).

13 JUNE

God chooses His labourers

'I have filled him with the Spirit of God, in wisdom, in understanding, in knowledge, and in all manner of workmanship.' Exodus 31:3

RECOMMENDED READING: Exodus 31:1–6

In Exodus 24, from v.12, God called Moses to climb Mount Sinai to give His servant instructions regarding the construction of the tabernacle.

In chapter 31, God gave Moses the final details, and then presented him with the two tablets of stone consisting of the Ten Commandments, before he departed.

Part of that final discourse dealt with the appointment of workmen who would be employed in the construction and furnishing of the tabernacle (vv.1–11). God had chosen the men to do it. Now the people had to be encouraged to provide the materials, most of which had been brought from Egypt.

Moses also needed men who would help in putting all these plans into operation. It is one thing to be aware of the task to be done, but another thing to find the people willing and able to do it.

Moses needed people who were reliable and trustworthy, as well as being gifted in the job that was required. God knew who they were.

First of all, we have Bezalel. Verses 2–5 tells us that he would be chief architect or master workman. He came from the tribe of Judah, a tribe God delighted to honour. His name means 'in the shadow or protection of God.' What a wonderful thought. God's own Son came from the same tribe.

Then we have Aholiab. He belonged to the tribe of Dan (v.6). He was appointed next to Bezalel and become a partner with him. Though Dan was one of the less honourable tribes, God used people from it. Another member of the tribe of Dan was Huram. When we move ahead to 2 Chronicles 2:13,14, we are told that he would become the head workman in the building of Solomon's temple.

God chose two men from the least of the tribes to perform important tasks in the construction of the tabernacle and the temple. Many times, God chooses the most unlikely people from the most unlikely places to do His work and carry His message, and often bypasses those who, to us, seem suitable and able. Look at the disciples our Lord chose. Some of those would not be in our second team.

God will reward all those who do their task to the best of their ability and to His glory.

14 JUNE

God calls and equips

'He has filled them with skill to do all manner of work.' Exodus 35:35

RECOMMENDED READING: Exodus 35:29–35

God gave Moses instructions regarding the construction and furnishing of the tabernacle. He then chose the people to lead this mammoth project. Today we see how He equipped them for this great task. There are three important things to note:

1. **Skill for the task is a gift from God.** Not only does God give the ability for the task, but also the development of that ability. In Isaiah 28:26 we read how God teaches the farmer in his employment, 'For he is rightly instructed; his God teaches him' (ESV).

God must have the praise for every gift and its improvement; we must never take the glory for ourselves. Whatever gift we possess, whether it is oratory, music, writing or leadership, comes from Him. We would be wise to remember that at all times.

(a) God gives His gifts to whom He pleases. One gift to one person, and another gift to another person. This is good for the advancement of both the local and worldwide church.

Moses was the most able to govern and lead the people, but Bezalel was more gifted to construct the tabernacle.

Never covet another person's gift; just thank God for your own. God has given to us different abilities—to some the gift of preaching; to others the gift of music; to others the gift of administration; to others the gift of computer technology (I'll try not to covet); to others the gift of practical abilities; to others the gift of finance; to others the gift of conversation and visitation. I could go on, but each gift is given at God's pleasure.

(b) Those whom God calls He will equip. Those employed were to work in gold, silver and brass. Others would make the fabric. God equipped each one for their particular task.

When Jesus sent out His disciples to tell people about the good news of the kingdom of God, He poured out His Spirit upon them. They were not to work upon metal or fabric but on the hearts of men.

We too have been given gifts. If you have buried them, then dig them up before it is too late. Never misuse your gifts, lest God removes them from you. We must use them but never abuse them.

Just one final thought; use your gift to God's glory. After all, they aren't really yours. God gave them to you.

15 JUNE

Willing hands are better than idle ones

'Then Moses called ... everyone whose heart was stirred, to come and do the work.' Exodus 36:2

RECOMMENDED READING: 1 Corinthians 3

During the past few days, we have looked at the men God chose for the construction of the tabernacle and the skills God had given them. Today we consider a further observation:

2. All the people had an important part to play in its construction. When the children of Israel became aware of the enormous challenge facing Moses in the construction of the tabernacle and its equipment, we read in chapter 36:2 that everyone whose heart was stirred came to do the work.

When we have a workday in our fellowship, it is so encouraging to see the numbers who come to help with the painting, cleaning and gardening. Even a 93-year-old lady comes to get her hands dirty.

In chapter 35:21 we notice not only those whose hearts had been stirred, but also those whose spirits were willing.

Some have hearts that have been stirred, but sadly their spirits are unwilling to be involved in the Lord's work.

Note that in the same verse they '... brought the Lord's offering for the work of the tabernacle of meeting, for all its service, and for the holy garments.'

They gave for the work willingly, and also abundantly. Chapter 36:7 tells us that in the end they brought more than was needed.

In some churches today there are those who give beyond their means, while some, sadly, seem too mean to give.

A minister informed his congregation one Sunday morning that he could share some exciting news with them. The extensive project the church had agreed upon could now go ahead as all the funds had become available. The congregation were absolutely delighted until he said, 'There is just one big problem holding the project up. The funds are still in your pockets.'

Hearing that story challenged me, as it should every believer. Unfortunately, it is not only the poor widow that gives the mite.

The children of Israel counted it a privilege to be involved in the construction of the tabernacle, so giving was not a burden to them but a delight.

It should be the same with us for the Lord loves a cheerful giver. Never forget that He did not withhold His Son from being a sacrifice, to save us from the punishment we were due because of our sin.

16 JUNE

Beginners and finishers

'Then Moses looked over all the work, and indeed they had done it; as the Lord had commanded.' Exodus 39:43

RECOMMENDED READING: 1 Corinthians 3

During the past few days, we have been considering the preparation and construction of the tabernacle and its furnishings, as God instructed Moses. We have also looked at the men God chose for heading up the work, and the skills they had for completing the task. We noted that all the people had a part to play in this construction, especially when it came to their generous giving towards this great project. We now come to our concluding thought on this great task God had given them.

3. God calls us to finish our task. It is one thing to begin a great work; it is another to finish it. No person can have a higher tribute paid to them than to be told, 'You have finished the work I gave you to do.'

Bezalel, from the tribe of Judah, and his assistant Aholiab, from the tribe of Dan, had been called and commissioned by God for one task only. That was to construct the tabernacle with all its furnishings using precious metals and various types of fabric.

Neither of them would ever become a celebrity. Moses, yes, but Bezalel and Aholiab? Most Christians have never heard of them.

Thankfully, God does not measure our effectiveness and success rate in the work of His kingdom by the number of times we make the headlines in the media. He measures it by accepting and fulfilling the responsibilities that He gives to us.

Bezalel and Aholiab are praised for having completed their assignments. Note again the words in chapter 39:43, 'Moses looked over all the work, and indeed they had done it; as the Lord had commanded.'

It can be so easy to volunteer for a particular task, but much more difficult to see it through to the end, especially if there are hindrances and challenges along the way that have to be overcome. All Christian workers should take note before embarking upon any assignment for the Lord.

Bezalel and Aholiab were not just beginners; they were finishers. That should be both a challenge and an encouragement to us all.

Galatians 6:9 says, 'Let us not grow weary while doing good, for in due season we shall reap if we do not lose heart.'

17 JUNE

Time is precious; handle it with care

'See then that you walk circumspectly, not as fools but as wise, redeeming the time, because the days are evil.' Ephesians 5:15–16

RECOMMENDED READING: Ecclesiastes 3:1–8

Our life is governed by time. I leave you with three thoughts to ponder:

1. What does it mean to redeem the time? To redeem is literally to 'buy back' at a price. Life is a precious possession which God has graciously given to every person on this earth. We are to invest in it and to use it wisely as God intended. We cannot bring back a day when it is over. It is gone for ever.

So here comes our responsibility. We can abuse it; ignore it; or we can put it to good use. Life presents to us with many opportunities. It is how we take them that is important. We can either waste them or take full advantage of them. Whatever we do, make sure we don't leave this world with regrets.

2. Why should we redeem the time?

(a) Because it is precious. This becomes very clear when we remember how much hangs upon our use of it. John Wesley put it like this: 'We only have this life to do all the good we can, to all the people we can, in all the ways we can.' You keep watch over a precious gem; do the same with your time.

(b) Because it is brief. For many of us who may be reading this, the past now seems so far behind, and eternity so near. The difficulty is, we don't know how near, because God can call us at any age, and He does. We cannot shorten our time on this earth and neither can we lengthen it.

Therefore, it is so important to ask God to 'teach us to number our days, that we may gain a heart of wisdom' (Psalm 90:12).

(c) Because it contains your only opportunity to secure salvation. If anyone is reading this who is outside of God's kingdom, then, 'Do not boast about tomorrow, for you do not know what a day may bring forth (Proverbs 27:1). The Bible contains no opportunity for salvation beyond the grave.

3. How do I redeem the time? Time cannot be recalled no matter how much we would love to do so. But the future can be redeemed.

- Sincerely repent of wasted years.
- Dedicate the remaining years that God may have left for you to Him and His service.

Time is precious; handle it with care and use it wisely.

Unceasing prayer

'Then Jesus came with them to a place called Gethsemane, and said to the disciples, "Sit here while I go and pray over there."' Matthew 26:36

RECOMMENDED READING: Matthew 26:36–56

Whenever I have been privileged to lead a tour out to Israel, I have enjoyed each day but the experience that moves me most is when I stand and read these verses in the Garden of Gethsemane. If there was no victory here, there would be no victory at Calvary or the tomb.

The prayer habit of Jesus has much to teach all Christians. Yes, some habits are good and should be maintained. It is worth noting the times, places and occasions of our Lord's prayers.

He prayed in the morning before a busy day began. Mark 1:35 says, 'Now in the morning, having risen a long while before daylight, He went out and departed to a solitary place; and there He prayed.'

He prayed in the evening after a busy day. Mark 6:46 says, 'And when He had sent them away, He departed to the mountain to pray.' We are told in Luke 6:12–13 that there were occasions when He spent all night in prayer.

Whether it was on a mountain, in some solitary place or in a friend's garden, He prayed. Communion with His Heavenly Father was essential.

He prayed when He faced a crisis; He prayed before making a decision, such as choosing His disciples; He prayed before and after great victories.

Throughout His ministry Jesus knew where His strength and support came from; it wasn't from earth, but from His Father in heaven. He enjoyed communion with His Father, and when facing a crisis His strength came from the same source.

Here, in the Garden of Gethsemane, Jesus is about to face His great hour of trial. He would soon feel the awful weight of the sins of His people, so He prayed.

The hymn-writer, Joseph Medlicott Scriven (1819–86) wrote the following words in his hour of need:

'O what peace we often forfeit,
O what needless pain we bear,
All because we do not carry
Everything to God in prayer!'

Tomorrow, as we look at this event in more detail, may we discover, through the example of our Lord, the secret of prayer.

19 JUNE

Teach us how to pray

'I do not pray for these alone, but also for those who will believe in Me through their word.' John 17:20

RECOMMENDED READING: Matthew 6:9–13

Today we consider our Lord's prayer in the Garden of Gethsemane just before His arrest. What lessons have we to learn from His prayer?

1. It was intimate. When you see great trouble ahead, you long for company, but also the need for solitude.

Jesus wanted to know that His close disciples were near at hand, but He also wanted that special communion with just his Father. No one must interfere with this precious time of intimate fellowship, for an intense battle was due to begin. Jesus did not lose sight of the fact of His Father's love and that the agony He was about to face was with His Father's permission.

How different it would be in our hours of trial if we too recognised this important fact. Never forget that God loves us too, and all we face is in His strength.

2. It was persevering. We read that, 'Again, a second time, He went away and prayed' (Matthew 26:42). But even that was not enough. We read that, 'He ... went away again, and prayed the third time (Matthew 26:44). Only then did the calm follow the storm and He was able to face what was ahead of Him.

We so quickly give up when the answer doesn't come immediately. We too need to learn to persist in prayer. God will answer when the time is right.

3. It was submissive. Matthew 26:39 says, 'Oh My Father, if it is possible let this cup pass from me; nevertheless, not as I will, but as You will.' He makes a similar request again in v.42. Jesus resigned Himself to the Father's will and placed Himself into His loving care. When trials come our way, we can do nothing more important than this.

4. It was triumphant. Despite being aware of both the physical and spiritual suffering that lay ahead, He did not turn from His mission, which was to save those who were lost through His sacrifice upon the cross. Everything was won at this point; there was no turning back from what was ahead. He was not only strengthened in His own spirit, but He could see the victory that lay before Him through the resurrection and His return to His Father.

May our Lord teach us through His prayers to be victorious over every challenge that comes our way, so that with Paul we may say, 'We are more than conquerors through Him who loved us' (Romans 8:37).

20 JUNE

Be sure that it is God who is speaking

'"Therefore I also have lent him to the Lord; as long as he lives he shall be lent to the LORD." So they worshipped the LORD there.' 1 Samuel 1:28

RECOMMENDED READING: 1 Samuel 1:20–28

These were dark days in the history of Israel. Yet God was at work preparing the way for the last of Israel's judges. His name was Samuel.

In the history of these islands, beams of light have shone through at the darkest times. There are too many to mention, but I thank God for men such as Tyndale, Wesley, Whitefield and many others who lifted the gloom and made the Word of God available to the common man in a language they could understand. They travelled throughout the land preaching the good news of the gospel of Jesus Christ. How we need beams of light today.

God had been preparing for a young man to become his spokesman during these difficult days. We must not forget the important part his mother played, for it was her prayers that God graciously answered.

'Give your maidservant a male child, then I will give him to the LORD all the days of his life' (1 Samuel 1:11). There is a great responsibility resting upon Christian parents to pray for their children that they may grow up to be servants of God in these challenging days. God answered the prayer of Hannah who kept her vow to the Lord. Samuel was taken to Shiloh to live and serve with Eli the priest.

Samuel and Eli had turned in for the night when the LORD called Samuel. The boy thought it was Eli who needed assistance but the old priest told him to lie down again as he didn't call. Shortly afterwards he heard the voice again but Eli assured him that he had not called.

It is so important that we are sure it is God who is calling and not man. If we are convinced it is God who is speaking then we must not delay in responding.

When God spoke a third time, Eli was convinced it was the LORD and told Samuel how he should reply.

When Samuel heard his name again spoken twice, he remembered what Eli had told him to say: 'Speak, for your servant hears' (1 Samuel 3:10).

God is still calling people. When He speaks it is wise to listen and obey.

> 'Master, speak! And make me ready,
> When Thy voice is truly heard,
> With obedience glad and steady
> Still to follow every word.'
>
> Frances Ridley Havergal (1836–79)

21 JUNE

A powerful and unforgettable message from God

'In that day I will perform against Eli all that I have spoken concerning his house, from beginning to end.' 1 Samuel 3:12

RECOMMENDED READING: 1 Samuel 3:10–15

We are considering the call of Samuel and have come to the moment when God speaks directly to His young servant. There are two things to note:

Firstly, this message from God was brief. It was much shorter than the message brought by the man of God in 1 Samuel 2:27–36.

There are occasions when a short and direct message can have a bigger impact than a long, drawn-out speech, which in the end is soon forgotten. This powerful declaration from God would not be forgotten.

Secondly, it was a distressing message that confirmed what was delivered by the man of God in chapter 2. It was clear, direct and could not be misunderstood. During the night, Samuel would have thought about the message God had given him to deliver to Eli.

God would punish the house of Eli. His two sons, Hophni and Phinehas, would face the anger of God for the sins they had committed, and their father himself would break his neck. To add to that devastating news, God made it clear that He would not atone for the sins of Eli's house. Things could not become more serious for Eli.

1 Samuel 3:13 says, 'For I have told him that I will judge his house forever for the iniquity which he knows, because his sons made themselves vile, and he did not restrain them.'

God would admonish Eli for neglecting to discipline his sons. This is a clear warning to all parents. While our children are young and vulnerable to the evils around them, we must do all we can to restrain them from wicked actions. As they grow older the task becomes even more difficult.

When Samuel woke the next morning, he knew what he had to do. He loved the old priest, but his obedience to the LORD must take precedence. It didn't become any easier when Samuel realised that Eli knew the LORD had spoken to him and told him to deliver this message. This would be no easy task, but he was obedient and delivered it.

The Christian life presents to us many challenges—some we would prefer to avoid if possible. Following God's instructions is not always straight forward. However, we must be obedient to His directions if we long to know His blessing upon us.

Growing old graciously

'Samuel told him everything, and hid nothing from him.' 1 Samuel 3:18

RECOMMENDED READING: 1 Samuel 3:16–20

As we conclude the early days of Samuel, we have God's message to Eli and the aged priest's reaction to it.

Firstly, we have Samuel bringing God's message to Eli. The time had now come for Samuel to be completely honest with him. This was not going to be easy because the news would undoubtedly distress the old priest. Yet, Samuel had to be faithful as there would be many more difficult tasks for him in the days to come. So young Samuel told Eli everything and left out nothing.

This is a clear example for every preacher of God's Word. They must not hold back that which God has laid upon their heart, even when the message is not palatable to the hearers. The message must be declared with authority, accompanied by a loving concern for the people. When we fail to do so, we are neglecting our responsibility and calling.

Secondly, we have Eli's gracious reaction to the message. In v.18 he said, 'It is the LORD. Let Him do what seems good to Him.' Eli never questioned Samuel's integrity; neither was he angry with him. Instead, Eli was quietly resigned to the sentence that was imposed upon him.

What a lesson that is for us! When we are rebuked, our first reaction is to bring a defence, even when we know we are wrong. If only we could have the gracious attitude of Eli and accept that God can do no wrong.

If we look ahead in time, it is interesting to know that the situation would be reversed. Now God rejected Eli's sons, but eventually Israel would turn their backs upon Samuel's sons.

When we are young, our decisions are not always wise and we can be slow to accept the advice offered to us. But when we are old some of our decisions can be unwise also. 1 Samuel 8:1 says, 'Now it came to pass when Samuel was old that he made his sons judges over Israel.' That decision was made despite the fact that v.3 tells us, 'His sons did not walk in his ways.'

How often we read of godly parents having ungodly children. It is heart-breaking for parents who have brought their children up the best way they could to ensure they grow to be godly Christians, and then see them not follow Christ as adults. It is hard but we must acknowledge God's sovereignty at all times.

Although this was a tough beginning for the young prophet, the Lord was with him wherever he went whatever he did and whatever he said, and the people honoured him. May that be an encouragement to all who seek to serve the Lord.

23 JUNE

The Saviour can solve every problem

'And they said to Him, "We have here only five loaves and two fish."'
Matthew 14:17

RECOMMENDED READING: Matthew 14:14–22

When we held our monthly prayer meeting for the persecuted church, we were shown brief clips of the challenges our brothers and sisters face in many countries throughout the world.

One particular clip showed the meagre amount of food some families were receiving that had to last a number of days. As we prayed for God to multiply that amount, my thoughts went to one of our Lord's miracles: the feeding of the five thousand. I want us to consider that miracle today—the only one recorded in all four gospels.

Our Lord is able to meet the needs of all people. But how?

1. **There must be an appreciation of the problem.** As this story commences (Matthew 14:14), there are significant problems to be faced. Our Lord appreciated them, as did the disciples.

(a) Verse 15 tells us it was a deserted place, far from the village where food could be obtained. It was also late in the day and many who came to hear Jesus were far from home.

(b) Verse 21 tells us that there was a hungry multitude. Over five thousand men were present, besides women and children.

(c) Verse 17 tells us that they had only five loaves and two fish.

In John's account, in chapter 6:9, Andrew notices a lad who had brought his own packed lunch with him, consisting of five barley loaves and two small fish. The lad may have been reluctant at first to part with his meal as he too must have been hungry. After all, why didn't people bring their own if they were going to stay so long?

In this story, the disciples could only see the physical hunger of the people. They could only see the problems before them.

Jesus, however, saw beyond the difficulties: He saw their spiritual hunger. They not only needed food to satisfy their bodily needs; they needed spiritual food to meet their hungry souls. Jesus saw these people as sheep without a shepherd. They were lost and facing spiritual danger.

As we look across this country of ours, do we also see people as sheep in need of a shepherd? Do we see the spiritual hunger in our cities, towns and villages? Problems cannot be ignored; they will not just disappear like a cloud. With God's help, these problems must be faced, for He has the answer to the needs of all people.

24 JUNE

Working with the Master

'There is a lad here who has five barley loaves and two small fish, but what are they among so many?' John 6:9

RECOMMENDED READING: Matthew 14:14–22

Yesterday we began looking at the problems that had to be faced as the day was drawing to a close. Before the disciples was a large crowd of people in a deserted place, and many of them a long way from home with only a meagre ration between them all. How do you solve this one?

2. We must be prepared to meet the demands which Christ puts upon us.

(a) Christ demands investigation. What have *they* got? The answer was clear—empty stomachs. What have *we* got? 'We have here only five loaves and two fish' (Matthew 14:17). What are they among so many people? They wouldn't fill the stomachs of one family never mind such a vast number of people.

(b) Christ demands co-operation. Matthew 14:18 says, 'Bring them here to Me.' When Jesus had the inadequate, He made them adequate. After Jesus had given thanks, the disciples distributed what Jesus had given to them (v.19).

Verse 16 says, 'You give them something to eat.' Jesus was not doing this by Himself, He wanted co-operation from his disciples. I wonder what was in their thoughts as they began distributing the small amount of food, watching a miracle take place before their very eyes. Would they have a look of bewilderment and amazement upon their faces, or a gentle smile knowing who was in charge of this feast? When the meal had concluded, the disciples collected the twelve baskets of fragments that remained.

Just imagine that lad's face when he arrived home and told his family all that had happened with his packed lunch. This was a day never to be forgotten.

What a privilege it is for us also to work together with our Lord. No task should be too menial for Him. What Jesus asks of His disciples, He also askes of us. He desires that we become willing workers with Him in feeding needy souls with the bread of life.

Imagine that a train accident occurred leaving many people seriously injured. A call was sent out for a doctor who might be on the train. A doctor was located, but as he took off his jacket to help the first patient he began to cry and said, 'If only I had my instruments!'

Is God saying the same thing today? You need to be willing to step up and be His instruments in the world.

25 JUNE

A never ending supply

'And my God shall supply all your need according to His riches in glory by Christ Jesus.' Philippians 4:19

RECOMMENDED READING: Ephesians 3:14–21

1. **'And my God …'** What a great privilege it is to be one of God's chosen children! We have a heavenly Father who was the Creator of this amazing universe and watches over everything that He created. We belong to the One who controls the affairs of all things in heaven and on earth and who can meet all the responsibilities placed upon Him. He can handle every crisis and control every created being no matter how great and powerful they may be. He is from everlasting to everlasting and will never be deposed from His seat of power, despite the fact that many throughout history have endeavoured to do so. I find it truly staggering to realise that this great, almighty God is my heavenly Father.

2. **'… shall supply …'** Whatever situation I find myself in, His supply is never ending.

I lived the early part of my life in a small village at the foot of the Pennine hills. Approximately forty yards from our home was a stream, which received its water through an outlet directly from the Pennines. As children we could collect the water and bring it home as it was pure, cool and fresh. It flowed throughout the winter months and even during extensive, dry summer spells. It could never be exhausted, and it never slowed down; it was a continuous flow. As King David longed for water from his hometown of Bethlehem, there are times when I long for the water from my village.

God's supply of knowledge, faith, mercy, love and grace are inexhaustible and as fresh as they have always been, and always will be. God's supply will never run out.

3. **'… all your need.'** If I gave you my username and passwords to my online banking, you would have complete access to the funds in my account. Don't get too excited—it won't provide you with much!

But I can tell you of one who has done just that and you can have unlimited access to all your needs. The wealth of heaven is daily at our disposal.

Philippians 4:6 says, 'Be anxious for nothing … let your requests be made known to God.'

Why then do we so often live as spiritual paupers when God's inexhaustible riches are constantly at our disposal?

26 JUNE

Preparing for the journey of a lifetime

'Then we who are alive and remain shall be caught up together with them in the clouds to meet the Lord in the air. And thus we shall always be with the Lord.' 1 Thessalonians 4:17

RECOMMENDED READING: 1 Thessalonians 4:13–18

During this coronavirus pandemic, the travel plans of many tourists and businesspeople have been severely disrupted. So, during the next two days I will present a guide for travellers to a very secure destination that will not be affected by any virus. It is the journey to heaven.

I came across the following headings many years ago, hoping that they could be developed on some future occasion. Now seems to be a very appropriate time to do so.

1. **Accommodation.** Arrangements are already being prepared for every born-again Christian. John 14:2 assures us that our Lord is preparing our new home and the accommodation will be beyond our wildest dreams. What is even more wonderful is the fact that there will be no cost to pay, for God has already paid it for us through the precious blood of Jesus poured out upon Calvary's cross.

Our new home is not temporary but permanent. It is guaranteed for eternity. There will be no eviction order, and I can assure you that we will never want to leave.

2. **Passports.** Revelation 21:27 tells us that only those who have the correct credentials, and have their names registered with the ruling authorities, will be permitted through the gates. I should also mention that the passport will not be renewed as you will not need it again.

How important it is to ensure that our names are written in the Lamb's Book of Life so that we have access into this great kingdom.

3. **Departure times.** Acts 1:7 informs us that the exact time of departure has not been announced. Travellers are therefore advised to be prepared to leave at a moment's notice. You will not leave a minute earlier or a minute later than God has planned, but we will never know when the Lord will call us.

Some people may have to wait until they reach a good old age, but some will be leaving while they are still young. Just be prepared for your departure, for it will come suddenly and, for some, unexpectedly.

We will continue our preparation for departure tomorrow.

27 JUNE

Preparing to meet our God

'And if I go and prepare a place for you, I will come again and receive you to Myself; that where I am, there you may be also.' John 14:3

RECOMMENDED READING: Revelation 21:1–7

We continue studying our travel guide in preparation for our journey home. We have secured our accommodation; have our passport; and ready for our departure whenever we are called. We conclude by making our final preparations.

4. Tickets. John 5:24 tells us that your ticket is a written pledge that will guarantee your journey. Just keep reminding yourselves of the promises that God has given to us in His Word.

I should mention that, as with your passport, there will be no return ticket given to you. To be honest, you won't want one!

5. Immigration. Hebrews 11:15–16 tells us that all passengers are classified as immigrants since they are taking up permanent residence in a new and far better country where there will be no more sin.

6. Luggage. 1 Timothy 6:7 tells us that no luggage will be taken with us. All your precious belongings will be left behind, including your wallet and credit cards—and to help my daughter-in-law, there will be no on-line shopping! What will await you will far outweigh those things you have left behind.

7. Vaccinations. Revelation 21:4 reminds us that injections are not needed, as diseases, such as COVID-19, are unknown at this destination. In fact, you will never know any form of pain ever again.

8. Air passage. 1 Thessalonians 4:17 tell us that those still alive at Christ's coming will go directly by air. We are always strongly advised to watch for indications of imminent departure (Matthew 25:13). While you are waiting, spend time preparing to meet your God.

Now prepare for take-off. There will be no turbulence and you are guaranteed a safe landing. I should add, finally, that you will take this journey alone though it won't take long. Jesus said to the thief on the cross, 'Today you will be with Me in paradise' (Luke 23:43).

This journey is only for those whose sins are forgiven and have peace with God through the Lord Jesus Christ. If you don't know Jesus as your friend and Saviour, your final journey will be far from pleasant. So, while you have time, change your destination at King's Cross and journey to a better country. Just look to Jesus and live!

28 JUNE

The Great Physician

'Jesus ... said to them, "Those who are well have no need of a physician, but those who are sick."' Matthew 9:12

RECOMMENDED READING: Matthew 9:10–38

During His earthly ministry, our Lord Jesus Christ was, among many things, the great healer. He was concerned for those who were sick in body and troubled in mind. But most of all He came to transform the lives of those who were spiritually in need of restoration. He came to seek and save those who were lost and needed His salvation. I want us to consider this amazing physician and realise how important He is to have as a friend and Saviour.

1. He knows our disease. There are certain diseases and viruses, including the coronavirus, that have baffled medical and scientific experts over many years. Even when a cure is found for these, in a number of years a new challenge will present itself with devastating consequences and our leading experts will again struggle in finding ways to eradicate it. If only they would acknowledge their limitations and look to the One who has the answer.

Sir Isaac Newton was congratulated for his scientific achievement. He responded, 'I seem to have been only like a little boy playing on the sea-shore, ... while the great ocean of truth lay all undiscovered before me.'[22]

Physicians often work in the dark. Even if they are aware of a disease, they can't always cure it. Jesus never works in the dark; He is the light of the world.

The greatest disease facing mankind is sin, and Jesus knows all about it. This is a far more serious pandemic than the coronavirus. Other diseases and viruses affect the body; sin affects the soul. Undetected diseases will kill the body; sin will eventually destroy the soul.

2. He is the tender physician. Some physicians have accumulated great wealth through their medical knowledge. To discover a cure for some life-threatening disease has brought them great accolades. When it comes to the greatest physician, He didn't become rich; to the contrary, He became poor. More than that, His own blood became His chief medicine, for it is 'by His stripes we are healed' (Isaiah 53:5).

This compassionate physician took the road to Calvary to spare our suffering. Our disease was laid upon Him so that we would be healed from further agony. The physician was full of love for His sinful patients. I know of no other physician who would take upon Himself our terminal disease, but Jesus did.

29 JUNE

Jesus always gives a correct diagnosis

'And Jesus went about all Galilee ... healing all kinds of sickness and all kinds of disease among the people.' Matthew 4:23

RECOMMENDED READING: Mark 1:32–45

Yesterday we began to look at Jesus as the Great Physician. We became aware of the fact that He knows our diseases, both physical and spiritual, but He is tender in His treatment of us. Today we consider two further aspects of this great healer.

3. He is a mighty and all skilful physician. A physician will diagnose your condition and then write out a prescription for your ailment, and both patient and doctor will trust your condition improves, thereby restoring you to an improved quality of health again.

Whether people had leprosy, useless limbs, blindness or even demonic illness, Jesus was never overwhelmed by it all. He just used His mighty power to bring healing and complete restoration.

He doesn't bring restoration to everyone, for reasons known only to Him, but He shows compassion and tenderness to His people, all supported by His prayers. Our prayers will never go unanswered.

Whether our ailment is physical or spiritual, Micah 7:19 says, 'He will again have compassion on us.'

4. There is no other physician like Him. If you are sick in body, you have a choice of physicians. A few miles from our home we have an excellent medical practice with doctors who specialise in different aspects of our welfare. We have a choice of whom we visit. However, despite our confidence in their expert ability, they are all human and have their limitations.

The Lord Jesus not only healed those who were sick in body and mind, but most of all He had the power to forgive sins and transform lives, and He does the same today. People struggling with alcohol, substance abuse and many other addictions have seen their lives turned around through Christ, who brings new purpose.

However, He will never flatter or deceive. He will always be honest in His appraisal of us and give His correct diagnosis. You will also find that He is always near at hand and ready to help in your lowest moments, whenever you call upon Him.

There is no other physician that can be compared with Jesus. In Acts 4:12 Peter reminds his hearers, 'Nor is there salvation in any other, for there is no other name under heaven given among men by which we must be saved.'

Thankfully we need no other!

30 JUNE

Praise the Lord, O my soul

'Let everything that has breath praise the LORD. Praise the LORD!' Psalm 150:6

RECOMMENDED READING: Psalm 100

David, the second King of Israel was responsible for composing approximately half of all the Psalms. They expressed his innermost thoughts and feelings. There were psalms of victory; psalms of failure; psalms of loss; psalms of gain; psalms of sorrow; psalms of joy.

I want to turn our thoughts to the closing psalm, which is one of praise. Psalm 150 contains only six verses, but the praise is directed solely to Almighty God. We too should ensure our praise and worship is to Him alone, for only He is worthy of it.

In every verse we are commanded to praise the LORD. In fact, twice in every verse the instruction is given to do just that! There are four things that we should consider:

1. It begins by telling us where to praise. Verse 1 says, '... in His sanctuary'. Whenever and wherever God's people meet, praise should come from their lips and expressed in their hearts. Wherever in the world we find ourselves, it is the right place to worship the Almighty, the King of Creation. Paul and Silas sang hymns in a prison in Philippi and, what is more, the prisoners heard them.

How I long to return to the House of God and open my lips and lungs without any restrictions.

2. It tells us why we praise. Firstly, because of who God is. Verse 2 tells us that we should praise Him for His 'excellent greatness'.

Secondly, because of all He has done and is still doing. Verse 2 tells us that He performs 'mighty acts'. We see these acts of power throughout the Scriptures. We also see them in everyday life.

3. How should we praise Him? We can praise God loudly, softly, enthusiastically, rhythmically and fearlessly. In other words, we can praise Him in many ways and on any occasion (vv.3–5). We must put our heart and soul into our worship.

4. Who should praise Him? Verse 6 tells us, 'Everything that has breath ...'. That includes young and old, rich and poor, strong and weak. God wills everyone, to whom He has given life, to use their breath and acknowledge that He is the on true Lord of heaven and earth. There is none beside Him.

1 JULY

The mount of safety

'Come and let us go up to the mountain of the Lord ... He will teach us His ways, and we shall walk in His paths.' Isaiah 2:3

RECOMMENDED READING: Genesis 22:1–14

I enjoy looking at mountains. The most spectacular view I have encountered was in South Africa. We were staying with our daughter and her husband for my wife, Kathryn's 70th birthday. We went for a few days to the Drakensburg Mountains, a range 620 miles in length from SW to NE with its highest elevation at 11,424 feet.

We stayed at the Cathedral Peak Hotel, which was wonderful, and served a variety of food that surpassed anything I have previously enjoyed. In the grounds it has its own beautiful church, and through the main window, behind the pulpit, is a view that you would travel many miles to see; it was magnificent. No, I don't work for the South African tourist board!

During the next two days I want to share with you three mountains that are mentioned in the Old Testament with the message they convey to us.

1. Mount Ararat. From Adam to Noah there are just ten generations, but we can see the steep decline into wickedness. So great was the fall that in Genesis 6:6 we read that the Lord was sorry that He even created man.

God had to act, so He instructed Noah to build an ark that would house not only his family but seven of every kind of clean animal and two of every unclean animal, both male and female (Genesis 7:2–3). These would be preserved during the flood that God was about to send upon the earth.

Judgement was to come for all mankind because of their iniquity, but Noah would find grace in the eyes of the Lord (Genesis 6:8).

Because of our sin and iniquity, we all deserve the judgement of God, which will one day come upon all people.

How thankful we should be today that God has demonstrated His love toward us, and that we also, like Noah, have found grace in His eyes and thereby been saved from condemnation.

This is all because of the Lord Jesus Christ, God's own Son, who took upon Himself our sin when He made the journey to Calvary's cross. Because He endured God's wrath for us, we now have peace with God.

2 JULY

The mount of holiness

'In the Mount of the LORD it shall be provided.' Genesis 22:14

RECOMMENDED READING: Exodus 20

Today we turn our thoughts to the mountains of Sinai and Moriah.

2. Mount Sinai. Most people are familiar with this mountain, but ignorant of the God who came down upon it.

The children of Israel had left Egypt three months earlier. The time had come for God to give His people laws to obey and follow. These consisted of the Ten Commandments.

God's appearance upon the mountain would be accompanied by thunder, lightning, earthquake, fire and a trumpet blast. The people were instructed to remain at a distance from the foot of the mountain and consecrate themselves for what was to come (Exodus 19:18–23). This would be a sacred moment as the people were about to meet with a holy God and receive His laws (Exodus 19:17).

When we gather to worship Almighty God, is it a sacred moment? Sometimes I fear we come with a casual attitude, totally unprepared for such an encounter with Him. Are we looking forward to meeting with friends more than we are in meeting with God?

Mount Sinai reveals to us the awesomeness and holiness of God. May our hearts be prepared for such an encounter with Him.

3. Mount Moriah. Abraham and Sarah had longed for the son God had promised to them. At the age of 100 and his wife Sarah being 90, Isaac was born. They enjoyed being parents and loved him so much that they would do anything for him. But would they do anything for the God who gave him to them? The test was about to begin.

In Genesis 22, God told Abraham to take his son Isaac and go on a three-day journey to the land of Moriah, and on the mountain sacrifice his son as a burnt offering. This was Abraham's greatest test of obedience and he did what God told him to do, but obviously with a very heavy heart.

The altar and wood were prepared, and only then was Isaac told that he would be the sacrifice. Isaac would have been strong and fit enough to resist his father, but he showed obedience too. As the knife was about to be plunged into Isaac's heart, a voice from heaven told him to withdraw his hand. Abraham had stood up to God's examination.

On that same mountain, where now stands the city of Jerusalem, a sacrifice did take place. Jesus was willing to give His life on that mountain to save sinners. He sealed our pardon with His blood.

3 JULY

Rebuilding the walls

'I went out by night.' Nehemiah 2:13

RECOMMENDED READING: Nehemiah 2:11–20

When I retired in 2010, we moved into the countryside. During most of my working life, we had lived in busy cities such as Brighton and London. These places are full of noise and activity, even during the night hours, and you learn to sleep with the constant hum of traffic in the background.

It took us sometime to adapt to the quietness of the night and the need to carry a torch wherever we went, for street lights were not a common sight. However, there are advantages because in the country, away from the pollution, the stars do shine and the heavens truly declare the glory of God.

When you turn to the Scriptures, we have recorded many events that took place at night when the darkness fell. During the next few days, I want to share some events that took place when it was dark.

1. **Nehemiah.** Here we have one of the most godly and courageous men in Old Testament history. Nehemiah served in the court of King Artaxerxes and held the prominent position of being cupbearer to the king (1:11).

When Nehemiah received news concerning the sad condition of Jerusalem and those who had survived the captivity, he was given permission to return and commence the rebuilding of the walls of the city.

Nehemiah was an independently minded man, and after three days he went out, at night, to view for himself the devastation and plan the rebuilding. Three times we are told he went out at night (2:12,13,15).

Nehemiah was his own man and didn't want to be influenced by others as he put his mind to the important task before him. The walls had been demolished; they now needed rebuilding.

As I look across the United Kingdom, it is clear to see that the spiritual walls of our nation have been crumbling over many decades. The foundations have been badly shaken and are in great need of repair.

Psalm 11:3 asks a question that needs an urgent answer: 'If the foundations are destroyed, what can the righteous do?' We need, for the sake of future generations, to pray and rebuild with God's help the spiritual walls of our land.

The people said to Nehemiah, 'Let us rise up and build.' I repeat that same message to Christians throughout our land. It is time we began to rebuild. Are you up for it?

4 JULY

God speaks in the night

'And a vision appeared to Paul in the night. A man of Macedonia stood and pleaded with him, saying, "Come over to Macedonia and help us."' Acts 16:9

RECOMMENDED READING: Acts 16:9–40

We are looking at a number of events recorded in the Bible that occurred at night. Yesterday we began with Nehemiah, who, when he had returned from captivity, went by night to view the walls of the city of Jerusalem with the intention of rebuilding them. Today we travel to Philippi to consider another event that occurred at night.

2. Paul and Silas. In Acts 16, the apostle Paul had a vision during the night urging him to go to Macedonia for they needed his help (v.9). After passing close to a number of cities along the journey, they finally arrived at Philippi, Macedonia. Paul didn't waste any time but immediately began to preach the gospel. As he did so, the Spirit began to move in the hearts of people and lives were being transformed. However, although people were being greatly blessed through Paul's ministry, it didn't go down well with everyone. The message that Paul preached began to affect people's evil businesses which led to a drop in income for many. This resulted in Paul and his companion, Silas, being brought before the magistrates of the city. The decision was that they should be flogged and imprisoned.

We may have reacted to this treatment with moans and groans, but they responded by singing hymns throughout the night. This was followed by an earthquake that not only shook the prison walls but also the people inside the prison. The tremors caused their chains to fall away, but their witness caused the jailer and his family to believe.

When Almighty God moves in the hearts of people, do not be surprised when opposition is the outcome. Satan will see to that!

Today, apathy among people is one of the great enemies of the church. Are we too comfortable? Do we need disturbing from our complacency? I find that there is no apathy among our persecuted family in other parts of the world who suffer so much for their faith in Christ Jesus; but see how the church is growing. If we are to see God move in the hearts of people in our cities, towns and villages, may we have the courage to face any adversity.

> 'Night with Him is never night;
> Where He is, there all is light;
> When He calls us, why delay?
> They are happy who obey.'
>
> Thomas Kelly (1769–1855)

5 JULY

Under cover of darkness

'This man came to Jesus by night and said to Him, "Rabbi, we know that You are a teacher come from God.' John 3:2

RECOMMENDED READING: John 3:1–17

We continue our consideration of the events in the Bible that occurred at night. Today we turn to our Lord's encounter with a Pharisee, Nicodemus, who met Jesus at night.

3. Nicodemus. So, who were the Pharisees? We could call them the fundamentalists of the old covenant church. They were a religious party among the Jews dating from the time of the Babylonian captivity. They believed in Scripture, in the supernatural, and in the resurrection. They were both earnest and zealous men but failed to understand the grace of God. Because of their man-made regulations, they were more concerned with what other people thought of them than what the Scriptures said to them. This was the reason Nicodemus came to Jesus at night. He did not want others to see him conversing with Jesus. So let us consider the account of the evening's meeting. Nicodemus made two important acknowledgements.

Firstly, in John3:2, Nicodemus acknowledged who Jesus was. He said, 'Rabbi, we know You are a teacher.' No one taught like this man. The common people heard Him gladly because they understood what He was saying. He didn't speak in riddles but was clear in everything He uttered.

His second acknowledgement in that verse was even more amazing: 'You are a teacher come from God; for no one can do these signs that You do unless God is with Him.'

Although the Pharisees, as a group, did not recognise this fact, it had clearly penetrated the mind of Nicodemus. He had now become a cautious enquirer, who clearly found the answers to his questions and soon became a follower of our Lord—as we saw in John 19:39 where he helped Joseph of Arimathea to prepare Jesus for our Lord's burial. He discovered that the new birth was essential to salvation.

There are lessons that we all need to grasp hold of to ensure that we do not go astray. Christians need to be careful and content with what God has said in His Word. In order to safeguard ourselves from error, we must never add non-biblical traditions to scripture, as the Pharisees did. Above all we must recognise that the law is nothing more than a tutor to lead us to Christ, though an important tutor. We must remember that the law has condemned us all and that our salvation is secure by trusting in the Lord Jesus alone. It is through Him that we have the guarantee of eternal life.

6 JULY

God often speaks to the unlikely ones

'Now there were in the same country shepherds living out in the fields, keeping watch over their flock by night.' Luke 2:8

RECOMMENDED READING: Luke 2:8–20

We continue to look at important events in the Bible that occurred at night. During the next few days, I want to turn our thoughts to the beginning and closing moments of Jesus' life, as both took place at night. I want to begin by thinking about His birth.

Luke 2 is a passage that is well known to many people, as it is read in churches throughout the world during the advent season.

So, who were these shepherds? They were not biblical scholars with degrees; they were not reared as princes in a palace, living among royalty; they certainly were not leaders in the synagogue. All these people God ignored.

These men were guardians of the sheep just like Abel and David. They were simple, humble labourers, yet honoured recipients of an amazing announcement direct from heaven.

God often speaks without warning, just as He did to Moses when he was looking after the sheep for his father-in-law, Jethro, in Midian; or as he did to Gideon when he was threshing wheat; or as he did to Elisha when he was ploughing. God often turns to the weak and unlikely ones, and makes them His chosen servants to declare His message of salvation and hope.

Now after 400 years of silence, God breaks through and speaks again, this time to shepherds guarding their sheep during the night shift.

The first broadcast across the air waves was not from Alexandra Palace in north London, but from fields outside a little town called Bethlehem.

But why were they afraid? Wouldn't you be? Luke 2:9 tells us that they saw, 'the glory of the Lord … and were greatly afraid'. They had been living through a period of time when true reverence and fear for the one true God was absent from the people.

We also are living in days when these two characteristics are absent in the nation, but particularly in the church. Is this why we fail to experience the true glory of the Lord?

When God came down in revival blessing throughout parts of the United Kingdom in the nineteenth and early twentieth centuries, people witnessed amazing things and felt the presence of God as never before.

Oh, revive us again, Lord!

7 JULY

The darkest night

'And it was night.' John 13:30

RECOMMENDED READING: John 13:1–30

We come to the closing hours of our Lord's life. It is now the final night before His crucifixion and many events were about to take place in a very short time.

1. The Upper Room. This was our Lord's final meal with His disciples before the Feast of the Passover. A number of things happened in the upper room that night—some of which continue to this present day.

Jesus taught His disciples an important and practical lesson in humility when He took a basin and towel and washed their feet. This was a task that slaves were given when their master returned home or friends came to visit.

That same night, Jesus instituted the Lord's Supper, which we continue to observe today in remembrance of His sacrifice upon the cross. His broken body and shed blood remind us of the heavy price that was paid for our redemption.

Also, this night the disciples argued yet again about which of them would be greatest in the kingdom. Would these men ever learn?

2. The Garden of Gethsemane. Following the Lord's Prayer in John 17, Jesus went out with His disciples across the Kidron valley into an olive grove or garden called Gethsemane. This place was very precious to our Lord as He brought His disciples here on many occasions. In this garden He would remove himself from the pressures of a busy day, rest from His labours and spend time in prayer and communion with His Father.

This night He did the same, but it turned out to be an intense battle, as He asked the Father if there was any other way mankind could be rescued from their sin apart from the way of the cross. Jesus resigned Himself to His Father's will and not His own.

But this particular night did not end with prayer as Judas, accompanied by a detachment of armed soldiers and officers from the chief priest, entered the garden and arrested our Lord. Judas had come that night to betray his Master—an act he would very soon regret.

Jesus was taken unceremoniously from the garden to face trumped-up charges and suffering that was totally unjustified. This was a long night for Jesus and it had only just begun. We will follow the events tomorrow which culminated in a glorious conclusion.

8 JULY

The dark night will see a bright dawn

'And it was night.' John 13:30

RECOMMENDED READING: Matthew 26:56–75

During the past few days, we have been looking at events that occurred at night. We centred our attention upon Nehemiah, Paul and Silas, Nicodemus and the shepherds outside Bethlehem.

Yesterday we began looking at some of the events that took place on the final night before our Lord's crucifixion, and today we conclude our thoughts on His night of suffering.

3. The Courtyard. Eventually Jesus was taken to the High Priest's house (Luke 22:54). We are told that, 'Peter followed at a distance'. It is always dangerous to follow Jesus at a distance.

That night, despite his promise to die with Him (Luke 22:33), became the darkest hour of Peter's life. Three times he denied any knowledge of being one of Jesus' disciples.

I am sure we can understand Peter's reaction to his failure when he wept bitterly. Could he, at that moment, have been looking back and recalling the memorable times he had spent with his Master? These would have been occasions when he experienced a spiritual high; now he knew what it was to experience a deep spiritual low.

Yet, despite all Peter was going through that night, the Lord loved him so much that Luke 22:32 tells us Jesus prayed for him that his '… faith should not fail'.

What a comforting thought that is for all God's children. When we also let our Saviour down and our faith seems to be hanging by a thread, Jesus is praying that our faith remains strong.

Yes, that was a dark night, and there would be three more dark nights to come. Even the following day, Matthew 27:45 tells us that, while Jesus was on the cross, there were three hours of darkness over all the land.

The suffering of our Lord brought darkness over that awful scene. The earth quaked in grief as its Creator bowed His head and died. We too should bow our heads in sorrow for it was our sin that held Him there.

But thank God the darkness would be lifted, as, early on that Sunday morning, the Light of the World would shine through the darkness and rise from the dead.

Hallelujah! He is risen; He has conquered; death is defeated; the grave is empty; Jesus lives for evermore.

9 JULY

Resting in the shade

'The righteous shall flourish like a palm tree.' Psalm 92:12

RECOMMENDED READING: Leviticus 23:39–43

The writers of Scripture often used visual aids to put across God's message more clearly. The Psalms are full of them, including Psalm 92. In v.12, the writer is comparing the life of the believer to both a palm tree and cedar tree.

I want to consider during the next few days some of the features of a palm tree and compare them with characteristics that should be evident in the life of the Christian.

1. Its height. There are over 2,500 different species of palm trees throughout the world, the tallest being the Quindío wax palm which can grow from 148 to 200 feet high (45 to 60 metres).

A desert palm in the Middle East will reach up to 90 feet high (27 metres) and sometimes more. Its unusual height enables travellers in the hot desert to see it from a great distance away.

The sight of the palm tree encourages the traveller because from the palm tree he knows he can obtain food to satisfy hunger and water to quench thirst.

The palm tree can also bring relief from the burning sun, as the traveller is able to rest under its shade. Food, water and rest are vital for those who spend a lot of time in a hot desert climate.

In John 6:35 Jesus said, 'I am the bread of life. He who comes to Me shall never hunger, and he who believes in Me shall never thirst.'

In John 7:37 Jesus said, 'If anyone thirsts, let him come to Me and drink.'

In Matthew 5:6 Jesus said, 'Blessed are those who hunger and thirst for righteousness, for they shall be filled.'

In Matthew 11:28 Jesus said, 'Come to Me, all you who labour and are heavy laden, and I will give you rest.'

Just like the palm tree, Christians should stand tall and be clearly seen in a spiritual desert. We should be there to inform sin-laden travellers, who journey through this life, where they can obtain food, water and rest. All these can be found only in the Lord Jesus Christ. His arms are open to receive weary travellers and provide for all their needs.

10 JULY

Strong roots result in good fruit

'... that Christ may dwell in your hearts through faith; that you, being rooted and grounded in love ...' Ephesians 3:17

RECOMMENDED READING: Ephesians 3:14–21

We are looking at the characteristics of a palm tree and likening them to a Christian's character. Yesterday we considered the exceptional height of palm trees that are found in the desert regions. Today we turn our thoughts to:

2. Its strong roots. The palm tree will flourish in a favourable fertile soil, but it is also resilient enough to endure a harsh desert climate and withstand powerful storms. The tree is adaptable to all conditions that nature will present to it and will thrive as it does so. Whenever I have watched a news report of violent storms hitting countries such as the Caribbean, I have noticed that great damage has been done to both property and the environment. But I have also noticed that the palm trees have remained firm, flexible and strong. Their deep roots have been strong enough to maintain it through the most ferocious conditions, whereas other trees have been uprooted and die.

In comparison, Christians should have strong roots in Christ and His Word so that they can withstand all that the world throws at them.

The apostle Paul says in Colossians 2:6,7, 'As you therefore have received Christ Jesus the Lord, so walk in Him, rooted ... in Him.'

The Christian is sustained by the hidden streams of God's grace and the strength and power of His word.

When God plants believers in lonely and spiritually desolate parts of the world, where persecution is a common experience, strong roots in Christ will uphold them.

Christians will not grow and develop spiritually, nor will they bear fruit, until they have strong, healthy and secure roots.

How do we obtain and develop strong roots?

(a) Through listening to and studying God's Word. We need to set aside time each day when we can listen to the voice of God through His Word, the Bible. We also need to take every opportunity to hear the Word preached through faithful ministers of that Word.

(b) Enjoying communion with God through prayer. We listen to God through His Word then we speak to God in prayer.

(c) By having fellowship with like-minded believers. Friendship with other Christians strengthens our spiritual roots as we learn from each other.

Strong roots bring good fruit and both come when, as Psalm 92:13 tells us, we are 'planted in the house of the Lord'.

11 JULY

Christians are to be fruit bearers

'Walk worthy of the Lord, fully pleasing Him, being fruitful in every good work.' Colossians 1:10

RECOMMENDED READING: Psalm 92

We continue by considering two more characteristics of the palm tree:

3. Its fruit yield. The fruit yield of the palm tree is practically 100%. The blossoms are tough, like a leathery substance. This enables them to withstand any destructive elements and insects. Also, its umbrella-like branches, which are anywhere between 6 to 8 feet (1.8 to 2.4 metres) in length, shade and protect the blossoms until they have developed into fruit. A good and healthy palm tree will produce up to 200lbs (90.7kg) of dates each year, which is a great yield of fruit.

The Christian, likewise, is assured of a great yield of fruit by Christ Himself. We are to be fruit bearers as we testify to the saving work of our Lord Jesus. John 15:8 says, 'By this My Father is glorified, that you bear much fruit; so you will be my disciples.'

As Christians, we must be fruitful. Sometimes we are like the vine and need to be pruned to bring forth much fruit. Pruning can be a painful experience but at times necessary.

'Every branch in Me that does not bear fruit He takes away; and every branch that bears fruit He prunes, that it may bear more fruit' (John 15:2).

Never complain when God prunes. It is for our good and the benefit of others. A Christian cannot be barren.

4. It sweetens with age. The palm tree reaches its peak after around thirty years of its life. It continues in strength and productivity for a further seventy years. After one hundred years it produces its sweetest dates.

We can therefore say that the sweetest dates are found on the oldest trees. I think that speaks for itself. We should produce sweeter fruit as we grow older. Though our outside casing may be a bit tough and leathery, the inside should be sweet and pleasant to the taste. From years of experience the aged believer shouts, 'Taste and see that the Lord is good' (Psalm 34:8). We have proved Him to be so.

Even in winter the palm tree remains green. Though we age in years, we should remain spiritually green. Don't think you have nothing to contribute now you are older. Psalm 92:14 says, 'They shall still bear fruit in old age.'

Whatever your age, you have still much to contribute within the life of the church and nation, so keep bearing good fruit and glorify your Father in heaven.

12 JULY

God loads us with benefits

'A faithful man will abound with blessings.' Proverbs 28:20

RECOMMENDED READING: John 12:12–16

Today we turn to a further characteristic of the palm tree:

5. Its many benefits. A man, whose home is in the Middle East, is considered well off if he possesses palm trees on his property.

Some years ago, I read about an American author who had stated that there is no part of a palm tree that cannot be used in some way by man. Of all the trees it is considered to be one of the most beneficially productive.

Likewise, the believer has been endowed with many benefits, and they are varied. The Christian's life is a continual source of blessing. Our verse at the beginning of today's thought should remind us of this fact.

The big tragedy is that, more often than not, we are unaware of the blessings we have and are able to share with others.

(a) The blessing of life itself. When we look back over the years gone by, we can thank God for His goodness to us in so many ways.

(b) The blessing of family and loyal friendships. Loved ones who have loved us, watched over us and encouraged us during difficult times have been a source of continuous thanksgiving.

(c) The blessing of Christian fellowship. How we should thank God for His church, which is not a building, but a body of Christian believers.

(d) The blessing of His salvation. To know that we are His children exceeds any other blessing we might possess.

(e) The blessing of His Word. The Bible is God speaking to us, so we need to read and listen attentively to all He says to us.

(f) The blessing of our future home in heaven. Ephesians 1:3 says, 'Blessed be the God and Father of our Lord Jesus Christ, who has blessed us with every spiritual blessing in the heavenly places in Christ.'

May we thank God every day for all the blessings He freely gives to us.

Psalm 129:8 is my prayer for you all: 'The blessing of the LORD be upon you.'

13 JULY

Secure in the storms

'And we know that all things work together for good to those who love God, to those who are the called according to His purpose.' Romans 8:28

RECOMMENDED READING: Matthew 7:24–29

During the past few days, we have been considering Psalm 92:12: 'The righteous shall flourish like a palm tree.' We have looked at five characteristics of a palm tree and all these should be evident in the lives of God's people. We have considered its height; its strong roots; its fruit yield; it sweetens with age; and its many benefits. We now turn to our final characteristic:

6. Its endurance. The best way of illustrating the endurance of the palm tree is by sharing the following story which took place off the coast of Florida.

The Rev. Earl Williamson told of an experience a friend and his family once had on an island during their holiday. The crew of a coastguard patrol boat had just circumnavigated the islands to warn of an approaching storm. Assuming there was no one left on the island, the skipper gave orders to return to the mainland at full speed before their boat was caught in the storm. Suddenly, one of his men noticed someone frantically waving their arms.

Immediately the officer called through the bullhorn, 'Sorry, it's too dangerous for us to return, but you will be all right as long as the palm trees stand.'

The hurricane hit with great fury, but the family, though terrified and badly shaken, survived by lying on the ground and clutching some of the palm trees.

Throughout this life the Christian faces many storms: physical, material and spiritual. Jesus commands us to take up the cross and follow Him. For many believers throughout the world, that cross can be an extremely heavy one to carry, but they do so in the strength which He provides for them.

We are living in a world that is insecure and full of uncertainty. The past eighteen months have shown that to be a reality. This world is fragile and it will not endure forever.

But a day is coming when every Christian will stand on eternity's shore proclaiming deliverance from every storm that has come our way because of God's mercy and abounding grace towards us.

14 JULY

How to ruin a perfect home

'The LORD God planted a garden eastward in Eden, and there He put the man whom He had formed.' Genesis 2:8

RECOMMENDED READING: Genesis 2:8–25

Eda Lord Murphy wrote these very relevant words:
'The beauty of the house is order;
The blessing of the house is contentment;
The glory of the house is hospitality;
The crown of the house is godliness.'[23]

A child who is brought up in such a home has been given the best start in life. They should be very thankful and treasure it for years to come.

Unfortunately, in the United Kingdom today, the opposite is usually the case. Ungodliness, disorder and discontentment are the common features within many homes, which sadly is often as a result of a dysfunctional family.

During the next few days, I want to consider a number of homes in the Bible and the people who lived in them.

1. The garden home. We read about this home in Genesis 2:15–18. Here was Adam's first home, a place to enjoy and look after. God gave to Adam a wife who was called Eve. They lived in the garden and enjoyed contentment and harmony. They had unbroken fellowship with their Creator, who had generously given to them all that they needed; they lacked nothing. This was perfect bliss. Could anything ruin this Utopia?

Once we come to chapter 3, the scene changes dramatically. What caused this transformation? In chapter 3:5,6 we notice a couple of things which caused this perfect home to be abandoned.

(a) Disobedience. 'She took of its fruit' (v.6). God had expressed love to this couple but, in return, demanded discipline. Love and discipline are vital to the running of any home. Leave out either and problems will soon arise.

(b) Power. 'You will be like God' (v.5). Today the home has become a power base where often parents are obedient to their children. If each member of the household accepted God's role for them, the home would be a more harmonious place to live. Unfortunately, the desire for power is evident throughout society and all walks of life are affected to some degree. When we consider the perfect home, we must be aware that sin is the destroyer of all that is good.

Husbands, wives and children: don't let the evil one break down the unity and harmony of the home.

15 JULY

Climb aboard and be safe

'And Noah did according to all that the LORD commanded him.' Genesis 7:5

RECOMMENDED READING: Genesis 7:1–24

The home should be the safest and happiest of environments for both children and adults. Today we continue to look at a number of homes mentioned in the Bible and their importance to the occupants.

Yesterday we began with the garden home recorded in Genesis 2. Now we turn to consider the life of Noah.

2. The floating home. We read the story in Genesis 6:5 – 9:17 with special attention to 7:7–10.

God's patience had finally run out. From the creation of Adam, God had seen the fall and removal of both Adam and Eve from the Garden of Eden because of their sin.

He had also witnessed the murder of Abel by his brother Cain. Now the 'godly' were marrying unbelievers. All this had taken place within ten generations.

This was too much for God to bear. He saw not only the wickedness that had taken place, but He knew the thoughts of man's heart was continually evil (6:5). Now the time had come for action which would result in God's judgement and the destruction of all that He had made (6:13).

However, among all the wickedness that was upon the earth, there was a man called Noah who walked with God. He was a just man who 'found grace in the eyes of the Lord' (6:8). Oh, may that be said of us!

Noah was instructed by God to build an ark which would be the home for both him and his family for over twelve months. It would be a place of safety and security from a great flood and the devastation and destruction that was to come upon the earth.

It would also be the home for seven of every clean animal, and two of every unclean animal, both male and female (6:2). Also included was seven of each of the birds, both male and female.

The home today should also be a place of security from the wickedness around us. It should be a place of love and happiness where God is in the midst and directs all the affairs of the family.

As God was in the ark with Noah during the flood, may God reside in our homes and be a great blessing to us.

16 JULY

A new home in a new country

'Wherever you lodge, I will lodge; your people shall be my people, and your God, my God.' Ruth 1:16

RECOMMENDED READING: 1 Samuel 3

We continue to look at homes in the Bible and lessons we could learn from the people who lived there. Today we turn our thoughts to a Moabite woman named Ruth, who began a new life in Bethlehem in the land of Israel.

3. The unexpected home. We read about this new home in the book of Ruth. The story began with a famine in the land of Israel. Elimelech, his wife Naomi and their two sons, Mahlon and Chilion, left their home due to a famine and journeyed to the land of Moab. Whilst there, following the death of Elimelech, the two sons married Moabite women named Ruth and Orpah. About ten years later both Naomi's sons also died.

Everything seemed to be going against Naomi, but during her grief she heard that the famine in Bethlehem was now over and she decided to return to her homeland.

On the journey she encouraged her two daughters-in-law to return to their homes and families in Moab. Orpah followed Naomi's instructions, but Ruth would not leave her mother-in-law. The words in Ruth 1:16–17 convey Ruth's deep feelings towards Naomi.

Chapter 2 begins with Ruth and Naomi back in Bethlehem. As Ruth was gleaning in the fields near the town, she met a wealthy member of Elimelech's family whose name was Boaz.

He became very quickly attracted to Ruth, admiring her for her unstinting loyalty to Naomi. Very soon a relationship developed between the couple and eventually they married.

God, in His mercy, had provided an unexpected home in Bethlehem for both Ruth and Naomi. Now, God provided a home for Ruth and Naomi with Boaz. You will discover the exceptional importance of this relationship in Ruth 4:17.

Wherever we live, our home is a divine provision from God. It doesn't have to be a six-bedroom mansion with swimming pool and all modern gadgets; it can be a simply constructed property that meets our needs. After all, it is only temporary and one day we will have to leave it for something far more beautiful with no bills to pay and no repairs necessary. It will be God's eternal provision for us.

17 JULY

At home with the Lord

'She took him up with her ... and brought him to the house of the LORD in Shiloh. And the child was young.' 1 Samuel 1:24

RECOMMENDED READING: 1 Samuel 1:20–28

We continue our brief series looking at homes in the Bible and the amazing people who occupied them. Today we turn our thoughts to the prophet Samuel, whose home was the temple in Shiloh.

4. A home in the temple. The judges had been ruling Israel but, despite God's mercy to His people, they did evil in His sight and served the Baals and Asherahs (false gods).

Not only was wickedness evident among the people, but we read in 1 Samuel 2:12 that the two sons of Eli, the High Priest, 'were corrupt; they did not know the LORD'.

If the leaders of the church are ignorant of the Lord and His ways, it is not surprising that the people are also living in ignorance and spiritual darkness.

We are told in 3:1 that, 'The word of the LORD was rare in those days; there was no widespread revelation.'

A certain man named Elkanah had two wives, Peninnah and Hannah. Peninnah had children, but Hannah was barren and she longed for a child.

After a long wait, God gave her a son who was called Samuel. Hannah knew where his future would be. She said in 1:27–28: 'For this child I prayed, and the LORD has granted me my petition which I asked of Him. Therefore, I also have lent him to the LORD; as long as he lives he shall be lent to the LORD.'

The temple in Shiloh had now become Samuel's home, and it was here that God revealed Himself to this young man.

In 3:19 we read, 'So Samuel grew, and the LORD was with him and let none of his words fall to the ground.' Samuel loved the temple, and it was here that the foundation stones of his life were set.

How often have we sat in the house of God and the Almighty has spoken to us through the faithful preaching of the Word?

As God spoke to young Samuel so long ago, let us pray that God will continue to speak to us week by week through His Word. May we soak it in as we come before Him with open ears and minds that are attentive to His every word. Then may our wills act in obedience to everything He wishes to say to us.

Christ the head of the home

'He entered a certain village; and a certain woman named Martha welcomed Him into her house.' Luke 10:38

RECOMMENDED READING: Luke 10:38–42

As we continue our brief series, we now enter a home that Jesus loved to visit. It was a spiritual oasis whenever He was in or around Jerusalem.

5. A welcoming home. This home is mentioned a number of times in the Gospels (read John 12:1–11).

Jesus found the home of Mary, Martha and their brother, Lazarus, in the village of Bethany, to have a more relaxing atmosphere than He seemed to find anywhere else on His travels. When He visited, He was received warmly, like a member of their family. He visited their home on a number of occasions and may even have spent some nights under their hospitable roof.

(a) It was a home of affection. It is clear when you read John 11:5 that Jesus loved Mary, Martha and Lazarus, and His love was reciprocated with great affection. It is also clear that there was a deep love for each other in this small family.

When we have love for Christ, it cannot fail to demonstrate love for people around us. 1 John 4:20 says, 'He who does not love his brother [and sister] whom he has seen, how can he love God whom he has not seen?'

A home where affection is clearly evident is always a good place to stay.

(b) It was a godly home. These friends of Jesus always looked forward to our Lord's visits when He was in or near Bethany. What He loved, they loved and so He took a central place in their lives and home.

I would have loved to have heard their conversation. I am sure their main topic would have centred on spiritual things as the Scriptures would have been important to them.

I wonder if we would be at ease if Jesus came to our house to spend a few days with us. I guess some books and magazines would be hidden out of sight and even the television hidden in the garage. All this would be unnecessary as He knows what we read and the programmes that we watch.

(c) It was a home of unity. Here was a united family that had a love for Jesus and a commitment to His work. A family that is held by ties of affection for Christ is one of God's greatest blessings.

When the Philippian jailer was converted, he was saved and his entire household (Acts 16:31–32,34). How we need to pray for families to be converted. When they are, the result is a home of spiritual unity.

19 JULY

God's wonderful provision

'Please, let us make a small upper room on the wall; and let us put a bed for him there, and a table and a chair and a lampstand; so it will be, whenever he comes to us, he can turn in there.' 2 Kings 4:10

RECOMMENDED READING: 2 Kings 4:8–37

We continue thinking of homes and the people who lived there. It is like looking through the keyhole and viewing the events taking place inside.

6. A home on the wall. Elisha was a very busy man with much work to do. It involved travel, study and fulfilling God's calling. There was little time to rest.

For many years, my work with Day One Christian Ministries has involved travelling many thousands of miles throughout different parts of the United Kingdom. During this time, I have greatly appreciated the kind hospitality that has been extended to me in providing both a comfortable bed and enjoyable meals. Many of these people I had never met before, but warm friendships have developed through these visits. When the travelling had to stop because of the COVID-19 pandemic, I greatly missed the fellowship with these kind friends.

Elisha went to Shunem, an important town during the period of Israel's monarchy. It was located in the tribal territory of Issachar, on the outskirts of the fertile plain of Jezreel. It was some fifteen miles from Mount Carmel.

A well-respected woman and her husband had provided hospitality for Elisha by making a room on their roof with three essential items:

Firstly, there was a bed which provided rest for the renewal of physical strength. Secondly, there was a table and chair for relaxation and studying the scriptures. Thirdly, there was a lamp which gave light, particularly on dark evenings. All these were basic items, but essential to help Elisha fulfil his calling.

A lady, who lived in a small, terraced house in South Yorkshire, once said to me, 'God has provided a roof over my head, coal for my fire, food in my pantry and a bed to rest on at the end of the day. What more do I need? I'm happier here than many who live in luxurious palaces.'

Elisha was content with what God had provided. May we know such contentment with God's provision for us.

The best home of all

'In My Father's house are many mansions; if it were not so I would have told you. I go to prepare a place for you.' John 14:2

RECOMMENDED READING: John 14:1–6

During the past few days, we have been travelling widely around the land of Israel and beyond, visiting a number of homes in the Bible and the people who lived there. We have visited the home of Adam and Eve; the home of Noah, the home of Ruth, the home of Samuel, the home in Bethany and the home in Shunem. Our final home is a long way from our current accommodation, yet it is the closest to our hearts:

7. Our heavenly home. John 14:3 says, 'If I go and prepare a place for you, I will come again and receive you to Myself; that where I am, there you may be also.'

What a remarkable future awaits the children of God! A day is coming when our Lord Jesus Christ will return to this earth once again to take those who are His to be with Him forever.

In this world we experience sickness, pain, sorrow, tears, separation and finally death. Along with this is our continual battle with sin and its consequences.

In heaven all the results of the fall will be removed forever. No evil thing will enter. Only those whom Christ died to save will be accepted.

God has prepared a home for us that no eye has seen and no ear has fully heard about. Heaven will be beyond our greatest expectation. Our puny minds cannot grasp the wonder that will be ours forever.

However, there is something even beyond all that has been mentioned. We will see our Saviour face to face.

The One who gave Himself upon the cross; who took all our sins and iniquities; who granted to us complete and undeserved forgiveness. He will be there to welcome us so that we can gaze upon His beautiful face and see the wounds in his hands, feet and side. We will be able to thank Him in a way we have never been able to do before. Oh, to just worship Him and cry out with all fellow believers and the angelic host, 'Worthy is the Lamb that was slain' (Revelation 5:12).

Oh, just to be home!

Let us today be thankful for the earthly homes God has provided for us; but the best home is yet to come!

21 JULY

True wealth is found in Christ alone

'Good Teacher, what shall I do that I may inherit eternal life?' Mark 10:17

RECOMMENDED READING: Mark 10:17–27

What shall I do? This is a question we all ask from time to time. It is asked by children when they are bored during school holidays. It is also asked by adults when they have to decide between various options and are unsure which is the correct one to take.

This question was asked on two occasions in the New Testament. I want to consider one of these occasions, which you will find in Mark 10.

Jesus was approached by a rich young ruler who asked Him, 'What shall I do that I may inherit eternal life' (Mark 10:17). During the next few days, we will consider his background, and his encounter with the Lord Jesus Christ. Here was a man who had many advantages before him.

1. He was rich. Wealth is desired on the cheap by so many people. That is why gambling is such a popular activity throughout our nation. We gamble on anything from sporting activities to the lottery. The rich gamble, the poor gamble. We even gamble with our lives. Gambling has become an obsession with many people of all ages. They believe wealth will make them happy. On the contrary, wealthy people are often the most unhappy and discontented people I have met.

The man who came to Jesus wasn't looking for wealth; he already had it. However, his life was empty. There was a deep void within him that couldn't be filled. Wealth could not satisfy his real need.

When your life is empty, it needs filling with something. Why do people take drugs? It is to fill the emptiness within them. Why do people drink to excess and make a fool of themselves? Because there is a void that needs satisfying.

One thing that is missing from society today is contentment. Jesus said, 'One's life does not consist in the abundance of the things he possesses' (Luke 12:15).

We brought nothing into this world, and it is certain that we will take nothing out. There are no pockets in a coffin. You leave this world empty-handed.

If there is emptiness in our lives, the things of this world will not satisfy that need. Only Jesus can fill that aching void. This man was rich, but poor and empty. Let us ensure that our treasures are where our heart should be—in heaven.

22 JULY

The years go quickly by

'Rejoice, O young man, in your youth, and let your heart cheer you in the days of your youth.' Ecclesiastes 11:9

RECOMMENDED READING: Ecclesiastes 11:7 – 12:1

Yesterday we began considering a man who approached Jesus seeking an answer to his longing for eternal life. This man had a very privileged background that he was reluctant to relinquish. We are told he was rich. We now consider two more aspects of his life.

2. He was young. Isn't it great to be young? Or should I say, it was great when I was young. A life ahead of me with great prospects. Dreams of a successful career; a healthy bank balance; a large house with the latest design in furniture; a big garden with a swimming pool; the latest model of my favourite car; a good healthy lifestyle and an attractive wife to enjoy it with. Dream on, boy! Now come into the real world (Well I did get the attractive wife but as for the rest …)!

Being young is not always rosy. It has its challenges and it has its temptations. A career can go to pieces; health can fail; problems can affect your happy family; you need to re-mortgage your house and you prang your new car. Youth has many advantages, so enjoy the early years while you can. However, if you are young, hopefully you will become wiser as you grow older and learn from those early rash mistakes. Life is an adventure but you need to take care and be wise so that you do not crash as so many have done. Be willing to take advice from those who have walked the path before you.

'Remember now your Creator in the days of your youth (Ecclesiastes 12:1). It has always been wise advice and still is today.

3. He was a ruler. We do not know his precise position or title but clearly, he was a young man of high social standing. However, even this did not blind him to his real need which was spiritual.

We live in a world where both men and women have a desire for power. It always has been, even from the Garden of Eden. There is never a shortage of candidates to fill positions of power and influence, in social, business and political life. People will do anything to achieve power and at anyone's expense. Throughout history, empires have risen and fallen. Leaders have come to power but eventually they too fall.

People must learn that, 'Power belongs to God' (Psalm 62:11). He is the only ruler of the universe and one day, not only this rich young man, but every knee will bow before Him.

23 JULY

Only Jesus can meet our needs

'Jesus, looking at him, loved him.' Mark 10:21

RECOMMENDED READING: Matthew 6:19–21

We have been looking at the characteristics of the rich young ruler. This morning we turn to his personal encounter with the Lord Jesus.

Many people write off this young man immediately, but he had some commendable points that are worth considering, even though he came to the wrong conclusion.

1. He came to the right person. This young man had a deep spiritual need that required immediate attention. He needed someone to handle his question. He could have gone to the Pharisees, who believed in the resurrection and eternal life; he could have gone to the rabbis or other notable religious leaders. But no, he went to this humble man from Nazareth.

He did not seek a private interview or approach Him under cover of darkness, as Nicodemus did. He was a young man who had courage and did not conceal his need. He knew something was missing in his life and only Jesus had the answer.

There are people today who investigate other religions or seek advice from educated leaders but it is to no avail. They find the cistern is broken and empty.

The only answer to a person's deepest need is to seek Jesus and then speak honestly to Him. He will listen to an honest cry for help.

2. He came with the right attitude. Mark 10:17 tells us that he came running. There was urgency in his mission. He could delay no longer. Jesus was in the vicinity and he could not miss this opportunity. He might not be in the same district again. If this chance was lost, there might be no other.

Also notice in v.17 that he came kneeling. This was a sign of deep respect for the Teacher. He recognised that Jesus was different from all the religious leaders he had met. He acted differently; He spoke differently, because no one spoke like this man; His face showed a peace that passed all understanding. He was no ordinary teacher.

If you have a spiritual need, then don't put it off; run to Christ and kneel reverently before Him. If you come in the right attitude, then He will welcome you.

24 JULY

Doing right but ending wrong

'He was sad at this word, and went away sorrowful, for he had great possessions.' Mark 10:22

RECOMMENDED READING: Mark 10:23–31

As we continue to consider the rich young ruler, we noticed yesterday how well he began. He came to the right person and in the right attitude. Today we will conclude with our Lord's response to him.

3. He came with the right question. After kneeling in respect before Jesus, he asked Him an all-important question, 'What shall I do that I may inherit eternal life?' (Mark 10:17).

During times of discussion with young people, many questions are asked, sometimes in a provocative manner. This young man, however, had a real spiritual concern. He believed there was eternal life, but clearly didn't know how or where to find it. He was very secure in the present life as he possessed an abundance of wealth but, for the future, he had no assurance or guarantee and he was looking for Jesus to help him.

4. He was given the right answer. First of all, in v.19, Jesus tested him on the second half of the Ten Commandments relating to his fellow men. In v.20 the young man responded with confidence. His reply may put many of us to shame. In v.21, Jesus then hit a sensitive nerve. Jesus will always hit the target with His reply, and sometimes it can hurt. 'Sell whatever you have and give to the poor … and come … and follow Me.' He knew this man inside out. He also knows you and me intimately. He will always give an honest answer in clear language that we cannot fail to understand.

5. He came to the wrong conclusion. This is sadly the situation for most people. They ignore the advice given to them, thinking they know better than their Creator. We are told that he went away sorrowful because he had many possessions. I believe Jesus was also sad because we are told in v.21 that He loved him.

If you are not a Christian, what is holding you back from following the Lord Jesus? Is it your possessions? Is it a wrong relationship? Or is it pride?

Can I encourage you to cast these aside? Don't think of what you may be giving up: think of the better things you will receive, including eternal life. Acknowledge your sin and turn your eyes upon Jesus, who willingly gave His life upon the cross, bearing your sin in His body. Look at Him and see the depth of His love for you. Have faith in Him. By doing so, both this life and your future destiny will be secure.

25 JULY

The love of money destroys lives

'What shall I do, since I have no room to store my crops?' Luke 12:17

RECOMMENDED READING: Luke 12:16–21

We have just considered the life of the rich, young ruler who wanted to find eternal life. The man in Luke 12 wanted to find room for his crops. There are some important things to note from this parable of Jesus.

1. It is centred on another rich man. It seems this man had prospered as an arable farmer. The recent harvest had been very successful and his land had yielded another excellent crop. In v.16 there is no problem or criticism of the man. He was using the land for the purpose it had been given and it had brought him success.

There is nothing wrong in being rich. There is nothing wrong in being a good businessman or businesswoman. Being rich is not the problem. The problem is how you become rich and what you do with your wealth. It is around this that God will judge us.

2. He thought only about himself. It is when we reach v.17 of Luke 12 that the challenge begins. 'What shall I do?' We ask this question on a regular basis and then come to a decision. The rich young ruler asked the same question and came to a decision.

Notice this farmer never once asked, 'Who helped me to get this wealth?' Or, 'Who can I help with my wealth?'

He never sought God's advice and wisdom. 'What shall I do? I have an abundance of crops. What is my next step?'

Each morning we should rise from our beds and face the challenge of a new day. It is wise to meditate and pray with regard to the hours before us. Then we should think within ourselves, 'How can I best use these hours that God has given to me? Who can I help and encourage? I have been blessed by God; how can I be a blessing to others? Can my time and possessions further the work of the gospel in my local fellowship?' Think within yourself, then pray again and act wisely.

In v.17, a great possibility lay before him. He was at the crossroads. Which direction would he take? That precise moment was crucial to his future.

When you think within yourself, always find room for God in your heart and mind. He will guide you to the right decision.

God always has the final word

'For where your treasure is, there your heart will be also.' Luke 12:34

RECOMMENDED READING: Luke 12:22–34

We are looking at a parable Jesus told about a prosperous farmer who wanted to find room for his crops after a successful harvest. We noticed yesterday that in all his thoughts God never came into the equation. His wealth was central in his thinking. We conclude with the farmer's response to his thoughts and God's reaction to his actions.

3. The decision is finally made. We have the farmer's response in Luke 12:18: 'I will pull down my barns and build greater, and there I will store all my crops and my goods.'

Business enterprise can be good. Many Christians have been successful and have helped others along life's journey.

The problem with this man's decision is that everything is centred upon him. Notice two words are repeated three times in v.18: 'I will'. Also note that 'I' is at the heart of vv.17, 18 and 19.

The decision he made was centred entirely upon himself. There is no mention of God, neither is there any reference to others. The middle letter in the word SIN is 'I'. The centre of sin is always 'I'.

4. God's response. We have the reaction of God to his decision in vv.20 and 21. Jesus continues with total honesty. He holds nothing back. He never holds anything back. As with the rich young ruler, so also with this farmer, Jesus lays the situation right on the line.

Jesus then turns to His disciples and urges them to always get everything in its right perspective. In v.31 of Luke 12, He says, 'Seek the kingdom of God, and all these things shall be added to you.'

There are many lessons for us to learn from this parable. I mention two:

(a) Don't centre life upon yourself and your possessions. Man's problem is that he is in love with what is vanishing. Be in love with Jesus and those things that will last forever.

(b) Ecclesiastes 5:19 instructs you to view wealth as a gift from God. Never regard it as your ultimate source of satisfaction. If you do, you will be greatly disappointed. Always get your priorities in the right order by putting Jesus first in everything.

27 JULY

Do not seek great things for yourself

'The Lord has sought for Himself a man after His own heart.' 1 Samuel 13:14

RECOMMENDED READING: Acts 13:13–26

During the next few days, we will be looking at a number of characteristics in the life of David. As we do so, let us apply them to our own lives, as they will help us in our Christian pilgrimage.

1. David the shepherd. In 1 Samuel 16:11 we read, 'There he is, keeping the sheep.'

At the direction of the Lord, Samuel took a journey to Bethlehem, to the home of Jesse, for the purpose of anointing the next king of Israel. Seven sons of Jesse were brought before Samuel, but none were suitable for this great task. When Samuel enquired if all the sons were present, he was told that the youngest was keeping the sheep.

To many people this was a menial task, but David carried out his duties with humility and care. God didn't want a proud leader for His people; He wanted someone who was willing to take on the responsibility with a quiet and humble spirit. James 4:6 says, 'God resists the proud, but gives grace to the humble.'

A young man had strong hopes of becoming the minister of a large, fashionable city church. He was invited to preach one Sunday and was told it would be a large congregation. The young man wasn't fazed by this as he was confident in his own ability.

The morning arrived. He left the vestry and climbed the steps into the high spacious pulpit. As he did so, his head was held high, proud of the thought that he would impress his congregation and be invited to become their future minister.

However, from the first hymn, he struggled throughout the whole service. At times he wished there was a trap door beneath him so he could escape, but he pressed on.

At the close of the service, he walked down the pulpit steps with his chin on his chest. An elderly deacon approached him and asked if he could give him some advice. He said, 'If you went up as you came down, you would have come down as you went up.'

How proud we can become of our abilities and achievements. Do not seek great things for yourself. Pride blocks out God's presence. It keeps Him in the background. If we thought less of self, God would reveal more of Himself.

David didn't seek great things for himself, but God exalted David to carry out great things for Him.

28 JULY

Keep your eyes on the real enemy

'Your servant will go and fight.' 1 Samuel 17:32

RECOMMENDED READING: 1 Samuel 17:20–51

Yesterday we began to look at a number of characteristics in the life of David. We saw him as a shepherd demonstrating humility. Today, we join him on the battlefield and see a young man with great courage.

2. David the soldier. Before David was ever introduced to King Saul, he was recognised for his bravery whenever his flock were in danger (1 Samuel 17:34,35).

In 1 Samuel 17:16, we read that for forty days, both morning and evening, Goliath, the champion of the Philistine army, issued a challenge to the men of Israel. By this time, Saul's courage had failed him and his army consisted of weak and unfit men.

David responded to Goliath's challenge with courage: 'Your servant will go and fight with this Philistine' (v.32). David was able to take up this challenge because he had confidence in his God.

The secret to David's life became clear when Samuel went to Bethlehem to anoint him in the presence of his brothers. We are told in 1 Samuel 16:13 that, 'The Spirit of the LORD came upon David from that day forward.'

David knew his God intimately and personally. Therefore, he would fight with all his energy for his God.

He knew the battle was the Lord's. Therefore, he was able to face Goliath with confidence, conviction and courage.

The true Christian Church consists of a family of believers who are at war with Satan and his followers. It is an intense and dangerous conflict.

In this battle, Christians need to be united in our aim and purpose. Unfortunately, sometimes we are so involved with fighting each other that we lose our focus and fail to recognise the true enemy.

We also need to possess a positive attitude in our conflict with the enemy. Someone once said that some Christians act like photographers: they spend too much time in the darkroom examining negatives.

It is regrettable to say, but we have some spiritually weak and unfit soldiers who should be strong and active for the cause of Christ. Remember, evil triumphs when Christians do nothing.

As Satan continues to issue his challenges, we, like David, need to prepare ourselves to face them. We do not do this in our own strength, for the arm of flesh will fail us; we do this in the strength which God supplies.

29 JULY

Time with God each day is essential

'Seek out a man who is a skilful player.' 1 Samuel 16:16

RECOMMENDED READING: 1 Samuel 16:14–23

We continue to look into the life of David. We have seen the shepherd and the soldier. Today we turn to look at two more areas of his life which became important to Israel.

3. David the psalmist. It is clear from 1 Samuel 16:18 that David was a gifted musician because, when Saul was overcome with a distressing spirit sent from God, David was immediately called to refresh him and bring temporary respite.

However, not only could he play, but the Psalms clearly show how he was able to put words to music.

For many believers, the Psalms have brought much comfort and strength in time of need. To neglect the Psalms is to neglect a treasure trove. They convey David's innermost feelings. We are permitted to go, as it were, behind closed doors and see a man opening his heart in devotion to God.

We see times of pain and helplessness; we see times of rejoicing and victory; we see times of sadness and loss. All of life's experiences are laid open before God in these verses.

Let God search us, every part of us. Let us be totally honest with Him as David was in the Psalms. Let us not try to hide things, because He can see the very thoughts of our heart.

How important it is to spend time daily in devotion with God. He must be at the centre of our thinking, praying and worship.

4. David the king. In 2 Samuel 5:2, the tribes of Israel came to David at Hebron to remind him that the Lord had said, 'You shall shepherd My people Israel, and be ruler over Israel.'

In his youth he was the shepherd of his sheep. Now he was to become the shepherd of a nation. David was now king, not just of Judah, but of the whole of Israel. He now had complete power in his hand. David loved his people and his people loved him.

David was a man of power, but he used it wisely for the benefit of his people. He was truly a man after God's own heart.

If that only could be said with regard to every pastor and the people of every church in our land today.

We may not be sovereign rulers on earth, but we do represent an even greater Sovereign. Therefore, we must stand tall for Jesus in a godless and alien world.

30 JULY

How easily the mighty can fall

'The thing that David had done displeased the LORD.' 2 Samuel 11:27

RECOMMENDED READING: 2 Samuel 11:1–27

We have seen David as a shepherd, as a soldier, as a musician and as a king. Now the scene changes dramatically through one serious lapse.

5. David the fallen. He had been a courageous soldier and a powerful sovereign over his people, but now we see his moral weakness. This king, whom the nation looked up to, is now seen as a fallen sinner. What a contrast!

There was a time when David would have led his army onto the battlefield ready for action. Now 2 Samuel 11:1 tells us that he remained in Jerusalem. In this one episode, David broke at least four commandments and, at each stage, sank into even greater sin.

First of all, he coveted what did not belong to him. He then took his neighbour's wife by force, while her husband was fighting for his country. He then committed adultery with her. To try and cover up his evil deeds, he arranged the murder of her husband.

Sin is a progressive, downward spiral. Once you are on the slide, you can soon find yourself at the bottom.

The Bible is totally honest about David. It gives details of his courage but it is completely open about his weakness and sin. The Bible hides nothing from us.

In v.27 of 2 Samuel 11, God makes it abundantly clear what He thought about David's actions: 'But the thing that David had done displeased the LORD.'

How true that the devil finds work for idle hands. If we are fully employed in the Lord's work, we will not find time for the devil's work.

Today we live in an age of great pressure. The television, advertising, loose moral standards and permissiveness, all have warning lights before them and it is usually red! How we need to make a covenant with our eyes lest we also fall into serious sin.

We need strong willpower to survive the evils of our society. Don't let Satan demolish our stronghold. If he does, it will lead to tragic consequences and the Lord's displeasure, just as it did with David.

I am so thankful the story doesn't end with his fall. We conclude tomorrow on a much brighter note; David rises again from the ashes.

31 JULY

Rising from the ashes

'I have sinned against the LORD.' 2 Samuel 12:13

RECOMMENDED READING: Psalm 51

We have been considering the life of David. He was a shepherd in the hills of Bethlehem. He was a brave and courageous soldier. He was the author of half of the psalms in the Psalter. He was king over Judah and Israel. He was a man who sunk into immorality and shame. But today we conclude by seeing him rise to new heights by experiencing God's mercy and forgiveness.

6. David restored. Following on from the solemn events of chapter 11, we read in chapter 12 of the prophet Nathan, who was instructed by God to visit David and rebuke him for his sin. He also had the grim task of informing David of the resulting consequence, namely the death of their son. Now follows David's repentance.

We have to turn to Psalm 51 to see the depth of David's grief and remorse for what had happened.

First of all, he acknowledged his sin (v4). This is where we all have to begin, for sin is the barrier between us and Almighty God. There can be no forgiveness without the acknowledgement of our sin.

David then made it clear that his sin was not just against Bathsheba, her husband Uriah and Israel, but primarily against the Lord (2 Samuel 12:13; Psalm 51:4).

He then prayed earnestly for God's cleansing from his sin (Psalm 51:1,2,7).

The stages of David's repentance are the same for us. It begins with conviction, then we make our confession, and finally receive God's cleansing.

Let us thank God this day that we have been shown a way by which we can be forgiven and cleansed from our sin. It is not through works of righteousness that we have done, but through the precious blood of the Lord Jesus Christ which was poured out for us on Calvary's cross.

We may not have the musical skills of David; we may not have the poetic genius of David; we may not have reached the height of royalty as David did, but we can know God's mercy and forgiveness, just as David did.

> 'The joy, O the joy of this glorious thought!
> my sin, not in part but the whole,
> Is nailed to his cross and I bear it no more;
> praise the Lord, praise the Lord, O my soul!'
>
> Horatio G. Spafford (1828–88)

Because of Jesus we can say, 'It is well with my soul.' Hallelujah!

1 AUGUST

Hold fast to the faith

'Seeing then that we have a great High Priest who has passed through the heavens, Jesus the Son of God, let us hold fast our confession.' Hebrews 4:14

RECOMMENDED READING: Hebrews 1:1 – 2:1

The letter to the Hebrews was written to Jewish believers who had come out of Judaism into Christianity but, in order to escape persecution, were considering returning to Judaism. The writer of this letter is encouraging them not to go back, but '… to go on to perfection' (Hebrews 6:1).

There are a number of words the writer uses on a regular basis throughout this letter such as, 'better' (e.g. Hebrews 7:19,22); 'perfect' (e.g. Hebrews 6:1; 7:19,28) and 'heavenly' (e.g. Hebrews 6:4; 8:5; 9:23).

However, there are two words that he uses a number of times in this letter and during the next few days I want to direct our thoughts upon them. They are, 'Let us …'.

We can link this with Hebrews 10:23: 'Let us hold fast the confession of our hope without wavering, for He who promised is faithful.'

The writer was very much aware that these young Christians were facing severe persecution and the temptation to return to their former way of life, under Judaism, was becoming very evident.

This letter was to encourage them not to lose their hold on their newfound faith which they had embraced and professed. He told them to hold firm; grip tight; not to let slip their beliefs, despite present and future circumstances.

He began this letter by exalting the Lord Jesus in the first chapter. In it he reminded them that the Lord Jesus is God's Son (1:2); He is our one and only Mediator (1:3); He is better than the angels (1:5); He is the eternal Creator of the universe (1:10); He is the unchanging one (1:12).

Then in Hebrews 2:1 he told them to give their full attention to the things they had heard so that they do not drift away.

It is sad when you hear or meet believers who are losing their grip on the faith and swerving in other directions.

My message today is the same that was delivered to these scattered young believers 2,000 years ago. Whatever your circumstances, now or in the future, hold fast to the faith you have professed without wavering. Do not go back to your old ways of living but 'go on to perfection' (Hebrews 6:1).

2 AUGUST

Always find time to pray

'Let us therefore come boldly to the throne of grace.' Hebrews 4:16

RECOMMENDED READING: Hebrews 4

We continue with our series on looking at the words 'Let us …' in the book of Hebrews. In Hebrews 4:14 we are reminded that seated at the right hand of the Father in heaven we have a great High Priest whose name is Jesus.

He is the One who is only too well aware of the temptations we face because He has already faced them and endured. The Lord Jesus knows what it is to suffer. He knows what it is to face persecution and ridicule. He knows what it is to be disappointed with people and to be let down, even by close friends. He has faced all the experiences that have come our way and many more beside, but has come through them victoriously.

He now invites us to approach Him and bring our pain, our temptations and our suffering to Him. He is only too willing to hear our cry.

We can come to Him just as we are and as often as we need, and lay our concerns, small or great, at His feet. He can handle them, so don't try to carry them yourself; some are just too heavy to bear.

Joseph M. Scriven (1819–86) wrote,

> 'Oh what peace we often forfeit, O what needless pain we bear,
>   all because we do not carry everything to God in prayer.'

The writer to the Hebrews knew the importance of spending valuable time with God, so he encouraged the believers who read his letter to approach the throne of God with total confidence. He is always ready to receive us and hear our prayers.

There is very little in the world today that we can be confident about but we can know for certain that God does hear our prayers. In fact, He is more eager to hear our prayers than we are to pray.

Therefore, 'Let us draw near … in full assurance of faith' (Hebrews 10:22).

As a good earthly father is ready to hear the requests of his children, so our heavenly Father is always ready to welcome us and listen to our petitions.

> 'Have we trials and temptations, is there trouble anywhere?
>   We should never be discouraged, take it to the Lord in prayer.
>   Can we find a friend so faithful who will all our sorrows share?
>   Jesus knows our every weakness—take it to the Lord in prayer.'
>
>   Joseph M. Scriven

3 AUGUST

Sin will only be a burden to you

'Let us fix our eyes on Jesus, the author and perfecter of our faith.'
Hebrews 12:2, NIV

RECOMMENDED READING: Hebrews 12:1–14

We continue our consideration of the words 'Let us' as we journey through the letter to the Hebrews. We now turn our thoughts to the words in 12:1, 'Let us lay aside every weight, and the sin which so easily ensnares us.'

Before we do, just note the last two verses of chapter 11. In this great chapter, the writer goes back to the dawn of history and lists those great giants of the faith, both men and women, who have overcome despite the great difficulties they faced. He then closes the chapter with the following words (vv.39–40):

'And all these, having obtained a good testimony through faith, did not receive the promise, God having provided something better for us, that they should not be made perfect apart from us.'

When I read those words, I am amazed to discover that you and I are included in this great company of believers. We will inherit the heavenly kingdom with these great men and women. I feel so unworthy of such an honour, especially when I discover that they are waiting for us before we are made perfect together.

As we are surrounded by such a great cloud of witnesses, we are then told to lay aside everything that would hinder us and the sins that entangle us.

Chapter 12:1 conveys to us that we are involved in a spiritual marathon with a precious prize to claim at the end.

Have you ever seen an Olympic athlete run in a race who is grossly overweight, wearing boots, trousers and a heavy jumper, and carrying an umbrella in case it rains? Of course, not

They run with the minimum of weight and with as light clothing as possible. They want nothing to hinder their efforts in attaining the prize they have trained for years to obtain.

In the spiritual marathon, we also are to throw off anything that hinders our progress, especially the sins that so easily entangle us. We are to run free from the burden of sin that so often drags us down so nothing holds us back.

4 AUGUST

Keep pressing on

'Let us run with endurance the race that is set before us.' Hebrews 12:1

RECOMMENDED READING: 2 Timothy 4:1–8

We continue with another occasion when we come across the words 'Let us' and it is also in 12:1.

Whenever I watch the Olympic Games, I am always impressed with the long-distance running. These athletes are so fit as they run marathons, and triathlons. I am impressed by both their stamina and determination to finish the course and win the race.

I would again remind us that these are not sprints, they are endurance races.

Do you remember when you were at school, running the cross country? Did you get a stitch? Did you have legs as heavy as lead as you ran through the mud? Did you ever feel like giving up, or finding a short cut back to school, or even letting everyone pass you, then thumbing a lift? You may have thought about it, but the thought of getting caught out made you carry on and persevere to the end.

You battled on through the pain barrier and the difficult conditions. You knew the rules and kept to them.

The Christian life can be very painful at times. You are let down by people, even those who are known to you; you face times of sickness and adversity, sometimes severe; people you trusted break their promises and disappoint you. Life at times seems so unfair.

So, do you give up and pack it all in? No, you press on; you persevere; you endure to the end, knowing that God will never let you down. He will support you and uphold you during your trial. He will never break His promises to you.

As someone once said, 'When God puts His children in the furnace, He keeps His hand on the thermostat and His eye on the thermometer.'

'Many of life's failures are people who did not realise how close they were to success when they gave up' (Thomas Edison, inventor).[24]

So, the message today is, keep running and never ever give up. No matter how difficult the race at times may be, persevere to the end and you will receive your reward. In the end you will thank God that He gave you the strength to endure to the end.

5 AUGUST

Seeing only Him

'Let us fix our eyes on Jesus.' Hebrews 12:2, NIV

RECOMMENDED READING: John 12:20–36

When we moved into our new home in Fairacre in 2011, our son Mark and his wife Sharon converted an outbuilding into a comfortable bungalow. The land around the bungalow is meadow and has been for hundreds of years.

Mark knew I loved vegetable gardening, so I was told to take as much ground as I needed. However, it was so hard digging it over into separate plots, as the ground was both hard and stony. My family were convinced I would give up but I kept at it day after day, until I had enough land for a variety of vegetables.

So, what kept me going when it was so hard? It definitely was a determination not to let it beat me and to prove my family wrong. But the main reason was the thought of the end product on my dinner table. My eyes were fixed on the finished article.

Why do we keep persevering in the Christian life when the race can be so difficult and demanding? Why do we keep enduring when we face ridicule, abuse and sometimes persecution, even from members of our own family? It is the thought of one day casting our eyes upon Jesus and looking into His wonderful face.

To fix our eyes upon the One who endured such fierce opposition; the One who was willing to bear the awful weight of our sin; the One who faced God's righteous anger instead of us having to face it. To see Him face to face enables and encourages us to keep pressing on.

So, when the battle becomes tough and the journey wearying, turn your thoughts towards Jesus and keep focused upon Him. He will inspire you to continue until your journey has come to its end.

When the apostle Paul wrote these closing words to Timothy in his second letter, he said in 4:7–8:

'I have fought the good fight, I have finished the race, I have kept the faith. Finally, there is laid up for me the crown of righteousness, which the Lord, the righteous Judge, will give to me on that Day, and not to me only but also to all who have loved His appearing.'

6 AUGUST

God accepts reasons but not excuses

'Let us not give up meeting together, as some are in the habit of doing.'
Hebrews 10:25

RECOMMENDED READING: John 20:19–29

When Jesus met with His disciples on the evening of His resurrection, all were present except Thomas. We don't know why he was absent but he was expected to be there. When the disciples brought a report of their meeting with the Lord, Thomas was sceptical and needed physical proof. If he had been present, he would have had the proof. He had to wait a further week before the Lord gently rebuked His disciple by revealing Himself personally to him. The response of Thomas was humbling indeed.

There has sadly been a significant decline in church attendance during my lifetime. This has, in some instances, resulted in the closure of church buildings and the abandonment of evening services. What is extremely concerning is that there is a decline in attendance even among professing Christians. I often wonder what they are doing instead.

How I feel for the pastor/preacher who spends hours in his study preparing food for the flock, who actually have no appetite to receive it. When you lose your appetite, it is a sign that you are sick.

I recently read this quote by Thomas Edison (1847–1931):

> 'Look at your Sunday morning service and see how popular the church is. Look at your evening service and see how popular the preacher is. Look at your prayer meeting and see how popular God is.'[25]

I am aware that there are genuine reasons for people being absent, and God accepts reasons—but not excuses. Remember, God knows where we are and what we are doing.

Let us take the Bible's admonition to our hearts. Don't; please don't give up meeting together, as some are in the habit of doing. If members of the body are absent, then the body can become disabled.

During this time of lockdown, it was good to meet together on Zoom, but as soon as the church doors reopened, I pray you were at the front of the queue. Don't be too comfortable on your sofa with your pot of tea, so that you don't want to leave it. Like the disciples, we should be in the building together to meet with our Lord.

To be back in the building will encourage your pastor, encourage our fellow believers and show we mean business with God. 'For where two or three are gathered together in My Name, I am there in the midst of them' (Matthew 18:20).

Let us be encouragers

'Let us encourage one another—and all the more as you see the Day approaching.' Hebrews 10:25, NIV

RECOMMENDED READING: Hebrews 10:19–25

During the past three days, we have been looking at six occasions where we have come across the words, 'Let us …'. Today we will consider two more, which will conclude our brief series. I will bring the final two occasions together as they convey to us a similar message.

Verse 24 reads, 'Let us consider how we may spur one another on towards love and good deeds' (NIV). Now look at the following verse. 'Let us encourage one another … as you see the Day approaching.' They are both messages of encouragement. We are to spur one another on and encourage each other.

Throughout the Bible we read of certain people who were great encouragers. In the Old Testament we have Caleb, who encouraged the Israelites to go in and possess the land of Canaan. Then we have Ruth from Moab, who was such an encouragement to her mother-in-law Naomi when they returned to Bethlehem.

In the New Testament we have Luke, who was a great support to Paul, caring for his physical needs as well as documenting his travels.

Finally, we have one of my favourite men, Barnabas, who encouraged both Paul and John Mark towards love and good deeds. There are many more we could mention if we had time and space. I fear this is an area where we fall down badly in our Christian ministry today. We tend to be so quick to complain and find fault. How about bringing words of encouragement and spurring one another on? What about a word of encouragement to your pastor and/or church leaders for their labours and the responsibilities they carry? What about a thank you to our youth leaders who faithfully prepare, teach and care for our children and young people? What about a word of thanks to our musicians who are so dedicated morning and evening? And don't forget to thank our church cleaners for keeping the premises clean and tidy?

So, let us encourage and spur one another on towards love and good deeds, for the day is fast approaching when our Lord returns.

Let us remind ourselves that we are not isolated individuals, but a body of believers: Christ's bride.

So let us labour together; let us pray together; let us feed upon God's Word together; let us be joyful together; let us please Him together, so that His Name is glorified throughout the earth. 'Now all who believed were together and had all things in common' (Acts 2:44).

8 AUGUST

Lord teach me how to pray

'Then I set my face toward the Lord God to make request by prayer.'
Daniel 9:3

RECOMMENDED READING: Daniel 2:17–23

Prayer is one of the greatest privileges that have been entrusted to the Christian. Can we fully understand and grasp what it means to address the great Creator of the universe, as a child would speak to their father?

How often we disregard or take lightly this open door into the very presence of God. There are many people, both in the Old and New Testaments, who have set us examples regarding the importance of prayer.

During the next few days, we will be considering the subject of prayer by first turning to the Old Testament and using God's servant Daniel as our model.

1. Daniel prayed in an emergency (Daniel 2:17,18). King Nebuchadnezzar had a dream which greatly troubled him. He called for all his wise men to interpret the dream and at the same time warned them of the consequences if they failed to do so (2:5). The problem for the wise men was that they not only had to tell the King the interpretation, but, also, the dream itself. It was impossible for any man to do such a thing.

The King, therefore, started to enforce his decree and the order to kill all the wise men began to be carried out (2:13). The concern for Daniel was that both he and his friends were also being sought, which would bring about a similar fate.

In v.16, Daniel asked the king for time and his request was granted. He returned to his house and shared the crisis with his companions. A vital time of prayer began, and Almighty God responded by revealing to Daniel both the king's dream and its interpretation.

When times of emergency come our way, who else can we look to? Where else can we turn? We can only turn our thoughts to the God of heaven from where all our help comes. Stephen, when making his defence before the Council of the Sanhedrin in Acts 7:55, didn't look towards his enemies for help, he looked towards heaven.

History confirms that all God's true servants, in times of great danger and uncertainty, looked towards the only One who could help them in their time of need. We should be doing exactly the same as our help comes from God alone.

9 AUGUST

Prayer should be personal and intimate

'And I prayed to the LORD my God.' Daniel 9:4

RECOMMENDED READING: Daniel 9:1–19

We are using God's servant Daniel as our model for prayer. Yesterday we saw how we need to pray in an emergency. Today we consider two further aspects of prayer.

2. Daniel prayed every day (Daniel 6:10). In fact, he prayed three times each day. Daniel kept in close and regular communion with God. He needed to know what the Almighty would say to him and would not take any action until he was entirely sure of the instructions that God conveyed to him. When he was certain, then there would be no delay in carrying them out.

How we need to keep in close contact with God on a regular basis throughout each day. A daily, regular quiet time is vital if fellowship with God is to be maintained. If we are not in constant touch with God, how can we know what instructions He wishes to convey to us?

3. Daniel prayed when situations demanded it (Daniel 9). There were regular times of prayer for Daniel, but also special times when the occasion required it. In chapter 9 we have Daniel confessing his sin and the sins of his people. But he is also making specific requests to his God.

In this chapter we are taught how to pray. Read it with care!

Here is a man who was regular, biblical, thoughtful, humble and specific in his prayer life. What an excellent pattern to follow!

- Daniel took prayer seriously: 'Then I set my face toward the Lord God' (v.3). He showed a clear sign of determination. He was doing important business with God. This was no casual and easy-going attitude. This was to be a serious encounter with the Almighty.

Do we take prayer seriously, or are we just laid back and come before God when we have the time and inclination to do so? We must approach God with confidence, but also with a humble and contrite spirit.

- Daniel made his prayer personal: 'I prayed to the Lord my God' (v.4). In Psalm 23:1 David talks about the Lord being my Shepherd. All the godly men and women in the Bible had this relationship with their God. It was close, intimate and personal.

May Daniel's prayer give us a longing for a close communion with God and a determination to take prayer seriously at all times.

10 AUGUST

A correct view of God

'And I prayed to the LORD my God, and made confession, and said, "O Lord, great and awesome God, who keeps His covenant and mercy with those who love Him, and with those who keep His commandments."' Daniel 9:4

RECOMMENDED READING: Psalm 103

One of the concerns I have is that, if we are not careful and biblical in our thinking, we can so easily present to people a distorted view of God. We create in our minds a God as we wish Him to be and not as He really is.

During the next two days I want us to consider four characteristics of God that Daniel refers to in his prayer. These should bring us much encouragement. Daniel presents to us a right view of Almighty God.

1. God is awesome. The word 'awesome' is being widely used by people today, but I fear out of context. If an athlete breaks a world record, that is awesome. If a footballer scores a great goal, that is awesome. When a new high-powered car comes off the production line, wow, that's awesome! Yes, it's a great feat of engineering … but awesome?

I have come to the conclusion that this word only applies to Almighty God. In v.4 of chapter 9, Daniel declares, 'O Lord, great and awesome God.' No one else, and nothing else is in that realm. Never make God smaller or less powerful than He is. Even His words cannot outshine Him. He is greater than even His creation. The sun, moon and stars cannot be compared to Him. God is powerful, majestic and glorious. God is truly awesome. There is none that can be compared with Him in heaven or on earth.

2. God is faithful. When we consider man, we have to acknowledge that the word 'unfaithfulness' is a better description of his character. We see this regularly in marriage, in politics and, sadly, even in spiritual matters.

But when we turn our thoughts and attention towards the Almighty, we say with total confidence that our God is faithful in all things and at all times.

In v.4, Daniel says, He 'keeps His covenant and mercy with those who love Him'. God is faithful to His Word, to His promises and to His covenant. He will not and He cannot break either. Even when we are unfaithful to Him, He remains faithful to us; He cannot change His character.

> 'Praise Him for His grace and favour To our father's in distress;
> Praise Him still the same for ever, Slow to chide and swift to bless;
> Praise Him! Praise Him! Glorious in His faithfulness.'
>
> Henry Francis Lyte (1793–1847)

God is always listening

'Now therefore our God, hear the prayer of Your servant.' Daniel 9:17

RECOMMENDED READING: 1 John 1

We are considering four characteristics in the prayer of Daniel. Yesterday we saw that God is awesome and faithful. Today, as we conclude, we note that God is forgiving and listening.

3. God is forgiving. In v.9 Daniel says, 'To the Lord our God belong mercy and forgiveness, though we have rebelled against Him.'

Despite His people's rebellion and wickedness, God continually demonstrated mercy and forgiveness to His people Israel. Throughout the Old Testament, God's servants acknowledged this remarkable attribute of God, but it first required genuine repentance on the part of His people. Forgiveness follows repentance. The same principle applies to us today.

1 John 1:9 says, 'If we confess our sins, He is faithful and just to forgive us our sins.' Here we have three attributes of God in one short verse.

All our sins, past, present and future are blotted out and removed from God's memory, never to be recalled. All this is possible because of Calvary. Forgiveness is found at the cross, where Jesus carried all our iniquities.

He took upon Himself God's anger; the anger that should have been directed towards us, but grace diverted it to Christ. The depth of God's forgiveness will never be fully grasped this side of eternity.

4. God is listening. The fact that God knows, sees and hears everything should bring terror to the unbeliever, but great comfort to the Christian.

Verse 19 says, 'O Lord, hear! ... O Lord, listen and act!' God hears the cry of His people day and night, whether we pray in private or in public. God listens and acts.

Governments have used a catchphrase: 'We are listening.' They may be, but they rarely act upon what they hear. Almighty God says to us, 'I am listening.' When He does, He always acts.

Daniel knew His prayer would be heard. Why? What gave him such assurance? In v.23 of chapter 9, God says to Daniel, 'I have come to tell you, for you are greatly beloved.'

Are you a Christian? Then God hears your prayers also. Why? Because you too are greatly loved by Him.

12 AUGUST

Spend time alone with God

'He went out to the mountain to pray, and continued all night in prayer to God.' Luke 6:12

RECOMMENDED READING: Matthew 6:5–13

During the past months we have considered a number of prayers recorded in the Old Testament, such as the prayer of Nehemiah and recently the prayer of Daniel. The next two days we will consider the example of our Lord as far as His prayer life is concerned.

There are many passages we could turn to, but I want to look at one particular event in the life of Jesus which is recorded in Mark 1. The day before the Sabbath, He had called four fishermen to follow Him (vv.16–20).

Now, being the Sabbath, He took His disciples into Capernaum and entered the synagogue to teach the people (Mark 1:21). He clearly impressed them with the words that He spoke. This man was so different from the scribes, who they heard on most Sabbath days. This man was understandable and His teaching was clear and direct. He also spoke with conviction and believed every word that He uttered. His message was also relevant to each hearer and applicable to their situation.

It is important that all preachers make their message understandable and relevant to people today. It should also go forth with enthusiasm and in the power of the Holy Spirit.

People, who heard Him, were not just impressed by His words, but they were amazed when He healed a man who had an unclean spirit. Even unclean spirits do what He tells them.

When He came out of the synagogue, He entered the house of Simon and Andrew, and found Simon's mother-in-law sick with a fever. When Jesus took her by the hand, not only did the fever leave her, but she was able to prepare a meal for them.

His fame was quickly spreading. By evening people had come with their sick friends, and Jesus healed them. What a day! No time to rest. Jesus was in need of a good night's sleep.

However, we read that early in the morning He was up and found a solitary place where He could have communion with His Heavenly Father.

In the busy world in which we live, we all need time for rest, but it is vital that we also regain our spiritual strength from times of communion with God.

13 AUGUST

We need discipline and devotion in prayer

'Now in the morning, having risen a long while before daylight, He went out and departed to a solitary place; and there He prayed.' Mark 1:35

RECOMMENDED READING: John 17

Yesterday we saw the need of our Lord for communion with God following a busy day preaching and healing those who were sick. We also need times when we can get alone with God following the stress and pressure which come from hectic lives.

There are three things we can learn from today's verse in Mark 1.

1. Jesus showed determination. 'Having risen a long while before daylight …' After a busy day doing His Father's work, one would have expected Jesus to have had a lie-in. But this had been a very short night, not because He was restless and couldn't sleep, but because He had an appointment with His Father that He couldn't and wouldn't miss.

It can take great determination and discipline to rise early. For most of us, rising early doesn't come naturally—staying in bed does! For some, rising early is a great struggle. I will not mention any names to protect the guilty! However, the benefits of rising early are immense.

There are some who prefer to have their quiet time with God later in the day. The most important thing is that we are disciplined in setting aside time each day to hear from God through His Word and speak to Him through prayer.

2. He showed detachment. 'He went out and departed to a solitary place.'

He went to a place where He was alone. He needed to be detached from a busy and corrupt society. He didn't want to be disturbed.

We must find time and space to be alone and undisturbed. Don't let anything encroach upon those precious moments.

Life today is so hectic and stressful. We need to come away from the rat race that demands much of our time.

3. He showed devotion. We are told, 'He prayed.' He didn't rise to catch up with the latest news—He knew that anyway. He rose early and went out to pray. Jesus was devoted to His Father, so communion with Him was vital.

A husband who is devoted to his wife longs to spend time with her. There can be little love in a marriage if a couple do not spend time sharing together. Sometimes we are just too busy, even for God.

If we, as believers, are devoted to Almighty God, then prayer should be a priority. Communion with Him can radically change every area of our life.

14 AUGUST

God meets our needs not our wants

'The LORD is my shepherd; I shall not want.' Psalm 23:1

RECOMMENDED READING: John 10:1–18

When I preached on the Psalm 23, I was asked to include it in this book. Of all the seventy-four Psalms that David penned, this is the most well-known, and was very personal to him. In the NIV it reads, 'The LORD is my shepherd, I lack nothing.'

During the next few days, I want to share with you a number of things that we shall not lack if the Lord is our Shepherd.

1. I shall not lack provision. 'I shall not want' (v.1). In v.2 we read, 'He makes me to lie down in green pastures.' The key word in that phrase is the adjective 'green'.

I have had the privilege over nearly forty years of taking parties to the land of Israel. I always visit during April/May when the winter rains have usually come to an end. In the spring the flowers are beautiful and the grass is lush and green.

The word 'green' signifies growth, abundance and provision. When I ponder over those words, I realise how good God has been to us. We all have far more than we deserve. If we had what we deserved we would be like paupers. God truly has been good to us, meeting all our daily needs.

Paul wrote in Philippians 4:19, 'My God shall supply all your need according to His riches in glory by Christ Jesus.'

We have many wants, but very few needs. God has not promised to meet our wants, but He has promised to meet our needs.

Our daughter, who lives outside Durban, sent us a recording of an interview with a delightful lady who lives in a poor township in South Africa. I am aware I have used this illustration earlier in the year but find it so relevant and challenging to us in these affluent days. Her home consists of one room, which is like a shack, closely packed together with hundreds more. She and her three children have no bathroom or shower; she just places a large bowl in the middle of the room and pour water over themselves. Her garden, which she is so proud of, consists of one plant which stands in a pot near a window. They sleep, eat, live and wash in this one small room. Yet in the recording she says, with a huge beam on her face, 'I am a Christian and God's economy is always good.'

May God forgive us when we complain and help us to be thankful for every provision that we receive from Him.

15 AUGUST

Knowing the peace of God

'He leads me beside the still waters.' Psalm 23:2

RECOMMENDED READING: Philippians 4:4–9

Yesterday we began considering Psalm 23 and the things we shall not lack if the Lord is our Shepherd.

2. I shall not lack peace. 'He leads me beside the still waters' (v.2). The key word to this phrase is again the adjective 'still.' We can also us 'quiet' or 'peaceful' waters.

In the autumn of 2019, we saw the counties of Herefordshire, Worcestershire and Gloucestershire experience severe flooding. The Avon and Severn rivers burst their banks with devastating force. Our local village of Wellington was cut off for a number of days with vehicles unable to enter or leave.

The power and force of water is amazing and we witnessed the damage first-hand. Yet these same rivers attract visitors from all over the country. The beauty, tranquillity and peaceful setting is difficult to equal anywhere else in the country.

We are living in a world that is turbulent and unpredictable. It is a world that is deprived of peace. However, despite the uncertainty outside, the Christian possesses the peace of God which passes all human understanding. This is a peace that only God Himself can give.

So don't let outside circumstances ever rob you of that peace. Just let God lead you beside the quiet waters and all will be well.

3. I shall not lack restoration. 'He restores my soul' (v.3). There are times in our Christian life when we fail and let God down badly. We grieve Him and know He is disappointed with us. Our relationship with Him is damaged and our spiritual walk is impaired.

I am so thankful that when we let Him down, He doesn't leave us to wallow in despair. He is a God who lifts up the fallen and raises those who are in the pit of despair. He is always encouraging us to do better and longs that we seek a closer relationship with Him.

I am so thankful that our God is so patient and merciful towards us. He encourages and helps us every step of the way. He brings us back to that relationship we once had with Him and never gives up on us. His peace is restored to us.

> 'Stayed upon Jehovah hearts are fully blessed,
> Finding as He promised perfect peace and rest.'
>
> Frances Ridley Havergal (1836–79)

16 AUGUST

Look to God for direction

'I will guide you with My eye.' Psalm 32:8

RECOMMENDED READING: Proverbs 3

We continue our thoughts on Psalm 23 looking at those things we shall not lack if the Lord is our Shepherd.

4. I shall not lack direction. 'He leads me in the paths of righteousness' (v.3). When I heard the call of God as a teenager, my desire was to follow Him. I thought the Christian life would be easy and my problems solved in a stroke, but I soon realised how challenging the future was going to be. I needed help—lots of it.

A dear elderly gentleman must have noticed I was struggling and gave me a verse of scripture that has been a blessing to me over the past sixty years: 'Trust in the LORD with all your heart, and lean not on your own understanding; in all your ways acknowledge Him, and He shall direct your paths' (Proverbs 3:5,6).

My message to you this. Trust in the Lord always, and though He may lead you around, He will never lead you astray. This especially applies to those who are young in the faith; seek God's direction and guidance in all things.

5. I shall not lack His presence. 'Yea, though I walk through the valley of the shadow of death, I will fear no evil; for You are with me' (v.4). This Psalm is often sung or read at funeral services—probably because the word 'death' is mentioned. Yet for me, *death* is not the key word: it is the word *shadow*.

Shortly after I was appointed General Secretary, of what is now Day One Christian Ministries, my first tour was to the Isle of Skye and northern Scotland. This was new territory for me so a map book was an important companion. When we reached Loch Lomond, the weather deteriorated considerably. We had to contend with pouring rain and poor visibility. As we journeyed through Glen Coe, those great mountains gave us both an eerie feeling. When we arrived at the end of Glen Coe, Kathryn asked me never to bring her on that journey again—I always listen to my wife.

Ten days later, I knew I had to take that same journey home so without a word I went for it. Kathryn loved the journey and wanted to stop regularly to take photos. On the return journey the sky was blue and the sun cast huge shadows across the mountains.

You will only see a shadow when the sun shines, so when we draw near to the end of life's journey, look for the shadow. When you see it, the Son will be shining.

17 AUGUST

God's rod to correct and staff to comfort

'Your rod and Your staff they comfort me.' Psalm 23:4

RECOMMENDED READING: 2 Corinthians 1:1–16

So far, we have thought about five things that we shall not lack if the Lord is our Shepherd. Today we look at another blessing that God gives to His children.

6. We shall not lack comfort. 'Your rod and Your staff they comfort me' (v.4). What a great comfort our Shepherd is to all His children. To know that He will never leave us, nor forsake us, gives great assurance and peace to troubled souls.

Loneliness can be an unpleasant experience for many people. Yet, for the Christian, though we feel it we also know that the Lord is near.

During my travels I have been privileged to share the home and fellowship with many elderly believers. In our conversations they will testify to the fact that, though they live alone, they never feel alone for the Comforter is always constantly with them.

There are times when we face anxiety and concern over friends and loved ones, especially when they are far away from us.

We also become anxious about our work; meeting financial obligations with little resources; ensuring the family are provided for during times of need; our health or the health of loved ones.

How thankful we should be that through all the changing scenes of our life, our Heavenly Father is the 'God of all comfort' (2 Corinthians 1:3).

Then there are times of bereavement when we greatly feel the loss of someone who, throughout life, has been very close to us.

We all handle bereavement in different ways but the greatest comfort for the Christian is knowing that we do not handle the experience alone. 2 Corinthians 1:4 says that He '… comforts us in all our tribulation'.

When we have experienced His comfort during difficult times, we can then comfort those who need comforting. Only those who have suffered loneliness can comfort the lonely. Only those who have endured great pain can comfort those who suffer. Only those who have battled with anxiety know what it is to help and support the anxious. Only those who have lost loved ones can truly comfort those who mourn.

Our Good Shepherd understands every experience we go though, and His rod and staff are always available to bring us the comfort we need.

18 AUGUST

Protection from the evil one assured

'You prepare a table before me in the presence of my enemies.' Psalm 23:5

RECOMMENDED READING: Philippians 4

We continue our journey through Psalm 23 and today see how secure and joyful we are in His care.

7. I shall not lack protection. 'You prepare a table before me in the presence of my enemies (v.5). God's servant David knew what it was to have His life constantly under threat. King Saul hunted him through the mountains of southern Israel but God protected him on every occasion. Even his own son, Absalom, planned to take David's life when he fled from Jerusalem.

Daniel, another of God's faithful servants, was protected when he was thrown into the den of lions. His close friends were also protected during their time in the fiery furnace.

Paul was protected by God from the Jews on the occasions when they tried to take his life. Our Lord Jesus was protected by His Father until His work was complete.

We too will be protected from the evil one until our work is finished here on earth. While we are here, He is before us, behind us, above us, beneath us, beside us, around us and, most of all, within us. Surely that must be good enough for every believer. We are safe in the hollow of His great hand, both for time and eternity.

8. I shall not lack joy. 'You anoint my head with oil; my cup runs over' (v.5). There is a close association between oil and joy. Hebrews 1:9 says, 'Your God has anointed you with the oil of gladness.'

Despite the persecution and trials that some Christians throughout the world have to face, their joy is evident through their trials. We also should be joyful people for we have much to be thankful and praise God for, especially our eternal destiny.

When I read the apostle Paul's account of his many trials in 2 Corinthians 11:23-28 and then read his letter of joy to the church at Philippi, I see a man who rejoiced in his sufferings and encouraged others to do the same.

Whatever our circumstances in life, we should be joyful people; for we have bread to eat of that the world knows nothing about. May our head be anointed with the oil of gladness.

19 AUGUST

A kingdom that will last for ever

'Surely goodness and mercy shall follow me all the days of my life.' Psalm 23:6

RECOMMENDED READING: Psalm 23

We now come to the conclusion of this well-known psalm of David. We have considered a number of things we shall not lack if the Lord is our Shepherd and today turn to the final two.

9. I shall not lack His divine blessing. 'Surely goodness and mercy shall follow me all the days of my life' (v.6). We may have been endowed with a beautiful house and great riches; we may hold a position of unrivalled power; we may have enjoyed excellent health; we may have a great personality that has made us popular with friends and colleagues. But what are these compared with knowing God's favour and divine blessing upon our lives.

I have been greatly privileged to meet Christians who have had little of the world's goods, but they have been clearly blessed with heavenly riches that cannot be bought or taken from them.

To experience God's favour and blessing upon our life exceeds anything this world can offer us.

Goodness and mercy are monuments of God's grace and cannot be compared with earthly treasures. These fade through time, but goodness and mercy will always follow us to the very end of our days.

10. I shall not lack a heavenly home. 'I will dwell in the house of the Lord for ever' (v.6). What a glorious prospect!

There we will have no more tears, or pain, or mourning, or sin, and no more death. But best of all is the knowledge that we will spend eternity with our Good Shepherd for ever. This is the Christian's guarantee.

Heaven is God's gift which cannot be bought or earned. It has grace stamped across the package and on the label are the words, 'With love'.

Motorbike stuntman, Evel Knievel, who died in 2007, said the following:

> 'All the money in the world can't buy your way into heaven.
> All the money in the world can't buy your way out of hell.'[26]

So let us use that money towards the growth of a kingdom that will last for ever.

Is the Lord your Shepherd? If He is, then you will lack absolutely nothing. No good thing will He withhold from those who trust Him. We have received much, both materially and spiritually. All God desires in return is our grateful and thankful hearts.

20 AUGUST

Working together for the gospel

'He [Paul] found a certain Jew named Aquila, born in Pontus, who had recently come from Italy with his wife Priscilla.' Acts 18:2

RECOMMENDED READING: 1 John 4:7–21

In Acts 18 the apostle Paul is introduced to a remarkable couple. They are always mentioned together; always sharing their daily work; always sharing in the Lord's work. Acts 18:3 informs us that they were tentmakers by profession. During the next few days, I want to share some thoughts about this amazing couple.

1. **They were often on the move.** Our first introduction to them is in the city of Corinth (Acts 18:1). They arrived there from Rome due to the persecution of the Jews (v.2). Paul lodged with them because he also was a tentmaker by trade. I can imagine the topics they covered in their conversation as they laboured together.

In v.18 Paul set sail for Syria, and Aquila and Priscilla went with him. In v.19 they journeyed to Ephesus. Paul continued on his journey but Aquila and Priscilla remained, as God had further work for them in the city.

It is worth noting that when Paul wrote his letter to the Romans, they were back in Rome once again (Romans 16:3). It was abundantly clear that they did not count this world to be their home. They did not settle permanently anywhere but were always on the move. As Hebrews 11:16 reminds us, 'they desire a better, that is, a heavenly country.' In this world they would settle where God could use them, or where His servants needed them.

It is of great concern that this world is becoming too much like home for many Christians. They build their palaces and extend them, but forget it is only temporary.

We need to be reminded over and over again that this world is not our home. We are citizens of a better country which will be our eternal home.

'Here we have no continuing city, but we seek the one to come' (Hebrews 13:14), and what a great day that will be when we take up permanent residence.

> 'When I stand before the throne,
> Dressed in beauty not my own,
> When I see Thee as Thou art,
> Love Thee with unsinning heart,
> Then, Lord, shall I fully know,
> Not till then, how much I owe.'
>
> Robert Murray M'Cheyne (1813–43)

21 AUGUST

An open home and open heart

'Do not forget to entertain strangers, for by so doing some have unwittingly entertained angels.' Hebrews 13:2

RECOMMENDED READING: 1 John 4:4–21

We are looking into the lives of Aquila and Priscilla who, throughout their lives, served the Lord so faithfully. Yesterday we saw the extent of their travels supporting Paul in his ministry. Today we consider two further characteristics which are an example to us all.

2. They had an open home. Paul wrote from Ephesus to the church at Corinth. In his first letter in 16:19 he says, 'Aquila and Priscilla greet you … with the church that is in their house.' Perhaps a year later, Paul wrote from Corinth to believers in Rome. In Romans 16:3,5 we read, 'Greet Priscilla and Aquila … likewise greet the church that is in their house.' We are to be people who are given to hospitality.

During my early childhood, my parents always had an open home. Evangelists, missionaries and others stayed with us. I remember Bible stories being read to me during the evenings. My young life was influenced by those who stayed in our home.

Could I give this message to young couples? Be hospitable and have an open home. You will be the ones who gain. You may be giving but will receive far more in return.

3. They were faithful in love and loyalty. Paul tells us, in Romans 16:4, that Aquila and Priscilla 'risked their own necks for my life'. That is the extent to which love should go.

Faithfulness—what a beautiful characteristic to possess. Yet, in society today, so few seem to demonstrate it in their relationship with others. To be faithful is to follow in the footsteps of our Saviour, who demonstrated this characteristic in every area of His life. Jesus wasn't gambling with his life. Jesus wasn't protecting His life; He freely gave it up. He willingly took the road to Calvary because He was faithful in love and loyalty to you and me. What an example He set us. We should follow in His steps, for that's exactly what Aquila and Priscilla did. They were faithful to God's servant and demonstrated it by the love and loyalty they showed him.

1 John 4:7 says, 'Beloved, let us love one another.' This is a sign of our love for God. Be loyal to the household of faith, for they are our brothers and sisters in Christ.

Could we go even to the extent of risking our lives for one another? I leave you with that question to ponder.

22 AUGUST

Guiding the wayward in the right way

'When Aquila and Priscilla heard him, they took him aside and explained to him the way of God more accurately.' Acts 18:26

RECOMMENDED READING: Acts 18:1–3, 24–28

4. They guided Apollos in the Scriptures. At Ephesus there was a man born in Alexandria called Apollos. He was a learned man, who preached with great fervour but, sadly, his theology was incomplete.

One day, Apollos was speaking boldly in the synagogue and Aquila and Priscilla heard him. He undoubtedly had the gift of oratory but needed guidance in doctrinal matters.

So, what did they do? Attack his preaching in public? No! Acts 18:26 tells us that, 'They took him aside and explained to him the way of God more accurately.'

How wise and gracious they were in dealing with his shortcomings. We need to learn from their example. How quickly we find fault with young believers when they don't live up to our expectations.

We can even do the same with mature believers. If they are incomplete in their theology, we so quickly go for the jugular and lay it on. So many then become discouraged and feel like throwing in the towel. We can be so ungracious and lack a loving spirit.

Let us take a leaf out of this couples' book and be wise and considerate. It is important to note that they did not correct Apollos publicly so that others heard; they took him aside and did it privately. How wise they were.

Note the results of their godly attitude. When Apollos crossed to Achaia, the brethren wrote to the disciples encouraging them to receive Apollos.

Also, in the latter part of vv.27 and 28: 'He [Apollos] greatly helped those who had believed through grace; for he vigorously refuted the Jews publicly, showing from the Scriptures that Jesus is the Christ.'

The question we could ask is this: would vv.27–28 have been written if Aquila and Priscilla had acted unwisely toward Apollos? We might be telling a different story.

I find this a great personal challenge. How we treat people can affect both their future and the future work of God. It can advance it or curtail it; strengthen it or weaken it.

Let us be people who are wise and gracious because our words and actions do affect others and, also, God's kingdom.

23 AUGUST

Labouring together for Christ

'Greet Priscilla and Aquila, my fellow workers in Christ Jesus.' Romans 16:3

RECOMMENDED READING: Romans 16

We have been looking at a godly couple who travelled widely for the cause of Christ; who had an open home; who were faithful in love and loyalty; and who guided Apollos in the Scriptures.

It is therefore not surprising that, when we read Paul's final chapter to the church at Rome, which lists those who had been a support to him, Priscilla and Aquila were top of the list. Paul had such a high regard for this couple that he says in Romans 16:4, '… to whom not only I give thanks, but also all the churches of the Gentiles'.

Today we turn our thoughts to one final attribute of this godly couple that meant so much to Paul and many others.

5. They worked together. This couple are mentioned seven times in the Bible and each time they are mentioned together. They worked in tandem. What a partnership! What an example to every married Christian couple.

It is worth noting that on five of the seven occasions, Priscilla is mentioned first. I thank God for the valuable ministry of godly women, whether they are married or single. I dread to contemplate the state of many of our churches today if it was not for the labours and enthusiasm of Christian women. I wish there were more men like them.

They have my utmost respect as they work in often difficult and discouraging situations. Never underestimate their contributions; we must never take their labours for granted. Our churches should value the role that both single and married women play in the church.

So here we have Aquila and Priscilla working together for the cause of Christ. They present a clear message to all married couples as to how they should live and work in unity for the growth of God's kingdom here on earth.

They were a great encouragement to the apostle Paul. He relished the times of fellowship he had with them.

The early church was strengthened by the example of this godly couple, who worked tirelessly together for the advancement of the gospel.

> 'Blest be the tie that binds
> Our hearts in Christian love;
> The fellowship of kindred minds
> Is like to that above.'

John Fawcett (1739–1817)

24 AUGUST

On to victory

'By faith they passed through the Red Sea as by dry land, whereas the Egyptians, attempting to do so, were drowned.' Hebrews 11:29

RECOMMENDED READING: Hebrews 11:23–29

Today we are turning to a very important event in the life of both Moses and the children of Israel. We will be considering the great victory which God gave to His servant and His people, Israel, as Moses led them through the Red Sea on dry land.

Immediately we notice in the account in Hebrews 11:23–28 that it is the faith of Moses that is emphasised. But, when we come to v.29, it is the faith of Moses and of the children of Israel which is emphasised. We read, 'By faith they passed through the Red Sea.' It was Moses' faith and their faith too.

How important it was for Moses to be obedient to the Lord. If he had disobeyed, then he would have led multitudes of others to do the same and Israel would not have survived.

A tremendous responsibility rests upon those whom God has appointed to positions of leadership. It is vital that those in leadership are living close to God and, 'by faith', carry out His will.

The children of Israel were often a foolish people but, under the leadership of Moses, 'By faith they passed through the Red Sea' (Hebrews 11:29). What a great Exodus that was!

Just imagine close to two and a half million people pursued by Pharaoh and his elite army. Picture that vast multitude of men, women and children hemmed in, with the Red Sea ahead of them and the enemy behind.

No wonder they were fearful and prayed for help. Exodus 14:10 says, 'And when Pharaoh drew near, the children of Israel lifted their eyes, and behold, the Egyptians marched after them. So they were very afraid, and the children of Israel cried out to the LORD.'

They had cried out before and they would do it again. This was yet another impossible situation facing them and there would be many more to come. Man's desperation is always God's opportunity to demonstrate His power.

In this triumphant victory over Pharaoh and his army, we will be considering during the next three days some aspects of a triumphant faith.

> 'Thine be the glory, risen, conquering Son,
>   Endless is the victory Thou o'er death hast won.'
> Edmond Louis Budry (1854–1932)

25 AUGUST

Faith overcomes our fears

'Have I not commanded you? Be strong and of good courage; do not be afraid, nor be dismayed, for the LORD your God is with you wherever you go.' Joshua 1:9

RECOMMENDED READING: Exodus 14:5–14

We return to the account of the crossing of the Red Sea under the leadership of God's servant Moses. This was an important event in the life of both Moses and the children of Israel.

Professor Verna Wright was a good friend of ours and also a vice-president of the Lord's Day Observance Society. Verna was professor of Rheumatology at Leeds University. He was also a founder of Young Life and United Beach Missions. All his correspondence concluded with the words, 'On to Victory.'

1. **A victorious faith is a faith that is far greater than our fears.** Just note the first words Moses spoke to the children of Israel (Exodus 14:13): 'Do not be afraid.'

It was natural for them to be fearful. I am sure if we had been among them our reaction would be no different. Yet, if our trust is in Almighty God, how unnecessary it is for us to be fearful.

It is said that there are 365 occasions in the Bible when the words, 'Do not be afraid', or something similar, are recorded: one for every day of the year. Many of these come at very critical times in the lives of God's people.

- *Our Saviour's birth:* 'The angel said to them, "Do not be afraid, for behold, I bring you good tidings of great joy which will be to all people"' (Luke 2:10).

- *Our Saviour's resurrection:* 'But the angel answered and said to the women, "Do not be afraid, for I know that you seek Jesus who was crucified. He is not here; for He is risen, as He said"' (Matthew 28:5–6).

A truly victorious faith removes any fear from us. This does not mean that we are careless and foolish with our own life or the lives of others. It means that when challenges come our way and the enemy is about to attack, we must learn to so trust in God, that we are able to say with Isaiah, 'Behold, God is my salvation, I will trust and not be afraid' (Isaiah 12:2).

When doubts and fears arise let us remember that we are, 'On to victory!'

26 AUGUST

Now was the time to act

'Moses said to the people, "Do not be afraid. Stand still, and see the salvation of the LORD, which He will accomplish for you today."' Exodus 14:13

RECOMMENDED READING: Exodus 14:21–31

We continue looking at the great victory God gave to His servant Moses and His people Israel.

2. A victorious faith trusts God to work. Exodus 14:14 says, 'The Lord will fight for you, and you shall hold your peace.'

When we find ourselves trapped at a dead end, with no way out, how difficult it is to just do nothing (v.13) and say nothing (v.14), if that is God's will. It is much easier to prepare to fight our enemies, than to wait and do nothing but trust.

A victorious faith leaves the whole issue in the hands of God. He has the power. He gives the victory. He alone deserves the praise. 1 Corinthians 15:57 says, 'But thanks be to God, who gives us the victory through our Lord Jesus Christ.'

Do you feel trapped with no way out? Have you issues that have no answer? Just turn your eyes upon the Lord and trust in Him. He won't let you down.

3. A victorious faith is ready to go into action. Exodus 14:15 tells us that there is a time when praying has to stop and action must begin: 'And the Lord said to Moses, "Why do you cry to Me? Tell the children of Israel to go forward."'

There are some people who go on praying about an issue when they should be doing something about it. There is a time to pray and a time to act.

Now prayer is vitally important and I would not want to underestimate its importance in any way. We must begin by pleading with God on our knees. But when He has made His will clear to us, the next step is to do what He tells us.

The Lord told Moses, 'Go forward', and there was only one thing to do, and that was to obey His instructions.

Is it possible that you are still praying about an issue, when God has made it very clear that now is the time to do something about it? What may be needed is action.

27 AUGUST

Keep right on to the end of the road

'He [Jesus] said to the man, "Stretch out your hand."' Mark 3:5

RECOMMENDED READING: Luke 6:6–10

We have been looking at an important event in the life of both Moses and the children of Israel. At the Red Sea they witnessed an amazing victory over their enemies. God's power was displayed before their very eyes. We conclude our thoughts with two final considerations.

4. A victorious faith steps out on the seemingly impossible. In Exodus 14:21 we read, 'Moses stretched out his hand ... the Lord caused the sea to go back.' When Moses obeyed the instructions given to him, he was showing his total confidence in Almighty God. He was relying on His promises.

Exodus 14:16 says, 'But lift up your rod, and stretch out your hand over the sea and divide it. And the children of Israel shall go on dry ground through the midst of the sea.'

Humanly speaking, the situation was quite impossible; nothing such as this had happened before. But faith laughs at impossibilities and cries, 'It shall be done!' So, despite the situation, Moses obeyed and God began to act.

Is there some impossible 'Red Sea' in your life? Remember, what is impossible to you is possible to Him. Depend upon Him and be obedient to all He says to you.

5. A victorious faith endures to the end. In Exodus 14:22 we have a picture of God's people passing through the Red Sea: 'So the children of Israel went into the midst of the sea on the dry ground, and the waters were a wall to them on their right hand and on their left.'

They needed a strong faith, not only to step out, but to step in, to step on, and to step through. Every step had trust written across it.

Fear said, 'Suppose the walls of water collapse and we are all drowned?' But faith replied, 'They cannot, for God has spoken and He will keep His promise to us.'

As we conclude, look up Numbers 23:19: 'God is not a man, that He should lie, nor a son of man, that He should repent. Has He said, and will He not do? Or has He spoken, and will He not make it good?'

God will never let you down. He who has promised is faithful to the end.

28 AUGUST

Lessons from the animals

'But now ask the beasts, and they will teach you.' Job 12:7

RECOMMENDED READING: Genesis 1:20–25

We often call them dumb animals, but Almighty God, in His great wisdom, has much to teach us through them, if only we are willing to listen.

1. The leopard. The leopard is mentioned eight times in the Bible, and we can see that it is an amazing animal. It is one of South Africa's big five. It is a very agile animal that can jump forward 20 feet (6 metres) and can leap upwards 10 feet (3 metres). It can run up to 36 mph (58 km/h).

The leopard is adaptable in its eating habits; it can eat beetles and zebras. It is also very cunning. It has a scent that is sweet and, because of this, other animals are attracted to its aroma. When they are in range, they are caught and devoured.

So here is our first lesson and it is a very important one, which gives to us clear warnings. The devil has an attractive aroma which is pleasant and tempting. However, when the victims are caught, it isn't long before they are devoured. Sadly, even Christians have been enticed and caught by his crafty schemes. The message to us all is this: be aware of him at all times.

Despite the many things a leopard can do, Jeremiah asks in 13:23: 'Can … the leopard change its spots?' It's a rhetorical question as the answer is obvious. A leopard was born with its spots. They can be neither scrubbed off nor scratched off. No amount of vanishing cream can get rid of these spots; they are permanent.

Human beings can be wise and clever. They have a will to make choices and the power to influence others. They have hearts that are brave and muscles that are strong. They have mouths that speak; ears that hear; and eyes that see.

But we have spots. In fact, we were born with them. These spots are called sin, and no human effort or personal cleansing can remove them.

Jeremiah states in 17:9, 'The heart is deceitful above all things, and desperately wicked; who can know it?' We are not only born in sin, but we also continue in it; it's our nature to do so.

However, there is hope, for God has provided a remedy for our sin in the gift of His Son, the Lord Jesus Christ. It is only through faith in Jesus and His sacrifice upon Calvary's cross, that we have the hope of heaven and eternal life.

29 AUGUST

Thank God for all you have

'The ox knows its owner.' Isaiah 1:3

RECOMMENDED READING: Psalm 145

We continue to consider lessons from the animals which God created. Yesterday we considered the leopard. Today we look at:

2. The ox. Because the ox is aware of its owner, it can depend on the good things it receives, such as food, shelter and care.

In Bible times, the ox was a very important animal and a good farmer would treat his possession with care, for it was valuable to him.

However, in Isaiah 1:3, God continues to tell His people exactly how He feels about their attitude towards Him. He says, 'But Israel does not know, My people do not consider.' What a startling contrast between God's people and the ox!

Regrettably, that picture is being repeated today. Human beings just do not think about the benefits and blessings which they receive from their Creator.

Acts 17:28 reminds us that, 'In Him we live and move and have our being.' Job 22:18 says, 'He filled their houses with good things.'

Yet we forget the Giver of all good things. You can prove that at a meal table or when you visit a restaurant. Just take a note of how many people bow their heads and thank God for their food before they eat. Sadly, we don't teach our children to do so either.

A number of years ago a Devon farmer came to London to visit the agricultural show. He travelled early in the morning and went to a café for a hearty breakfast. When his food arrived, he bowed his head to thank God for what He had provided.

A group of young people in the café noticed him praying. They began to laugh and poke fun at the elderly farmer. The farmer looked at them and asked, 'Don't you thank God for your food before you eat?' 'No' they replied in unison. 'That's funny' he said. 'When I fed my pigs early this morning before I left, they didn't either.' He continued his breakfast in silence. His message had got through to them.

Sadly, most humans are unthankful people. Hosea 13:6 says, 'When they had pasture, they were filled; they were filled and their heart was exalted. Therefore, they forgot Me.'

Remember, God gives blessings to us but He can also take them away. So, thank Him for what you have. Ask the ox; it will teach you.

30 AUGUST

We meet a loving Saviour or an angry God

'I will meet them like a bear deprived of her cubs.' Hosea 13:8

RECOMMENDED READING: Hebrews 10:23–39

In this brief series we continue to look at the lessons from the animals. So far, we have considered the leopard and the ox.

3. The bear. A friend and colleague of mine, from our college days, came from Toronto in Canada. One day he told me of an experience he had that would never be forgotten:

'One day I was driving my car through a remote part of the country when, suddenly, a huge bear strolled onto the road ahead of me. I had never encountered one before in the wild so I came to a sudden stop. It just stood in the road staring directly at me. Goose pimples emerged on my arms, and I admit I was afraid.

'After what seemed quite a long time, to my relief, it sauntered away into the forest. It was the most frightening experience I have ever encountered. I then wondered what it must be like to meet a bear deprived of its cubs; terrifying.'

When I heard my friend's experience, I then began to think what it must be like for an unbeliever to meet an angry God on that great judgement day.

Over recent decades, we have created a false picture of heaven. When a famous personality dies, someone on the media will tell us that they will be looking down on us and having the time of their life in heaven. Those in heaven will not be looking down upon us on earth; neither will they have any desire to do so. Their eyes will be fixed on Jesus only.

Let me clear up any misunderstanding over this important issue and do so as directly as possible. Heaven is a place that God has prepared only for those who have acknowledged their sin and have placed their trust in the Lord Jesus for their salvation. It is only through the cross and the precious blood that He shed for us that we are assured of a home in heaven.

It also needs to be made clear that God has also prepared a place for those who have rejected His love and turned their backs upon Him. This is a place to avoid at all costs.

Hebrews 10:31 clearly reminds us that, 'It is a fearful thing to fall into the hands of the living God.'

While you have life and breath, fix your eyes upon Jesus; repent of your sins; seek His forgiveness; and live for Him.

31 AUGUST

Be aware of our enemy

'The king's wrath is like the roaring of a lion, but His favour is like the dew on the grass.' Proverbs 19:12

RECOMMENDED READING: 1 Peter 5:1–11

As we continue to study the beasts and the lessons we can learn from them, we now turn to a fourth example.

4. The lion. In 1 Peter 5:8, the apostle reminds us that our, '… adversary the devil walks about like a roaring lion, seeking whom he may devour.' This presents to us a picture of ferocity and great danger.

(a) He often prowls silently. We can go through the day totally unaware of his presence. When we think all is safe and cosy, then we are lulled into a false sense of security. Worse than that, some people don't even recognise him or believe in him and he delights in that. His silence says all is well. It is often still before the storm.

On 26 December 2004, while many people were enjoying the sea and sand of Sri Lanka's coast, the tsunami struck with great devastation. Over 230,000 people died that day, which will be long remembered. All was calm and peaceful, then sudden destruction.

You can't hear or see the devil but let me assure you he is there and will strike suddenly, without warning. He must be resisted at all costs.

(b) He often waits secretly. Psalm 10:9,10 contain some very thoughtful words: 'He lies in wait secretly, as a lion in his den; he lies in wait to catch the poor … he draws him into his net … he crouches, he lies low.'

Yes, there are times when he searches for us. There are times when we seem to search for him. Beware of the places you go to; be careful of the people you associate with.

Be alert! Be watchful! Psalm 7:2 tells us he will tear us to pieces.

May I give a special warning to Christians, especially those in leadership roles. How many good men and women, who were doing good work for God's kingdom, have been drawn into his net with one careless lapse and torn to pieces. Their testimony has gone and great damage has been done to the church.

I say to all: the roaring lion is watching and seeking to devour you. Be alert! Be watchful!

1 SEPTEMBER

A Lamb came to destroy a roaring lion

'I looked, and behold, in the midst of the throne ... stood a Lamb as though it had been slain.' Revelation 5:6

RECOMMENDED READING: 1 Peter 1:13–25

During the past few days, we have been looking at the words in Job 12:7: 'But now ask the beasts and they will teach you.' We have considered some lessons from the animals that God created, such as the leopard; the ox; the bear and the lion. We conclude with the most docile of all, but one that our Lord Jesus Christ portrays in both Old and New Testaments.

5. The Lamb. John 1:29 says, 'John saw Jesus coming to him and said, "Behold! The Lamb of God who takes away the sin of the world!"'

A Lamb (The Lord Jesus Christ) came to this earth to destroy the roaring lion (Satan). He came to take us out of his clutches. We, who are bound through sin, are released by Christ.

Almighty God, who cannot look upon our sin because He is so pure and holy, sent His only begotten Son to take the punishment which was due to us. God's righteous anger fell upon Jesus as He, who knew no sin, became sin for us. When He died upon the cross at Calvary, our sins died with Him. Because the Lamb of God was slain, our sin is not charged against us.

1 Peter 1:18–19 puts it like this: 'You were ... redeemed ... with the precious blood of Christ, as a lamb without blemish and without spot.'

A lamb was slain so that a sinner could live.

The apostle John in Revelation 5:6 wrote, 'I looked, and behold, in the midst of the throne...stood a Lamb as though it had been slain.'

John continues in Revelation 5:9 with these words, 'And they sang a new song, saying, "... For You were slain, and have redeemed us to God by Your blood."' The Lamb died for you.

Without the Lord Jesus as your Saviour, you are depicted as a leopard with ugly, unchangeable spots of sin. You are being devoured by a roaring lion. You are facing an angry God as a bear deprived of its cubs. But the good news is that you can be redeemed to God by the blood of the Lamb, who came to take away the sin of the world.

He can do that for you.

We all need encouragement

'Encourage him.' Deuteronomy 1:38

RECOMMENDED READING: Acts 4:32–37

Moses is coming towards the end of a very exciting and active life. He had been a prince in Egypt for forty years. He had spent forty years in the land of Midian, where he met his wife Zipporah, who gave him two sons, Gershom and Eliezer. It was while he was in Midian that he received God's clear call to return to the land of his birth and bring the children of Israel out of bondage. For a further forty years he had, under God, brought the Israelites through the wilderness towards the land of Canaan.

As the book of Deuteronomy opens, we see Moses looking back and recounting the many experiences he had during those challenging years.

In the first chapter, he reminds the children of Israel of their rebellion and lack of faith when a whole generation had to die in the wilderness because they were reluctant to cross into Canaan. Only Caleb and Joshua were faithful and trusted the Lord.

The time had now come for Moses to step down from his position of leadership. The responsibility of leading this great nation would fall upon the shoulders of Joshua who would lead them into the Promised Land.

In v.38 of the first chapter, we have two important words that Moses says to the people with regard to Joshua. He asks them to, 'encourage him'.

This would be an enormous challenge for Joshua, and he needed their support and encouragement as they would face many difficult challenges ahead.

Leadership in the church can be a lonely work, but it can be made easier and more enjoyable if the pastor has the support and encouragement of the people, especially through difficult times such as the COVID pandemic.

Unjustified criticism doesn't help anyone in the Lord's work. Instead, it discourages and makes the work twice as hard. Yes, decisions are made that, with a little more thought and prayer, could have been wiser, but don't pull the leader down. Build him up and encourage him. He doesn't make mistakes intentionally. A good leader will always have the people's interests as a priority.

When difficulties come, as surely, they will—for the devil will see to that—don't pick up your bags and look for another church, taking your complaints somewhere else. Get behind the leader, offering a word of thanks after a service or sending an email.

We must not place burdens on people's backs but seek to lift them from their backs. Let us take to heart the words of Moses and, 'Encourage them!'

3 SEPTEMBER

Be careful how you walk

'...that you may walk worthy of the Lord.' Colossians 1:10

RECOMMENDED READING: Ephesians 5:1–17

The letters 'www.' are a common feature for most people today. It is the system of communication and gathering information. It is commonly known as the 'web.'

Now whether we like it or not, it has become a very real part of the world system, and a large majority of people are now using this technology.

However, no one can deny the fact that it is also used for the most corrupt and evil purposes. Young people, especially, are vulnerable when they can have access to pornography and other evil temptations.

On the other hand, Christian organisations avail themselves of this system to make known the various aspects of their ministry. Churches also use this technology to gain important and helpful information, as well as communicating the gospel to countless numbers of people. During lockdown, the gospel message has gone far and wide.

However, my message is not based on modern technology, but upon five other w's which are a vital part of the Christian's spiritual life. All these are found in Paul's letter to the Colossians. Today's word is:

1. **Walking.** The word 'walk' refers to the way we conduct ourselves as Christians.

Paul used this word often in his letter to the Ephesians. In fact, in chapters 4 and 5 he uses it five times (Ephesians 4:1, 4:17, 5:2, 5:8, 5:15). He is setting out the believer's conduct, encouraging them to please God in all things.

John in his first letter (1 John 2:6) says we are to walk even as Christ walked. The prophet Amos asked in 3:3, 'Can two walk together, unless they are agreed?'

If we desire to be like Christ, we should walk with Him. One of the greatest commendations paid to anyone was given to Enoch and Noah. They '... walked with God' (Geneses 5:22, Genesis 6:9).

Do you long for a Christ-centred life? If so 'walk in Him' (Colossians 2:6). Do you desire to live an honest life? Then 'walk honestly toward them that are without' (1 Thessalonians 4:12, AV).

Do you not desire to live a holy life? Genesis 17:1 reminds us that we are to 'walk before Me [God] and be blameless'.

The challenge for every Christian is to be careful how we walk because the world is watching closely.

4 SEPTEMBER

Wiping the slate clean

'... having wiped out the handwriting of requirements that was against us, which was contrary to us. And He has taken it out of the way, having nailed it to the cross.' Colossians 2:14

RECOMMENDED READING: Colossians 2:6–15

Yesterday we looked at the word 'walking'. We now turn to our second 'w':

2. Wiping. The NIV reads, 'Having cancelled the written code, with its regulations, that was against us and that stood opposed to us' (Colossians 2:14). The NKJV uses these words: 'Having wiped out.' What a wonderful thought! Our sins have been wiped away.

According to Matthew Henry, Adam Clarke and many other commentators, the written code—or the handwriting of ordinances as the AV and NKJV puts it—clearly means the ceremonial law. In Colossians 2:15, reference is made to food and drink, and observing religious festivals. None of these can save us.

We are changed through Christ's work, not ours. The observance of ceremonial laws is man-centred: it is what we do. Faith in Christ's finished work at Calvary is God-centred: it is what He has done.

We can thank God this morning that the ceremonial law was nailed to the cross, so it is no hindrance to us. The slate has now been wiped clean. We have a new beginning. The old has passed away; He has made all things new.

However, I need to clarify an important point. The moral law, which represents God's holy character, has not been annulled. His required standards are unchangeable. Some say the moral law is for unbelievers only but, when we see the lowered standards of some Christians, we must question that viewpoint strongly. Even God's people need to be reminded of God's standards. The moral law has not been wiped away, but thank God our sins have been. Christ alone kept that law perfectly for us, so that we would not face God's anger and wrath. We have broken God's law but, without Christ, the law would have broken us!

God's holy standard, which cannot change, is a constant reminder of our utter failings and our need for His mercy. We see the law; we cannot keep it; we turn to the one who can. Jesus is the tutor to lead us to safety. There is no cane, no slipper and no punishment from the school master, for Christ has taken the punishment for us.

I may not know much about www. but I do know my sins have been cancelled, blotted out, wiped away, and never to be remembered against me anymore.

5 SEPTEMBER

The alarm is sounding

'Him we preach, warning every man and teaching every man in all wisdom, that we may present every man perfect in Christ Jesus.' Colossians 1:28

RECOMMENDED READING: Ezekiel 33:1–11

We are looking at important words in the letter to the Colossians that commence with the letter 'w'. So far, we have considered walking and wiping.

3. Warning. We live in an age of warnings. Smoking damages your health; eat more fruit and vegetables to lower your cholesterol; wear safety helmets on this building site.

To reduce vehicle accidents, we have warnings in abundance. Do not exceed speed limits; wear your safety belts; do not use your phone whilst driving; do not drink and drive (I wish some sober people would not even drive). We have become very familiar with warnings during the COVID pandemic.

Now, some people take warnings seriously and obey the rules but others ignore them and treat them as irrelevant. Sometimes those who disregard the warnings pay the price. It may be a fine but, in some instances, it can cost an innocent life.

I have sat in an aircraft that is due for departure and seen passengers appear totally oblivious to the safety instructions being given prior to take off. They are sleeping, reading, or in deep conversation but certainly not listening.

However, there is an area where warnings are crucial. These are found in many passages of the Bible, and God is the One who is instructing us. To ignore these clear warnings can affect our souls and, maybe, our future destiny.

It is the Christian's duty and responsibility to warn and to teach, and this means to believers and unbelievers alike.

Our warning has to be positive as well as negative. We must warn unbelievers to flee from the wrath to come, for the wages of sin is death—people must be warned. But the gift of God is eternal life—people need to be taught.

We must also warn believers of the danger of drifting and backsliding. But we must also teach with wisdom to present the church perfect in Christ.

Warning is a responsibility we must fulfil. To not do so is to fail in our duty both to God and also our fellow man.

6 SEPTEMBER

We are made to work as well as rest

'To this end I also labour, striving according to His working which works in me mightily.' Colossians 1:29

RECOMMENDED READING: Nehemiah 2:11–18

Following on from walking, wiping and warning we now turn to the fourth 'w' in Paul's letter to the Colossians:

4. Working. Colossians 1:10 says, 'Walk worthy of the Lord, fully pleasing Him, being fruitful in every good work and increasing in the knowledge of God.' We should not only be walking with God, such as Enoch and Noah. We should also be working for God as did Nehemiah in rebuilding the walls of Jerusalem. Be willing to get your hands dirty for God's kingdom.

Ephesians 2:8–9 makes it very clear that no one can become a child of God by works. However, when we become children of God, our desire is to be 'fruitful in every good work' (Colossians 1:10), whatever that work may be.

It was Martin Luther who eventually discovered that works are not the root of salvation; they are the fruits of our new life in Christ. The apostle James clearly reminds us that faith without works is dead. Ephesians 2:10 tells us that we are 'created in Christ Jesus unto good works' (AV). The word 'unto' means 'for the purpose of'. Patrick of Ireland (dates unknown) wrote these lines:

> 'I would not work my soul to save; for that my Lord has done;
> But I would work like any slave; for love of God's dear Son.'[27]

Unfortunately, we do have in many churches those who just come to occupy a pew but do little else to further the cause of Christ. As we say in Yorkshire, 'Some will work, and some will let them.' It is love that spurs us on to good works. We have a great example in our Lord Jesus Christ. He ministered through every part of Israel doing the work His Father had sent Him to do. His time was limited, and so is ours. But He left this testimony: 'I have finished the work which You [My Father] have given Me to do' (John 17:4). Believer, there is a work for Jesus none but you can do.

We all face a task that is unfinished. However, be encouraged, because Hebrews 6:10 reminds us that, 'God is not unjust to forget your work and labour of love.'

In his second letter to the church at Thessalonica (2:17), Paul prayed that the church would be established 'in every good work.'

So, my friends be encouraged and keep pressing on, for our labour is not in vain if it is in the Lord.

7 SEPTEMBER

Keep your eyes looking upwards

'When Christ who is our life appears, then you also will appear with Him in glory.' Colossians 3:4

RECOMMENDED READING: 1 Thessalonians 5:1–11

During the past few days, we have been considering the 'w's of Colossians. Today we come to our fifth and final word.

5. Watching. One of the most wonderful promises we have in the Bible is the assurance that our Lord Jesus Christ will return and He will appear. What a glorious prospect for the Christian! We need to keep watching and waiting. Don't be unwise but ensure you keep your lamps trimmed.

The church in Thessalonica was encouraged not to sleep but to keep spiritually alert. Paul also warned them not to be idle. We have a dual responsibility to both watch and work.

We are to keep one eye on the task before us, for there is much work to be done. But we need to keep the other eye on his return, for He will come and we must be prepared for that great Day.

We must also encourage one another so that we don't become idle in our work or lose sight of His coming. The apostle Paul was always encouraging believers.

1 Thessalonians 4:18 says, 'Therefore comfort one another with these words.' 1 Thessalonians 5:11 says, 'Therefore comfort each other and edify one another, just as you also are doing.'

We are living in evil and godless days. We are witnessing a downward drift in spiritual values, both in the church as well as in the nation. Lines that would not have been crossed are now being crossed. Things and places that would have been avoided at all costs are now permissible. It is much easier to lower the standard than to maintain it.

The days are becoming even more challenging. Therefore, we must not pull each other down but, like Paul, encourage our fellow believers to keep our eyes on what we are doing and where we are going.

Colossians 2:2 says,'... that their hearts may be encouraged, being knit together in love'.

So, the slate has been *wiped* clean. We are to issue clear *warnings* to unbelievers and believers so that we may be perfect in Christ. We are to *walk* in our Lord's footsteps. We are to *work* untiringly in His service. We are to keep *watching* and waiting, for He will come and we need to be always ready for that great Day.

8 SEPTEMBER

Enter the right gate

'Open to me the gates of righteousness; I will go through them, and I will praise the Lord.' Psalm 118:19

RECOMMENDED READING: Psalm 122

David ruled as king over Israel with his capital in Jerusalem. He was also a prophet and by faith saw the day of Christ. Following the sacrifice of our Lord, the gates of salvation were opened to all who sought forgiveness of their sin and had faith in Him. I want to consider three gates that are important to us all.

1. The gate of salvation. Matthew 7:13–14 says, 'Enter by the narrow gate … Because narrow is the gate … which leads to life'. The Bible also talks about a broad road and a narrow road. The broad road leads to death and destruction and the narrow road to eternal life and glory.

Unfortunately, many travel on the broad road, either through ignorance or with a clear intention. The end of this road brings people to a wide gate which takes them to destruction. Regrettably few travel on the narrow road, which has a number of difficulties to negotiate along the way. At the end is a narrow gate which leads to heaven and everlasting life.

2. The gates of hell. Matthew 16:18 says, 'You are Peter, and on this rock I will build My church, and the gates of Hades shall not prevail against it.'

Since the birth of the early church in Acts 2, followers of Satan have sought by any means to bring down the church of Jesus Christ and continue to do so today. They have no chance! The enemies of our Lord are fighting a losing battle. The church is more than a conqueror because it has Jesus as its foundation and its head.

A day is coming when the gates of hell will be permanently shut upon Satan and his followers. Until then we seek, with God's help, to save the lost from eternity without Christ.

3. The gates of heaven. Revelation 21:21 says, 'The twelve gates were twelve pearls …'.

When you read about our eternal home, the brain goes into overdrive. The wonder of it all is too difficult for our puny minds to grasp. No more pain, no more sorrow, no more death, and no more sin. But best of all is to see Jesus and be in His presence throughout eternity.

Today the gate is still open for all who renounce their sin and seek His forgiveness. Jesus still welcomes sinners and those who are living in darkness and the shadow of death. I urge you to look to Jesus and live.

9 SEPTEMBER

There is much more to be told

'And there are also many other things that Jesus did, which if they were written one by one, I suppose that even the world itself could not contain the books that would be written. Amen.' John 21:25

RECOMMENDED READING: Acts 1:1–12

The Gospel of John contains a record of the things that Jesus both did and said but, at the close, John was overwhelmed at the thought of how little he had told.

The greatest writer fails to tell the full story of Christ's life on earth because the words He spoke and the miracles He performed were more than John could record.

Some who heard Him preach said He was Elijah; others thought he was Jeremiah or perhaps another prophet. Every person who came into contact with Jesus, whether it was a king such as Herod, or a diseased leper, was taken in with Him. No one who met Him went away the same as they came. Whether they responded to His teaching, or completely rejected what He said, they knew deep down in their hearts that this man was not of this world.

When we first went to South Africa to stay with our daughter and her husband, I took hundreds of photographs. During our visit we were taken to the Drakensberg Mountains. I took some pictures and told people where they were. I failed to tell them that the mountains stretch over 400 miles in length.

John's description is like my photos. They fail to convey the full picture of the life of our Lord. However, I am thankful for my photos but more thankful for the accounts in the Gospels. Jesus' birth, teaching, miracles, death, resurrection and ascension give me all I need for salvation.

Whole libraries have been written on the person and work of our Lord. There is no end to writing books about Him and yet, there is so much more to say.

If everything Jesus did both in heaven and on this earth were recorded, the world itself could not contain the volumes that would have to be written.

A day will come when Christians can sit at His feet and hear the full story from His own lips. We will have all eternity to discover and hear about the rest of His life.

10 SEPTEMBER

A girl on a mission

'Now a certain woman named Lydia heard us.' Acts 16:14

RECOMMENDED READING: Acts 16:11–15

How thankful we should be for our female workers in the church. Many of our smaller fellowships depend on them. Some are so precious that they are like nuggets of gold or pearls on a necklace.

The early church was so thankful for the labours of women such as Dorcas and Priscilla, and now we have another, named Lydia.

Paul came across a small company of believers in Macedonia and took the opportunity to preach the gospel to them. As he did so, the Spirit of God began to move in Lydia's heart. Here we have clear lessons as to what redemption is all about.

1. Conversion is God's sovereign work of grace. Verse 14 says some very simple yet important words: 'The Lord opened her heart.'

God never deals with us the same, as we are so different. He dealt with Lydia so gently as she responded to God's call. Yet soon afterwards, while Paul and Silas were in prison, it took an earthquake to shake the heart of a Philippian jailer.

God deals with some of us with gentle persuasion while, with others, it has to be earth shattering because our hearts are so stubborn.

2. Conversion leads to transformation. Immediately following Lydia's conversion, she was baptised and her household with her (v.15). When the Lord becomes our Master, we long to please and obey Him, for our entire character is transformed. We are no longer our own; we are His. Lydia began to grow spiritually by responding to the doctrine Paul taught her.

If there is not an evident change in our life, then we must question whether we have experienced a true conversion. The fruits of the Spirit should become visible to those we encounter whether it be in the home, at work or in the fellowship of the church.

3. Conversion leads to fellowship with the Lord's people. Verse 15 says, 'Come to my house and stay.' She shared her home and those things God had graciously provided for her. She followed the teaching of the early church by having an open home.

Acts 2:42 (NIV): 'They devoted themselves ... to fellowship.' Verse 46 (NIV) says, 'They continued to meet together.'

If we are able to use our home for the blessing of others, let us welcome the church into it. You may be entertaining angels without realising it.

11 SEPTEMBER

Laws are needed for our good

'Whoever breaks through a wall will be bitten by a serpent.' Ecclesiastes 10:8

RECOMMENDED READING: Isaiah 5:1–7

A common Bible practice is to take a fact from nature and illustrate it with a moral truth. This was frequently done by the Lord Jesus and by many of the writers of Scripture.

The writer of Ecclesiastes is probably thinking of an eastern vineyard, which would be surrounded by a loosely built wall and hidden among the stones, there would be a deadly viper. As the thief draws near, he is sure no one has seen him, so he begins to break down a small section of the wall. Unexpectedly, a viper gives the victim a nasty bite and deadly poison enters into his blood. The desire for pleasant fruit has resulted in his downfall. As the wall protected the vineyard, so laws are also for our protection.

1. We are given laws for our benefit. We all live in a world that is governed by laws, and these are to protect us and keep us safe.

Our physical lives are governed by laws. These are to aid the health of our bodies as well as develop the mind. The neglect of these laws can bring sickness and, on some occasions, even death.

Our moral and spiritual lives are also governed by laws. They are embedded in our conscience and we become aware of this whenever we break them.

But you will also find laws in God's Word. The Ten Commandments in Exodus 20 have been given by God for our good.

2. There is a penalty to pay when laws are broken. There is a reason why laws have been given to us. When we break them there will be a sting to encounter and a penalty to pay.

A number of years ago, I was stopped by the police for carelessly breaking the speed limit. I was only a few miles per hour over that limit but I had to face the penalty of three points on my licence. I was not annoyed with the law but with myself, for the law was there to protect myself and others.

This is also true with regard to our spiritual life. We cannot, and should not, ignore God's laws. If we do, there will be a penalty to pay.

However, for the Christian there is much to be grateful for because the penalty for our sins has been paid by God's only begotten Son, the Lord Jesus Christ, upon Calvary's cross. There is no further penalty for us to pay.

12 SEPTEMBER

Only Jesus can lift us up from the pit

'He also brought me up out of a horrible pit, out of the miry clay, and set my feet upon a rock.' Psalm 40:2

RECOMMENDED READING: Psalm 40

I was born in Barnsley, South Yorkshire. The region was known for its coal-mining industry with fifty-six collieries throughout the county. The mines are known as pits, with some nearly half a mile deep. Our verse today has an important spiritual message to convey to us.

1. **Sin. 'A horrible pit.'** Coal mines were unpleasant places to work in, especially during the early part of the last century. Some men had to work for most of the day in darkness, always aware of the possibility of flooding and sinking into soft ground or collapsing tunnels. These were unpleasant and dangerous conditions for any miner. In this verse the Psalmist describes unbelievers being in a horrible pit, with the darkness of sin always surrounding them. They are always aware of sinking into new sinful and ungodly ways, which will lead them deeper into iniquity.

2. **Rescuer. 'He ... brought me up.'** When pit disasters have occurred, miners have needed colleagues at the pit head to rescue them. They cannot rescue themselves; they are totally dependent upon others.

There was a time in our lives when we were deep in the horrible pit of sin, unable to help ourselves, and gradually sinking deeper into the mire. We cried out to God for help, and He did what we could not do; neither could anyone else do it for us. We were too deep to get out unaided; we needed a rescuer.

If anyone is reading this who is deep in that horrible pit of sin and iniquity, then look to Jesus and cry out to Him. He is the only one who can deliver you and lift you out.

3. **Security. 'Set my feet upon a rock.'** When miners were brought out of the pit, they had to adjust to the bright sunlight after being so long in darkness. They had to remove the foul air from their lungs and breathe in clean, fresh air. Then they steadied their feet on firm solid ground. They now felt secure and safe.

What a blessing to have been delivered from the pit of sin, feel the fresh breezes of heaven and to behold the bright light of the glory of God. What a joy to have the filth washed away and feel clean throughout.

We now have something to truly sing about, for He has 'put a new song in my mouth' (Psalm 40:3). The Christian faith is a singing faith. We were born again to sing.

13 SEPTEMBER

It is how you finish that is important

'And Samuel said to all the people, "Do you see him whom the Lord has chosen, that there is no one like him among all the people?"' 1 Samuel 10:24

RECOMMENDED READING: 1 Samuel 10

Whether it is sport, politics or business, it is not just how you begin but how you finish that is most important.

A good start but a bad end sums up the life of King Saul. What caused this decline after such a promising beginning? We will try and answer this question during the next two days.

The children of Israel demanded a king like the other nations. The prophet Samuel had clearly warned them of the changes this would bring but the warnings were completely ignored.

Despite all that God had done for them in delivering them from bondage in Egypt; providing for them during their wandering in the wilderness; demonstrating His great power in battle; and giving them the Promised Land, they still demanded a king. God gave them their request.

It can be a matter of great concern when God gives to us what we want (Psalm 106:15). It does not always turn out to be the best for us. I would rather He provided for our needs than ask Him for our wants.

Saul was chosen to be their future king and much was expected from him.

Yes, he had a very promising beginning; he had a sincere heart and God was with him. What a great deal could have been accomplished if he had kept his heart right with God.

In 1 Samuel 10:6 we are told that the Spirit of the Lord would come upon him. God was preparing Saul for his future work.

The opportunities before him were great. He also had the support of the people, but pride entered with his position and slowly, but surely, he departed from God and that promising early beginning.

Unfortunately, Saul was not the only one to begin well but end in grief. A number of the kings, particularly in Judah, began their reign promising great things but ended their time on the throne in failure because they did not keep their thoughts centred upon Almighty God.

If we are Christians, it is so important that in this spiritual race we keep our eyes upon Jesus at all times. If we do, we will end well.

Tomorrow we will look at where it all went wrong for Saul.

14 SEPTEMBER

When you are going down start looking up

'As long as he sought the Lord, God made him prosper.' 2 Chronicles 26:5

RECOMMENDED READING: 2 Chronicles 26:1–23

We continue to look at the downward path of King Saul, who was similar to some other kings of Judah, such as Uzziah in today's reading. So, what led to Saul's downfall?

1. Impatience. In 1 Samuel 13 the Philistines were in the ascendancy and when the Israelites saw the danger, they went into hiding. Saul at this time was in Gilgal and the prophet Samuel told the king he would meet him in seven days. When Samuel was delayed, Saul became impatient and disobeyed the command of God. He offered a burnt offering, which was the sole responsibility of the priests. But the situation was urgent, and after all, he was now the king!

2. Disobedience. In 1 Samuel 15:16–17 Saul's disobedience was just the beginning of other transgressions. He was clearly told to punish the Amalekites and not spare any of them. But he spared the king, Agag, and also the very best of the flock. When he was made aware of his disobedience, he tried to cover his sin with a lie. This resulted in God's rejection of him as king.

3. Jealousy. In 1 Samuel 18:8-10, Saul was clearly losing favour with the people, and what made matters worse was that David was winning it. The evil in Saul's heart was becoming even more evident. Beware of jealousy when someone becomes more popular then you. This will only lead to anger and a sinful heart. Kill the root of jealousy before it grows and bears fruit.

4. Attempted murder. In 1 Samuel 19:9–10, it has become clear that the devil had got such a stranglehold on Saul that he sought opportunities to remove David permanently. Firstly, he tried to nail him to the wall with his spear. Then he hunted David among the mountains near En Gedi. But God protected David in many amazing ways.

5. Inconsistency and unfaithfulness. In 1 Samuel 28, Samuel had died and Saul had removed all mediums and witches from the land. Despite that action, he then tried to look into his future by visiting a medium at En Dor. Despite the encouraging beginning, we can now see how dark his mind had become.

The clear message for us is to begin well but, most of all, to end well. Keep walking close to the Lord and never wander from the path He has planned for you. Just keep your eyes upon the Saviour at all times.

15 SEPTEMBER

An active life of service

'Other little boats were also with Him.' Mark 4:36

RECOMMENDED READING: Matthew 8:23–27

The Lord Jesus Christ had three active years of ministry, which are recorded in all four Gospels. He walked many miles each day covering every part of the land of His birth. He visited towns and cities teaching in the synagogues but also spent much time in the countryside preaching the Gospel of the Kingdom of God.

During his ministry He told many parables, healed those who were diseased, and performed many miracles on land and sea. Many of these have been recorded by faithful writers such a Matthew, Mark, Luke and John.

Over the next few days, I want to consider one such miracle: the stilling of the storm. As well as being recorded in Mark and Matthew, it is also found in Luke 8:22–25, but it is only Mark's account that refers to other boats being with Him.

Jesus had been speaking to large crowds and He was now physically and mentally weary. As evening was approaching, He told His disciples to take a boat and cross over to the other side so He could get some rest before He faced a further day of activity.

During the night's crossing a strong wind disturbed the waters of Galilee so that waves began to fill the boat. Jesus, however, continued to sleep in the stern, undisturbed by the wild conditions around Him.

The disciples, on the other hand, were in an understandable panic. These experienced fishermen, who had spent much of their lives around and on this lake, had seen and endured storms before but had never faced anything quite like this. They were truly terrified.

It is quite understandable, when reading this story, that our attention should be centred upon the boat in which Jesus was sailing but Mark, in his account, emphasises that during the night there were other boats crossing the lake.

The disciples who sailed with Jesus had the advantage of His presence and the privilege of calling upon him in their time of danger, but what about the other boats that were on the lake battling alone on that stormy night?

As we look carefully at this story, I will be making a number of simple but important observations that I trust will both comfort, encourage and challenge us as we journey often through stormy seas.

A busy night at sea

'Now when He got into a boat, His disciples followed Him.' Matthew 8:23

RECOMMENDED READING: Mark 4:35–41

We are turning our thoughts to the storm on Galilee and noticed from Mark's account that other boats were on the lake that night.

1. There are always many ships at sea. When I was preaching in Kent just prior to the COVID lockdown, friends took Kathryn and me to see Dover Castle, as we hadn't been before. The castle looks down upon the English Channel, which is the busiest waterway in Europe with boats and ferries continually on the move to and from France and Belgium. Whatever the weather conditions, it affects them all. The storm that breaks on one ship, breaks upon them all. That was the situation on Galilee that eventful night.

But this is also true of those who are exposed to the winds and storms of life. However troubled you may be by circumstances that you think are peculiar to you, out on the stormy sea are 'other little boats'. The storm of adversity does not break upon you alone.

There may be some reading these thoughts who are having a hard time these days and things are in a chaotic mess. You can't work out what has gone wrong, or how it has gone wrong, or why it has gone wrong, particularly for you.

I would remind you that you are not alone in your adversity. There are other little boats and we must resist the urge to grumble and complain about our own circumstances.

As we look around, it is clear to note that the storm is sweeping over every sea. We have no monopoly of present-day difficulties on this troubled surface. There are still 'other little ships.'

I know for some this will bring little comfort but I think it helps to know that no strange thing has happened to us. We are in good company.

It is foolish for anyone to think that all the fates are against them. Unfortunately, there are people who think this, and they become hard and bitter.

Trouble and adversity are common to us all. When the storm breaks, the whole sea is disturbed. We are in it together. With us are 'other little ships.'

The comfort Christians have is that Jesus is with them in the boat and in control of all circumstances, so in Him we place all our trust.

17 SEPTEMBER

Fight your way through the storm

'He said to me, "My grace is sufficient for you."' 2 Corinthians 12:9

RECOMMENDED READING: 2 Corinthians 11:23–28

Yesterday we began looking at the storm on Galilee and noticed that there were other boats on the lake besides the one Jesus was in. All were affected by the storm.

2. This is true of physical affliction. I cannot count the number of times people have said to me, 'What have I done to deserve this?' or, 'Why has this trouble come upon me?' In September 1996, my wife Kathryn was diagnosed with Multiple Sclerosis. Initially we also asked many questions. Then we were able to say, 'Why not?' Is there a lot of pain? Yes. Is there weariness? Yes. Are there questions? Yes. But there is now acceptance.

Over the years we have met other ships in their twenties and thirties who are confined to wheelchairs and even beds. Yes, there are other boats, not as well constructed, that are in the midst of the storm. Thankfully in our boat is a supportive family and our Lord.

'He [Jesus] said to me, "My grace is sufficient for you, for My strength is made perfect in weakness"' (2 Corinthians 12:9).

Those who continually complain about their troubles are so seasick that they cannot get on deck to see other little ships. They take great delight in magnifying all their ills and persuading themselves that all the trouble in the world is just theirs. Nothing could be further from the truth.

We sympathise with those in trouble, as we should, but we must always remember that, when the storm breaks and water starts filling our boat, we are not the only ones at sea.

I thought grave digging was a new business when, at the age of thirty-three, I buried my father whom I loved very much. However, through my tears I noticed the pathway through the churchyard had been worn with many feet. Others had been there before me. As I came away, I noticed others were still coming.

Life is a journey and we must fight our way through what sometimes is a stormy sea. But always remember that there are other little ships with us.

There are times when temptations seem to be multiplying. You get over one storm and another is approaching, and no one seems to understand. Friend, you are not alone; there are other little ships. But thank God today that you are in the boat with Jesus and He will bring you safely to the other side.

We often say that calm comes before the storm. A day will come when calm will follow the storm and we arrive safely in our heavenly haven.

18 SEPTEMBER

Cheer up; Jesus is with us!

'Therefore now, O LORD, please take my life from me, for it is better for me to die than to live!' Jonah 4:3

RECOMMENDED READING: 1 Kings 19:1–8

We continue to look at Mark's account of the storm on Galilee in chapter 4 with special consideration of v.36: 'Other little boats were also with Him.' We have seen that in the storms of life we are not alone. Yesterday we saw how it is true of physical affliction and today we consider another aspect.

3. It is true of spiritual affliction. We are living in days of spiritual decline which is affecting many small fellowships throughout our land. We often find ourselves just drifting through the storm, constantly being tossed about in every direction.

We see larger ships coping so much better than ours, even picking up passengers from smaller ships.

The problem is that some of these larger boats are flying a different flag. There are the flags of liberalism, ecumenism, socialism and many other unknown flags.

There are times when we think we are the only boat at sea as the storm rages. Has the storm swept similar boats such as ours against the rocks? Are we the only ones using the divine compass?

Though they may be hidden by the high waves and obscured by the night mist, there are others, just like yours, battling through the storm.

Elijah was full of self-pity thinking he was the only ship on the lake. You were wrong Elijah! There were 7,000 other little ships in Israel who were steering through the storm. You were not alone. Don't sink in spiritual despondency.

The storm is around us and the tempest is raging. How we can easily sink in despair and leave the rowing to the few when all hands need to be working together.

Yes, it is true that human beings are lovers of pleasure more than lovers of God. Yes, it is true that many will not endure sound doctrine but turn their ears to fables. Yes, it is true we are battling against the waves of ungodly legislation, which is hurting our children and breaking marriages.

We must always remember that there are other little ships besides ours battling hard against the elements. So don't become downcast and despondent and full of self-pity.

Raise your flag once more and secure your masts. Commence rowing again, for the Master is not far away. The storm will calm and soon you will see the shore.

19 SEPTEMBER

Whose boat are you in?

'When they had left the multitude, they took Him along in the boat as He was.' Mark 4:36

RECOMMENDED READING: Matthew 14:22–23

We have been considering the storm on Galilee, recognising that other boats were on the lake during that stormy night. We have centred our thoughts on words from v.36, 'Other little boats were also with Him.' This shows that the disciples were not the only ones on the lake battling against the violent waves. Though they were experienced fishermen, they had never encountered a storm as bad as this one.

4. There were advantages sailing with Jesus. Of all the boats that were on Galilee that night, I know which one I would rather be in. Those who sailed in the boat with Jesus were conscious of His presence during the storm, even though He was asleep during it.

The occupants of the other boats shared the miracle; they experienced the benefits of Jesus stilling the storm. But to hear His words and be with Him when the amazing miracle occurred was something very special.

Millions of people today cope with the rough seas of life, because Jesus is in the boat with them. They realise how indebted they are to Him.

Some may say, 'I have seen Christian people just as fearful as I have been.' That may be true as we all have to sail through the same sea and we are just as fearful in the storm. But the Christian has the Lord, who created the sea, holding their hand. Although they are filled with fear, they know He will never fail them because He is Master over the elements.

Remember what they said when they woke Him? Verse 38 tells us: 'Do you not care that we are perishing?' The Lord does not command the storm to cease at the first gust of wind. He lets it blow for a while and some suffer seasickness before they are rescued from their difficulties. But He is there; He is always there. The boat that Jesus sails in will always outride the storm.

It's always a privilege to sail with the Master mariner but, as we do so, remember to pray for other little boats, that the occupants may be aware of the One who stills the storm. Our responsibility is to inform others that Jesus' boat is large enough to take them also.

Tomorrow we will take our final voyage; but as we do so, let us make sure we are in the right boat, with Jesus for company.

20 SEPTEMBER

Our final voyage into calm waters

'Then He arose and rebuked the wind, and said to the sea, "Peace, be still!" And the wind ceased and there was a great calm.' Mark 4:39

RECOMMENDED READING: Luke 8:22–25

The Sea of Galilee lies 680 feet below sea level. It is surrounded by hills, especially on the east side where they reach 2,000 feet high. These heights are a source of cool, dry air. In contrast, around the sea the climate is semi-tropical with warm moist air. This extreme difference causes large temperature and pressure changes, which result in strong winds funnelling through the hills and dropping to the sea.

As Galilee is small, these winds descend directly to the centre of the lake with often violent results. As it is a relatively shallow lake, the winds cause it to be whipped up more quickly than deep water.

Our Lord Jesus Christ, the Creator of heaven and earth, is in total control of all the elements of nature. The storm on Galilee was under His control from beginning to end. All the boats on the lake that night were blessed through His intervention. Today I want to turn to my final thought.

5. There is to be a voyage only one boat can take.

One day a major storm will break and there will be only one boat that will survive. There will be no other little boats.

In the book of Genesis, we read of a storm where there was only one ship that was built according to God's instructions. At God's command, Noah and his family went into the ark, and God shut them in.

When the windows of heaven opened and the foundations of the deep were broken up, this ship proved that it had been built for a stormy day and rough waters.

When the storm of God's wrath broke upon a sinful world that had rejected Him, the waters rose until the tops of the mountains were covered. All perished except those who were hidden safely in the ark.

A day is coming when heaven and earth will pass away. Salvation is in Christ alone. There will be no other ships to rescue you. There is salvation in no other. We need to ensure that we are found in the ship with Him.

We need to be in Christ, so that we can make that last great voyage to the land, where storms are past and there is joy and peace for evermore. Christ in you is the only hope of glory.

21 SEPTEMBER

We need a daily spiritual workout to be strong

'But as for you, be strong and do not give up, for your work will be rewarded.'
2 Chronicles 15:7, NIV

RECOMMENDED READING: Joshua 1:1–9

Asa was king of Judah. He came to the throne when the country was experiencing a time of peace. This peace continued for ten years (2 Chronicles 14:1).

We are told (vv.2–3) that he did what was right in the eyes of the Lord by removing foreign altars and destroying the many idols that Judah had erected.

In 2 Chronicles 15:1–2 the prophet Azariah was instructed by God to meet Asa with a clear message containing valuable advice. We would do well to heed it ourselves.

1. Be strong. Asa had an important task ahead of him and he needed to be strong in carrying out his responsibilities. As these two words are important for all of us, both physically and spiritually, we are to:

- *Eat Well.* A child is always encouraged to eat well to develop physically. When we have been ill, we are advised to improve our intake of food to gain strength once again.

  For the Christian, the Bible is our spiritual food, but if we neglect it, we will become spiritually impoverished. If we feed regularly upon God's Word, our faith matures and we become stronger.

- *Exercise.* A lack of exercise is not good for our health and can be a danger to the heart and other vital organs. Regular exercise strengthens the muscles and we feel the benefit of it, though there are times when we prefer to remain sedentary. The Christian needs spiritual exercise, though knee bends can be a challenge when we have other things pressing upon us. Yes, prayer can be a battle sometimes but well worth the effort. When you don't feel like praying, that is the time to pray.

- *Rest.* Some people are workaholics, but times for rest are essential. Constant work will eventually catch up with you. God created us to work and rest. Even Jesus took time alone to rest awhile during a busy schedule. God instituted one day in the week when we should put aside our daily tasks and responsibilities and turn our thoughts to higher and better things.

Yes, we are to be strong in our faith. Tomorrow we will look at the remainder of the verse.

22 SEPTEMBER

Keep persevering to the end

'But as for you, be strong and do not give up, for your work will be rewarded.'
2 *Chronicles 15:7*, NIV

RECOMMENDED READING: Ephesians 6:10–17

We are looking at advice given to King Asa that we also would be wise to remember. Yesterday we were told to be strong. We do this by feeding regularly upon God's Word, being in communion with God through prayer, and weekly resting from our labours on His day.

We now turn to the second piece of advice given to king Asa.

2. Do not give up. I don't watch a great deal of television, but I do enjoy quizzes—my favourites being *Mastermind* and *University Challenge*. No, I'm not clever, but I love to watch with great admiration those who are. *Mastermind* is famous for its black chair and catchphrase, 'I have started so I'll finish.' Those two words, 'started' and 'finish', are so important to the Christian.

When I read about the kings of Judah, so many began well, but failed to end well. They started well but failed to finish as they began. It is so sad when you know of, or hear of, believers who start with such enthusiasm but fail to maintain it to the end.

May God give us courage, determination and perseverance to endure to the end and not give up when the journey becomes difficult.

3. Your work will be rewarded. As we labour for God during the years of this life, there are many ways in which we are rewarded, but the greatest is knowing that our labour is not in vain if it be in the Lord.

We have this great assurance in Isaiah 55:11 which says, 'So shall My word be that goes forth from My mouth; it shall not return to Me void, but it shall accomplish what I please, and it shall prosper in the thing for which I sent it.'

But our greatest reward is in heaven. Listen to what the apostle Paul said in 2 Timothy 4:7–8:

'I have fought the good fight, I have finished the race, I have kept the faith. Finally, there is laid up for me the crown of righteousness, which the Lord, the righteous Judge, will give to me on that Day, and not to me only but also to all who have loved His appearing.'

23 SEPTEMBER

Lessons from Noah

'But Noah found grace in the eyes of the LORD.' Genesis 6:8

RECOMMENDED READING: Genesis 9:8–17

From the time of the fall, in Genesis 3, human beings have constantly rebelled against their Creator. They have rejected God's commandments, ignored His Word, spurned His love and turned their backs upon his Son.

Throughout history, God's righteous anger over sin is clearly visible. We see that especially when we come to Genesis 6:6 which says, 'And the LORD was sorry that He had made man on the earth, and He was grieved in His heart.'

God will not ignore our sin but will, in His good time, bring judgement against it. The result of man's sin and corruption was a flood over the whole earth. This would be so devastating that it would destroy every living thing that had breath.

Among all the people on the earth at that time, there was only one man whom we are told in v.8, 'found grace in the eyes of the Lord'.

Noah was instructed by God to build an ark, not only for himself and his wife, but also for his three sons and their wives. They would enter the ark along with seven of every clean animal and two of every unclean animal that was on the earth.

There are a number of things about life that we can learn from Noah's ark. We will look at one of these today and the remainder tomorrow.

1. **Prepare for the future.** There was a great deal of preparation to be done before God finally sent the flood upon the earth. Not only had the ark to be built, but they had to get the animals and living creatures on board and settled. They also had to ensure that provisions were gathered and stored safely away, for a long time, aboard the ark. Much planning and preparation had to be done before God finally shut the door of the ark.

Today we plan for many things, from the birth of a child to the days of our retirement. However, there is one important thing that we give little time for preparation, and that is eternity. How unwise we can be for something that is so important.

We all need to prepare to meet our God.

Noah the master builder

'... the flood came and took them all away.' Matthew 24:39

RECOMMENDED READING: Matthew 24:36–44

We continue to look at life lessons from Noah's ark. Yesterday we considered the need to plan ahead. Today we have four more lessons from the ark.

2. Remain active. At the age of 600 years, Noah was asked by God to do a major task. He never expected to be involved in such a huge project, but, when God had given him the starting orders, he followed the instructions carefully and built this huge floating vessel to the best of his ability.

We must never be surprised at the tasks God asks us to do, or where he asks us to go, whatever our age. Retirement isn't appropriate for the Christian. You are always on His Majesty's service, ready for the next instructions.

3. Ignore the critics. Noah would face much criticism and opposition as he began to build the ark. Remember it wasn't raining when he built it. As it came to completion, he would face even more sarcasm and ridicule. In answer to this, Noah and his sons would just continue to follow God's instructions and keep building.

If you stand entirely upon the truths of God's Word, criticism will come, and sometimes from unexpected quarters. Don't flinch or be swayed by it; just stand by God's principles and keep building His kingdom. In the end all will be well if we stand firm.

4. Use what God has given to you. We do not know what gifts and talents Noah and his sons possessed, but God enabled them to construct a safe and secure vessel.

You may not possess many gifts and abilities. God knows what you are capable of doing, so just use the talents He has given you. Remember, the ark was built by amateurs, the Titanic by professionals.

5. Keep your eyes heavenward. Do not worry and concern yourself about the storm. When you belong to God's family, there is always a rainbow in the sky. The rainbow is not man's invention, or the monopoly of any organisation. The rainbow is a reminder from God of His covenant with His people.

No matter how severe and long the storm lasts, God's people are always safe and secure within the ark of His love. So, keep your eyes looking up to where your help comes. God always watches over His people and, in His good time, will bring us to our calm and secure resting place.

25 SEPTEMBER

A man of exceptional courage

'Let us go up at once and take possession, for we are well able to overcome it.' Numbers 13:30

RECOMMENDED READING: Numbers 13:27–33

There is so much to encourage us, in the life of Caleb. He was a great man of God—one from whom we can learn much.

In Numbers 13, the Lord instructed Moses to select a leader from every tribe, who would spy out the land of Canaan. They were to find out if the people were strong or weak, few or many, whether the land was rich or poor, whether the cities were like camps or strongholds.

From the tribe of Judah, Caleb was selected. The twelve spies spent forty days covering the land gaining valuable information.

Yes, there were encouragements. The land flowed with milk and honey. They brought back figs and pomegranates to prove it.

However, there was a sting in the tail, for the people who occupied the land were strong and lived in fortified cities. There were also giants in the land (vv.28,32,33).

Ten spies told Moses that they would be unable to take the land because the people were much stronger than the Israelites (v. 31).

But Caleb showed great courage by silencing the people and encouraging them to go up at once and take possession of the land (v.30). In Numbers 14:9 he said, 'Do not fear them.' It took great courage to stand out against ten negative spies, who had already influenced the people.

Times have not changed; people have not changed. Unfortunately, within the church we have those who are great discouragers, who keep reminding us that we are fighting a losing battle and that things have never been as bad. How ignorant they are of our history!

Some Christians soon give up when the battle becomes intense and, what is worse, they discourage those who are still fighting. Apathy, defeatism and cowardice are catching, so be warned.

Christians follow a Saul or a David. Saul was a weak and unfit king. David was a strong and inspirational leader. If the leader is weak and unfit, the followers are likely to be so also. If the leader is strong and inspires others, nothing is impossible.

Caleb was a man of great courage despite the strength of the opposition. 'We should go up and take possession' (v.13).

Despite the strength of the opposition which the church faces today, may these words and Caleb's enthusiasm inspire us to accomplish great things for God.

26 SEPTEMBER

He was a man of faith

'The LORD is with us. Do not fear them.' Numbers 14:9

RECOMMENDED READING: Numbers 14:1–29

Yesterday, we began to consider the characteristics of a man named Caleb. Today we will think of his great faith.

When ten leaders of the tribes of Israel told the people that they were not able to go against the inhabitants of Canaan because this nation was stronger, Caleb said to the people in 13:30, 'We are well able to overcome it.' What confidence he showed; what faith he displayed in God!

There was no talk of fighting a losing battle. There was no sense of discouragement. Caleb showed a clear and positive attitude.

Was his confidence misplaced? Was he showing a sign of foolish optimism? Was he too self-assured? Not in the least!

When we read Numbers 14:9, we see clearly where his faith was centred. It was in the LORD. He reminded the people, 'The LORD is with us.' Without the assurance of the LORD's presence, he would not even consider embarking upon such an encounter. But with the LORD's support, why be afraid?

The opposition has always been greater in number. The opposition has always had far more human resources, but we must never forget where our resources are found. We must also remember that one person, with God's help, is in the majority.

Why then are we so easily overwhelmed? Why are we so weak and cowardly? Why do we run at the first sign of conflict? Our problem is that we often look at things and situations from a human perspective. Caleb had his sights in another direction. What a faith!

Here we have a man who was governed, not by fear, but by faith. He was a man who was willing to go against the flow. He was a man who motivated others. He was a man who did not underestimate the difficulties, nor overestimate his own ability. Here was a man whose faith was in God.

How often our faith feels weak when challenges come our way and the enemy seems set to overpower us. We are ready to run and hide to avoid any conflict. Then Jesus looks at us and says, 'O, you of little faith' (Matthew 6:30).

When I consider the life of Caleb, my prayer is: Lord, increase my faith.

27 SEPTEMBER

He was unashamed to be different

'My servant Caleb ... has a different spirit in him and has followed me fully.'
Numbers 14:24

RECOMMENDED READING: John 12:21–26

We continue our consideration of the life of God's servant Caleb. We have seen his courage and his strong faith. Today we look at his faithfulness to his God.

Chapter 14 recounts God's punishment upon His people Israel. Following the negative report of the spies, the people began, yet again, to complain. They regretted leaving Egypt and agreed to select a leader to take them back into bondage.

Again, Caleb begged them not to rebel against the Lord, nor to fear the people of the land, but they ignored his plea and prepared to stone him.

At this point, God stepped in and reminded Moses of all that He had done for Israel. Because of their disobedience and rebellion, He told Moses that He would strike them with pestilence and disinherit them (v. 12).

From vv.13–19, we see Moses interceding for Israel. What a mediator he was, and the result is seen in v.20: 'Then the LORD said, "I have pardoned, according to your word."'

God did not disinherit His people. However, because of their continued rebellion—despite the signs which He did in Egypt and in the wilderness—and because they would not listen to His voice, God made it clear that those who rejected Him would not see the Promised Land. They would die in that barren wilderness.

Then we come to v.24: 'but Caleb ...'. This man had 'a different spirit'; he was God's chosen servant and he followed Him wholeheartedly. According to Ephesians 1:4, Christians are called to be different.

One of the greatest concerns I have for the church today is that we don't stand out in the world as we should do. We are not different. There should be a chasm between the man of the world and the man of God. Caleb had a different spirit—do we? Can people see the difference? That difference was clearly seen in the life of Caleb.

We can be so half-hearted in our service for God. Caleb was wholehearted. It is not always easy to be fully committed and different, but that is what God expects from us; that is what He has called us to be.

In the city of Antioch, the people who followed Jesus Christ were called Christians because they were noticeably different. May people see that difference in us.

28 SEPTEMBER

Strength beyond his years

'I am as strong this day as on the day that Moses sent me; just as my strength was then, so now is my strength for war, both for going out and for coming in.'
Joshua 14:11

RECOMMENDED READING: Joshua 14

We have been considering the life of God's servant Caleb. We now consider two further aspects of his life that I trust will inspire us to continue in our work for the Lord.

- **He was given a promise.** Numbers 14:24 closes with a promise from Almighty God: 'him … I will bring into the land where he went, and his descendants shall inherit it.'

Because he had a different spirit and followed the Lord fully, he was guaranteed this reward. What God promises He fulfils. Deuteronomy 1:35–36 confirms this promise.

When we are wholehearted in our commitment to the Lord, He is wholehearted in His commitment to us. Those who honour Him, He honours.

However, one amazing aspect of God is that He remains faithful, despite us and our half-heartedness.

When we study the Scriptures, God's promises are on every page. There is one aspect of God's nature that is comforting to all Christians; His promises are reliable, dependable and trustworthy. God never breaks His word, His covenant or His promises.

- **Caleb remained strong in faith.** He remained strong in faith though now old in years. Joshua 14:11–12: 'I am as strong this day as on the day that Moses sent me; just as my strength was then, so now is my strength … Now therefore, give me this mountain of which the Lord spoke … The Lord will be with me, and I shall be able to drive them out.' And he did!

One of the most discouraging statements I hear from older Christians is when they tell me they can't accomplish any more tasks and their work is finished. My friends, God will decide that!

One of the most encouraging verses in the Psalms is found in 92:14: 'They shall still bear fruit in old age.'

It is always good to hear of elderly Christians who are as enthusiastic for the Lord's work now as when they were first converted. In fact, many accomplished more in their later years than they did in their former ones.

When the Lord calls us to be with Him, may we be able to say with Jesus, 'I have finished the work which you have given me to do' (John 17:4).

29 SEPTEMBER

He was an unselfish man

'So she said to him, "Give me a blessing; since you have given me land in the South, give me also springs of water." And Caleb gave her the upper springs and the lower springs.' Judges 1:15

RECOMMENDED READING: Judges 1:12–15

In Hebrews 11, we have the great chapter which looks back on the heroes of the faith. There are eighteen different names that the writer mentions in that account.

If you were invited to present a list of eighteen people, who have helped and inspired you in your Christian life, who would you include? I would certainly include Caleb in mine.

During the past four days we have been thinking about the life of Caleb, son of Jephunneh. We have seen his courage, his faith, his different spirit, God's promise to him and his determination to be strong in faith though old in years. Today we come to the final chapter in his long life.

He was an unselfish and generous man.

Caleb had a daughter named Achsah and one day she asked him a favour. There is nothing new in that, as every father will know.

Caleb had already given her land in the south and now she was asking for springs of water. We are told he responded positively to her request. What a generous father; what an unselfish man.

Regrettably, Caleb's descendants did not always live up to his standards. In 1 Samuel 25:3 we read, 'The name of the man was Nabal, and the name of his wife Abigail. She was a woman of good understanding and beautiful appearance; but the man was harsh and evil in his doings. He was of the house of Caleb.' Unselfishness is not hereditary; it doesn't automatically run in families.

However, a characteristic that should dominate the lives of Christians is unselfishness. We should possess a generous spirit.

Our perfect example is the life of our Lord Jesus Christ. He was unselfish in laying aside His heavenly robes and coming down to this sinful world. He was unselfish in His ministry, always concerned about others.

Jesus was unselfish on the cross, willing to take our sins upon Himself and giving to us His spotless robe of righteousness.

Jesus has given, is giving, and promises to continue to give. What wealth we possess from such an unselfish and generous benefactor. What a generous Father we have.

Yes, Caleb was a giant in spiritual terms. May our lives reflect these aspects of his character and, as the Lord used him, may he use us to His glory.

30 SEPTEMBER

Be careful what you ask for

'And Jabez called on the God of Israel saying, "Oh, that You would bless me indeed."' 1 Chronicles 4:10

RECOMMENDED READING: 2 Kings 20:1–6; 21:1–12

When you have a personal longing and desire, and you bring this before the throne of God in prayer, we should always qualify it with these words, 'Not as I will, but as You will' (Matthew 26:39). Otherwise, we might receive what may be dangerous for us to accept. If we persist in the request God could give it to us in anger which would not be a blessing to us but bring us grief.

I am always reminded of the children of Israel in the wilderness asking for flesh and God gave them quail. It was while the meat was still in their mouths that God's anger came upon the people.

When we ask God, it would be wise to add that if our request is not going to be a blessing to us then please withhold our petition.

C.H. Spurgeon used the following illustration[28] to help us understand this better:

A kind mother had a son who was ill, and the child was close to death. She pleaded with her Puritan minister to pray for his life and his healing. He prayed very earnestly, but at the end of the prayer added, 'If it be Thy will save this child.' The woman said, 'I cannot bear that: I must have you pray that the child should live. Do not include any ifs or buts'. The pastor kindly responded, 'Woman, it may be you will live to regret the day that you ever wished to set your will against God's will.'

Twenty years later she was carried away in a fainting fit from under Tyburn gallows-tree, where that son was put to death as a criminal. Although she had lived to see her child grow up to be a man, it would have been infinitely wiser for her had the child died and she had left it to God's will.

We should never be sure that what you think is an answer to prayer is any proof of God's divine love.

King Hezekiah was told by the prophet Isaiah that he would die from his sickness. Hezekiah asked God to heal him. God granted his request and added fifteen years to his life. These extra years were the most spiritually barren years of his reign. Manasseh was born three years after God had extended his life and you can read about the evil he did in 2 Kings 21:1–12.

We should always qualify any request with those words, 'Not as I will, but as You will.' God always knows what is best for us.

1 OCTOBER

Let us be honest with ourselves and God

'We have sinned and committed iniquity, we have done wickedly and rebelled, even by departing from Your precepts and Your judgements.' Daniel 9:5

RECOMMENDED READING: Romans 3:10–18

Reading Daniel's prayer in chapter 9, one point comes out clearly; Daniel had a right view of man. During the next two days I want to look through the eyes of Daniel to see ourselves as we really are.

As I have prepared these daily thoughts I have tried to be as positive as I can, but we must at all times be faithful to the teaching of the Bible. If we are honest, when we look at ourselves, it is not all pleasant reading. However, there is always light at the end of a dark tunnel.

1. Man is a sinner. Daniel is very clear regarding this characteristic of human nature. In his prayer in v.5, he says, 'We have sinned and committed iniquity.' In v.8 he says, 'O Lord, to us belongs shame of face ... because we have sinned against You.' Then in v.11 he adds, 'We have sinned against Him.' Finally in v.15 he acknowledges that, 'we have sinned, we have done wickedly!'

This is not pleasant reading, but Daniel could not be clearer. This picture is not just Old Testament teaching. The apostle Paul gives numerous examples in his letters, such as Romans 3:23 where he says, 'For all have sinned.'

I thank God for that glimmer of hope when we come to Romans 5:20: 'But where sin abounded, grace abounded much more.'

Despite our sin, 'God demonstrates His own love toward us, in that while we were still sinners, Christ died for us' (Romans 5:8).

But Daniel has more to say about man.

2. Man is unfaithful. In Daniel 9:5 he says, 'We have ... rebelled ... by departing from Your precepts.' In v.7 he adds, 'because of the unfaithfulness ... committed against You'.

Unfaithfulness is a characteristic of man. We see it in the political realm which has become cut-throat politics. We see it in international relations and ask, 'Who can you really trust?' We also see it in the marriage vows, which for so many are entirely irrelevant. But, most serious of all, we see it in the spiritual realm where ministers of Christ's church deny the fundamental principles of the faith.

How thankful we should be that, in the midst of unfaithfulness, there is One who is faithful in all things and at all times.

Forgive our sin and bless us

'All this disaster has come upon us; yet we have not made our prayer before the LORD.' Daniel 9:13

RECOMMENDED READING: Daniel 9:1–19

We are looking at Daniel's prayer in chapter 9. In it he portrays a right view of man. Yesterday we saw man as a sinner and unfaithful to God. Today he brings out two further aspects of man's character.

3. Man is disobedient. Daniel says in v.10, 'We have not obeyed the voice of the Lord our God.' In v.14 he emphasises, 'We have not obeyed His voice.'

Disobedience began in Eden, bringing the downfall of Adam and Eve and with them the entire human race. It eventually led the children of Israel into captivity, even after strong warnings from faithful prophets.

Disobedience is still a characteristic that forms part of our nature, and this will remain with us from the cradle to the grave. Children are disobedient to parents, employees rebellious to employers, and citizens disobedient to lawmakers. But the most serious of all is our disobedience to Almighty God.

We should be thankful for One who demonstrated obedience at all times to His Father, even to death on the cross. The will of Jesus was not paramount; He came to do His Father's will no matter what the cost, even His own blood.

4. Man is prayerless. Daniel sums up his view of man in v.13, 'All this disaster has come upon us; yet we have not made our prayer before the LORD our God.'

We usually assume that when trouble strikes, man turns to prayer, but not according to Daniel. Even when disaster comes, prayer is neglected; man is still defiant against His Creator.

A lesson from history tells us that when God's people turn to serious prayer, He listens. We have numerous examples of this during times of revival.

Our country today is in total disarray morally and spiritually, and this includes much of the organised church. The prayer meeting is the least attended meeting in the church's diary. We can so easily find excuses, but God knows those who want to do business with Him. We are active, but not prayerful. We put duty before devotion. We should therefore not be at all surprised if God removed the lampstand from many of our churches. How can we look God squarely in the eyes when his word condemns us so clearly?

If we are serious about it, God will show mercy and forgive. We need to be like Jacob who, when wrestling with God, said, 'I will not let You go unless You bless me' (Genesis 32:26).

3 OCTOBER

Never despise the small things

'There are four things which are little on the earth, but they are exceedingly wise.' Proverbs 30:24

RECOMMENDED READING: Proverbs 6:6–8

We live in an age of big things. Projects have to be on a big scale, surpassing previous achievements. Skyscrapers are becoming higher, with the Burj Khalifa dominating the skyline in Dubai. It stands at 828 metres which is nearly half a mile high.

Transport is becoming faster with high-speed rail; two-tier jets take to the air regularly with large passenger numbers.

Sport has now become big business with players earning immoral amounts of money at such a young age, but often failing to find true contentment.

Even church buildings are being built on a grand scale seating thousands of people.

Despite all this, the Bible very rarely speaks about big things, but has much to say about little things. Let me explain:

A spark is only a little thing, but it can kindle a forest fire. It was only a little bowl of stew, but it cost Esau his birthright. A tongue is a very small muscle, but it can cause untold damage when let loose. It only takes a little faith, but it can move mountains. Remember it is the little foxes that destroy the vines. It is the little sins and habits which, if not controlled, can lead to far greater ones. It was only a little town called Bethlehem, but its local inn witnessed a premier birth.

A cross-country traveller, who had walked many miles through a number of countries, was once asked what his greatest hindrance was. He replied, 'It is not the wide rivers I have to cross, or the great mountains I have to climb, not even the storms I try to avoid. My greatest hindrance is the little grains of sand that get into my shoes and between my toes.'

What does the Bible say about little things? Zechariah 4:10 says, 'Who has despised the day of small things?' Psalm 37:16 says, 'A little that a righteous man has is better than the riches of many wicked.' Proverbs 15:16 says, 'Better is a little with the fear of the LORD, than great treasure with trouble.'

Many, who may be reading this, belong to small fellowships throughout the land. You have struggled for many years with little, if any, results that you can see. Don't give up! God sees the effort you put in and you will be rewarded. You never know what an influence you have been to those around you.

4 OCTOBER

Lessons from the ant and friends

'The ants are a people not strong, yet they prepare their food in the summer.'
Proverbs 30: 25

RECOMMENDED READING: Proverbs 6:6–8

1. The ant. The ant gives us a lesson in preparation. It knows the bright days of summer will soon be past and then it is too late to search for life's provisions, because winter will soon be upon them.

The ant lives today in view of tomorrow. It utilises the present to prepare for the future. Read again Proverbs 6:6–8.

It teaches us that we should all be preparing for that great day when we meet our God. This applies to both Christians and unbelievers.

The big question that needs an answer is, 'Are we as wise as the little ant?' Today people seem so preoccupied with the pleasures of this life that the cries of the ant go unheard. People give little or no thought at all for their future after death.

Their ruling passion is the materialistic gain and pleasures of this present world. Fame, fortune and fun are what they are taken up with and not a thought that, one day, they will meet their Creator.

How dangerous it is to live for the present only, and not prepare for the life to come. Listen to the ant!

2. The rock badger. These are also known as coneys or hyraxes. They are very timid, defenceless and often clumsy little creatures which are no bigger than rabbits.

They are not strong enough to dig and make their home in the earth, so they live in the rocks and crags. Psalm 104:18 tells us, 'The cliffs are a refuge for the rock badgers.'

In the rocks they find protection from the elements of nature, and they find safety and security from the marauder or invading enemy. Psalm 94:22 reminds us that, 'The LORD has been … the rock of my refuge.'

The Lord Jesus Christ is our Rock, and when we hide in Him, we are safe and protected from the storms of life and the power of the evil one.

We cannot trust and rely upon our own skill and ability to keep us safe. We tried to do that before we met the Saviour, and the evil one showed just how vulnerable we are. Our trust is not in ourselves but in the Lord and He will guide us safely to our eternal home.

5 OCTOBER

We must fly together

'The locusts have no king, yet they all advance in ranks.' Proverbs 30:27

RECOMMENDED READING: Joel 2:1–11

We are looking at the wisdom of four little things on the earth which are exceedingly wise. We have considered the ant and its lesson in preparation. We have also thought about the rock badger that makes its home in the crags. Today we conclude with two more little creatures and the lessons they teach each one of us.

3. The locust. The message of the locust is one of unity. You will rarely find a locust flying alone; they fly together. Locusts work in a similar way to the devastating description of the 'Day of the Lord' in Joel 2:1–11.

Ants have a queen, bees have a queen, but the locusts have no king. If the locusts, who have no king, can fly together in unity, what about Christians who have a king—in fact, the King of all kings?

Have you heard the argument about the kite? Who flies the kite? 'I', said the boy. Who flies the kite? 'I', said the wind. Who flies the kite? 'I', said the string. Who flies the kite? 'I,' said the tail.

Who does fly the kite? Well, they were all wrong, yet they were all right, for they all fly the kite. While we are all individuals in the church of our Lord, yet we are all one in Christ and therefore we should be flying together.

We should all be working together in harmony towards the extension of God's kingdom and the glory of His name. We must learn to fly together.

4. The lizard. Proverbs 30:28: 'The lizard you can take in your hands, yet it is in kings' palaces' (ESV). What can be more out of place than a lizard (which should be in a desert) in a palace? (Some translations have the word 'spider' but this can also be translated as 'lizard'.)

The type of lizard Solomon refers to is found in Israel. Under each toe of the lizard is a sponge-like container which holds adhesive liquid. As it runs up the slippery walls, the liquid helps it to hold on to the smooth surfaces.

Faith is the hand by which we take hold of the promises of God, securing ourselves to them. Faith in God will hold on when everything else has let you go.

Faith laughs at impossibilities and cries, 'It shall be done.' Faith bypasses obstacles, removes the immovable and does the impossible. Faith never says, 'I can't.'

If your doubts are high and your faith is low, then listen to the lizard as it proclaims, 'Have faith in God.' If we do this, we shall be as wise as these four little creatures.

6 OCTOBER

If we don't move forward, we drift backwards

'And the sons of the prophets said to Elisha, "See now, the place where we dwell with you is too small for us."' 2 Kings 6:1

RECOMMENDED READING: Ephesians 4:1–6

Many events recorded in the Bible involve people who are well known to us. However, this story we are about to consider involves a young man who remains anonymous.

1. The task of the anonymous young man. The first thing to notice is that he was involved in expansion. Chapter 6:1 tells us that the place where they lived was too small for them. The school of the prophets had outgrown its accommodation. There was an immediate need for more room, so a building project was about to begin.

This was good, for they were not content with things as they were; they wanted to extend their influence and usefulness. This should always be the motive of the members of Christ's body, the church. It is so easy to get into a rut and lose the plot, and therefore miss the vision. We must never become complacent or satisfied with things as they are.

The church of Jesus Christ must be a growing concern, as should the life of each individual Christian. If we don't move forward, the danger is that we drift backwards. There is no such thing as holding your own.

The task of the anonymous young man was to see that not only he should be involved in expansion, but that others should help him. Verse 2 says, 'Let every man take a beam.'

There was clear unity among the sons of the prophets. They worked together as a team. When the early church began to expand in Acts 2, we are told in v.44, 'All who believed were together.'

Here is another lesson as we work for the Lord. It is so easy to leave God's work to a few. Some will work, others will let them. As members of the local church, we work together in a spirit of unity.

As I write this, we have just lost a 93-year-old member of our congregation called Kath. She attended every work day in the church and was willing to do anything with a cheery disposition. Such people are invaluable.

We must have enthusiasm in our employment. This young man caught the vision and was willing to do his share. He was keen, zealous and enthusiastic.

May we be equally keen for the things which matter most—God's kingdom and its growth.

7 OCTOBER

You can't cut trees with just an axe head

'As one was cutting down a tree, the iron axe head fell into the water.'
2 Kings 6:5

RECOMMENDED READING: 2 Kings 6:1–7

We are looking at a story of an anonymous young man who witnessed a miracle with his own eyes. Yesterday we considered his task. Today we look at another element of the story.

2. The tragedy of the anonymous young man. Not only did the iron axe [spelt ax in NKJV] head fall into the water, but we are told it was borrowed. To lose or do damage to one of your own tools is unfortunate, but, when it belongs to someone else, it can be very embarrassing.

He lost his axe head, not the whole of the axe, but the most effective part of it. A tragedy had undoubtedly occurred. Only the handle was left in his hand. It may have been an expensive tool with a carved handle, but you cannot cut down a tree with a wooden stick, no matter how ornate it looks. It is vital that you have a cutting edge attached to the handle if the tool is to be useful.

There are many Christians today who are trying to cut down trees with axe handles. In other words, the most important part of their tool is missing.

There are those who believe that if they are articulate in speaking with an attractive and appealing personality, plus a good education, that is all that is necessary in being successful in Christian ministry. Whoever we are, we all need the most important possession of all, and that is God's Spirit and the cutting edge of His Word.

It is always sad when youth workers, church leaders and members lose their power for service.

Here was a known tragedy. As soon as the axe head had gone, the young man was aware of the problem. It would be a waste of energy swinging a headless handle. Are some Christians trying to accomplish God's work without His power to support them?

The young man acknowledged what had happened. He did not try and hide his loss. Despite the humbling experience, he confessed his axe head was lost.

We always find it difficult being upfront with God, but there is no advantage in hiding our mistakes, because He knows anyway. To be open and honest with Him is the first step to recovery.

8 OCTOBER

Always wise to be honest with God

'The man of God said, "Where did it fall?" And he showed him the place.'
2 Kings 6:6

RECOMMENDED READING: 2 Kings 6:1–7

Today we conclude with two further points concerning the anonymous young man in 2 Kings 6.

3. The honesty of the anonymous young man. When Elisha was told about the tragedy, he asked, 'Where did it fall?' And he showed him the place. This was a very important question to ask. Elisha wanted to know where he lost the axe head.

Could Almighty God be asking a similar question? 'Where did you lose your power and enthusiasm for My work?' It can only be recovered when you are truthful with the Lord. Where did you lose your cutting edge? Was that power lost when you developed an unhelpful relationship with someone? Or was it when the Lord was no longer central in your thoughts and desires?

Was it some bitterness, jealousy, or unkind criticism towards another Christian that did the damage? Perhaps it is something deeper which is affecting your relationship with Him, such as neglecting your prayer life, or you have become intermittent in the reading of His Word. When did your axe head fall, and where did you lose it? Be truthful and tell God the occasion and show Him the place.

4. The triumph of the anonymous man. Elisha threw a stick into the water where the axe head had fallen in and the iron head floated. When the man was told to pick it up, he just reached out his hand and took it. The axe head was not only in sight but also within reach, thanks to this miracle of God. The result was triumph. When Christians are truthful about their spiritual condition, triumph is usually the outcome. Failure can soon turn to victory.

A Christian worker returned home from a series of meetings. His two little daughters rushed to greet him. The eldest reached him first, and hugging him said, 'I've got all there is of Daddy.' The youngest began to cry, but when her father put his arms around her in a comforting way she said, 'You got all there is of Daddy, but Daddy has got all there is of me.'

A very simple story, but it carries a profound message. In the spiritual realm, has God got all there is of you or are you just living for yourself?

'The iron floated.' Then go and pick it up!

William Carey, missionary to India, said, 'Expect great things from God and attempt great things for God.'[29] How great are your expectations?

9 OCTOBER

A doctor who kept out of the limelight

'Luke the beloved physician and Demas greet you.' Colossians 4:14

RECOMMENDED READING: Acts 16:9–15

A strong friendship has often been forged through a casual introduction. There are occasions when God works providentially and often unexpectedly in bringing two people, or even families, together who had never met before.

This has been our experience over many years of itinerant ministry. As we have travelled from place to place, we have met people for the first time and developed a relationship that has continued over many years.

Throughout the apostle Paul's life, he was brought into contact with believers who became a great support to him as time went on. There are too many to mention, but one man stood out as exceptional, sticking with Paul through thick and thin.

In addition to that, God used him to write two of the New Testament books: the Gospel of Luke and the Acts of the Apostles. Yes, his name was Luke. I want to share three commendable characteristics about Paul's friend and God's servant.

1. Luke was a humble man. To my surprise, his name is only mentioned three times in the Bible. When we read through the Acts of the Apostles, we only know that he was actually there because he used the word, 'we'.

Acts 16:10 says, 'Immediately *we* sought to go to Macedonia.'

In Acts 21:18 we read, 'On the following day Paul went in with *us* to James, and all the elders were present.'

In Acts 27:27 it says, 'Now when the fourteenth night had come, as *we* were driven up and down in the Adriatic Sea.'

We will look at the occasions when his name is mentioned, but clearly, we have a man who was willing to play the second fiddle well and work quietly in the background. Luke was a humble man who didn't push himself into the limelight; he knew his role and he stuck to it.

As well as his links with Paul, Luke must have had a close relationship with the family of our Saviour. In the first chapters of his Gospel, he gives a lot of important information about their lives and God's dealings with them. Yet, he records his information in a quiet unobtrusive way, giving glory to God, and not in any way exalting himself.

May we be constantly reminded that God's glory should be our sole aim in life. We must never take any of the glory from Him, for He alone is deserving of all praise.

A doctor on call to the end

'Only Luke is with me.' 2 Timothy 4:11

RECOMMENDED READING: Philemon 19–25

We conclude our consideration of the life of Luke who was Paul's friend and God's faithful servant.

2. He was Paul's loyal and trusted companion. When Paul was a prisoner and about to commence a dangerous sea voyage to Rome, Luke voluntarily joined the ship to accompany his friend on the journey. When Paul was in prison in Rome, Luke was with him. When Paul wrote to the Colossians, in chapter 4:14, he said, Luke the beloved physician and Demas greet you.' In v.24 of his letter to Philemon he wrote, 'Mark, Aristarchus, Demas, Luke, my fellow labourers.' What a beautiful description that is of another believer. When writing to the Philippians, in 2:25 he refers to Epaphroditus as his 'brother, fellow worker and fellow soldier'.

With Paul there is a genuine desire to work together in both good times and bad times. There is a striving for unity in the same cause, having the same purpose in mind. It isn't difficult obtaining friends and fellow workers when things are going well, but for them to join you on a dangerous journey, and stay with you when you are in prison, is a great blessing and encouragement. Such companions as these are hard to find but, when you find one, you possess a great and valuable treasure.

3. He was loyal to the end. Paul was in prison on two occasions. He spent two years in Caesarea and then, six years later, he was in Rome. When Paul wrote his second and final letter to Timothy, in 4:11 he tells him, 'Only Luke is with me.' Right at the end, Luke was still at Paul's side. What an encouragement he must have been to Paul when others, for whatever reason, had left him. Paul needed support and companionship throughout his ministry, especially during his final days in Rome. He longed for loyalty, and Luke was the man to give it. Loyalty, in these days, seems to be a scarce commodity. Politics and the business world are cut-throat. However, the church should be different. It is sad when pastors and leaders are betrayed and under attack by members of their own congregation. This is becoming a common occurrence. They plough a lonely furrow and often become discouraged and disheartened over some of the issues and people they have to handle. Disagreement should not be a problem, and it should never break loyalty and unity.

Just as Paul needed the friendship and loyalty of Luke at this difficult time, may we show that same loyalty to those who carry a heavy burden in the work of the gospel.

11 OCTOBER

Take your faith with you

'The Syrians had gone out on raids and had brought back captive a young girl from the land of Israel. She waited on Naaman's wife.' 2 Kings 5:2

RECOMMENDED READING: 2 Kings 5:1–3

One of the most interesting stories in the Old Testament is the story of Naaman. It is so easy to understand, full of detail and grips the imagination of all who read it.

But this story doesn't just involve Naaman and the prophet Elisha, important though they are. This story might not have occurred if it hadn't been for a young servant girl, who the Syrians captured during a raid into Israel (v.2). So, what do we know about this girl?

1. This young girl did not forget her faith when she was taken from home. Though she was in a foreign country, she still remembered her father's God and the prophets who taught them.

This is an important lesson especially when travelling was so common before the outbreak of the coronavirus and will hopefully be again one day. Unfortunately, the motto with some Christians is, 'When in Rome, do as the Romans do.' When they travel to other countries, they act as though God is not looking down upon them as he does at home.

A number of years ago I was having lunch with a deacon and his wife and they told me that when on holiday they didn't go to church on a Sunday. When I asked why, they said a holiday gives them a break from it.

The Lord's Day is the Lord's Day wherever you are. Meeting with the Lord's people should be the highlight of any holiday. Begin it in the right way, in the right place, and it sets the tone for the days ahead.

Never lock up your faith when you turn the key in your door. As well as taking guidebooks for the journey, don't forget to take the greatest guide of all—your Bible.

No matter where you go, take your faith with you. Joseph took his to Egypt; Daniel took his to Babylon; this little Hebrew maid took hers into Syria.

When you just ponder about it, this young maid had strong temptations to give up her faith. No doubt it would have pleased her new master if she had turned to his gods, but here was a girl who would not disown the only true God whether she was at home or away.

Proverbs 3:6 says, 'In all your ways acknowledge Him, and He shall direct your paths.'

12 OCTOBER

Always seek to do good

'Repay no one evil for evil.' Romans 12:17

RECOMMENDED READING: 1 Samuel 24:1–15

Yesterday, we began to look at the story of the healing of Naaman from leprosy (2 Kings:5), concentrating on the important role a young servant girl from Israel played in his recovery. We saw how she did not leave her faith at home when she was taken captive from her homeland.

Today we consider a second commendable aspect of her character which we would do well to emulate.

2. The young girl did not look for revenge. She had been torn from her home and family by the hands of Syrian soldiers who would have shown little sympathy or mercy towards her. Her father may have been murdered by these same men during the conflict.

Yet, despite all this, we do not find her demonstrating a spirit of revenge—in fact the opposite. Instead of rejoicing to see her master suffer, she had sympathy for him. She longed to see him healed of this terrible disease, so she informed her mistress that he could receive help from Elisha, a prophet in Israel.

Have we ever rejoiced inwardly in the suffering of another, especially when they have been unkind towards us, or has revenge been a part of our plan?

Have we ever harboured a secret thrill of satisfaction when someone, with whom we have had a strong disagreement, has things go wrong for them?

A spirit of revenge—however natural it may be to our sinful nature—is not how a Christian should behave, no matter how much we may have been offended. Jesus clearly teaches us to do unto others as we would wish them to do unto us.

Jesus says. 'Love your enemies, bless those who curse you, do good to those who hate you, and pray for those who spitefully use you and persecute you.' (Matthew 5:44).

These things are not always easy, but we are told that they bring glory and pleasure to our Father in heaven. Surely that is what Christianity is all about.

We certainly cannot do these things in our own strength, as we do not have the ability, or often the desire, to do so. If we try, we will fail miserably. But with God's help all things are possible.

> 'A heart in every thought renewed
> and full of love divine;
> Perfect and right and pure and good—
> a copy, Lord, of thine.'
>
> Charles Wesley (1707–88)

13 OCTOBER

Never too young to stand up for Jesus

'You are not able to go against this Philistine to fight with him; for you are a youth, and he a man of war from his youth.' 1 Samuel 17:33

RECOMMENDED READING: 1 Samuel 17:32–51

We continue to look at the life of a young Israelite girl who was captured by the Syrians and became a servant to Naaman's wife. The commander of Syria's army had been struck down with leprosy and this young girl came to his aid (2 Kings 5:1–3). Yesterday we saw she did not seek for revenge. Today we look at one more commendable attribute.

3. Although she was young, she became a blessing to others. She did not say to herself, 'I'm too young, there is nothing I can do.' Neither did she wait for some greater task to do in the future. She just did the work that was nearest to her. She saw a way by which she might be useful and took the opportunity to act without delay.

She said to her mistress (v.3): 'If only my master were with the prophet who is in Samaria! For he would heal him of his leprosy.' That was all she said. She just told her mistress where healing could be found.

This is a lesson for all young people, for none are too young to do something for Jesus. He may want you to stand up for him in school, college or university. If you don't, who will?

He may want you to show some kind act to the sick or elderly. He may want you to think of others and not always yourself. Do the work that is nearest to you.

But this is a lesson for all of us, no matter what age we are. What are you doing to be a blessing and encouragement to others? Could there be a poor family that you support? Is there not a troubled person that you might be able to comfort and talk with? Is there not some struggling Christian you could sit and pray with? Is there not some unbeliever that you might share this life-changing message with?

There are so many people in need, extremely lonely and afraid in these difficult days. We need courage to speak up for Jesus, so when the opportunity presents itself let's stand up for Him and never be ashamed of him.

Be available so that God can use you, even in a small way. God needs those in the orchestra who can play the second fiddle well.

14 OCTOBER

Even the greatest can be vulnerable

'He was also a mighty man of valour, but a leper.' 2 Kings 5:1

RECOMMENDED READING: Luke 7:1–10

We have been looking at the lessons that can be learnt from a young girl who was captured from the land of Israel. Now we turn our attention to her master Naaman.

1. Naaman was a great man. Most people come into this world in virtual obscurity. They work and struggle; they live and die; they achieve nothing of great importance. They remain ordinary and obscure individuals.

Then there are others who rise to fame, and very quickly make a name for themselves. Soon their achievements are known by all. This was the position of Naaman. Wherever he went he was recognised and given enthusiastic adulation. If he walked through the streets, I am sure he would soon be surrounded by adoring crowds.

Now read the description of this man again in v.1. He was commander of the Syrian army, the highest soldier in the land. Everybody looked up to Naaman. He was truly a great man. We are told he was honourable. He could be relied upon and trusted. Through him, the Lord had given victory to Syria, which meant that God had fulfilled His purposes through Naaman. Almighty God had been at work in his life. Also note that, 'he was a mighty man of valour.' He was brave and courageous and recognised for it.

2. He had a life-destroying disease. The closing words of v.1 tell us he was 'a leper.' Underneath that splendid uniform, cut and fitted no doubt by the best tailor in Syria, was a dreadful, and life-destroying disease. Hidden behind those medals of honour was a body infected with leprosy.

When the great physician, Sir James Simpson, was given a title from the Queen, he received numerous letters of congratulations that came from all over the world. One would have thought it would have made him the happiest man in the world. But behind the adulation was the realisation of an underlying disease that would eventually take his life. He died when he was 59 years of age. Many a broken heart is obscured by a smiling face.

There are many throughout our land today who are popular and successful, but the greatest disease of all is ruining their lives—sin. Sin may be hidden from even our friends, but God sees it.

Let us thank God today that He provided a cure for our sin through the sacrifice of His Son the Lord Jesus Christ, who freely gave His life upon Calvary's cross, carrying our sin and thereby assuring us of complete forgiveness.

15 OCTOBER

God's way always brings the best results

'So he went down and dipped seven times in the Jordan, according to the saying of the man of God; and his flesh was restored like the flesh of a little child, and he was clean.' 2 Kings 5:14

RECOMMENDED READING: 2 Kings 5:1–16

As we look at the life of Naaman, we see a man, who was great in the eyes of the Syrian people, but he had a serious disease; he was a leper.

3. Naaman made three serious mistakes. Initially, he was wise in listening to the advice of a young servant girl from Israel, but he was foolish in not following her advice.

Firstly, he thought he could buy the cure (v.5).

There are so many people today who ignorantly think that they can purchase or earn their salvation. They sincerely believe that if they give generously to charity, or say special prayers, or occasionally attend a place of worship, they will be admitted to heaven. But they are totally deluded! God's salvation is a free gift that cannot be bought or earned.

The Lord Jesus Christ paid the price at Calvary. The cost was His precious blood which was freely poured out for us. The price has now been paid in full.

Secondly, he went to the wrong place for healing (v.6).

Instead of going to Elisha, God's prophet, he went to the king of Israel. Many people, who seek to be healed from sin, knock on the wrong door. They seek forgiveness from a priest, but he is only a man. Only God can forgive our sin.

Some seek peace through other religions or false sects, but they also are hammering hard on the wrong door. There is only one place where true forgiveness can be found and that is at Calvary's cross.

Thirdly, he sought healing his way, not God's (vv. 10–12).

If we are to receive forgiveness, it is through God's way only. Isaiah 45:22 says, 'Look to Me, and be saved.' Is that too difficult? Verse 10 tells us how simple it was for Naaman: 'Go and wash in Jordan seven times.' God's way always brings the best result.

4. The story concludes with an amazing miracle. With his servants and men all around him, he steps into the water and dips below the surface seven times. When he went down so did his pride (v.14). The result was amazing. He was restored completely.

When we turn to Christ, He makes a new person of us.

16 OCTOBER

He made all things beautiful

'Therefore we must give the more earnest heed to the things we have heard, lest we drift away.' Hebrews 2:1

RECOMMENDED READING: Hebrews 1

Whenever I meet someone for the first time, I usually ask: 'Where do you come from? What do you do for a living? What plans do you have for the future?' I'm interested in knowing about them and what makes them tick.

In Acts 9, we have the account of Saul's conversion on the road to the city of Damascus. In v.4, he hears a voice speaking to him. In v.5, Saul asks, 'Who are You Lord?'

When we turn to the first chapter of the letter to the Hebrews, we find the answer to that all-important question. However, it was the first verse of chapter 2 that caught my attention.

Throughout the history of the Christian church, believers have faced attacks upon their faith from the enemies of our Lord. During recent decades the attacks have been directly aimed at our Saviour as well as His followers. Books have been written by well-known authors and scientists, seeking to discredit the authority of our Lord. Sadly, even some clergy have also seriously watered down their theological position regarding our Saviour.

They have done what Paul warned about in Romans 1:25, exchanging the truth of God for a lie. Therefore Hebrews 2:1 is relevant for them.

During the next few days, we will be considering some aspects of our Lord's character and ministry, clearly laid out in this letter, that are being undermined. I will only be touching upon them briefly but do consider them in more detail.

1. He is the Creator of the world. Hebrews 1:2 says that God 'has ... spoken to us by His Son, whom He has appointed heir of all things, through whom also He made the worlds'. Hebrews 1:10 says, 'You LORD, in the beginning laid the foundation of the earth.'

During my travels I have met professing believers who sincerely believe that Jesus came into existence as a baby in Bethlehem 2,000 years ago. The truth is that Jesus came to earth through the incarnation in Bethlehem's manger, but not into existence.

If you read through the Psalms and the prophets, He is there. In the book of Genesis you have a number of pre-incarnate visits to this earth. He is there back in the first chapter of the Bible. In Genesis 1:26 God said, 'Let *us* make man in *our* image.' The Father, the Son and the Holy Spirit were all there in the beginning, creating this amazing world in which we live.

17 OCTOBER

Jesus is God's only Son

'God ... has in these last days spoken to us by His Son, whom He has appointed heir of all things, through whom also He made the worlds.' Hebrews 1:1–2

RECOMMENDED READING: Matthew 3:13–17

We are looking at some aspects of our Lord's character and ministry as laid out in the first chapter of the letter to the Hebrews. We are, sadly, living in days when these aspects of our Lord are being challenged and undermined, but must be held onto by Christians at all costs.

Yesterday we saw that the Lord Jesus was the Creator of the universe. Today we consider briefly a further aspect of His character.

2. He is the Son of God. In Matthew's Gospel there are two very important occasions in the life of our Lord where His deity is confirmed by Almighty God.

On the occasion of his baptism in the river Jordan, as He came up out of the water, we read in Matthew 3:17, 'Suddenly a voice came from heaven, saying, "This is My beloved Son, in whom I am well pleased."'

Then, towards the close of His ministry, we read of our Lord's transfiguration. In Matthew 17:5 we read, 'Suddenly a voice came out of the cloud, saying, "This is My beloved Son, in whom I am well pleased. Hear Him!"'

It saddens me greatly when I hear and read of leaders within our churches that openly question, and even deny, the deity of our Lord. I have to be clear that I find it impossible to believe that anyone who denies our Lord's deity can be a truly born-again believer.

No finite man could ever die to forgive our sin, no matter how holy they were. It had to be One who was perfect and spotless, without any trace of sin; only God's Son was capable of fulfilling that task.

I want to proclaim loud and clear that I believe the Lord Jesus Christ to be the only begotten Son of the Father, full of grace and truth. Hold onto that truth, my friends, because our faith is centred upon it and godly men were even willing to die for it.

> 'Thou art the Everlasting Word, the Father's only Son;
> God manifestly seen and heard and heaven's beloved One.
> Worthy, O Lamb of God, art Thou,
> That every knee to Thee should bow!'
>
> Josiah Conder (1789–1855)

18 OCTOBER

He prays for His people

'When He had by Himself purged our sins, sat down at the right hand of the Majesty on high.' Hebrews 1:3

RECOMMENDED READING: John 17

We continue to look at some of the characteristics and ministry of our Lord found in Hebrews 1. We have acknowledged Jesus as the Creator of the world and everything in it. We have recognised Him to be the Son of the living God. We now turn to another important aspect of His ministry which continues today.

3. He intercedes for us at the right hand of God. Throughout the Bible we come across certain men of God who interceded for God's people when difficult situations arose. One of these was Moses.

In Numbers 14, Almighty God was angry with His people and was about to disinherit them because they didn't believe they could go into the land and conquer it. At this point Moses stepped in and pleaded with God to show mercy and forgive their unbelief. God answered the prayer of Moses but had to punish the people by extending their time in the wilderness by forty more years.

However, we have a greater intercessor than Moses in our Lord Jesus Christ. Following His death upon Calvary's cross and His glorious resurrection from the dead, Jesus ascended into heaven to sit at the right hand of His Father.

Hebrews 10:12 says, 'But this Man, after He had offered one sacrifice for sins forever, sat down at the right hand of God.' The Christ of truth returned to the Father. The Spirit of truth came to dwell with men.

So, what is His ministry at God's right hand? I just want to mention two things:

Firstly, He is waiting for the Father to announce His return to earth a second time. Jesus will return to earth at a time known only to the Father. When He comes, He will gather His people to be with Him for ever. This heaven and earth as we know it will be no more. Our future will no longer be here, but with Him in glory for evermore.

Secondly, until that day comes, He is at God's right hand interceding on our behalf. He is there praying for His people. It is good to intercede for one another, but the greatest comfort is to know that Jesus prays for us. Whatever our concerns, may we today know that He prays to the Father on our behalf. May that thought comfort us until He comes again.

19 OCTOBER

Jesus is conqueror over the evil one

'... that through death He might destroy him who had the power of death, that is, the devil'. Hebrews 2:14

RECOMMENDED READING: Romans 8:31–39

We have looked at three aspects of our Lord's character and ministry. We have seen Him as Creator of the universe; we acknowledge Him as the Son of God; we have noted His intercessory work at God's right hand. We now turn our attention to a fourth aspect, which should cause our hearts to rejoice with thanksgiving.

4. He has power over the evil one. We need to be regularly reminded that we have an adversary. There are some today who do not believe in the devil. Well, if he isn't around, I would love to know who carries on his evil work because, whoever they are, they are doing a great job. The devil is delighted when we don't believe in him. Then there are others who say he is just a force of evil.

According to the Bible, the devil possesses a real personality, and his task is to undermine the work of God. He is a real person and is not just a force of evil: he is evil. The Bible describes him as a murderer, a deceiver, a liar and a cheat—to name a few. When you look at the world today you can clearly see the results of his work.

However, his work is not just conducted outside in the world, but sadly, inside the church also. He is not just a roaring lion; when it suits him, he becomes an angel of light. If he can cause mayhem among God's people he is delighted. Sometimes we even do his work for him. His aim is to bring disunity among the people of God by any means possible and, unfortunately, there are times when he succeeds.

We must resist the devil with all our spiritual strength. We must strive for true unity at all costs. This was one of the apostle Paul's key messages to the churches. As unity doesn't come naturally, we must work at it, demonstrating humility in the process.

However, let me conclude positively. Our enemy, the devil, is defeated already. He may be powerful, but our risen Saviour is all-powerful. The devil may be mighty, but our Saviour is Almighty. Jesus is stronger than Satan and sin, and Satan to Jesus must bow. Keep that thought before you throughout this and every day.

20 OCTOBER

Jesus is unchanged and unchanging

'But He, because He continues forever, has an unchangeable priesthood.'
Hebrews 7:24

RECOMMENDED READING: Hebrews 2:1–9

Today we continue with a further attribute of our Lord Jesus Christ.

5. He is unchanging. In Hebrews 1:11–12 we read the following words which refer to the heavens and the earth as we know them: 'They will perish, but You remain; and they will all grow old like a garment; like a cloak You will fold them up, and they will be changed. But You are the same, and Your years will not fail.'

We live in a world of change. If my parents were able to come back today, they would be stunned by the changes that have taken place in just forty years.

We have seen amazing changes in technology, which has allowed us to be able to communicate by email and hold services through social media. Our daughter who lives in South Africa can contact us regularly free of charge through these social media platforms. There have also been changes in travel, in science, in fashion, in the environment and in education.

I can just about cope with these, but what causes me the greatest concern is the changes we have seen in lowered attitudes, principles, morality and respect for authority. I could regrettably name many more. And where is the respect we once had for the church and God's holy laws?

The great hymn writer, Henry Francis Lyte (1793–1847), wrote these words in one of his well-known hymns:

> 'Change and decay in all around I see:
> O Thou who changest not, abide with me.'

Despite the continual change we witness even in our own generation, I am thankful today that the Lord Jesus Christ does not change.

His word is unchanging; His power is as strong as ever; His love never diminishes; and His truth will endure for evermore.

Malachi 3:6 says, 'For I am the LORD, I do not change.'

In Hebrews 13:8 it says, 'Jesus Christ is the same yesterday, today, and forever.' Truth unchanged, unchanging.

> 'How good is the God we adore,
> Our faithful unchangeable Friend
> His love is as great as His power
> And knows neither measure nor end.'

Joseph Hart (1712–1765)

21 OCTOBER

There is only one Saviour and his name is Jesus

'For God so loved the world that He gave His only begotten Son, that whoever believes in Him should not perish but have everlasting life.' John 3:16

RECOMMENDED READING: John 3:1–17

During the past few days, we have been considering some of the attributes and work of our Lord Jesus Christ found in the letter to the Hebrews. We have seen Him as the Creator of the universe; as the Son of the living God; as our one and only Mediator who sits at the right hand of God; as the one who has power over the evil one; and as the unchanging One. We conclude with one further attribute.

6. He is the only Saviour. Despite the many religions and sects throughout the world today, Jesus stands unique in the fact that He alone is the Saviour from sin. Only Jesus can meet the needs of man's sinful heart. He did that by giving His life upon Calvary's cross, bearing in His body all our sin. He shed His blood that we might be forgiven of all our iniquity and offers us hope of everlasting life.

Though the cross many be offensive to many people, for the Christian it is central to our faith. Without the truth of the cross and the empty tomb, the Christian has no hope to offer people. But, because of the fact of His death and bodily resurrection, our message is full of hope.

I have made many important decisions during my lifetime, some of which I sadly regret. However, the greatest decision was when God spoke to me as a young man and I became a follower of the Lord Jesus Christ. That will never be regretted!

To have peace with God and know the forgiveness of all my sin, is the greatest experience any person can have.

However, in Hebrews 2:3, we are presented with a clear warning: 'How shall we escape if we neglect so great a salvation?' The answer to that question is very simple and also crystal clear. We can't.

Therefore, if God speaks to you through these brief messages, I plead with you to respond to His call and look to Jesus Christ and live!

I can assure you that there is hope in no other but Him. In John 14:6 it says, 'Jesus said to him, "I am the way, the truth, and the life. No one comes to the Father except through Me."'

Always strive for unity

'Now I plead with you, brethren, by the name of our Lord Jesus Christ, that you all speak the same thing, and that there be no divisions among you, but that you be perfectly joined together in the same mind and in the same judgement.' 1 Corinthians 1:10

RECOMMENDED READING: 2 Samuel 3:1

When I retired as director of Day One in 2010, our son Mark and his wife Sharon suggested that we come and live with them. There was an outbuilding that could be made into a one-bedroom bungalow, which would be ideal for us. We are now thirty yards from their house. We are able to live independently, but close if needed. It has proved to be a successful arrangement and we thank God for this provision.

Unfortunately, relationships between some people are at their most healthy when the parties do not live so close together and do not see each other too often.

For many years there was constant friction between the house of Judah (David), and the house of Benjamin (Saul). The two tribes may have enjoyed better relationships had they lived further apart, next to the house of Asher or Naphtali in the north of the country. The fact was that Judah and Benjamin did live next to each other and the tension between them was great.

The first king of Israel was Saul who was from Benjamin. David, who came from the house of Judah, was always viewed with suspicion as the tribe of Benjamin thought he was planning to take over the throne by removing Saul. That was not his intention initially at all (It was obviously God's intention though as he did become king after Saul).

It is a sad situation and thwart with danger when one part of the body says, 'I am of Saul' and another says, 'I am of David.'

The apostle Paul had a similar challenge when some people within the church said, '"I am of Paul" and others said, "I am of Cephas" or "I am of Apollos"' (1 Corinthians 1:12).

When things like this happen, it is a sure sign that there is going to be trouble ahead. It is therefore necessary to take decisive action immediately.

Throughout his letters to the churches, Paul constantly emphasised the need for unity among God's people. We are all different in personality and in stages of growth in the faith. We are not to usurp one another but have one aim and purpose and that is to bring glory to our one and only Head of the church, the Lord Jesus Christ.

23 OCTOBER

Jesus cares for every lamb in His flock

'I will feed my flock, and I will make them lie down.' Ezekiel: 34:15

RECOMMENDED READING: John 10:1–18

I come from a farming background, as my mother was a farmer's daughter. Sheep are a common sight in many parts of Yorkshire; in fact, there are 2.1 million of them. It is always an interesting experience when you hear stories from the lips of a shepherd.

There were many shepherds in the Bible, Abel and David being just two of them. I want us to consider a third, being none other than our Lord Jesus Christ.

1. He is the Good Shepherd.

Firstly, He knows His sheep. John 10:14 says, 'I am the good shepherd; and I know My sheep, and am known by My own.' This is a two-way relationship. He knows the sheep and the sheep know the shepherd.

We live close to a number of farms which are mainly arable, but one field has a flock of sheep. One morning as I was walking past the field, I noticed the sheep had gathered by the gate. I began to talk to them, but within minutes they raced to the other end of the field. I clearly didn't possess a Herefordshire accent; they didn't know my voice. John 10:4 says, 'The sheep follow him, for they know his voice.' I was a stranger, so they ran as fast as they could from me.

John 10:27: 'My sheep hear My voice, and I know them, and they follow Me.' What a comfort it is to be aware that He knows us. Every lamb in His flock He knows and has a concern for them.

Secondly, He gives His life for the sheep. John 10:11 says, 'I am the good shepherd. The good shepherd gives His life for the sheep.' Verse 15 says, 'I lay down My life for the sheep.' Verse 18 says, 'No one takes it from Me, but I lay it down of Myself.'

From His birth in Bethlehem, His eyes were set towards Jerusalem and Calvary's cross. He came to give his life as a ransom for many; He came to carry the heavy burden of our sin upon Himself; He came to face the anger of a holy God, so that we would be spared from facing that anger ourselves. Instead of facing death, which our sins deserve, we would receive everlasting life. He died that we might live.

24 OCTOBER

He who died now lives for evermore

'Now may the God of peace who brought up our Lord Jesus from the dead, that great shepherd of the sheep.' Hebrews 13:20

RECOMMENDED READING: 1 Peter 5:1–4

Yesterday we saw our Lord Jesus Christ as the Good Shepherd. Today I want to share two more characteristics of the Shepherd.

2. He is the Great Shepherd. Hebrews 13:20 reminds us that our Good Shepherd is also the Great Shepherd. The One who died upon Calvary's cross and three days later rose again from the dead. The grave could not hold Him. Death had been swallowed up in victory; it had finally had its sting removed. Victory was assured through the work of the Lord Jesus Christ. He who rose from the dead lives for evermore. Because He lives, we shall live also.

This great victory, which He accomplished for us, means that we are now safe and secure in His hands. John 10:28 says, 'They shall never perish; neither shall anyone snatch them out of My hand.' We are safe and secure for eternity, and it is a double security. No one can snatch them out of His hand (v.28) and no one is able to snatch them out of the Father's hand (v.29).

Though the devil lies, cheats and deceives, we are safe if we remain in the security of our great Shepherd's fold.

3. He is the Chief Shepherd. 1 Peter 5:4 says, 'When the Chief Shepherd appears, you will receive the crown of glory that does not fade away.' What a wonderful hope awaits God's people.

A day is drawing near when the Lord Jesus Christ, who after His resurrection returned to His Father, will once again return to us and for us.

We will not be left in this world for ever. What a comforting thought that is, for this sinful world is not our home. We are not citizens of this earth; our citizenship is in heaven.

The thought that Jesus will appear for us should fill the heart of every believer with unending joy and anticipation.

He is our chief Shepherd. He is coming for us.

> 'Goodness and mercy all my life
> Shall surely follow me
> And in God's house for evermore
> My dwelling place shall be.'

Francis Rous (1579–1659)

25 OCTOBER

The new birth should be clearly evident

'Unless one is born again, he cannot see the kingdom of God.' John 3:3

RECOMMENDED READING: John 3:1–7

One evening Jesus met a Pharisee named Nicodemus. During their conversation Jesus made it abundantly clear that he must be born again.

1. The importance of the new birth. The new birth is not a take-it-or-leave-it option; it is a vital necessity. If, like the rich young ruler, we seek eternal life, we must be born again. There is no other option as far as God is concerned.

There are two concerns that people have with regard to salvation which leads them to ask these questions:

Firstly, how far can a person go into sin and still find salvation?

Let us consider one of the kings of Judah to discover the answer. King Manasseh had a godly father named Hezekiah, but he had little influence upon his wayward son. Manasseh was one of Judah's most wicked kings who, when he came to the throne, introduced all forms of evil and idolatry, both in Jerusalem and throughout Judea. He opposed the worship of Almighty God by murdering the prophets.

To save further carnage from this evil king, he was taken prisoner and removed from his own land. God had to humble this king, but it brought him to his senses, and he eventually repented of all the evil he had done.

However, we need to be careful, for there is a clear and solemn warning before us. The example of Manasseh, and others like him, should not cause people to think that they can sin with impunity. There are numerous examples of people who did fall deep into sin and never sought or found God's forgiveness.

Secondly, how far can a believer sink through backsliding?

There are many examples we could use, but one of the greatest can be found in the life of another king, David. The second king of Israel was responsible for breaking at least four of God's commandments, for he was guilty of coveting, stealing, adultery and murder. However, when he repented of these sins, God showed mercy and restored David to a relationship with Himself. But I have an important piece of advice; don't put God to the test.

I cannot imagine any sensible Christian wanting to backslide intentionally or wanting to stay in that condition any longer than necessary. An immediate recovery should be of paramount importance to us. Always keep in mind that you will not sink into a backslidden condition if you continue to keep walking in the steps of the Saviour.

26 OCTOBER

There must be a change that can be seen

'Unless one is born of water and the Spirit, he cannot enter the kingdom of God.' John 3:5

RECOMMENDED READING: John 3:5–17

Yesterday we considered the importance of the new birth. We will now consider the evidence of the new birth.

When a person is born again, they are given a new heart. The hard heart of granite has become a heart of flesh. This change cannot be brought about through good deeds, but only through the work of the Spirit of God. Let us now consider:

2. The evidence of the new birth. There should be a dramatic change in our lives that should cause the world to sit up and take notice. If a change is not clearly seen, then we must question if one has truly taken place. So, what is the evidence before us?

(a) The blind can now see. If I took a group of people to the summit of a hill to view one of the most beautiful scenes in the country, that picture would be breath-taking to most people. But if there was a blind person among them, no matter how well I described the panorama, it would be impossible for my friend to be completely enthusiastic about it.

A preacher can speak with great enthusiasm and passion about the Saviour whom he loves and express the wonder of all that Jesus has done for him, but if, in that congregation, there are people who are spiritually blind, they will never grasp or understand what he is talking about.

Their spiritual eyes need to be opened so they can see for themselves the wonderful truths that are being conveyed to them. Only the power of God can open blind eyes to enable people to see.

What a difference it makes, however, when those blind eyes are opened, and people can clearly see the wonderful truths that are contained in the Bible.

(b) The deaf can now hear. When you have difficulty in hearing, it can be most frustrating not being able to join in a conversation.

There are millions of people throughout our land who are spiritually deaf. God speaks through His Word, but so many fail to hear the message that is being explained to them. I am never sure what the worst condition is; being blind or being deaf. For the unbeliever they have both conditions.

What a difference it makes when both eyes and ears are open and we can see and hear and respond to God's call. Don't shut your ears but open them wide and listen to Him. He is still speaking.

27 OCTOBER

The dead in Christ shall live again

'For as in Adam all die, even so in Christ all shall be made alive.'
1 Corinthians 15:22

RECOMMENDED READING: 1 Corinthians 15:12–58

During the past few days, we have been looking at the importance of the new birth, and now we are looking at evidence of the new birth. This involves a noticeable change seen by yourself and other believers.

You have now come from death to life. You are no longer in darkness but in the light. You are no longer blind to spiritual realities but can see them. You are no longer deaf to the voice of God but can hear Him speaking through his Word. This has brought not just a minor change, but a significant change in your life. A miracle has taken place. We conclude by considering two further pieces of evidence regarding this change.

*(c) **The dumb can now speak.*** All forms of communication with the outside world are lost when a person cannot see, hear or speak. Some people live in a very lonely world when all forms of communication are cut off.

There is a far more serious condition when people are separated from their Creator. They have no desire to worship Him with their lips and have no urgency in making Him known to others.

What a difference it makes when our silent tongues can speak audibly and we are no longer mute. We can now sing His praises and share the good news with others.

*(d) **The dead can now live.*** To be blind, deaf, dumb and mute is a desperate condition to live with. However, there is one state that is far worse and many are in that condition. They are lifeless. They cannot breathe; they cannot move; they are cold and still. They are physically alive, but spiritually lifeless.

When a person discovers life in the Lord Jesus Christ, they are born again. They can see, hear, speak and live.

Has a change taken place in your life? Is the evidence of this new life seen by those who know you? Are you spiritually alive?

Two thousand years ago at a hill called Calvary, Jesus Christ, the Son of God, died upon a cross, carrying the burden of your sin. He took upon Himself the punishment that you deserved. He bravely faced God's anger over sin that you should have faced. He died so that you could be born again and have a new life, a new beginning. Today look toward that cross and live!

28 OCTOBER

Where do you place your trust?

'But God will redeem my soul from the power of the grave, for He shall receive me.' Psalm 49:15

RECOMMENDED READING: 1 Corinthians 15:1–11

Psalm 49 is clearly a message for all people throughout the world. It comes with a clear warning to be very careful where you place your trust.

The Psalm gives a description of the confidence of the foolish man who places his hope and future in this life only. This is a warning to us all whether we are high or low; rich or poor (v.2).

The Psalmist is about to share the deep thoughts of his heart, and his lips will convey to us the wisdom he has gained from his own experiences.

1. He trusts in his wealth (v.6). How many people in the world today, particularly wealthy nations in the west, fall into this same trap? We constantly need to be reminded of the words of our Lord when He said, 'One's life does not consist in the abundance of the things he possesses' (Luke 12:15).

Towards the end of the Psalm in v.17, we are reminded that, 'When he dies, he shall carry nothing away.' There are no pockets in a coffin, no matter how ornate it may be.

Where are you placing your wealth? In pockets that have holes in them? In the Sermon on the Mount in Matthew 6, Jesus gives some very helpful advice we would all do well to follow. In v.19 He says, 'Do not lay up for yourselves treasures on earth where moth and rust destroy and where thieves break in and steal.'

He then advises us where to place our wealth in v.20: 'but lay up for yourselves treasures in heaven, where neither moth nor rust destroys and where thieves do not break in and steal'.

He then concludes in v.21 with words that are relevant for us all: 'For where your treasure is, there your heart will be also.'

2. He trusts in his knowledge. In v.10 the Psalmist reveals some important facts about life. 'For he sees wise men die; likewise, the fool and the senseless person perish, and leave their wealth to others.'

Both the fool and the wise will one day perish. Both of them will descend to the grave and be no more. In Job 12:2, God's servant says, 'Wisdom will die with you.'

There are people who, throughout their life, have used their intellect for the good of others, which I commend. Sadly, others have used their knowledge to the detriment of others. If God has given to us the gift of knowledge, then use it to His glory.

29 OCTOBER

There is hope in the midst of despair

'When he dies he shall carry nothing away; His glory shall not descend after him.' Psalm 49:17

RECOMMENDED READING: Psalm 49

As we continue to look into this Psalm, we see the confidence and hope that the foolish man has is in this life only. We have seen how he trusts in his wealth and his knowledge. Today we consider three more:

3. He trusts in property and land. In v.11 we read, 'Their inner thought is that their houses will last forever, their dwelling places to all generations.'

We need to realise that we cannot take our beautiful homes and gardens with us. If we are Christians, who would want to? I was once reminded by my mother-in-law that, 'we own nothing in this life. When we die, we just pass it on to somebody else.'

Our main concern should be to reach our heavenly home, where no repairs will be needed and all expenses have already been paid.

4. He trusts in beauty. In v.14 we read, 'Their beauty shall be consumed in the grave.' People spend hours of their time and huge amounts of their money trying to improve their looks with make-up, clothing, jewellery and cosmetic surgery. These are the order of the day and always have been throughout history. How we appear to the world is so important to most people, which is why we have mirrors in every room. When you see a beautiful looking woman about to be interviewed, as soon as she opens her mouth I often think, 'I'm glad she is not my wife.' Read Proverbs 31:10–31 with special consideration for v.26. Looks are just skin deep.

But growing old brings declining beauty, no matter how much we spend or how hard we try. We cannot put the brake on ageing. In the end, beauty is consumed in the grave.

5. He trusts in adulation (v.18). People long to receive praise from others and to be congratulated for their achievements. People love to be in the company of the successful, and the successful revel in it. When we fail we are soon forgotten as a dream. Adulation can be very dangerous. It has ruined the lives of many people.

So, we have seen the confidence of the foolish, and this psalm is very direct in reminding him, or her, where their end will be.

However, in v.15 we have a glimpse of hope in the midst of despair. Our bodies will decay in the grave, but our souls will be redeemed from the power of the grave. Hallelujah!

30 OCTOBER

There is only one message to proclaim

'In those days John the Baptist came preaching in the wilderness of Judea.'
Matthew 3:1

RECOMMENDED READING: Matthew 3

As I was thinking about John the Baptist and our Lord Jesus Christ, I was reminded that they were related, being half-cousins. They often say that similarities can be seen among relatives. I want to look at a few important likenesses between these two men.

1. **They both preached the same message.** At the start of Matthew 3 we read, 'In those days John the Baptist came preaching in the wilderness of Judea, and saying, "Repent, for the kingdom of heaven is at hand!"'

Shortly after this, we have the baptism of our Lord, followed by His temptations in the wilderness. After John had been put in prison (4:12), Jesus went to live in Capernaum. We then read in 4:17, 'From that time Jesus began to preach and to say, "Repent, for the kingdom of heaven is at hand."'

It is important to note that both men preached a message of repentance. They called people to turn from their sins, seek God's forgiveness and follow Him.

Ministers and preachers are nothing more than a voice, often in the wilderness, through which God communicates His mind. Preaching is the most responsible task that any man can undertake. Sometimes, the responsibility of conveying that message can weigh heavily upon them.

Every minister of the gospel must follow the example of both John the Baptist and our Lord Jesus Christ and preach with passion for a verdict. The seed must be sown, and then left to Almighty God to bring the increase.

The preacher may not have all the skills of oratory, nor may he have reached the heights in education, but give me a fool on fire for God any day than a cold scholar on ice.

If a medical consultant discovered a medicine that would cure all forms of cancerous disease but kept his findings just for his own family and friends, that man would have a great deal to answer for one day.

The Christian church has within its hands a book that contains a life-transforming message that cannot and must not be kept to ourselves. We are instructed to follow the example of John, and our Lord, and go out into the wilderness declaring a life-changing message to a desperate and dying world.

31 OCTOBER

Never be proud of your humility

'Therefore humble yourselves under the mighty hand of God, that He may exalt you in due time.' 1 Peter 5:6

RECOMMENDED READING: Philippians 2:1–11

We are looking at similarities between John the Baptist and our Lord Jesus Christ. Yesterday we noted that they both preached the same message. Today we conclude with two further similarities.

2. They both demonstrated a humble spirit. John was a true servant of God. Matthew 11:11 says, 'There has not risen one greater than John the Baptist.' John 5:35 says, 'He was the burning and shining lamp.'

You see this man as a humble believer. When Jesus came to the Jordan to be baptised by John, he said to Jesus, 'I need to be baptised by You, and are You coming to me?' (Matthew 3:14).

He was a man who put away the honour that the Jews were ready to pay him. He declined all flattering titles. Even his disciples left him to follow Jesus (John 1:37). To exalt Christ was his mission, and he accomplished it.

When we consider the Lord Jesus, Philippians 2 says it all. Read again vv.5–8. Jesus never thought of Himself but doing His Father's will. All He was concerned about was keeping His eyes in the direction of the cross, despite the cost.

To do anything for Jesus is a great honour. To serve Him should be our greatest delight.

3. They were both great. In Luke 1, an angel of the Lord was speaking to Zacharias in the temple. In v.15 he said, 'He will be great in the sight of the Lord.'

In the same chapter, Gabriel visited Mary at Nazareth and announced that she would have a Son. In v.32 he says, 'He will be great, and will be called the Son of the Highest.'

The greatness of John—human. The greatness of Jesus—Divine. We will never attain the latter, but we can strive to become great in the eyes of the Lord.

The world's definition of greatness is to be conformed to the image of the world. To be powerful, wealthy and popular is the aim of so many.

God's definition of greatness is to be conformed to the image of His Son.

We have just had a brief glance at a remarkable servant whose only task was, not to put himself in the limelight, but to exalt the Name that is above every name: the Name of Jesus. That is your task and mine! May God give us the strength and determination to do so.

1 NOVEMBER

A guide that never leads astray

'Israel said to Joseph, "Behold I am dying, but God will be with you and bring you back to the land of your fathers."' Genesis 48:21

RECOMMENDED READING: Genesis 48

When we come to the close of the book of Genesis, we also come to the end of Jacob's life. He is first mentioned in 25:26. In chapter 50 Jacob returns to Canaan and is buried in the field of Machpelah, which Abraham, his grandfather, had bought years earlier. The life of Jacob covers half the book of Genesis.

In chapter 48, Jacob blesses Joseph's two sons, Ephraim and Manasseh. Then in v.21, after acknowledging that he was dying, issued a prophetic statement: 'But God will be with you and bring you back to the land of your fathers.'

As Joseph looked back over his life, God had certainly been with him. When his brothers intended to kill him, God implanted into the mind of his brother Reuben the desire to rescue him. He was lowered into a dry pit. God was with him as he journeyed into the land of Egypt. God was with him in the house of Potiphar to ensure he did not sin with the Captain of the Guard's wife. God was with him in prison when he interpreted the dreams of Pharaoh's butler and baker. God was with him as he also interpreted Pharaoh's dreams. God was with him as he gathered corn for seven years of famine. God was with him as he revealed himself to his father and brothers.

We may not have had such an adventurous, challenging and exciting life as Joseph, but as we look back over our lives, we can say, despite all the challenges and difficulties, whether they be few or many, 'But God has been with me and helped me.'

He helped me when I didn't know which way to turn. He has given to me far more than I deserved. He saved me and protected me from the evil one. His presence has been with me every step of the way. That is what I see as I look back over the years of my life.

However, we can say with absolute confidence that God will be with us today and for evermore.

Despite our many failings, despite our glaring sins, God will never fail us, nor leave us. He will continue to be with us to the very end of our days.

One day we too will complete our earthly journey and God will bring us safely to the home of our Heavenly Father. Then we can truly settle down for the last time in peace and security.

2 NOVEMBER

No one is too wicked to be saved

'All that the Father gives Me will come to Me, and the one who comes to Me I will by no means cast out.' John 6:37

RECOMMENDED READING: 1 Timothy 1:12–17

Where would we have been this day if God had not poured out His grace upon us? This grace cannot be earned and is totally undeserved.

When the reformer, John Bradford, witnessed a wagonload of men making their way to Tyburn, for people to witness their hanging, he said, 'There goes John Bradford, but for the grace of God.'

Who knows what our lives would have turned out to be like, if it was not for God's wonderful grace? There are those who have said to me over the years, 'My life has been so bad; God would never give me one glance, let alone pour out His love upon me.' John 6:37 says, 'The one who comes to Me I will by no means cast out.'

Saul of Tarsus was responsible for the imprisonment and deaths of many godly believers and consented to the stoning of the first Christian martyr, Stephen. When he was on his way to Damascus, Jesus made Himself known to him in a most dramatic way. Despite Saul's ungodly life, he was not cast out.

John Newton, the violent blasphemer and renowned slave trader, was to many people beyond God's reach. Yet God, in his mercy, took this man and changed him into a new person. He became a renowned preacher and minister of the gospel, and also one of our most prolific hymn writers. He witnessed the conversion of many souls, both in London and in other parts of England. Despite being a notorious slave trader, God did not cast him out.

If anyone, reading these words, thinks they are beyond God's saving grace, let me assure you that, whatever your past record may show, you are never, ever, beyond God's saving power and grace.

Those who are made aware of our Lord's sacrifice and come to Him in sincere repentance, confessing their sin with a willingness to turn from their wicked ways, He will forgive and cleanse, no matter how scandalous they may have been.

Jesus will never cast you out. Instead, like the father of the prodigal son, He will welcome you with open arms, and saturate you with His love. That's what He did for me and has done for countless others throughout the centuries.

'The one who comes to Me', Jesus said, 'I will by no means cast out.'

3 NOVEMBER

We must go where He sends us

'Now the LORD had prepared a great fish to swallow Jonah.' Jonah 1:17

RECOMMENDED READING: Matthew 12:38–50

When we turn to the book of Jonah, we are faced with a number of questions that sceptics present to us. Is the book history or fiction? Was Jonah a real person? Was he swallowed and kept alive in a big fish? Did his message save Nineveh from God's judgement?

Now these questions are vitally important because the answers confirm or deny the authority of the Bible, including the words of our Lord.

So, was Jonah a real character? There is no doubt Jonah was a real man (Jonah 1: 1). 2 Kings 14:23–25 supports this as we are told that he lived in the days of Jeroboam who was the longest reigning king in Israel. But then we have the words of our Lord who, in Matthew 12:38–40, tells the story of Jonah's experience to support His own resurrection.

But could a great sea creature swallow a man? Yes, if you believe the Bible. When I was young, the skeleton of a whale was displayed in my hometown of Barnsley and curiosity made me go and see the display. There is no question that a man could survive in such a mammal.

But did it happen? No question about it if you believe the Bible. However, this is not the important part of the story. The central message is the miracle of a city like Nineveh turning in repentance toward God. I want to consider four events in this story.

1. Jonah and the storm. Twice in the first ten verses we are told that Jonah tried to escape from obeying God's instructions.

'The word of the LORD came to Jonah' (Jonah 1:1). God spoke to Jonah and told him to take His message to the people of Nineveh. But in v.3 we are told that he ran away from the Lord. We are also told he had to pay his own fare. When we disobey the Lord there is a price to pay.

In v.4 God uses His creation to bring His servant back to Himself and in v.5 Jonah falls into a deep sleep.

In v.12 Jonah admits his error. All that has happened is due to his disobedience. Someone once said that Jonah had to get wet before he got right.

Has God asked us to do something and we have run from the task before us? If so, we need to acknowledge our sin and repent. The next task God asks us to do, let us be obedient to His instructions.

4 NOVEMBER

Prayer in the belly of a big fish

'Then Jonah prayed to the LORD his God from the fish's belly.' Jonah 2:1

RECOMMENDED READING: Jonah 2

2. Jonah in the belly of a fish. We began yesterday looking at Jonah's disobedience to God's instructions which led him to ending up in the belly of a big fish. Chapter 2 records Jonah's prayer and testimony.

Before we continue, it needs to be made clear that Jonah did not find himself in the big fish as God's punishment for his disobedience. God intended to keep Jonah safe so that he could have another opportunity to follow God's instructions and sail to Nineveh.

So here was Jonah praying to God inside the big fish. This proves to us that we can pray to God absolutely anywhere, even in the depths of the sea within a fish. God is not tied down to time or place. His ear is always open to hear our cry.

Now this prayer did not consist of asking God to rescue him. He had already done that. This was a prayer thanking God for deliverance. It was a prayer full of praise to his God. He was thanking God for His great mercy. This was another opportunity God had given him to fulfil the task he had been given. He must not rebel against God again.

While he was in the fish, Jonah realised once again God's amazing love and protection for him. He also realised that beneath him, over him, and encircling him were the everlasting arms of his God.

How stupid he had been in thinking that he could trick Almighty God and escape from His presence. Jonah came to realise that God knows everything and is everywhere. No one, not even Jonah, could run from His presence and hide from His all-seeing eye.

During his time in the fish, Jonah recommitted his life to his God and then spoke those often-used words in v.9: 'Salvation is of the LORD.' He had now proved it to be so.

Once he had spoken these words, the great fish spewed Jonah out of his mouth. Jonah found himself safe on dry land and was immediately ready to resume his journey to Nineveh.

There are lessons to learn from the reading of this chapter. Firstly, it is important to realise that we cannot thwart God's plan for our lives. It will only bring pain and grief if we try to do so. A second lesson to learn is that, if we think we can outwit God and try to live without Him, we will be bereft of His presence.

The wonderful thing is that, when we come back to him in sincere repentance, He will restore to us the fellowship with Him that we once enjoyed.

5 NOVEMBER

The good news is for all people

'So Jonah arose and went to Nineveh, according to the word of the LORD.'
Jonah 3:3

RECOMMENDED READING: Jonah 3

3. Jonah enters Nineveh. We have seen Jonah's disobedience to God's instructions, which caused him to be thrown overboard into the sea, and seen him being rescued by a big fish. While in the belly of the big fish he prays to his God seeking his forgiveness. He then makes a firm decision to do what the LORD asked him to do in the first place, which was to go to Nineveh.

We now come to the heart of the book of Jonah, which centres on Nineveh's repentance and God's mercy upon this great city.

Before we consider what happened to the city, it is helpful to consider the size of Nineveh. On three occasions it is described as 'that great city.' In 3:3 it is described as, 'an exceedingly great city, a three-day journey in extent.'

When we come to the last verse of the book, we are told that Nineveh had a population of 120,000 people including much livestock. This was a huge assignment God had given to Jonah, so we can understand in some measure why he was reluctant to go.

Professor Keil, who is an Old Testament archaeologist, said that Nineveh comprised of four large primeval cities. If you walked round them, you would cover a distance of 60 miles which, by doing an average of 20 miles a day, would be a three-day journey. Some archaeologists would disagree saying Nineveh was much smaller, but they are describing the inner city of Nineveh and not the surrounding area of Nineveh (think of the City of London as opposed to Greater London). This would be far from a gentle stroll in the park for Jonah.

In 3:1 we read that, 'the word of the LORD came to Jonah a second time.' How thankful we should be that God doesn't cast us off when we fail Him the first time. Many of us, including John Mark, who we read of in the Acts of the Apostles, are thankful for that second opportunity after our first- time failure.

God clearly directed Jonah to proclaim the message He had given to him. When we do what God asks, remarkable things can happen. The result of Jonah's obedience in bringing God's message to the people is seen in v.5: 'The people of Nineveh believed God.'

The king instructs the people of Nineveh to repent, and God responded in mercy and not judgement.

However, God has not finished with Jonah just yet. He has still lessons to teach God's servant.

6 NOVEMBER

Our concern must be for all people

'And should I not pity Nineveh, that great city ...?' Jonah 4:11

RECOMMENDED READING: Jonah 4

When we come to the final chapter of the book of Jonah, we are permitted to listen to the discussion between Jonah and the Lord. This has been a rollercoaster ride for God's servant. He has experienced the highs and the lows of being God's prophet.

In chapter 1, Jonah rebels, disobeys and even tries to run away from God. Psalm 139:7 should have been a lesson for Jonah: 'Where can I flee from Your presence?' The Psalmist even adds, 'And dwell in the uttermost parts of the sea' (Psalm 139:9). Well, Jonah certainly had experience of that. The lesson for Jonah, and us, is that no matter how we may try, we cannot escape God's presence; He is everywhere and His eye misses nothing.

In chapter 2, Jonah repents, and makes a new and firm commitment to the Lord. He is then obedient to God's instructions.

In chapter 3, he is restored and becomes the faithful preacher, boldly declaring God's word to the people of Nineveh.

4. Jonah has lessons to learn. Now in chapter 4 he is nearly back to where he began. He is sulking because his pride has been punctured. Things have not turned out as he wanted or expected. He would have preferred it if Nineveh had rejected God's message and been destroyed.

Jonah was a passionate Israelite, and fully aware that God was merciful. He just did not want Israel's enemies to receive God's salvation.

It is when we come to the close of this book that the last verse reveals both Jonah's character and also the Lord's.

Jonah was self-centred and only concerned about his own comfort and getting his own way. God is so opposite in that He was concerned about these lost people in the city of Nineveh. He is concerned for all people, both Jews and Gentiles.

This is such an important message to the church as a whole. We must never lose sight of our commission to convey the message of the gospel to all people. Our task is to sow the seed; God, and Him alone, will bring the increase.

Someone said, 'A class-conscious church is a church with limited vision'.

Let us be obedient to God's instructions and go where He sends us. If God is concerned, so must we be.

7 NOVEMBER

God acts in mercy and with judgement

'Who knows the power of Your anger?' Psalm 90:11

RECOMMENDED READING: Psalm 90

Every preacher has a responsibility to declare the whole counsel of God and that includes His anger over sin. Recently I have been reading about God's act of judgement in the great flood. I then read of God's judgement over the cities of Sodom and Gomorrah.

One thing became abundantly clear; man's sin brought about God's judgement. These were not acts of nature as some lead us to believe; they were acts of Almighty God. So, what do we understand about God's judgement?

1. **Righteous anger.** We read of this in Psalm 90:7,11. Almighty God cannot and will not turn a blind eye to sin. Evil has to be dealt with sooner or later. Upon the cross Jesus experienced God's righteous anger. If sin is not dealt with at the cross, it has to be dealt with in hell. There is no other alternative. That is why we should urge sinners to seek the Lord now, while He may be found. God demonstrated patience with people before the flood and with the citizens of Sodom and Gomorrah; now action had to be shown.

We should pray earnestly for our nation while God's patience is evident. We still live in days when the message of the cross and God's salvation in Christ can be preached, but God is righteous and one day He will act.

It has been said that non-Christians do not have to choose a special road to go to hell; they just have to stay on their present road long enough.

2. **God's judgement is catastrophic.** When God finally acts, the results will be devastating. In Genesis 7:23 we read that all living things were destroyed apart from those who entered the ark. In Genesis 19:25 we read that all the inhabitants of Sodom and Gomorrah perished apart from Lot and his two daughters, who were rescued.

When disasters take place, we must be brave and honest to ask, 'What is God saying to us through them?' Regrettably, that is often the last question we ask, as we are seeing in our own nation at this time.

Many events that have occurred throughout history have been called catastrophic, but an event is coming that will make all these seem insignificant. Only those who trust in the Christ of Calvary will be secure.

If you do not have the assurance of salvation, then I urge you to look to Jesus, repent of your sin and seek His forgiveness. He will not turn any away who sincerely come to Him in faith.

8 NOVEMBER

Troubles often come unexpectedly

'Escape for your life! ... lest you be destroyed.' Genesis 19:17

RECOMMENDED READING: Genesis 19:15–29

We are considering God's judgement, and yesterday we noted that it is catastrophic. A.W. Pink said, 'The wrath of God is as much a divine perfection as is His faithfulness, power or mercy.'[30] Today we consider a further aspect of God's judgement.

3. God's judgement is unexpected. Let us first of all consider the flood. Though numerous warnings had been given, when the flood eventually came it was unexpected. The people were totally unprepared.

I can imagine their response when they were told that a flood was coming. 'Why waste all this effort and time building an ark? When did we last see rain, never mind a flood? Look, there is no sign in the sky of rain.'

Then turn your thoughts to the cities of the plain. Although the people had been warned, the destruction of the cities was totally unexpected. Even Lot's sons-in-law thought it was a joke (v.14).

It has been said: 'People believe that if they destroy the one who preaches danger, they will destroy the danger itself. You can remove the messenger, but you can't destroy the message.'

We are told not to live in the past, but to learn from it. The problem is that we don't. Disasters often come unexpectedly. When the initial shock is over and the press and media finally move away, we continue as if nothing happened.

One thing is clear, God's final judgement will come and, when it does, we will not be expecting it. There will not be time to turn to God and put things right with Him. While the warnings are still coming, I plead with you to listen to them and act before it is too late.

4. God's judgement will come and not delay. When God says something, He will always carry it out. God never breaks His word and never makes mistakes.

With regard to the flood, we read that every living thing was destroyed (Genesis 7:23). With regard to Sodom and Gomorrah, the cities are no longer to be seen (Genesis 19:25).

The results of sin are terrible. God's judgement over sin is frightening. It is a fearful thing to live opposed to the living God.

I therefore say to you again, flee to Christ. Seek His forgiveness without delay. He will receive and welcome all who turn to Him, and will not send any away. Those who come to Him He will not cast out.

9 NOVEMBER

In His wrath God remembers mercy

'Have you anyone else here? ... take them out of this place!' Genesis 19:12

RECOMMENDED READING: Genesis 19:15–22

We have been considering the judgement of God. This is a characteristic we prefer to ignore, but it is an integral part of God's holy character. We ignore it at our peril. We now consider those who experienced God's mercy. What a blessed relief that is to unforgiven sinners.

It was a godless age during the time of the flood, but God remembered Noah and demonstrated mercy to him and his household.

Despite the evil that was prevalent in Sodom and Gomorrah, God did not forget Lot and showed mercy to him and his wife and daughters. We are told he extended mercy to others but they ignored His offer. They thought the destruction of the city was a joke. Judgement is far too serious to be laughed at.

How many people today make light of, or ignore, the message God's people declare to them? God is offering a way of escape at the final hour, but they reject His offer of mercy.

In v.16 of Genesis 19, the Lord demonstrated the depth of His mercy, when the angels grasped the hands of Lot's family while they delayed.

In Luke 17:32 we have those poignant words: 'Remember Lot's wife.' There are lessons for us to learn from those words. We see clear disobedience. She was told not to look back. She disobeyed a message that would have saved her.

She clearly longed for what she had left behind. No matter how important it was, it was no good for her now. The result of disobedience was to reject a pillar of mercy for a pillar of salt. What is sad about her is that she was on the way to safety but rejected God's mercy. The message is clear: don't look back but persevere until you reach the place where you are safe—in the arms of God.

Let me conclude by asking you again to consider what the Lord Jesus Christ has done to save you from that great day of judgement.

The Lord Jesus Christ came from heaven to show us the way to heaven. He carried our sins upon the cross and gave to us His spotless robe of righteousness.

He has done this for countless numbers of people; He can do it for you. The gate of heaven is still open to all who turn in repentance and faith to Him.

You are only a breath away from destruction, but just a prayer away from eternal security.

10 NOVEMBER

The devil will always seek to hinder progress

'But the eye of their God was upon the elders of the Jews.' Ezra 5:5

RECOMMENDED READING: Nehemiah 4

The book of Ezra opens with Cyrus, the king of Persia, announcing that, under the direction of the God of heaven, a temple is to be built in Jerusalem.

In chapter 2, under the leadership of Zerubbabel, 49,897 people returned to their homeland. In chapter 3 we are told that, within seven months, the worship of the true God had been restored. It was two years later when the rebuilding of the temple commenced.

In chapter 4, the enemies of Judah and Benjamin approached Zerubbabel and cunningly suggested that they also become involved with the rebuilding. Zerubbabel was alive to their craftiness and told him that they alone would rebuild, as Cyrus had directed. The enemies of God did not accept his reply and soon opposition became apparent. When God's work progresses, be sure that the enemies of the Lord will do all they can to hinder it.

In Ezra 4:4, they first discouraged the people. Then in v.5, they hired counsellors to frustrate their work. In the end they sent a letter to Ahasuerus, who had succeeded Cyrus, accusing the people of rebellion by not paying taxes. They also assured the king of their continued loyalty. The king responded, assuring them that a search would be made of the archives. In the meantime, the work would cease until he had the necessary information.

The work ceased until the second year of King Darius. When it resumed, Tattenai, the Governor of the area, challenged Zerubbabel about the recommencing of the work (5:2–3).

What a relief to read v.5: 'But the eye of God was upon them.' And the work continued.

When we come to chapter 6, Darius confirmed the decree that Cyrus had made previously and so the work proceeded without any more delay. Despite all that had happened to God's people, His eye was upon them.

God will not let His work stop indefinitely. There will be delays for various reasons, but the work will proceed to its conclusion. Let us be encouraged in our own work for the Lord as we consider this event in the history of God's people.

There will be occasions when God's enemies oppose and discourage us. But God has His eye always upon His people to support them, despite the enemy's opposition to the work.

God's plans will succeed despite the opposition. He will never be thrown off track, so be encouraged as you labour for Him.

11 NOVEMBER

We should build up, not pull down

'Joses, who was also named Barnabas by the apostles (which is translated Son of Encouragement).' Acts 4:36

RECOMMENDED READING: Acts 9:10–28

There is a great need to encourage each other as we serve the Lord in the life of His church. One man who constantly followed that practice was Barnabas. During the next few days, we shall consider the life of this godly man.

1. His background. We do not have a great deal of information about his background, but what we have is very helpful to us. We are told in Acts 4:36 that he was a Levite who originally came from Cyprus to settle in Jerusalem. It was the disciples that gave him the nickname Barnabas.

In many ways he had a similar background to the apostle Paul. They both had a strong religious background and were called of God to take the gospel to the Gentiles. They both came from Gentile countries; Paul came from Cilicia and Barnabas from Cyprus. It didn't take long for them to become acquainted with each other. God, in His great wisdom not only arranges the place of our birth, but also where we live and the friends we meet. This was so with Paul and Barnabas.

Here we have two men with different gifts and both used by God in different ways. Someone said that Paul searched for the wound while Barnabas bound that wound up.

Barnabas had a cousin called John Mark, whose mother lived in Jerusalem and hosted the church in her own home (Acts 12:12). Could this relationship have been a reason why Barnabas showed understanding to his young cousin when he returned early from Paul's first missionary tour?

2. His generous spirit (Acts 4:36–37). The Levites did not possess any land in Israel, but they could purchase land further afield. When Barnabas decided to come and live in Jerusalem, he sold the land he possessed and distributed it according to the teaching in Acts 2:44–45. It is clear from these verses that he had a generous hand.

When we become followers of Jesus Christ, it is important to remember that all we possess is on trust from the Lord. We are stewards of our time, our wallet and our possessions. We leave this world with nothing, so it is wise to use what God has given towards the growth of a Kingdom that will last forever.

The local church cannot continue on good will alone, so we should show support to the Lord's people by having a generous spirit. The Lord loves a cheerful giver but He is no man's debtor.

12 NOVEMBER

Barnabas intervenes to help Paul

'But Barnabas took him and brought him to the apostles.' Acts 9:27

RECOMMENDED READING: Acts 11:27–30

As we consider the life of Barnabas, we have already seen what a generous man he was. Now we see further attributes in his character.

3. His role as mediator (Acts 9:26–27). Throughout the Old Testament we read of a number of people who acted as mediator between groups of individuals. Moses in Numbers 14 acted as a mediator to turn away God's anger, when he was about to destroy His people for failing to enter the Promised Land.

Now we read of another mediator who came to help Saul of Tarsus. Shortly after his conversion experience on the road to Damascus, Saul came to Jerusalem in an attempt to join the disciples. However, because of the persecution he had caused to God's people before his conversion, the disciples were naturally sceptical of his testimony and, therefore, afraid of his real motive in wanting to join them. Was he sincere or was this a ploy to plan a further attack against them?

Similar things happen today. In our work with Day One we have come across prisoners who found Christ during their confinement, but then find it difficult being accepted within a local church following their release.

I thank God for Barnabas, who intervened, and personally took Paul and introduced him to the disciples. It was not only courageous of him to do this, but it showed just how much he was trusted, not only by Paul, but also by the disciples. Barnabas acted as a mediator to reconcile the persecutor with those who had been persecuted.

Today I thank God for an even greater Mediator in the Lord Jesus Christ. At just the right time God intervened and sent His Son to bring us back to a personal relationship with God. That reconciliation came through His death upon Calvary's cross.

Following His resurrection and ascension He continues to mediate on our behalf at the right hand of His Father. Today in heaven He pleads with the Father on our behalf, receiving the prayers that we both individually and corporately bring before Him.

There have been many mediators throughout history who have played an important role in reconciliation, but there never has, nor ever will be, a Mediator as important to the Christian as our Lord Jesus Christ, for He stands between sinful people such as us and a holy, righteous God.

We need more encouragers in the church

'When he came and had seen the grace of God, he was glad, and encouraged them all that with purpose of heart they should continue with the Lord.' Acts 11:23

RECOMMENDED READING: Isaiah 41:8–13

We continue with a further characteristic in the life of Barnabas. We now see why he was nicknamed Barnabas.

4. His encouragement. In the city of Antioch, the Spirit of God had begun to move in the hearts of many people so that a great number believed and turned to the Lord. When the church in Jerusalem became aware of this, Acts 11:22 tells us that they sent Barnabas.

They sent a reliable man who could adapt to the changing situation and very quickly assess what help and support were needed. They sent a man who was recognised for his wide range of gifts and abilities; a man in whom they had complete confidence that he could do what was required.

During the years I have been travelling around the United Kingdom, I have come across many men and women who serve the Lord in very challenging situations. Most of them are just ordinary people, but they have proved to be reliable and trustworthy in the role God has given them. They just get on with the job before them, with humility and zeal for the Lord. Even though some of them may have limited abilities, they are always dependable and ready to be of service. They are invaluable within the church to which they belong.

I thank God for those within our churches who give us so much encouragement. Could you be a Barnabas in your fellowship and be a great encourager to others?

Barnabas encouraged the church in Antioch to keep praying and to keep labouring, for it will not be in vain if it is for the Lord. He would have also encouraged young believers to hold fast and not waver when persecution threatened to come their way.

Just notice the words in v.23: 'When he came and had seen the grace of God, he was glad.' He was not envious because God had blessed the labours of others. There are some people who cannot rejoice in the conversion of others because they have not been part of it. How tragic when that is the case.

We must be glad to see the grace of God at work in others, especially where we did not expect it. Thank God for transformed lives whether we have been part of that change or not.

14 NOVEMBER

Humility is a test of true greatness

'For he was a good man, full of the Holy Spirit and of faith.' Acts 11:24

RECOMMENDED READING: Acts 11:24–30

We continue to look at three further attributes in the character of God's servant Barnabas.

5. His spiritual legacy. No finer testimony could be accorded to any Christian than that which was given to Barnabas in Acts 11:24.

The big questions for us to consider before we leave this world is this: 'What testimony will we pass on to the next generation?' Would the words of v.24 apply to us when we have left this world? Would we be known for our godliness? Did we possess a great faith that was evident to others? Were we full of the Holy Spirit as we served the Lord?

When we display those characteristics, it will be clearly evident to people, just as it was to the people at Antioch.

6. His adaptability. In 11:27–30, we read of Agabus giving a clear warning that a famine was to spread throughout the world. The disciples agreed to send relief to those who lived in Jerusalem. Barnabas and Paul were chosen to be the ones who would deliver it.

Barnabas was sent to encourage the church in a time of great blessing. He was now sent to encourage the church during a time of testing. It's amazing how the church knew who to choose.

Do we possess the abilities that enable the church to send us when a visit is needed; when comfort is required; when prayer is vital; when encouragement is necessary?

I imagine Barnabas was a man who was good to be with, and when he was with you, he did you good. Can we fit into that category?

7. His humility. We see that clearly in Acts 11:25, 'Then Barnabas departed for Tarsus to seek Saul.' Barnabas showed the attribute of humility in bringing Saul to Antioch. Saul was already a leading speaker and would be likely to outshine Barnabas. But the building up of the church was more important than preserving his own reputation.

People were being saved; now they needed to be taught and Saul was just the man to do it. Preaching is not only for the conversion of those without Christ, but also for the sanctification of those within His fold.

There is a ministry for unselfish men and women. So many want to be the conductor. We need to be content to play the piccolo.

15 NOVEMBER

Don't let disagreements fester

'Be kind to one another, tenderhearted, forgiving one another, even as God in Christ forgave you.' Ephesians 4:32

RECOMMENDED READING: Ephesians 4:1–7

During the past two days we have been considering the life of Barnabas, the great encourager. There is just one final point I want to leave with you.

8. His new role.

Firstly, this is shown as he steps away from his prominent position with Paul. Just notice the following verses. In Acts 12:25, Barnabas and Saul had returned from Jerusalem. In Acts 13:2, the church sent Barnabas and Saul on a missionary journey. In Acts 13:7, Sergius Paulus called for Barnabas and Saul in order to hear the word of God. However, by vv.46 and 50, it is no longer Barnabas and Saul, but Paul and Barnabas. Like John the Baptist, the time had come for Barnabas to decrease, while Paul increased and became more prominent. There may come a time when we have to be willing to step aside and let others, perhaps much younger than ourselves, take a leading role and encourage them as they do so.

Secondly, his new role involved Mark. Acts 15:36–40 tells of a sharp disagreement between Paul and Barnabas over John Mark. On the first missionary tour, Mark had let Paul down and left the tour early. Barnabas wanted to give Mark another opportunity as he believed his cousin was now more mature. Paul was unwilling to risk another calamity and so disagreement came. I am aware that many will disagree with me on this point, but I was thankful to be given a second opportunity when I had failed badly on earlier occasions.

If we are discarded because of our earlier failure, we might never be where we are today. Mark needed encouragement and Barnabas was just the man to give it. This time Mark didn't let the church down. We must never discard a first-time failure in the life of the church. Those who are, or feel to be, a failure need our encouragement. Like Mark, they can be a success. Always remember, we could be the next to fail, and may just need encouragement from one who was once a failure.

I'm pleased the disagreement between Mark and Paul was healed. Note 2 Timothy 4:11 where Paul is in prison and says, 'Get Mark and bring him with you, for he is useful to me for ministry.' We must never let disagreements continue to fester. Read Ephesians 4:32.

May God raise up more people such as Barnabas. You could be one. The church certainly needs them.

16 NOVEMBER

Stand by your principles

'The LORD was with Joseph.' Genesis 39:2

RECOMMENDED READING: Genesis 39

Our young people are facing many new challenges in today's society. Some they will be prepared to encounter; others will be unexpected. With our young people in mind, I want to consider a young man who upheld his integrity in challenging circumstances.

Joseph was in his late teens when he was sold by his brothers to Midianite merchants who were travelling to Egypt.

When he arrived in the country, he found himself as a slave in the marketplace waiting to be bought by the highest bidder. This turned out to be one of Pharaoh's officials by the name of Potiphar.

We are told, in Genesis 39:2–3, that the LORD was with him and that he prospered in all that he did. Because of this Potiphar placed him in charge of all his affairs. The result was that Potiphar also prospered.

However, there was one significant problem looming on the horizon. Potiphar's wife was attracted to this good-looking young man, and she longed for a physical relationship with him. Joseph, being aware of the dangers, resisted her advances. This woman was very dangerous and a major threat to Joseph's integrity.

A day came when she was alone in the house and accused Joseph of trying to assault her, when he had done no such thing. This resulted in her husband being very angry and putting Joseph in prison.

Here was a young man finding himself in prison for being honourable and standing by his principles. But God had not forsaken him, even in prison (vv.20–21).

In the end his character was shown to be impeccable and, through interpreting Pharaoh's dreams and warning of a severe famine, God made him second in command to Pharaoh.

Here is a clear message for us all, particularly our young people, who are living in an age of declining moral principles. God has a standard for us all. Sexual relationships should only occur within marriage, and between one man and one woman. We must never place ourselves in a position where we become weak and vulnerable because of temptation.

We are to respect the opposite sex, whether it is girlfriend or boyfriend, or husband or wife. But most of all we must honour the Saviour and never grieve Almighty God. If we do, problems will come and our reputation ruined.

If we face temptation with our integrity intact, we will be assured of God's blessing upon us. As He was with Joseph, so He will be with us.

17 NOVEMBER

Keep pressing on!

'And the LORD said to Moses, "Why do you cry to Me? Tell the children of Israel to go forward."' Exodus 14:15

RECOMMENDED READING: Exodus 14:10–18

Moses, under the powerful hand of God, had brought the children of Israel out of bondage in Egypt to the border of the Red Sea. However, Pharaoh's obstinacy led him yet again to forget the warnings he had experienced, and he came thundering after the escaped nation. The Israelites, in fear and dismay, expressed their fury against Moses.

People have stated to me that they would not have wanted to be in the Prime Minister's shoes with all the pressure he has faced during the coronavirus pandemic. Very few, if any, would have wished to take the place of Moses when both Egypt and Israel were against him, with no way out of their dilemma. But God told Moses this was the time for action.

1. To go on was the safe way. It certainly did not look that way, but there would be no safety for them if they had not gone forward. There are times in our lives when we see no path ahead. We hesitate, even compromise, but we know we must press ahead. The weaker we are, the more reason for pressing on. The only way is obedience.

2. To go forward was clearly God's will. God did not work so many miracles to bring Israel out of Egypt in order that they might return. From the moment God heard the cry of His people, His plan was to lead them forward until they arrived in the land of Canaan. God's plan for us is to lead us forward until we reach our Promised Land.

3. No victory is to be obtained by turning back. The future of the entire nation of Israel hung in the balance. Had they wavered or delayed Egypt could have wiped them out on the spot.

The past two years have been very challenging for most people, but we must press forward. The past is behind us, the future is before us. Let us put our hand into the mighty hand of God and go forward together.

> 'Thy way, not mine, O Lord,
> However dark it be!
> Lead me by Thine own hand,
> Choose out the path for me.'
>
> Horatius Bonar (1808–89)

18 NOVEMBER

Putting your back to the task

'And I told them of the hand of my God which had been good upon me.'
Nehemiah 2:18

RECOMMENDED READING: Nehemiah 2:11–18

Earlier in the year we looked at Nehemiah as cupbearer to the king. Now I want to consider his new role and the example he set to the people on his return to Jerusalem.

The wall builder. Nehemiah's main objective was the rebuilding of the city walls around Jerusalem. Having been given royal approval, with the assurance of God's blessing, he began his task fully aware of the challenges before him. He set off for Jerusalem in 445BC, escorted by Persian soldiers, and completed the journey in about three months. On his way, he had to pass through the provinces of certain Persian governors, one of these being Sanballat. Sanballat had a servant called Tobiah, who also could have been his secretary. Chapter 2:10 indicates that these two men were about to give Nehemiah a great deal of trouble. Three days after his arrival in Jerusalem, Nehemiah saw for himself the ruins of the city. He toured the walls at night and was in no hurry to do so. He wanted to assess the huge task before him. Once fully surveyed, Nehemiah would not stop until God's work was completed. He wanted to make Jerusalem a safe and pleasant city in which the people could live. He didn't share his plans until he was sure the task could be completed within a few weeks (2:12–18).

Although he had to face significant opposition, the wall was completely rebuilt within fifty-two days. This was 142 years after its destruction in 586BC (Nehemiah 6:15). There were forty-two working groups who all worked upon the sections nearest to their home (3:10,23,29,30). This would have given them a special incentive. Another lesson that comes from this book is the close link between the practical and the spiritual (See 4:9): *Pray* and *Watch*. A simple strategy but most effective.

It's the Nehemiahs that God uses. It is important for us to blend the practical and the spiritual. Oliver Cromwell's famous words are still relevant today. He said, 'Trust in God and keep your powder dry.'[31]

In our church life we can present attractive programmes, but where is the real spiritual burden? The practical has in many instances taken over the spiritual. We need to get the balance right again.

> 'Give me the faith which can remove and sink the mountain to a plain;
> Give me the childlike, praying love, which longs to build thy house again.'
> Charles Wesley (1707–1788).

19 NOVEMBER

The attacks kept coming

'Hear, O our God, for we are despised.' Nehemiah 4:4

RECOMMENDED READING: Nehemiah 4:1–6

There are many lessons we can learn from a book that is so practical, yet so spiritual. One lesson was the hindrances and opposition that Nehemiah and the people had to confront. They came from outside, which was expected, but also from within.

1. Derision. Sanballat presented a derisive attitude towards Nehemiah and the people by referring to them in v.4 as, 'these feeble Jews'. That is often the world's opinion to those involved in the Lord's work. So how did Nehemiah respond to this sarcasm? They just continued to pray and to build. How embarrassed must Sanballat and Tobiah have felt when they saw the walls of the city rising higher and higher!

When the enemies of the Lord ridicule and undermine our efforts, the only response is to keep on praying and keep on serving the Lord. It is the best way to answer our critics. But there were more attacks to come.

2. Plots. When derision did not succeed, Sanballat made plans to form an alliance against God's people. This came in the disguise of threats and plots. Read 4:7–9. Things were beginning to look really bad. The battle was certainly becoming more intense and the dangers more acute. The people needed to be alert. The enemy was not going to relax in its endeavour to undermine the rebuilding programme.

This alliance not only involved Sanballat and Tobiah, but also the Arabians, Ammonites and Ashdodites. It is amazing how mutual enemies can become mutual friends if, together, they can confound God's people. We are told in Luke 23:12 that even Pilate and Herod became friends, who were formerly at enmity with each other prior to Jesus' crucifixion.

So, when people work together against us, what should our strategy be? Keep praying and keep building, but always be watchful. At the same time, we must also be ready for spiritual warfare and put on the complete armour of God. We do not necessarily look for confrontation but, if it comes, we cannot ignore what the enemy is planning. There is a time when we must take our stand and expose sin and error. Never run away from your responsibilities whatever the consequences may be.

> 'Christian, seek not yet repose, cast your dreams of ease away:
> You are in the midst of foes—watch and pray.'
>
> Charlotte Elliott (1789–1871)

20 NOVEMBER

The enemies came with their box of tricks

'All of them conspired together to come and attack Jerusalem and create confusion.' Nehemiah 4:8

RECOMMENDED READING: Nehemiah 6

We have seen the derision and plots Nehemiah had to confront. But when these failed, they finally turned to:

3. Cunning tactics.

(a) Deceit. Read vv.1–4. In these verses, Sanballat issued a seemingly friendly invitation to Nehemiah, but there would be a nasty surprise awaiting him. He asked Nehemiah to come to the plains of Ono for a vital conference as they needed to get together and talk, but he planned to do Nehemiah harm. Today the church would jump at it. Nehemiah was not hoodwinked or misled by such hypocrisy. His reply was in v.3: 'I am doing a great work, so that I cannot come down. Why should the work cease while I leave it and go down to you?' Nehemiah might have been a dead man if he had agreed to Sanballat's request. They were persistent and asked Nehemiah four times but Nehemiah did not get worn down. His love of work probably saved his life on a number of occasions. It may have done here.

Nehemiah's reply should be our reply when we are faced with such deceit. We should not become involved.

(b) Bribery. Read vv.10–14. They even bribed Nehemiah's relatives and the prophets. Regrettably the prophets betrayed Nehemiah and the people.

Has the nature of people changed? I think not! There are people in some congregations today, who would betray their pastors and/or elders in certain situations and they bring grief and sadness to Christian ministers.

So how do we react to crafty tactics? Continue building and praying. There is no other alternative.

(c) Compromise. Read vv.17–19. What a horrible and dangerous situation they were in! The cunning Tobiah had become the son-in-law to one of the leaders in Israel. Then, to make matters worse, Tobiah's son took a Jewish girl to be his wife. There were those within Jerusalem who had clearly allowed family ties with Tobiah to supersede their spiritual responsibility.

Compromise is so dangerous. Many believers have given way for the sake of an easy ride or popularity and corruption has been the result. We must hold our position and never undermine our Christian heritages which have been so passionately fought for. Faithfulness to God should be our goal. Therefore, keep building and praying, and keep our eyes fixed upon Jesus.

21 NOVEMBER

Dispose of all the rubbish

'Then Judah said, "The strength of the labourers is failing, and there is so much rubbish that we are not able to build the wall."' Nehemiah 4:10

RECOMMENDED READING: Nehemiah 4

We have been looking at the challenges Nehemiah and the people had to face following their return to the city of Jerusalem, particularly from Sanballat and Tobiah. Yet Nehemiah rose to the challenges with great determination and enthusiasm.

But now, more drawbacks came to his attention, this time from within, and they were just as threatening.

The first challenge was to clear the rubbish that had built up over the years (4:10).

Even Sanballat had remarked about it earlier. To tackle this would be a huge challenge, especially as some of the workmen would have to be employed as guards.

When we consider Christian work today, there is so much rubbish, such as disunity and false doctrine, to be removed and many Christian workers find themselves spiritually drained and physically worn out trying to clear them. All this time and effort hinders the real work of rebuilding but the task has to be done.

The second challenge was to confront the fear within the hearts of the people (4:11–14).

The people who resided outside the walls of the city informed Nehemiah that their enemies were about to attack at any moment. When the workers on the walls became aware of this, they became discouraged and fearful.

We can become just like them. We see the size of the enemy and become afraid. This is always the case when we take our eyes away from the One who has all power in heaven and on earth.

We must never forget that God's power can bring down governments and turn the hearts of men just as He pleases. The only antidote to fear is faith.

When the battle becomes intense, look to God. Chapter 4:14 says, 'Do not be afraid of them.' Then remember why you are fighting. For the Israelites, everything was at stake, from family to property.

I thank God for those great men and women of the faith who were willing to sacrifice their lives to preserve and protect our Christian heritage Are we willing to make our stand for future generations?

Eventually all the setbacks were overcome and the work was finished. I pray that this will be so in our work for the Lord. So let us arise and build and finish the work God has sent us to do.

22 NOVEMBER

You can always rely on God

'Behold, God is my salvation, I will trust and not be afraid.' Isaiah 12:2

RECOMMENDED READING: Psalm 27

Having a reliable friend in whom you can trust is one of life's great blessings. To have someone to share a problem with, or seek advice on some important concern, is a valuable asset, especially when you can feel assured it will go no further than the ears of your friend.

Yes, you can trust a loyal friend but, in many ways, they are just like you. They have their weaknesses and frailties and, though not intentionally, they can fall short of your expectations.

However, when we consider Almighty God, we can fully trust in Him at all times and with everything that concerns us. He never fails the soul that trusts in Him. Why can we be so confident?

1. He is great. God is all-powerful and nothing is beyond His ability to help in time of need. From the dawn of time, He has proved to be forever victorious. He can never be defeated no matter how strong the enemy may be.

His power is seen in the life of His Son, the Lord Jesus Christ, who had control over nature and could heal all forms of diseases, but most of all had power over the evil one, the devil. We see the power of God so clearly displayed at the cross and the tomb when He raised His Son from the dead.

Yes, the one true God is invincible and unconquerable and He longs to be our trusted friend.

2. He is true. This great God is also reliable. He is true to His word. When we read the Scriptures, every promise He makes can be depended on. He will never go back on His word; it is completely trustworthy. What He says He will do as He has proved on so many occasions.

God is true to His character. He is a faithful friend in whom we can have total confidence for He will never fail the one who trusts in Him. In a world where people can be unfaithful to others, even in close relationships such as marriage, He will stick fast to you at all times. God never acts on impulse but is wise in his dealings with us.

To have a God who is all-seeing, all-knowing and all-listening as a close friend is a great blessing indeed. We can trust Him at all times and never be afraid.

23 NOVEMBER

Treat others as you wish them to treat you

'For He knows our frame; He remembers that we are dust.' Psalm 103: 14

RECOMMENDED READING: Romans 16

C. H. Spurgeon tells the story of a faithful minister of the gospel by the name of John Berridge. Around his room he had a number of pictures of well-known Christians such as John Calvin and John Bunyan. Among the pictures he had a mirror hanging on the wall. As he showed his visitor the pictures, they would come to the mirror and he would say, 'and that is the devil'. Before they became offended by his comment he would add, '... remember there is a devil in us all'.[32]

How quick we are to condemn other Christians. Our lack of patience towards others shows how imperfect and judgemental we are. If we portrayed the image of our Saviour, we would be able to show compassion towards others and endure their annoying habits.

Let us never forget that our fellow believers, with whom we tend to quickly find fault, are also God's children and if God in his mercy chose them, why do we so often disdain and reject them? They are just like you, saved by the precious blood of the Lord Jesus. As He died for you, so He also gave His life for them. If He thought so much about them that He rescued them from hell, why do we think so little of them?

Yes, they may have significant weaknesses. They are proud of their achievements and at times their temper is quick to react. But these same believers clearly put you to shame in their generosity and in their zeal for those who are lost. Yes, they might complain about others from time to time and find fault with the pastors preaching and his lack of vision, but are you guilty too?

Would it not be a good resolution to look at the best side of your fellow Christian? We need to remember that we all have our faults and weaknesses so let us consider their good points and perhaps we could learn a great deal from them.

Let us try to see the best in them and trust they will do the same with us.

> 'All praise to our redeeming Lord, who joins us by His grace
> And bids us each to each restored, together seek his face.
> He bids us build each other up; and, gathered into one,
> To our high calling's glorious hope we hand in hand go on.'
>
> Charles Wesley (1707–88)

26 NOVEMBER

We need to know Him better

'I know My sheep, and am known by My own.' John 10:14

RECOMMENDED READING: Ezekiel 34:11–24

We have seen that the Shepherd knows his sheep. Today we turn that statement around.

2. The sheep know the Shepherd. There may have been a time when to us the Good Shepherd, our Lord Jesus Christ, was just a person that we would read about in books. We may have been taught about Him when we attended Sunday school, or stories about Him were read to us by our parents.

Regrettably, for some, His name is only heard in the form of blasphemy, as is too often the case today. The television and film companies have much to answer for in the way that they have demeaned His holy character.

Despite all this, the big question that people need to ask is, 'How can I know the Shepherd?' How can this person of history become real to me? How can I be sure I am a Christian and possess eternal life?

This chapter is very clear on this issue. The Bible is not just any book; it is a talking book. It is a book that speaks. It is Almighty God who is communicating to us. Just note the following verses:

Verse 4: 'They know His voice.' Verse 5: 'They do not know the voice of strangers.' Verse 3: 'The sheep hear His voice.' Verse 16: 'They will hear My voice.' Verse 27: 'My sheep hear My voice.'

God is speaking to us through His Word. If we don't read it, we are not going to hear Him. Many times, we are too busy, or just can't be bothered. That is why the Christian is often confused and bewildered.

Communication is a neglected part of life today. Parents and children seem to spend little time in conversation with each other, especially with the advent of social media. Even husbands and wives don't really know each other, living like ships that just pass in the night.

How well do the sheep know the Shepherd? Just count the hours in a week when we seek to be entertained; then add the hours spent reading God's Word and talking to Him in prayer. The difference could be very significant indeed.

The Good Shepherd wants to get to know His sheep, and the sheep need to know the Shepherd.

I say to all Christians, 'Get to know your Shepherd better.' When you do you will be amazed by the result.

27 NOVEMBER

Beware of false shepherds

'The thief does not come except to steal, and to kill, and to destroy.' John 10:10

RECOMMENDED READING: John 10:1–14

Today we have a clear warning and an encouragement.

3. The Shepherd protects his sheep. Always watch out for false shepherds. Note the words of John 10:12–13: 'But a hireling, he who is not the shepherd, one who does not own the sheep, sees the wolf coming and leaves the sheep and flees; and the wolf catches the sheep and scatters them. The hireling flees because he is a hireling and does not care about the sheep.'

So how can we differentiate between the true and false shepherds?

They speak differently. The words of the true Shepherd are trustworthy, reliable and utterly dependable. We know that His words are true.

As for the false shepherds, note v.5: 'Yet they will by no means follow a stranger, but will flee from him, for they do not know the voice of strangers.'

Any words that contradict the Bible and the words of Jesus are false. They are the words of strangers. In this chapter the leaders of the temple rejected the words of Jesus. They even called Him a demon (v.20).

We need to be aware of leaders in the church today who do not accept the authority of God's Word. Such people are false shepherds. They are the voice of strangers, so ignore them. They do not enter by the true and living way (v.1). Jesus said, 'I am the way'—the only way (John 14:6). Neither do they care about the sheep (v.13). When the wolf comes, they only care about themselves.

Now let us turn to the true Shepherd. In v.7 Jesus said, 'I am the door of the sheep.' During the night, when the wolf prowled, the shepherd would lie across the opening of the fold. The only way the wolf could get to the sheep was across the body of the shepherd. He was their protection and security.

We are so spiritually weak and fragile that he holds us in the hollow of His hand, and no one can snatch us out.

In Northern Ireland a farmer bred very small birds. They would nestle down in his powerful hand where they were secure and protected.

We are so like those birds—weak and defenceless—but in the Shepherd's hands we are safe from the devil's grasp.

Let us thank God that as His children we are protected from the enemy by One who knows every trick of the enemy and who is always one step ahead of him.

28 NOVEMBER

He loves the Gentiles also

'Other sheep I have which are not of this fold; them also I must bring, and they will hear My voice; and there will be one flock and one shepherd.'
John 10:16

RECOMMENDED READING: Matthew 12:15–21

We continue to look at our Good Shepherd who knows His sheep and the sheep know Him. Thankfully, the Shepherd also knows the enemy and protects His sheep.

4. The Shepherd has many sheep. Throughout the Old Testament, the prophets were sent by God to minister to the Gentiles as well as the Jews. The apostle Paul was chosen by God to take the gospel into Gentile countries.

Here, and in other passages, our Lord made it very clear that believers would not come from Israel only, but from every nation under heaven. From the day of Pentecost, the message of the gospel spread throughout Africa, Asia and into Europe, eventually reaching the shores of Britannia.

In 1982, I was privileged to lead my first tour to Israel. We were in Jerusalem on Easter Sunday, so we went to the Garden Tomb for the early morning service. Then some of us decided to join with a local church for their Easter service. This was a service we would never forget.

It was an Arab Baptist Church and the spacious building was packed. Into the pulpit came the Arab pastor followed by Richard Wurmbrand, the persecuted Romanian pastor. As there were many nationalities from all over the world, there were numerous interpreters throughout the building.

To begin the service, we were asked to rise and sing, 'Christ the Lord is risen today' (Charles Wesley 1707–1788), but in our own language. It was one of the most moving experiences I have had. To sing about the heart of our faith with brothers and sisters from every corner of the globe, moves me even now when I recall it.

Let us thank God that the message of salvation was not just confined to the House of Israel but has spread beyond that fold to other hungry sheep who today are hearing His voice.

There is one Shepherd and one flock comprising people from every nation, colour, tribe and language throughout the world, and God is still building his church today.

29 NOVEMBER

Safe forever in His hands

'My Father, who has given them to Me, is greater than all; and no one is able to snatch them out of My Father's hand.' John 10:29

RECOMMENDED READING: Romans 8:28–39

During the past few days, we have been considering the Good Shepherd. There is one final point that I want us to consider before we conclude.

5. The sheep have double security. Just read carefully vv.28–29: 'And I give them eternal life, and they shall never perish; neither shall anyone snatch them out of My hand. My Father, who has given them to Me, is greater than all; and no one is able to snatch them out of My Father's hand.'

In these verses we see the Godhead at work. Today every Christian can rest securely in the fact that we are in the hand of the Son and the Father.

Verse 28: 'Neither shall anyone snatch them out of My hand.' That is security.

Verse 29: 'No one is able to snatch them out of My Father's hand.' That is double security.

Jesus said, 'I and My Father are One.' (v.30).

If we are His blood-bought children, then please rest assured in this firm promise that in Christ you are safe, whatever your circumstances now or in the future. But there is just one final point to note before we conclude.

We are safe for eternity. In v.28 Jesus says, 'I give them eternal life.' Our present is safe and secure, but so is our future. We are His forever.

Time as we know it will not break our link with Him. The relationship we have with Him now will never end; it will only grow deeper and stronger.

Let us be thankful this day that we are His sheep. He knows us; He loves us; He leads us; He gave His life for us; He protects us; and now He prepares an eternal home for us.

> 'Let every creature rise and bring
> blessing and honour to our king,
> Angels descend with songs again
> and earth repeat the loud "Amen!"'

Isaac Watts (1674–1748)

30 NOVEMBER

We can change

'Nevertheless they did not depart from the sins of the house of Jeroboam, who had made Israel sin, but walked in them.' 2 Kings 13:6

RECOMMENDED READING: 2 Chronicles 33:1–16

What a profoundly significant and hope-filled fact lies before us; we can change. We can come to a point in our lives when we can stop and take a new direction. Despite others continuing in their old ways, we can have a new beginning. We have a number of people in the Bible who turned their lives completely around. Instead of opposing Almighty God, they began to follow Him. I want to consider some of these people whose lives were dramatically transformed when they came face to face with the Lord.

1. **Manasseh.** Manasseh was the son of the godly king of Judah, Hezekiah. Sadly, children do not always follow in the steps of godly parents. There are many pastors and church workers whose hearts are heavy with grief because their children do not follow the ways of the Lord—what a blessing it is to both children and parents when they do.

Manasseh was described as one of the wicked kings of Judah. God spoke to him on a number of occasions but he would not listen. Eventually, God had to take action to bring this man to his knees in repentance.

The Assyrians bound Manasseh with bronze fetters and took him with hooks to Babylon. It was when he was in great affliction that he pleaded with God and humbled himself before him. God heard his prayers and brought him back to Jerusalem. In v.13 of 2 Chronicles 33, we see a changed man. 'Then Manasseh knew that the Lord was God.' His life began to change and this also affected the people of Judah in a very positive way.

2. **Nicodemus.** One of the most well-known chapters in the New Testament is centred on Nicodemus. In John 3:1 we are told that he was a Pharisee and a ruler of the Jews. Despite his religious upbringing, he was deeply troubled about his spiritual state. He decided to meet with Jesus as he had heard much about him. He came by night, probably so that he would not be recognised having this encounter with Jesus of Nazareth.

In this chapter Jesus explains to him in clear language that he needs to be born again. In fact, Jesus told him that if this did not happen, then he would not see the Kingdom of God. Despite the man's high standing, Jesus did not compromise His message but made the issue clear and plain. The good news is that Nicodemus did change and became a follower of the Lord Jesus.

The best news of all is that you too can change. Be born again and become a new person.

1 DECEMBER

A spiritual transformation

'He who believes in Him is not condemned; but he who does not believe is condemned already, because he has not believed in the name of the only begotten Son of God.' John 3:18

RECOMMENDED READING: Acts 9:1–16

We do not need to continue living as we are doing; we can change. Today we conclude with two more examples of changed lives.

3. The jailer. We are not told his name, but clearly God knew all there was to know about him. What we do know is that he was in charge of prisoners in the jail at Philippi. It was just another day, but one he would never forget.

He may have become aware of the uproar in the city. The news of the conversion of Lydia was beginning to spread, but this seemed nothing compared to what had happened to a young slave girl, who had been possessed with a spirit of divination (16:16). It had caused uproar in the marketplace.

Paul and Silas had been arrested and beaten for preaching the good news about Jesus which was changing lives. Eventually they found themselves in the prison under the responsibility of this jailer. The treatment they received had not dampened their spirits because around midnight they were singing hymns and the other inmates heard them. While they were doing this, an earthquake shook the prison foundations and doors flew open. The chains binding them came loose. When the jailer saw what had happened, he thought the prisoners had escaped and he was going to be punished severely for this. He was about to commit suicide when Paul stopped him, reassuring him that they were all still there. The result was not his death, but new life in Christ. This was a night he and his family would never forget. A midnight transformation had taken place.

4. Mary Magdalene. I want to conclude with this very special lady. I have read many descriptions regarding Mary, but they are not recorded in the Bible. What we are told in Mark 16:9 is that Jesus met her and cast out seven demons from her. The most important thing about Mary was that her life was turned around after her encounter with the Lord Jesus. From that decisive moment she followed her Lord and gave Him her complete devotion. She was with Him at the cross (Mark 15:40), and she was among the first to be at Jesus' tomb (Mark 16:1). Jesus had done much for Mary, and Mary did all she could for her Lord who had changed her by His power.

You can also be changed. Whether you are as religious as Nicodemus, or utterly ashamed of your sins, Jesus can give you a new beginning if you look to Him, repent and seek His forgiveness.

2 DECEMBER

Prayer is a great privilege

'Inquire at the house of Judas for one called Saul of Tarsus, for behold, he is praying.' Acts 9:11

RECOMMENDED READING: Acts 9:1–12

There are a number of dramatic conversions recorded in the New Testament, but none as dramatic as the account which centred on a man called Saul of Tarsus. We have the story in Acts 9.

Many sermons have been preached on the early verses of this chapter, which have stirred the hearts of many people. During the next few days, I want to consider the life of Saul following his conversion. As a young believer, what were his priorities? What characteristics became evident in his life?

1. **Prayer.** The desire for prayer—communion with God—is evidence of a changed life. One of the first unexpected surprises for Ananias was to find Saul praying (v.11).

He continued as he began. It soon became clear that Saul, or Paul as he became known, would be a man of prayer. Whenever he wrote to the churches, or individuals, he assured them of his prayers. It is noticeable that, in the first chapter of every one of his letters recorded in the Bible, Paul told the recipients that he prayed for them.

In Philippians 1:3–4 he counted it a joy to intercede for them. We need to ask ourselves if intercession is a burden, a duty, or can we truthfully say it is a joy to pray for our Christian family.

When we go back to the birth of the early church in Acts 2:42, we find that prayer is one of the main aspects of church life and growth. In talking to many pastors and church leaders, it is sad to find that our emphasis has changed. The message I hear constantly is that the church prayer meeting is the worst attended meeting of the week.

We must never lose the desire to pray, personally and corporately. Don't lose the joy of praying and joining with others when you do so.

We should all long to see conversions in our churches, but sadly they seem so rare. Every preacher laments that, but we must not always blame the preaching when we have lost the desire for prayer.

Let us pray for, and expect, transformed lives in villages, towns and cities where we live, and throughout our land and the world.

From his conversion, prayer took a central role in Paul's life. He just couldn't exist without communion with his God.

Lord, teach us how to pray, and find joy in doing so!

3 DECEMBER

We need each other

'I make mention of you always in my prayers, making request if ... I may find a way in the will of God to come to you. For I long to see you.' Romans 1:10–11

RECOMMENDED READING: Romans 16:1–16

Today we look at a further priority in the life of Saul of Tarsus who soon would be known as the apostle Paul.

2. Fellowship. Acts 2:42 reminds us that fellowship was an integral part of church life and growth. If there has been one area in our life that we have missed during lockdown, it has been that personal fellowship with the Lord's people. We have been reminded that no one is an island; we need each other.

Acts 9:19 tells us that Saul, 'spent some days with the disciples at Damascus'. In Acts 9:26 we read, 'When Saul had come to Jerusalem, he tried to join the disciples.' Saul longed for support, encouragement and fellowship. However, it wasn't initially reciprocated. In v.26, when he came to Jerusalem in an attempt to join the disciples, they were afraid of him and didn't believe his conversion. This was when noble Barnabas intervened and introduced him to the apostles assuring them that Saul was a true believer (v.27).

It was approximately three years after his conversion that, according to Galatians 1:18, he met with the apostle Peter and spent fifteen days with him. I would have loved to have been the proverbial 'fly on the wall' and listened to their conversation. I am sure Paul would have spent the time throwing loads of questions in Peter's direction. Those fifteen days would have flown by. Paul would have longed for more fellowship, such as he had with that great apostle. Galatians 1:19 tells us that the only other apostle he saw was James. I can imagine the questions coming again.

What a blessing it is to have Christian fellowship. It has been such a help in our own Christian lives. Those whom we have met and stayed with over many years have been such a blessing and we thank them for their fellowship in the Lord.

My heart goes out to Christians in many parts of the world who are isolated and unable to enjoy fellowship with other believers. How they need our prayers.

From his conversion on the Damascus Road to the final days in a Roman prison, fellowship was vital for Paul. He longed for it. In his letters he yearned for it. In Philippians 1:8 Paul says, 'How greatly I long for you all.' What a privilege to have fellowship with those of like mind. Take advantage of it; It is a precious blessing that we should never take for granted.

4 DECEMBER

The persecutor became persecuted

'I will show him how many things he must suffer for My name's sake.'
Acts 9:16

RECOMMENDED READING: 1 Peter 5

We continue our consideration of the life of Paul following his conversion. A third aspect of his life affects many true followers of the Lord Jesus throughout the world.

3. Suffering. Before his conversion, Saul had caused much suffering to the Christian church, including giving his assent to and witnessing the death of Stephen. But now the tables had been turned and he was about to suffer for the faith he had embraced.

Today I want to leave you with verses of scripture which show how many things this man had to suffer for upholding the name of Jesus, because it would not be long before Acts 9:16 would become a reality.

In Acts 9:23, 'The Jews plotted to kill him.' In 9:24, 'They watched the gates day and night, to kill him.' Verse 25 tells us that to save his life they let him down through the wall in a basket. He then made his way to Jerusalem. However, that intervention was only a brief respite for Saul.

We read in v.29, 'He spoke boldly in the name of the Lord Jesus and disputed against the Hellenists, but they attempted to kill him.' Again, the disciples intervened (v.30) and brought him to Caesarea and then sent him to Tarsus.

The book of Acts then devotes its account to the life of Peter until we come to 12:25 where Saul took centre stage once again. It wasn't long before Paul had again to suffer for the faith. Notice by this time his name had been changed to Paul. Chapters 13 and 14 give further examples of the reality of the Lord's words to Ananias in Acts 9:16.

Just spend some time reading the remainder of Acts and Paul's letters to see how this Christian had to suffer for the cause of Christ, and did it joyfully. When he wrote to the church at Colosse, in Colossians 1:24, he said, 'I now rejoice in my sufferings.' What an amazing statement!

In many parts of the world today, Christians suffer much persecution for their strongly held beliefs. They lose their homes and possessions, are separated from their families, are imprisoned, persecuted and even endure death itself for their faith. In the United Kingdom, it is mainly verbal persecution that we have to endure, but who knows what the future may bring?

My prayer this morning is that Almighty God will give us the resolve to suffer for the cause of Christ if ever we are called upon to do so!

5 DECEMBER

The church grows through persecution

'Saul increased all the more in strength.' Acts 9:22

RECOMMENDED READING: Acts 2:40–47

We conclude our look into the life of Saul/Paul with one very important aspect of his life.

4. Growing. When we read Luke's account of the early church in Acts, we see growth, not only in numbers coming to a saving faith in the Lord Jesus, but in the lives of individual believers. Even Paul experienced a significant change. Acts 9:22 tells us that, 'he increased all the more in strength.'

Spiritual growth in the life of believers is so important. We cannot, and we must not, remain spiritually stagnant. No matter how long we have been in the faith, we must grow in the knowledge of our Lord Jesus Christ. Unfortunately, we can start to resemble a river that has become stagnant because of the debris, and this leads to pollution.

Acts 2:42 shows us how the individual believers were strengthened in their faith. May that be our experience as we grow closer to our Lord.

But we also see how the early church grew numerically. From a human point of view, one would have expected Saul's sufferings to have had a detrimental effect upon the church. To the contrary, in 9:31 we read that the church multiplied.

It is the same throughout the world today. Where the church faces persecution, the church multiplies. It sends the devil crazy. Some are killed here, and twice the number spring up over there. Not all the forces of evil can stem this growth.

Remember, the Christian church is the only organisation on earth that never loses a member through death. The National Secular Society cannot say that! Neither can any other religion throughout the world.

So, in the life of Paul we have a man who prayed, who longed for fellowship, who was willing to suffer for his faith and who grew in grace. All this resulted in a growing church. Isn't that what we all long to see?

Paul eventually comes to the end of his life and he finds himself on death row. He was a Jew by birth and a tentmaker by trade, but he was called by God to be an apostle. He wasn't afraid of death; he was just longing to be with his Lord and Saviour and to finally rest from his labours.

In the last letter he wrote, he said to his friend Timothy, 'I have fought the good fight, I have finished the race, I have kept the faith' (2 Timothy 4:7). May we be able to say the same.

6 DECEMBER

All our sins have been blotted out

'Therefore, having been justified by faith, we have peace with God through our Lord Jesus Christ.' Romans 5:1

RECOMMENDED READING: Romans 5:1–9

There are many wonderful doctrines in the Bible that cause the Christian to rejoice. One of these doctrines, which the apostle Paul refers to on numerous occasions in his letter to the church at Rome, is the doctrine of *justification*.

Preachers often use this word but rarely explain its meaning. So, what exactly does this word mean, and what message is it seeking to convey to us?

You may have come across this explanation for the word justification. Some well-intentioned people say it means, *just as if I'd never sinned*. There is an element of truth there but it is only partly correct.

It is impossible to explain to people such a great doctrine and reduce it to six words. In fact, the more I think about it, the more I realise it falls a long way short of its full meaning.

So, what does *being justified* really mean? What are we trying to convey to people when we use this great word? *Justify* is a forensic term which means *acquit* or *declare righteous*. It is the total opposite of the word *condemn*.

When I was in my teens, I looked forward to watching programmes such as *Ironside*, *Perry Mason*, *Matlock*, and the forensic scientist *Quincy*. I loved the court case drama, waiting eagerly for the judge to pass the sentence. The one on trial would either be condemned or acquitted.

In the spiritual realm we know that the 'judge of all the earth [will] do right' (Genesis 18:25).

However, for the Christian, God does much more than pass a favourable verdict: He blesses those He has acquitted in ways unimaginable.

God does not justify His people by a series of steps, but the moment we confess our sins, repent of them, seek his forgiveness, and turn to Christ, we are fully justified.

What blessings being justified brings to the child of God. May this word encourage your heart as it has mine and make us realise what privileged people we are in having this remarkable relationship with the One, true, living God whom we can now call our Father.

> ''Tis finished! The Messiah dies, Cut off for sins, but not His own;
> Accomplished is the sacrifice, The great redeeming work is done.
> 'Tis finished! All the debt is paid; Justice divine is satisfied;
> The grand and full atonement made; God for a guilty world hath died.'
> Charles Wesley (1707–88)

7 DECEMBER

Loved with everlasting love

'Yes, He loves the people; all His saints are in Your hand.' Deuteronomy 33:3

RECOMMENDED READING: Isaiah 49:7–18

I hope you find pleasure in both giving and receiving. God does! In this verse we discover four gifts which God gives to His people, and He is delighted to do so.

1. He gives love to his people. Forty years earlier, through the leadership of Moses, Almighty God had brought the children of Israel out of Egypt following four hundred years of slavery and persecution.

Now, at the border of the Promised Land, Moses addresses this huge company of people for the last time before he leaves them. Soon he will go to Mount Nebo and rest from his labours. His days of leadership will be over and Joshua will take his place.

However, before he goes, he takes this opportunity of reminding the people of all that God has done for them, and the love that He has shown to them on numerous occasions.

Jeremiah says in 31:3, 'Yes, I have loved you with an everlasting love; therefore, with lovingkindness I have drawn you.'

Despite their persistent moaning and rebellion; despite the constant breaking of His commandments; despite the worship of other gods; despite their unbelief on numerous occasions, God's love for them has always been evident. They are His special people whom He has redeemed, and His love for them exceeds even a mother's love for her child.

Isaiah 49:15 says, 'Can a woman forget her nursing child, and not have compassion on the son of her womb? Surely, they may forget, yet I will not forget you.'

We can easily forget that, as Christians, God's love for us reaches even greater heights. Yes, we are loved with an everlasting love, and that love far exceeds that of a mother's love. But He also loves us with a love that led Him to give His only begotten Son. Despite our rebellion, disobedience and unbelief, God still loves us.

To give the Son He loves, to allow Him to suffer at the hands of cruel Roman soldiers is astounding. For Jesus to bear our sin and iniquity, to endure God's divine anger over sin instead of us, is truly amazing.

Does God need to go any further to show the true depth of His love? Christian, remember at all times and through all circumstances, that God loves you.

8 DECEMBER

Every Christian is a saint

'Yes, He loves the people; all His saints are in Your hand.' Deuteronomy 33:3

RECOMMENDED READING: Ephesians 1

In Deuteronomy 33:3 we have four gifts which God willingly gives to His people, and He is delighted to do so. Yesterday we saw how He gives love to His people. We are loved with an everlasting love, and we realise how deep and strong that love is when we fix our eyes upon His Son, our Lord Jesus Christ, who freely gave his life for us all. Today we consider the second part of that verse.

2. God gives a privileged title to His people. We are called 'His saints.' Over the centuries this word *saint* has been greatly misused and, in some cases, abused.

We visit some of our beautiful cathedrals and churches throughout the United Kingdom, and stand admiring the great architecture and stained-glass windows—many of which portray characters with haloes around their heads—and these are known as 'saints'. We also see figures made of stone or precious metals that adorn these buildings and people pay homage and worship these 'saints'.

From time to time, an announcement comes from the Vatican in Rome to say that a particular person, who may have been dead hundreds or even thousands of years, is about to be elevated to the position of a 'saint'. This is usually due to the good works or miracles they performed during their days on earth.

Many people have the impression that a saint is someone who is extra special; the elite of heaven; those who have a special place in God's presence.

If that is how you think let me encourage you because, if you are a Christian who has been saved from your sin through trusting in the Lord Jesus and His work at Calvary, you are a saint.

Ephesians 1:1 says, 'To the *saints* who are in Ephesus, and faithful in Christ Jesus.' Philippians 1:1 says, 'To all the *saints* in Christ Jesus.'

So, who is a *saint*? You are!

If we are His children, He has given us a very special title. We are *His saints*. Therefore, each of us must live like one.

> 'But saints are lovely in His sight;
> He views His children with delight;
> He sees their hope, He knows their fear,
> And looks, and loves His image there.'
>
> Isaac Watts (1674–1748)

9 DECEMBER

God is our teacher

'All His saints are in Your hand; they sit down at Your feet; everyone receives Your words.' Deuteronomy 33:3

RECOMMENDED READING: Proverbs 1:1–9

We have looked at two gifts that God has given to his people. We have received His everlasting love, and we are now His saints. Today we conclude with two more gifts.

3. God gives instructions to His people. 'They sit down at Your feet' (Deuteronomy 33:3). In Luke 10:39, we read of Mary who sat down at the Saviour's feet to learn from Him.

There is a time to labour; there is a time to learn. Martha, her sister, was so busy, involved with many things. There was nothing wrong with the tasks she was doing. It was just not the right time to be doing them. Jesus would not be with them much longer and Mary was right to take full advantage of this opportune moment to sit at His feet and receive His instruction.

There is no question about the importance of duty, but not at the expense of listening to the words of our Lord.

Luke 6:47 says, 'Whoever comes to Me, and hears My sayings …'. This reminds us of the need to sit and learn from Him. How hungry are we for spiritual food?

The pastor spends hours in his study preparing food. Should we not take every opportunity of eating it? How is your appetite?

Sunday and midweek should see us there with eyes, ears and hearts wide open to hear what God has to say to us. He may only speak once, so don't miss what He has to say.

4. He gives His precious word to His people. Everyone shall receive of His words. Jesus said in Matthew 11:29, 'Learn from Me.'

Men of God, such as William Tyndale, gave their time, and even their lives, to ensure that the scriptures were available to all people in their own language. When we take the Bible into our hands, do we realise what it cost to translate it so that we can read the Word of God in our native tongue? The cost was not in monetary terms; it was often in blood.

Today that same book is being translated into countless languages throughout the world. What a privilege it is to have this book and understand its message. It truly is a lamp to our feet, and a light to our path (Psalm 119:105).

May we treasure it, read it, love it, and proclaim its message to those near and far until everyone shall receive His words (Deuteronomy 33:3).

10 DECEMBER

Trials are sent to improve us

'Now it came to pass after these things that God tested Abraham.' Genesis 22:1

RECOMMENDED READING: Hebrews 11:8–10

One of the key events in the early chapters of the Bible is found in Genesis 22. It involves two of the Patriarchs, Abraham and his son, Isaac.

We are first told about Abraham in Genesis 11:26. He lived for 175 years, and it was a life filled with excitement, adventure and at times great danger. But throughout it all, he constantly cast himself on the faithfulness and promises of Almighty God.

Chapter 22 is a major event in his life where we see his faith tested to the limit—a test he had to face alone.

1. The time of his trial. Let's go back about eighteen years when Isaac, the precious child Sarah and Abraham had longed for, would have been about three years old. His stepbrother Ishmael, who was the son of Hagar, and Egyptian slave, was now about seventeen years of age. Ishmael was presenting himself as a real threat to Isaac's right of inheritance. His bullish attitude was a real concern to Sarah and she pleaded with her husband to cast out Ishmael along with his Egyptian mother.

Abraham was naturally reluctant to comply with Sarah's request, not only because he was the father of Ishmael, but also because the law forbade the expulsion of a slave wife and her children. However, God clearly instructed Abraham to do as Sarah requested, but at the same time assured him that it was through Isaac that the Hebrew nation would come (Genesis 21:12). He also assured Abraham, in the following verse, that a nation would come through Ishmael.

So, in chapter 21:14, Ishmael and his mother were sent away, and they wandered through the desert region. In time the water they were given ran out, but God met with them, provided a well of water and personally assured them that Ishmael would be the father of a great nation.

During this time, Isaac grew from infancy, through childhood into his teenage years. He had become a great joy to Abraham and Sarah, but that joy would be short-lived.

Men and women of great faith must expect to face difficult trials. Abraham was about to face his greatest test of all. Isaac's life was going to be on the line.

We also face times of great trial, thankfully rarely as difficult as Abraham faced, but we must be aware that God will never leave us nor forsake us. In our time of trial, He will be our constant companion.

11 DECEMBER

Strong faith is often brought about by strong trials

'Take now your son, your only son Isaac, whom you love.' Genesis 22:2

RECOMMENDED READING: Hebrews 11:17–19

We are looking at an event in the life of Abraham that proved to be his greatest test of faith.

2. The trial itself. Verse 1 tells us that, 'God tested Abraham.' This test was not to lead him into sin, but to discover how strong and firm his faith in God was. Abraham had faced storms in the past, but this would be like a tsunami—greater than anything he had previously encountered.

There is an important point to note from this verse. God knows His people by name. In Luke 22:31, just before Peter's denial, Jesus said, 'Simon ... I have prayed for you.' In John's account of the resurrection in chapter 20, Jesus meets Mary Magdalene. When she supposed He was the gardener, in v.16, He simply said, 'Mary'.

Abraham had heard God's voice speaking to him on a number of occasions. What would God ask him to do this time? Where would God ask him to go?

God knows all His people by name. He knows you by name. You are personally important to Him if you are His child, bought with the precious blood of His Son. We must therefore listen when He speaks, and act upon His instructions.

Verse 2: 'Take now your son, your only son Isaac, whom you love.' God made His instructions short, clear and plain. Abraham could not misinterpret them in any way. God never wastes words. Why was God asking him to do this?

Maybe Abraham's confidence is in Isaac rather than God's promises. Was He asking Abraham to put Him first? Was God testing Abraham's obedience?

There was another issue that may have been confusing Abraham. Human sacrifices did take place among the Canaanites, but not among God's own people. Why was God asking for a human sacrifice? This didn't seem right.

But there was one more matter that must surely have troubled him. If he did what God was asking him to do, how would God's promise to him and Sarah be fulfilled? We will soon see how all this becomes clear.

There are times in our Christian journey when we cannot fully understand God's plans and purposes for us. 'Why?' so often becomes the common question in our thoughts. God always knows what He is doing and it is always for the best. Let us leave our times and events in God's safe hands; that is the most secure place for them to be.

12 DECEMBER

Unquestioning obedience is all God asks from His children

'So Abraham rose early in the morning and saddled his donkey, and took two of his young men with him, and Isaac his son.' Genesis 22:3

RECOMMENDED READING: Genesis 22:1–6

We continue this amazing story and the dilemma that confronted Abraham. Was Abraham's confidence still in Isaac rather than God's promises?

Where is our confidence resting today? Is it in a close friend? Does it lie in our own talents? Or does it lie in our bank balance or our pension pot? If that is so, be ready for a challenge, for God will not share His glory with another person or thing.

3. The person to be sacrificed. God's instruction was clear to Abraham. I don't want bulls or lambs. Neither do I want your servants. I must have your son; the son who came from the womb of your wife Sarah; the one you both longed for, that you waited so long to hold in your arms; the one you trusted would be the start of the great nation that I promised to you. He is the one I want.

Abraham could not be left in any doubt whatsoever. God's message could not be spelt out any clearer. You can imagine Abraham's inward response. Surely not! You can't be serious! Is my hearing deteriorating so badly? Is this the Almighty speaking to me?

One big advantage we have is that we know the end of the story. Abraham didn't. So, can we put ourselves in his sandals for a moment? If you have children, would you not bring a defence against this instruction? Would you not discuss it with God? Would you not seek an alternative way out of the situation?

As I have read these verses, I cannot find any record of Abraham debating with God. Verse 2 is God's clear instruction. Verses 3 to 6 are Abraham's response. All we have before us is obedience. That is all God asks of us—unquestioning obedience.

The task before him was to offer his son as a sacrifice—the most difficult task God had ever asked him to perform.

There are occasions in our life when God tests our faith. He gives us instructions to fulfil that seem beyond us. If we were thinking only of our own wellbeing, we would run away—fast! But we know deep down within our heart that to obey Him is the best and wisest route to take, however painful it may be. We have no right to question our sovereign God. As God said to Job in 38:4, 'Where were you when I laid the foundations of the earth? Tell Me, if you have understanding.'

The mountain of sacrifice

'My son, God will provide for Himself the lamb for a burnt offering.'
Genesis 22:8

RECOMMENDED READING: Genesis 22:5–14

Abraham made his painful journey aware of the solemn task that was before him. Despite the horror of what he was about to do, he did not flinch from carrying out God's instructions.

4. The place of sacrifice. He was to journey to the land of Moriah. God had made this instruction abundantly clear. He was near Beersheba, but he had to take a three-day journey with plenty of time to ponder over the task before him. God was not making this easy.

When God appoints a place for us to go to, He makes it possible for us to go there, even if the journey is to be a painful one.

In 1973, God called us into a new ministry, but it meant leaving our home near Barnsley and travelling to our new house in Brighton on the south coast. We would be leaving our family and friends to travel to a place that was foreign to us, and to live in a house that Kathryn hadn't even seen. At the time it was tough, but God was good and met our needs.

But why had Abraham to travel to Moriah?

Around 2,000 years later, on that same mountain, God would ask of Himself the same thing that He asked of Abraham. I will sacrifice My Son, My only Son, the Son that I love. Not a lamb from the flock, but a lamb after My own heart.

Try and picture Abraham and Isaac climbing those last few steps to the summit. Remember Abraham was now 120 years of age. His body was tired and his heart heavy with the thought of what he was about to do.

But Isaac had a question to ask: 'Where is the lamb for a burnt offering?' (Genesis 22:7). Although Abraham was to pierce Isaac's heart, this was like a knife into his own. As he struggled to speak, he said, 'My son, God will provide for Himself the lamb' (v.8). So, the preparation began.

Throughout this story, Abraham demonstrates obedience. But what about Isaac?

Abraham was an old man. Isaac was young and strong and would easily have been able to overpower his father. But he was resigned to this untimely death. He didn't resist but was willing to be bound and laid upon the altar they had built together. Isaac showed a level of obedience and submission to God's will that we would all also do well to emulate. My prayer is that we would attain that same level of submission to Christ's will in our lives.

14 DECEMBER

God did provide a Lamb

'When they had come to the place called Calvary.' Luke 23:32

RECOMMENDED READING: Luke 23:26–47

We have followed Abraham on a very difficult journey. God had instructed him to offer his son as a burnt offering. He took the three-day journey from Beersheba and finally arrived at the appointed place. Everything was prepared for the sacrifice. Isaac had been bound and now lay on the altar waiting for his life to expire.

5. The trial comes to a sudden conclusion. As Abraham was about to plunge the sharp knife into the heart of his son, an Angel of the Lord spoke his name yet again. Not once did he hear it, but twice. 'Abraham! Abraham!' (v.11). Can you imagine the sudden relief that came from the heart of God's servant? It was all so different 2,000 years later. When Jesus hung on Calvary's cross, God could have called 10,000 angels to rescue His Son, but that day God did not intervene.

Jesus had to endure all the horrors of the cross so that we might be rescued and spared God's righteous anger because of our sin. Yes, Calvary was all planned for us before this world was ever brought into being. Jesus was to become our substitute. God's anger, instead of being deservedly directed towards us, was directed at Jesus. He faced the full force of God's wrath.

Philip Paul Bliss (1838–1876) could not have explained it more clearly when he wrote, 'In my place condemned He stood. Sealed my pardon with His blood. Hallelujah, what a Saviour!'

When God called a halt to the sacrifice of Isaac, God provided Abraham with a ram as a substitute. But why was it a ram? And why caught by its horns? A few years ago, I was preaching in Derbyshire and stayed for lunch with a sheep farmer. During the afternoon we were talking about farming and this story came into our discussions. He told me that he had been looking after sheep all his life and he had never seen a ram caught by its horns because they are so strong and powerful. Caught by the wool and the flesh, but not the horns. This brought home to me a wonderful truth. The sacrifice that day had to be a perfect sacrifice. If the flesh had been torn or bruised in any way it would have been imperfect.

So it was with Christ. No other person could have taken our place. Only a perfect, spotless sacrifice was acceptable to God. The good news is that three days after his death was His glorious resurrection. What a wonderful, positive, life-changing message we have for a dying world. May our lips and our lives proclaim it.

15 DECEMBER

Light shines through in the darkness

'The word of the LORD was rare in those days; there was no widespread revelation.' 1 Samuel 3:1

RECOMMENDED READING: Isaiah 9:1–7

When we turn to the book of Samuel, the people of Israel had been settled in the land of Canaan for over 200 years. The tribes had received their possession following the amazing victories that had been accomplished through Joshua's leadership. These should have been exciting days for God's people. They had everything they needed to make life pleasant and enjoyable. The land was good and God had proved to be very patient and merciful.

Unfortunately, these were not good times as chapter 3 makes very clear.

1. **The condition of the nation.** Verse 1 says it all. The priest Eli was one of the final judges that ruled Israel. When you read the book of Judges, it soon becomes clear that Israel had turned their backs upon God. Wherever you cast your eye, idolatry and immorality are clearly visible, even at the temple doors. Eli's two sons, Hophni and Phinehas, were involved and setting a diabolical example to all who came near the temple.

Had God forsaken His people? Dark clouds were certainly hanging low over the land. Israel was in moral and spiritual darkness. Even if the people listened, they were disobedient to God's instructions. Judges 21:25 says, 'Everyone did what was right in his own eyes.'

Would not this describe our own nation? God has blessed these islands. He has helped us during the dark days and given to us far more than we deserve. But, as with Israel, we have turned our backs upon Him and gone after other idols. We have become immoral and godless. The word of the Lord is becoming rare, and the lamp is burning low.

2. **Minute chinks of light.** Verse 1 does not leave us without hope. God has not totally rejected His people. His word was rare, but not completely gone. Even through the heavy clouds, a shaft of light breaks through to lift the gloom. Verse 4 says, 'The LORD called Samuel.' He was a shaft of light in the darkness of Israel's history.

In Egypt, Moses was a beam of light that brought hope to God's people. In Persia, Esther became a shaft of light to save Israel from annihilation.

In Bethlehem's manger, the Lord Jesus would come to be the light of the world removing the darkness from the hearts of the people. Isaiah 9:2 says, 'The people who walked in darkness have seen a great light.' God's word is that shaft of light that we have today, along with faithful Christians who obey that word. Be part of the solution and shine that light brightly!

16 DECEMBER

Never doubt this wonderful fact

'I will come again.' John 14:3

RECOMMENDED READING: Mark 13:21–37

We are now in the season of Advent when we prepare for, and remember, the coming of our Lord Jesus Christ. But this is also the time when we can focus our minds on His second coming.

One of the greatest promises of our Lord is found in John 14:3: 'I will come again.' The return of our Lord is clear Bible teaching. However, despite that, one of the many things to be regretted in certain sections of the church is her indifference to the second Advent of Jesus Christ. If these are the last days, surely the importance of the second coming cannot be over-emphasised.

In Mark 13 we are told about the last days, so let us consider this important subject.

1. A truth to be grasped. All Christian beliefs are based upon the authority of Scripture. Although many today deny its truth, the Holy Spirit has revealed and continues to reveal its wonders to God's people.

The Christian knows that the Bible contains facts that are authentic, and one of these is the return of our Lord Jesus Christ. It is the most certain fact in the Bible. This event is referred to over 300 times in the New Testament alone.

There are many strong reasons why I believe that Jesus is coming again.

- It is predicted by Christ Himself. It is impossible to read the New Testament without observing what our Lord had to say about His coming again. In His parables and teaching there is a great deal said about His return. We have the parables about *The bridegroom and the virgins* (Matthew 25:1–13), and *The lord and the talents* (Matthew 25:14–30), to name just two. These both teach us that Jesus is coming again. But, in addition to the parables, we have His plain teaching. There are too many to list but I mention one. In John 14:2–3 Jesus said, 'I go to prepare a place for you. And if I go and prepare a place for you, I will come again.' In Mark 13:31 Jesus made it very clear that every word He spoke would come to pass.

- It is taught by the apostles. The apostles are equally clear and emphatic in their teaching of the return of our Lord. 1 Thessalonians has been called, 'The book of the Second Coming'. It is also referred to in: James 5:7–8; 1 John 2:28; Revelation 1:7—to name a few.

Since the birth of the early church all evangelical Christians have followed the example of the apostles and preached this great truth. It cannot be ignored.

17 DECEMBER

Can you keep a secret? God can!

'But of that day and hour no one knows, neither the angels in heaven, nor the Son, but only the Father.' Mark 13:32

RECOMMENDED READING: John 14:1–3

Yesterday we began considering the return of our Lord Jesus Christ. We saw that the second coming was a truth to be grasped. Today we look at a second important fact in this great doctrine.

2. A secret to be kept. Throughout the history of the Christian Church, predictions have been made regarding the physical return of our Lord.

Dates have been set and people have gone to great lengths to suggest not only the year and the month, but even the time of day. Many questions have been asked, but each prediction has proved to be a clear misjudgement.

It is time to stop asking questions and making predictions because there are some things God never intended us knowing and the return of our Lord is one of them. This has not only been kept from us, but also from the angels and even from the Lord Himself. This is known by God alone.

Some people, however, would say, 'If Jesus is God, how can He be ignorant of this important fact?' Jesus possesses a divine nature but also a human nature. He is the God man. Here He speaks as a man.

When He came to this earth with His human nature, He took on limitations. He was weary, hungry and He had to endure temptations. He was also limited as far as knowledge is concerned.

With regard to His return, the time is only known to the Father so we need to keep on our spiritual toes and be always alert. The Lord says, 'Be ready, for the Son of man 'is coming at an hour you do not expect' (Matthew 24:44; Luke 12:40).

However, Jesus did say there would be signs (Mark 13:28–29). There would be a falling away. Verses 6, 21 and 22 tell us that there will be false teachers and false sects and these are often ready with their false predictions. Then v.8 informs us that there will be disasters, famines and wars. In v.10 we are reminded that the gospel must be preached to all nations. These are signs, but they must not lead us into the danger of predicting His return.

We must be content with the knowledge that God does know, so let us be willing to leave this secret in His capable hands. After all, we are not meant to know everything.

18 DECEMBER

We must never leave Christ out of Christmas

'For unto us a Child is born, unto us a Son is given.' Isaiah 9:6

RECOMMENDED READING: Isaiah 9:1–7

Very soon we will be remembering the birth of our Lord Jesus Christ. What would you say to people who ask you what Christmas is about? For many people it is about cards, presents, turkeys, food and drink. For others it is about shepherds, wise men, a manger and a star. This is where we are completely going astray. It is not, *what* is Christmas about, but *who* it is about.

1. The Nativity reveals God's almighty power. The One who created the world from nothing, the One who hangs the stars on nothing, the One who holds back the waves of the sea, the One who maintains gravity to keep this earth in its place, the One who keeps our amazing bodies functioning, became a **Man**. Christmas is just a further demonstration of God's almighty power. Almost 2,000 years ago God stepped into history and, yet again, released His power. History is His story.

2. The Nativity reveals God's amazing plan. We humans have a major problem with sin. We have been condemned by God because of it. We have broken God's moral laws. We have been separated from God. That is the condition we find ourselves in, and the situation could not be more serious. Now God had three alternatives:

- He could annihilate us. Do you recall what happened in the days of Noah because of man's sin? Do you remember what happened to the cities of Sodom and Gomorrah because of man's sin? We deserve no less!

- He could just overlook it. That is a common practice today. Those who are in debt declare themselves bankrupt; then start over again as though nothing had happened. If those who commit a crime plead guilty, they can get their sentence reduced or, better still, removed. But God is holy and doesn't act as we do. God cannot, and will not, just overlook our sin. We are all responsible for our own personal sin.

- He could rescue and save us. As someone once said, 'you don't give life-jackets to sunbathers on the beach'. You give them to people who are drowning and need rescuing. Thankfully God chose to do the latter. Christmas is about God coming to rescue us (Matthew 1:21).

Jesus came to this earth to take your sin upon Himself, to offer you forgiveness, to give you eternal life. That is who Christmas is all about.

19 DECEMBER

See God's amazing plan being worked out

'And it came to pass in those days that a decree went out from Caesar Augustus that all the world should be registered.' Luke 2:1

RECOMMENDED READING: Micah 5:1–4

Let us go back to the land of Israel 2,000 years ago and be reminded of the events surrounding Christ's coming into this sinful world.

1. The time. We read in Luke 2 that Jesus was born in the days of Caesar Augustus, who was the first Roman emperor. This empire was vast and extended to Parthia (north-eastern Iran today) in one direction and Britain in the other. It was known as *the empire of the whole earth*. Luke 2:1 calls it, 'the entire world', because the entire civilised world depended upon it.

Also at this time, the Jewish people were coming under the dominion and taxation of a foreign power and Israel did not have a government of its own. Rome was beginning to show its muscles with great authority. The time had surely come when the promised Messiah would show Himself to the people.

There was never a better time for the gospel of Christ to be declared openly. Nothing could prevent a preacher from travelling throughout the country or even further afield if they wished to do so. Assyria, Persia, Greece, Egypt and even Rome itself were revealing the truth of 1 Corinthians 1:21: 'The world through wisdom did not know God.' This was a period of great change, but idolatry was still practiced openly. Could this be the time for God to reveal Himself and send His only begotten Son to this needy world that He had created?

It is so comforting to know that Almighty God is in complete charge of all events and circumstances. Every part of our lives is in His powerful hand.

Some people say that they are in control of their own life and destiny. This is so far from the truth. God controls our destiny and it would be well for us if we acknowledged this fact.

He also knows the best time to send help to the world, the church and to ourselves. We must never fret about any situation that confronts us, for God will step in when the time is right.

We must not try and govern the world by ourselves, for we will surely fail.

God has always been in control of the world He created. He remains in control, so trust Him and do not be afraid. He knows what He is doing.

20 DECEMBER

Wealth destroys more souls than poverty

'But you, Bethlehem Ephrathah, though you are little among the thousands of Judah ...' Micah 5:2

RECOMMENDED READING: Matthew 1:18–25

Yesterday we considered the time of the birth of our Lord, acknowledging that God is in control of time, events and people.

2. The place. Micah, hundreds of years before the birth of Jesus, foretold the place where this event would take place. Bethlehem was a humble location with under 1,000 inhabitants.

However, the name was significant. Bethlehem means, 'House of Bread', which is a very relevant name for the One who came to be 'The Bread of Life' (John 6:35).

The census that was issued was to satisfy the pride of Augustus in knowing the numbers of his people. Little did he know who was among that number!

Once again, we see the overruling providence of God in evidence, not only in the time, but also the place. God directs all things, both in heaven and on earth. He turns the hearts of kings and rulers as He desires. Caesar Augustus was just a pawn in the hand of the Almighty God. He didn't realise that he was helping to lay the foundation of a great Kingdom.

Luke then tells us in 2:7 that Jesus was born in a stable next to an inn.

An inn is a place where different people congregate. Jesus came to identify Himself with all conditions of people. Colour, nationality or status meant absolutely nothing to Him. Jesus never forgot His reason for coming: to seek and save the lost.

When you visit an inn, you have to pay. Very rarely are you given free accommodation. It cost a great deal for our Lord to stay in a stable attached to an inn. He came into this world in the poorest part. The King of the universe, who owns not only the cattle on a thousand hills, but the hills themselves and owns the gold in every mine, demonstrated humility by coming into our world by the means of a common stable. He became poor for our sakes.

We must never despise the poor because of their poverty. God looks at the hearts of men, not their incomes. It is no disgrace to be poor.

When the love of money begins to creep over us, let us think of the stable at Bethlehem, and the One who was born in it. To do so may save us much grief and unhappiness. Let us make sure our treasure is laid up in heaven.

21 DECEMBER

God often reveals Himself unexpectedly

'Now there were in the same country shepherds living out in the fields, keeping watch over their flock by night.' Luke 2:8

RECOMMENDED READING: John 10:1–18

We have been considering the time and place of the birth of our Lord. Now we turn our thoughts to the recipients of an amazing announcement.

3. The witnesses. Who were these shepherds? They were not biblical scholars with letters after their name; neither were they occupants of a palace with royal status; nor were they connected with the religious establishment. All the elite people of that day were bypassed and ignored.

These men out in the fields that eventful night were guardians of the sheep that were under their care. We have similar examples in the life of Abel, the son of Adam, and David who was to become the second king of Israel.

Shepherds were simple, modest labourers who were often unrecognised by man. However, this group of men were honoured by being the recipients of an amazing visit from heaven.

God's voice had been silent for some 400 years, but this night His voice rang out when His angels unexpectedly paid a visit, not to the religious establishment or royalty, but to humble shepherds on what was known as *the graveyard shift*. The weak and unlikely ones are often called before the mighty.

Why were they afraid? If we saw what they saw we too would shake in our boots. These men were privileged to hear from heaven and see the glory of the Lord.

This was a time when true reverence for the Almighty God was absent from Israel. People did what they thought was right in their own eyes. The United Kingdom today is no different. Awe and godly fear are by and large absent in both the church and throughout the nation. Is this why we fail to see the glory of the Lord?

The shepherds also saw the greatness of the Lord. Do we make our God too small? Do we fail to elevate Him as we should in our preaching, in our worship and in our daily living? We need to make our God as big and as great as forgiven sinners can. Even then we fall short, as He is far beyond human understanding.

After this experience these men would never be the same again. As we prepare spiritually for the Nativity of our Lord, may we have just a glimpse of His glory and the greatness of His being.

22 DECEMBER

Jesus came to banish fear and bring faith

'And behold, you will conceive in your womb and bring forth a Son, and shall call His name Jesus.' Luke 1:31

RECOMMENDED READING: John 1:1–14

We now consider the message as it was told by the angels.

When you listen to the news it can be so depressing. We hear of such devastating loss of life and debilitating illness due to COVID, not forgetting loved ones forced to isolate from each other. Then we have all the drama that Brexit has brought to the nation. On top of all this are the scandals, riots and general world problems.

Well, let us put all this to one side for a moment and consider some exceedingly good news. Most people believe the first broadcast across the airwaves took place at Alexandra Palace. I would respectfully disagree. The most exciting broadcast took place 2,000 years ago in fields outside the town of Bethlehem. It was a live broadcast given to a select few—humble shepherds.

This broadcast is now meant for us all to hear. It is a message that will affect your future. It is a message of hope. It was truly good news from God to the world. Luke tells us why the gospel is such good news.

1. The gospel is good news because it banishes fear. Luke 1:13 says, 'Do not be afraid.' After 400 years of silence these were the first words uttered to fearful people.

Through sin, fellowship with God had been broken. God longed for that fellowship to be restored. He had spoken through judges and prophets, but the people did not listen.

Now God spoke again when people were gripped by fear. Silence can be frightening, which is why people prefer noise. In silence the conscience speaks. With noise it is dulled.

Today people are gripped by fear. There is the fear of powerful nations and rogue states throughout the world. There is the fear of pain and loneliness, especially as the years tick by. There is the fear of unemployment, business closures, and financial concerns. But there is also the fear of death and the unknown beyond the grave.

Christmas is a time when many people camouflage the real world and just eat, drink and be merry. However, within a fortnight the camouflage is removed and we return to the real world once again.

The Christian message is a message of hope. The angel said, 'Do not be afraid.' Jesus Christ came to remove fear and, in its place, bring faith.

Tomorrow we will look further into this message from heaven.

23 DECEMBER

The joy of the Lord is our constant strength

'Do not be afraid, for behold, I bring you good tidings of great joy which will be to all people.' Luke 2:10

RECOMMENDED READING: Galatians 4:4–7

Yesterday we began to consider the angel's message to the shepherds. We saw that the gospel is good news because it conquers fear. Today we continue with the angel's message.

2. The gospel is good news because it brings great joy. Verse 10 says, 'I bring you good tidings of great joy.' There was a time when there was little joy in Israel. They were occupied by a foreign power and evil men ruled the people. Where fear reigns in the hearts of people there is little joy.

The angel's message was a difficult one to grasp considering the situation the people were in. What did this message really mean? Would Rome be overthrown and Israel released from tyranny? If this was people's expectation, they would soon be disappointed.

The joy the angel was referring to, was a different joy altogether. It was a joy the world could not give, neither could it take away. The people had to realise that this joy only Jesus could bring. It was a joy that could be experienced even through trials and difficulties.

For Christians, this joy doesn't stay for a couple of weeks over Christmas but is a companion throughout the year and throughout your lifetime, whatever the circumstances.

3. The gospel is good news because it is for all people. It is relevant to the needs of everyone. We live in a multicultural society with people from numerous backgrounds and nationalities. It is a mixed world in which we live. The gospel is for all people.

It is for the educated and scholarly, but also for the unlearned and ignorant. It is for the wealthy landowner as well as the homeless person on the streets. It is for the highly respectable and for those who are despised and outcasts in society. It is for those whose tables are overladen with good food, but also for those who are hungry with empty stomachs. It is for the Jew as well as the Gentile; for people in the east as well as in the west.

God is no respecter of status. He longs that all conditions of people should come to repentance and find forgiveness in Him.

May our churches offer a welcome to the respectable in the area where we live, but also put an arm around the destitute and those rejected by society. May we love them as Jesus loved them.

24 DECEMBER

God descended to earth so that we would rise to heaven

'For there is born to you this day in the city of David a Saviour, who is Christ the Lord.' Luke 2:11

RECOMMENDED READING: Luke 2:1–12

We have been considering the message the angels brought to the shepherds in the fields near Bethlehem. We continue to look at reasons why the gospel is good news.

4. The gospel is good news because it emphasises the value of the individual. Verse 10 reminds us that the gospel is good news to all people, yet v.11 tells us, '… to you'.

Today society caters for the masses. We are no longer a name but a number on a computer system. We have lost sight of the individual, but thankfully God hasn't. He knows us personally and is fully aware of our fears, our problems and our concerns.

Throughout His earthly ministry, Jesus always found time and showed interest in the individual. Yes, He preached to many thousands at one time, but one of His greatest sermons was spoken to one man, Nicodemus.

He travelled to Samaria to speak to one woman who He met at a well. He told three parables relating to one lost coin, one lost sheep and one lost son. In Acts 9 He challenged one man named Saul as he travelled on the road to Damascus.

If you have never met Him, He wants to meet with you to put your life on the right track and give it purpose and meaning.

5. The gospel is good news because it saves. Verse 11 says, 'For there is born to you this day in the city of David a Saviour, who is Christ the Lord.'

The angel could have said that Jesus had come to be a reformer, a teacher, or even a king, but His main purpose for coming into this world was to save us from our sin.

It is sad to see people recognising Jesus just as a babe at Bethlehem, but then rejecting Him as the Saviour of Calvary. Yet it was here He took the punishment that should have been ours. He became our substitute to save us from hell and its reality.

Because of our sin, we have been separated from our Creator. Therefore, it is impossible for anyone to reach up to God. There was only one way for us to be united with Almighty God and that was for Him to come down to us. That is who Christmas is all about. He came down to earth so that forgiven sinners would one day rise to heaven.

25 DECEMBER

Only God deserves the glory

'Glory to God in the highest, and on earth peace, goodwill toward men!'
Luke 2:14

RECOMMENDED READING: Luke 2:13–20

Our minds over the past few days have been focused upon the angel's message. Today is the climax of our meditations.

6. The gospel is good news because it glorifies God. Verse 14: 'Glory to God in the highest.' After the angel of the Lord had made the earth-shattering announcement, a multitude of the heavenly host joined him in praise to the Almighty One. What a moment that would have been for those shepherds! This would have been an unforgettable experience.

Our sole purpose in life should be to glorify God! May that be our aim throughout this day.

There are those who proudly say they are 'religious'. They give to good causes, even Christian ones, particularly at Christmas. They remind us that they live a good life and are always willing to help those in need. They will be there at the Carol Service singing their heart out. These can be commendable characteristics, but the main test is: 'Do we glorify God or not?' He should be glorified in our work, in our home, and in every aspect of our life.

Let us, with the angels, put Him first in everything, and at all times. 'O come let us adore Him, Christ the Lord.'

7. The gospel is good news because it gives real, lasting peace. Verse 14: 'On earth peace, goodwill toward men.' We all long for peace, but how will peace come to a troubled world like this? It will certainly not come through political pacts, treaties or agreements. On most occasions they are not worth the paper they are written on. True peace will only come when people recognise and receive Christ into their hearts and homes.

So, we come to another Christmas. With Christ in His rightful place, it could be the best you have ever had. On a cold winter's day, a man was walking down a street and noticed some grain on the ground. A flock of sparrows were having an unexpected feast. As the man took a step towards the birds, they became uneasy. After another step their nervousness increased and they suddenly flew away. For a few moments the man stood reflecting upon what had happened. Why had the sparrows flown away? He had meant them no harm. Then he realised he was too big.

Another question then came to his mind. How could he walk among those birds without frightening them? It would only be possible if he were to become a sparrow and fly down among them. Have a happy, peaceful day!

26 DECEMBER

Never be too busy for God

'Now after Jesus was born in Bethlehem of Judea in the days of Herod the king, behold, wise men from the East came to Jerusalem.' Matthew 2:1

RECOMMENDED READING: Matthew 2:1–6

Christmas is not just about receiving; it is also about giving. Which gives you the greatest pleasure? For children it has to be receiving, but for adults it must be the joy of giving and seeing the pleasure on people's faces when they open their gifts.

We don't often hear messages about the wise men. Today I want us to consider the part they played in the coming of Jesus.

As we think of giving, these high-ranking officials gave four important and meaningful things to the Lord Jesus.

1. They gave their time. For most people, time is very important and precious. It passes by very quickly and we need to make the best use of this valuable gift.

These men would have spent many days planning and preparing for this arduous journey. They had to ensure that they had ample provision, not only for themselves, but for the entire caravan who would be accompanying them.

The journey itself would have taken many weeks. For the shepherds, it was only crossing a few hills; for the wise men it would be crossing at least three countries.

They were willing to give their time to honour the King of the Jews. What about us? If we are too busy for God, then we are just too busy.

Did you find time to sincerely thank Him for the good food you have eaten over this festive period? Do you find time to attend a place of worship each Sunday, or do other things crowd into your life and take priority? Do you find time to serve Him in the life of the church?

When I was younger, I made a list of my activities for the Lord and the time I devoted to them. I then listed my personal priorities which gave me pleasure and the time I devoted to them. The scales weighed heavily in the latter. I needed to make urgent readjustments.

Are you too busy to give your time for God? Do you need to make further readjustments? I can tell you it is worth doing so for you will have no regrets.

These men gave their time. Let us do the same.

27 DECEMBER

Tired in God's work, but never tired of it

'When they had opened their treasures, they presented gifts to Him: gold, frankincense, and myrrh.' Matthew 2:11

RECOMMENDED READING: Matthew 2:7–12

Yesterday we turned our attention to the wise men and the account in Matthew 2. They gave four important things to Jesus apart from the gifts they brought. Yesterday we considered the first, which was their time. We now consider the second.

2. **They gave their energy.** Travelling can be very tiring. At the end of a long journey, whether by air or car, you can feel exhausted. Our daughter and her husband live near Durban in South Africa and when we have visited them it can take thirty hours from door to door. When we arrive, all we want is a bed!

Now just spare a thought for these men. We do not know for certain their exact route, but it would have taken them through a number of countries before reaching Israel. The journey would not be by air, but all the way on camels. From personal experience, they are not the most comfortable beast to travel on. They must have been exhausted at the end of the journey and then, in a short time, they would have to return to their homeland. There is no doubt that these men gave their energy to honour Jesus.

The early apostles, including Paul, travelled long distances by both land and sea taking the message of the gospel into Gentile countries. They gave their energy for the task because they believed in the message they were commissioned to declare to others.

Our Lord Himself walked the length and breadth of Israel preaching the gospel of the Kingdom of God. He only had three years of public ministry, yet He didn't waste a moment of time, expending His energy in seeking to save those who were lost.

How do we spend our energy? We always find energy for pleasure and many other things in life, but do we willingly offer our energy for God's work?

Yes, we may be tired when we are involved in God's work; tired in it, but never of it. It's far better to wear out for Jesus than just rust out.

There is no greater cause to give your time and energy to than sharing the good news of the gospel with others. Your efforts will never be in vain.

28 DECEMBER

He wants the best that we can give

'Let each one give as he purposes in his heart, not grudgingly or of necessity; for God loves a cheerful giver.' 2 Corinthians 9:7

RECOMMENDED READING: 2 Corinthians 9

We have been considering the visit of the wise men as recorded in Matthew 2. We have noted that they gave their time and their energy. We conclude with two more gifts.

3. They gave their wealth. We can see from v.11 that they brought on their journey the best gifts they could give: gold, frankincense and myrrh. They were givers not getters.

Our Lord Jesus Christ gave up so much for us. He was willing to leave the security of His Father's presence. He was willing to leave the worship and adoration that the angelic host of heaven continually gave to Him. He was willing to lay aside His heavenly robes and come down to a manger and be wrapped in swaddling clothes.

Throughout His life, He continued to give to all who came in contact with Him. He then gave up His life on a cruel cross outside the city walls of Jerusalem. His precious life-giving blood was poured out for us so that we might know the forgiveness of our sins and receive the gift of everlasting life. Jesus gave up everything so that we might have everything.

4. They gave themselves. Verse 11 tells us that they, '... fell down and worshipped Him.' Though they were wise men, they recognised that before them was the King of all kings.

Yes, these wise men gave their time, their energy and their wealth, but they gave the most important gift of all—themselves.

Just pause again and consider all that Jesus has done for you and given for you. This is the time to think not of what you haven't, but what you have. We have received from His hand far more than any human being deserves.

Now think of what you have given to Him. He doesn't want your sacrifices or rituals. The greatest gift any of us can give to Jesus is ourselves. He wants the very best that you can give. He wants you.

Today, let us bow down before that manger and give to Him what He longs most of all to receive: our grateful, thankful hearts.

29 DECEMBER

Always looking for something new

'For all the Athenians and the foreigners who were there spent their time in nothing else but either to tell or to hear some new thing.' Acts 17:21

RECOMMENDED READING: Acts 17:15–33

Wherever the apostle Paul travelled, the message he brought always divided people. When he came to Thessalonica, he preached on three consecutive Sabbaths in the Jewish synagogue. He tried to show to them that Jesus was the Christ, the Son of God.

Some were persuaded by his message and a large number followed Paul and Silas. These were mainly devout Greeks, but the Jews were not convinced by his argument. In fact, they became so angry that it resulted in an uproar within the city.

He was then sent to Berea, to people who were willing to search the Scriptures to verify Paul's message. Many believed in the words Paul spoke to them, but the Jews from Thessalonica came to Berea and stirred up the crowds. This resulted in Paul sailing to Athens. Here he had an audience that was willing to listen. The Athenians loved to 'tell or hear some new thing' (v.21), and Paul's message was certainly new to their ears.

Within human nature there is the craze for something new. It not only applied to Paul's day, but is also relevant to our own.

How quickly we become tired and bored with our possessions and look for something new.

A child soon becomes tired of their old toys and wants something new, especially when they see it advertised on television or the internet.

But adults are not exempt from this desire for something new. Mum gets the urge to dispose of her clothes at the charity shop and purchases a new outfit. Dad has had his car for three years and wants an up-to-date model. He also wants a new job with fresh challenges.

Within a few days we begin a new year. For some last year was nothing special, so they look with great expectation to the first day of January thinking the New Year will change their fortunes. We always look for better days.

What about the Christian? As we soon embark upon a new year, make the most of it. Consecrate it to God and use the days to serve Him and be a witness to others. Never miss an opportunity to tell people about your Saviour. For many the sands of time are sinking fast so make this year very special to you and others.

30 DECEMBER

Leaving the past behind

'Choose for yourselves this day whom you will serve.' Joshua 24:15

RECOMMENDED READING: Joshua 1:1–9

Joshua was now an old man as he gathered the tribes of Israel to Shechem. As he looked back over his life, he thanked Almighty God for His many mercies both to him and to Israel. God had brought them through many battles and difficult encounters and now he called the people to make a further consecration of themselves to His service.

Tomorrow is New Year's Eve and many people will be making resolutions for the coming year. Unfortunately, for the vast majority their resolutions will only last a few weeks, others a few days, and some won't even survive the night.

For the Christian, it will be a day to review the past, and then dedicate themselves to God's service for the coming year. Today we will consider the year that is coming to a close, and tomorrow look to the future.

As we look back over the past year, the vast majority of people—including me—will be glad that it is drawing to a close! COVID has brought untold pressure on families, the health service, care homes, the police, fire and ambulance services, just to name a few. It has had an impact upon people's employment, businesses and finances.

But most of all, this Christmas has left vacant seats in many homes due to loved ones who have died because of this dreadful virus. Most of us will have known of someone who has suffered during these past two years.

This year, 2020, has seen the worst in people who have completely ignored the rules, despite the many warnings given to them. But it has also brought out the best in people who have shown love and compassion to those in need.

It has also brought extra pressure on pastors and leaders of churches throughout the UK and the world. The ones we know have worked tirelessly trying to keep their congregations safe, as well as maintaining their regular duties. We thank you most warmly for your faithful labours and the care you have shown.

But how have you done spiritually? What have you done with the talents, the time and the opportunities God has given to you? Have you maintained close fellowship with the Lord which is vitally important at all times?

If we are honest, both with ourselves and with God, there are times when we have failed miserably. But despite this, God has been so good to us all and brought us safely through this year. May we be grateful for the many undeserved mercies He has shown to us!

31 DECEMBER

Stepping into the future with God

'Behold, God is my salvation, I will trust and not be afraid.' Isaiah 12:2

RECOMMENDED READING: Isaiah 12

We now come to the end of another year. Within a few hours the calendar will turn and we will enter a new year in our earthly journey. Yesterday we looked back over the year and acknowledged God's faithfulness to us despite our many failings and shortcomings.

Soon we will embark on a new beginning. One thing is abundantly clear: the future is unknown to all of us. We do not know what the coming year will bring, but we have our hopes and longings.

The big question facing us all is, 'What will we do with the coming year if God spares us?' Will we learn from our past mistakes or just repeat them as we have in previous years? Will our love for Christ grow stronger or just remain stagnant?

Today we can commit ourselves, not only to the Lord's service, but to the Lord Himself. Let us give more time to studying His Word; more time to prayer; more regular attendance in God's house. If it was our Lord's custom to be in the synagogue, may it be ours to be with His people. Let us begin the year as we mean to go on and not become slack in our commitment to Him.

As we welcome a new year in, let us step forward knowing the future is in the hands of Almighty God, and there it is safe.

It has been good to spend the year with you and I wish you and your loved ones a very peaceful and Christ-centred year.

> 'Standing at the portal of the opening year
> Words of comfort meet us, hushing every fear;
> Spoken through the silence by our Father's voice,
> Tender, strong and faithful, making us rejoice.'
> He will never fail us, He will not forsake;
> His eternal covenant He will never break;
> Resting on His promise, what have we to fear?
> God is all-sufficient for the coming year.'
>
> Frances Ridley Havergal (1836–79)

ENDNOTES

1. 4 January
Ruth Paxson, *The Wealth, Walk and Warfare of the Christian* (www.bookministry.org, 1939).

2. 15 January
St Augustine of Hippo (354–430), https://www.brainyquote.com/quotes/saint_augustine_165165. Retrieved: 09/06/21.

3. 25 January
C. H. Spurgeon, *365 days with C. H. Spurgeon*, Vol.2, 23 April (Day One Publications).

4. 25 January
C. H. Spurgeon, *365 Days with C. H. Spurgeon*, Vol.2, 23 April (Day One Publications).

5. 29 January
C. H. Spurgeon, *365 Days with C. H. Spurgeon*, Vol.6, 18 June (Day One Publications).

6. 29 January
W. David. O. Taylor, *The Theater of God's Glory* (Grand Rapids MI: Wm. B. Eerdmans Publishing Co., 2017).

7. 5 February
D. L. Moody (1837–1899), 'The Seven Walks of Ephesians', Cited in: *Our Daily Bread*, https://odb.org/ZA/1995/11/16/walk-your-talk-2 by Joanie Yoder. Retrieved 10/06/21).

8. 7 February
J. C. Ryle (1880–1900), (https://www.jcryle.info/2018/01/the-best-of-men-are-men-at-best.html. Retrieved 10/06/2021).

9. 12 March
Ruth Paxson, *The Wealth, Walk and Warfare of the Christian* (www.bookministry.org, 1939).

10. 20 March
Robin Knox-Johnston, Cited in: Bear Grylls, *A Survival Guide For Life* (London: Bantam Press, 2012), p. 136.

11. 23 March
Brian H. Edwards, *Grace, Amazing Grace* (Leominster: Day One Publications, 2003).

12 24 March
Source Unknown.

13 14 April
See Clive Anderson, *Travel with C. H. Spurgeon* (Day One Publications, 2012), p. 22, and C. H. Spurgeon, *Autobiography, Vol.1: The Early Years* (The Banner of Truth Trust, 1973), p. 87.

14 24 April
Christopher Hitchens, (http://www.bbc.co.uk/pressoffice/pressreleases/stories/2010/11_november/26/hitchens.shtml). Retrieved 16/06/2021.

15 24 April
Carey Francis of Kenya, Source unknown.

16 24 April
John Wesley, Source unknown.

17 3 May
Dr W. E. Sangster, (1900–1960), Source unknown.

18 11 May
Rita F Snowden, *While the Candle Burns—A Book of Devotions* (London: The Epworth Press, 1944).

19 22 May
Phillip Yancey, *Disappointment with God: Three Questions No One Asks Aloud* (Grand Rapids, Michigan: Zondervan, 1988).

20 30 May
C. H. Spurgeon, *365 days with C. H. Spurgeon*, Vol.3, 5 April (Day One Publications).

21 11 June
George Washington, Source unknown.

22 28 June
Isaac Newton, 1642–1727, (https://www.goodreads.com/quotes/30410-i-do-not-know-what-i-may-appear-to-the-world), Retrieved: 22/06/21.

23 14 July
Eda Lord Murphy (1922) 'The glory of the house is hospitality.' *The Iowa Homemaker. Vol 2: No 7*, Article 6, (Available at https://lib.dr.iastate.edu/homemaker/vol2/iss7/6, 1922).

24 4 August
Thomas A. Edison, 1847–1931, (https://www.brainyquote.com/quotes/thomas_a_edison_109004), Retrieved: 23/06/21.

25 6 August
    Thomas A. Edison, 1847–1931, Source unknown.

26 19 August
    Evel Knievel, 1938–2007, (https://vn800rider.wordpress.com/). Retrieved: 24/06/21.

27 6 September
    Patrick of Ireland, Dates unknown, (http://www.blessedquietness.com/journal/housechu/patrick.htm). Retrieved: 28/06/21.

28 30 September
    C.H. Spurgeon, *365 days with C.H. Spurgeon*, Vol.3, 15 June (Day One Publications).

29 8 October
    Paul Pease, *Travel with William Carey* (Day One Publications, 2005), pp. 5, 104.

30 8 November
    A.W. Pink, 1886–1952, *The Wrath of God* (www.gracegems.org/Pink2/wrath_of_god). Retrieved 30/6/21.

31 18 November
    Oliver Cromwell, 1599–1658, 'Trust in God and keep your powder dry', (https://en.wikipedia.org/wiki/Trust_in_God_and_keep_your_powder_dry): Retrieved 07/06/2021.

32 23 November
    C.H. Spurgeon, *365 days with C.H. Spurgeon*, Vol.3, 17 July (Day One Publications).